Suicide
Across the Life Span
Implications for Counselors

Edited by
David Capuzzi

American Counseling Association
5999 Stevenson Avenue
Alexandria, VA 22303
www.counseling.org

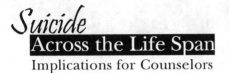
Suicide Across the Life Span
Implications for Counselors

10   9   8   7   6   5   4   3   2   1

American Counseling Association
5999 Stevenson Avenue
Alexandria, VA 22304

Director of Publications
Carolyn C. Baker

Production Manager
Bonny E. Gaston

Copy Editor
Elaine Dunn

Cover design by Martha Woolsey

Cover poem by David Capuzzi and Mark D. Stauffer

Library of Congress Cataloging-in-Publication Data
Suicide across the life span: implications for counselors/David Capuzzi (ed.)
    p.   cm.
    ISBN 1-55620-232-6 (alk. paper)
    1. Suicide—Prevention. 2. Suicidal behavior. 3. Counseling. 4. Suicidal
behavior—Treatment. 5. Suicide victims—Psychology. 6. Life cycle, Human—
Psychological aspects. I. Capuzzi, Dave.

HV6545.S819   2004
362.28—dc22   2003023713

Table of Contents

1
Background

Chapter 1

Mark D. Stauffer

Chapter 2

Jonathan W. Carrier and Kay Ennis

Chapter 3

Fred J. Hanna and Alan G. Green

2
Examining the Issues Counselors Must Address

Chapter 4

Melinda Haley

3
Counseling Suicidal Clients and Survivors

Preface

Ashley, a 19-year-old freshman at a large state university, met his counselor in May, just as he was studying for final exams after completing his first semester of enrollment. Ashley could have matriculated at the university in late August, but he deferred his admission by one semester because he was so nervous about leaving his family and the small town he and his parents had always called home. Ashley was a much wanted, only child born when his father was 48 and his mother was 46. Ashley's mother had a difficult pregnancy and a complicated, early delivery. Ashley was a low-birth-weight, premature baby and did not come home until he was 7½ weeks old. He was always small for his age and was often picked on and made fun of by his peers. He felt comfortable at home with his parents and enjoyed socializing with the friends of his parents because they were all middle-aged and older adults. If his parents' friends brought their children to a dinner or party at the home of his parents, Ashley found them to be easy to talk with because they were older and nothing like his own peer group. Ashley had never been able to establish close friendships with any of his peers because he rarely had been allowed to spend time at the homes of classmates and had not been allowed to attend summer camp, participate in athletics, and do the normal "kid" things because of his asthma, severe allergies, and his parents' concern for his safety and welfare.

When the counselor met Ashley, he noticed how different Ashley was from the typical freshman at the university. Ashley dressed like a much older person, did not seem interested in doing the things most young undergraduates enjoyed, and had not made any friends. Ashley had come to the university's counseling center because of the anxiety attacks he was experiencing since enrolling. He had worked with a doctoral intern who referred him to the counselor, employed by the counseling center, when her internship was ending. Ashley's intern-counselor, a woman in her early 40s, thought Ashley would benefit by seeing a younger counselor and learning he could be comfortable while doing so.

Ashley saw the counselor every week for almost a year even though, at first, he was afraid of the counselor. The counselor was in his mid-20s; Ashley initially wished he was still being seen by the intern, who was more like his parents and the people he had spent time with as he grew up. After a few counseling sessions with his new counselor, Ashley began to feel more comfortable and asked the counselor to help him learn to talk with the other young undergraduates at the university. He shared his feelings of low self-esteem and poor self-confidence. He told the counselor he chose to rent a room in a small, off-campus boarding house when he enrolled because the idea of living in a university residence hall was "scary" because he did not know what to say to people his own age, and the boarding house had some older graduate students and only one young undergraduate. He began to like the young counselor and even asked for suggestions for how to dress more like a younger person and not so much like his dad.

During his sophomore and junior years Ashley gradually developed his social skills and made a few friends. He still was troubled with anxiety attacks, usually at night after a stressful day or after encountering a social situation during which he behaved in an awkward manner. Even though his slowly developing feelings of increased self-confidence could easily be shaken, he felt better about residing away from home and did not miss his parents and their friends like he did when he was a freshman . He saw his counselor less frequently now, and often let 4 or 5 months lapse between sessions; sometimes, he missed his appointments entirely and did not reschedule for 2 or 3 weeks. He had started to date a young woman he met during the middle of his junior year and was amazed and delighted that someone his own age seemed to like him.

One day Ashley's counselor noticed that he had scheduled an appointment and the counselor wondered how close to graduation it might be for Ashley. The counselor also wondered if Ashley was experiencing fears and anxieties about transitioning out of the university that were similar to those he experienced as he left home and made the transition to the university. Ashley did not keep his appointment that day, and the counselor wondered how long it would take him to reschedule.

On the way home that afternoon, the local radio station reported the story of the attempted suicide of a university student. The headline was "University student becomes human torch." The counselor wondered what residence hall the student lived in and anticipated being asked to accompany other counseling center counselors into the residence hall to work with student "survivors." When the counselor arrived at the counseling center the next morning, he found out that Ashley was the student and that he had doused himself with gasoline and lit himself.

The counselor was overcome with grief and flooded with feelings. He could not understand why he did not see what was coming and blamed himself for what had happened. He was angry with Ashley for not keeping his appointment, angry at himself for somehow not knowing what was happening, and even angrier that he had not been required to take courses solely focused on assessing and treating suicidal clients while he did his graduate work. After talking with colleagues and gaining perspective, he decided to spend time with Ashley at the hospital.

Ashley was severely burned, and the counselor had to put on sterile garb and open Ashley's tracheotomy each time Ashley tried to communicate with his counselor. Ashley was so burned that he had lost parts of his fingers, nose, and ears. His counselor found it difficult, at first, to be with Ashley but knew Ashley needed to talk about what had happened. It seems that the precipitating event had been twofold: Ashley's girlfriend had ended their relationship that morning, and when Ashley returned in a shaken state to his boarding house residence, he was stressed and said and did some awkward things and was made fun of by some of the other residents.

The counselor went to the hospital twice each day. The first 3 days Ashley talked with his counselor about what had happened and how he had been feeling. The last 7 days Ashley and his parents, who stayed by Ashley's bedside, wanted the counselor to help Ashley die and to help the family during the process. Ashley died on the afternoon of the 10th day.

I was the counselor in that scenario. Shortly afterward, I began my "journey" in terms of learning all I could about working with youth at risk of attempting or completing suicide. I attended trainings, read widely, and began accepting referrals of potentially suicidal youth from colleagues who knew of my interest and developing expertise in this area. Twenty years later I thought I knew enough to offer trainings to school districts, mental health center staffs, and other community groups. Then I began developing interest in learning how to work with youth at risk for other behaviors that could harm them. As time passed, I began working with counselors who were dealing with youth who were becoming eating disordered, violent, confused about their sexuality, and so on. This eventually led to the writing and editing of *Youth at Risk: A Prevention Guide for Counselors, Teachers, and Parents* with my coauthor and coeditor Douglas R. Gross. This book is now in its fourth edition (2004) and is also published by the American Counseling Association (ACA).

Not too long ago I was asked by the chairperson of ACA's media committee to submit a proposal for a book focused on suicide across the life span because so many counselors are called on to provide assistance to clients of all ages who are experiencing depression and preoccupation with suicidal ideation. This book is an attempt to provide counselors with a life span approach to counseling clients at risk of suicide attempts or completions. Every effort has been made to develop a comprehensive reference for members of the profession who are faced with helping clients who have lost hope and need help to reestablish the will to live.

Part One of this book contains three chapters that provide foundational material to counselors working with this clientele. Chapter 1 discusses suicide in both Western and Eastern cultures and analyzes how voluntary death has been conceptualized in various cultures over the centuries. Trends, statistics, and major approaches to counseling suicidal clients are highlighted. Chapter 2 stresses the relationship between suicide and depression and the process of developing counseling/treatment plans for depressed, suicidal clients. Finally, this section ends with a chapter focused on hope and suicide. It is based on the contributing authors' belief that the old adage "Where there is life, there is hope" really needs to be changed to "Where there is hope, there is life," to be applied to the context of counseling suicidal clients.

Part Two of this book examines the issues counselors must understand and address when counseling those who are suicidal. Risk and protective factors, assessing suicidal risk, assisted suicide and associated ethical issues, and suicide and the law are addressed in chapters 4 through 7. As is the case in the first section of the book, the contributing authors are all experts in these areas.

Part Three of the book contains four chapters (chaps. 8–11) that are written with the sole purpose of applying preceding chapter content and other concepts to counseling suicidal children, adolescents, and adults. The concluding chapter was written to provide guidelines for counseling survivors of those who have taken their lives.

As this book was being conceptualized, written, and edited, every effort was made to address adaptations for diversity and to provide a helpful and comprehensive reference for members of the profession. It is my hope that more and more counseling, social work, and psychology programs and departments *require* students to take courses and acquire supervised practice in this area. No practitioner, new to or experienced in the helping professions, should ever see clients without expertise in this area.

This book, in so many ways, has been in the making for years and symbolizes my own development through the decades. Since the 1960s, this developmental process has enriched my understanding of suicide as I have tried to learn more and more about this subject for use in the context of my roles as counselor and counselor educator. It also, I believe, represents the parallel process that has occurred during this time span in the profession of counseling as members of the profession have increased the expectations for competence they have for themselves as counseling professionals.

—*David Capuzzi*

Acknowledgments

I wish to thank all of the contributing authors to this important resource for members of the helping professions. Without their willingness to work with me on this project, I would not have had the
support I needed. Without their input, expertise, and commitment to
carry through, this book would not have been published.

To my colleagues and friends in the Graduate School of Education
at Portland State University, I extend my appreciation for their
support and patience as I labored on this project to "birth" this book.

Special recognition must be given to Mark Stauffer, my research assistant and a graduate student in counselor education at Portland
State University in the couples, marriage, and family specialization. Mark
is a talented and scholarly master's student who aspires to a career as a
counselor educator. He has provided invaluable assistance in the editing of the manuscript for this book and contributed an outstanding first
chapter. In many ways he symbolizes the great hope I have for the future
of counselor education and the impact competent young professionals
will have on the helping professions.

Meet the Editor

David Capuzzi, PhD, NCC, LPC, is a past president of the American Counseling Association (ACA) and is professor and coordinator of counselor education in the Graduate School of Education at Portland State University in Portland, Oregon.

From 1980 to 1984, Dr. Capuzzi was editor of *The School Counselor*. He has authored a number of textbook chapters and monographs on the topic of preventing adolescent suicide and is coeditor and author, with Dr. Larry Golden, of *Helping Families Help Children: Family Interventions With School-Related Problems* (1986) and *Preventing Adolescent Suicide* (1988). In 1989, 1996, 2000, and 2004 he coauthored and edited *Youth at Risk: A Prevention Resource for Counselors, Teachers, and Parents;* in 1991, 1997, and 2001, *Introduction to the Counseling Profession;* in 1992, 1998, and 2002, *Introduction to Group Counseling;* and in 1995, 1999, and 2003, *Counseling and Psychotherapy: Theories and Interventions* with Douglas R. Gross. *Approaches to Group Work: A Handbook for Practitioners* (2003) and *Sexuality Issues in Counseling,* the latter coauthored and edited with Larry Burlew, are his two latest texts. He has authored or coauthored articles in a number of ACA-related journals.

A frequent speaker and keynoter at professional conferences and institutes, Dr. Capuzzi has also consulted with a variety of school districts and community agencies interested in initiating prevention and intervention strategies for adolescents at risk for suicide. He has facilitated the development of suicide prevention, crisis management, and postvention programs in communities throughout the United States; provides training on the topics of "youth at risk" and "grief and loss"; and serves as an invited adjunct faculty member at other universities as time permits. He is the first recipient of ACA's Kitty Cole Human Rights Award and also a recipient of the Leona Tyler Award in Oregon.

Meet the Authors

Mary Boylan, PhD, is a counselor educator and is currently working with the National Training and Development Institute in Ireland. This institute provides education and training to people with disabilities. She has had experiences in the United States and Ireland working with families in mental health, school, university, and agency settings. Her primary area of research is suicide and suicide prevention. This research interest resulted in her completing her doctoral dissertation on "The Self-Efficacy of Irish Guidance Counselors in Identifying and Assessing Students at Risk for Suicide."

Jonathan W. Carrier, MS, is currently a doctoral student in counseling psychology at the University of Louisville in Kentucky. His counseling and research interests include behavioral interventions, multicultural studies, evolutionary psychology, and early influences on psychopathology.

Tamara Davis, PhD, is an assistant professor at Marymount University in Arlington, Virginia. Her counseling experiences with children and adolescents spans the last 15 years. Prior to her position at the university, she was an elementary school counselor for 8 years and a high school counselor for 1 year in Manassas, Virginia. She has authored a book about school counseling titled *Exploring School Counseling: Professional Practices and Perspectives.* She is president of the Virginia Association for Counselor Education and Supervision and a member of the Board for the Virginia School Counselor Association. Dr. Davis presents at national, state, and local conferences on a variety of topics on counseling children and adolescents.

Kay Ennis, MA, is pursuing her doctoral degree at New Mexico State University. Her career goals include teaching at the university level, providing therapy, and authoring books and journal articles. Her research interests include the areas of hope, depression, and moral as well as spiritual values as they relate to both personal and professional life. Her experiential endeavors include cofacilitation of groups, individual counseling for college-age individuals, and assisting as instructor for multiple college courses.

Alan G. Green, PhD, is an assistant professor and coordinator for the School
Counseling Program at Johns Hopkins University. He is the principal
investigator of Project Inspiration, a federally funded grant for the development and refinement of an urban elementary school counseling
model being implemented in the Baltimore City Public School System
of Maryland. Previously, Dr. Green was a research assistant and adjunct
professor at the Metropolitan Center for Urban Education at New York
University. Here he worked as project director of a federally funded
Safe and Drug Free Schools data collection project with New York City
Public Schools. Dr. Green's research interests are in urban education,
academic underachievement among African Americans, and the use of
data to improve schools.

Douglas R. Gross, PhD, NCC, is a professor emeritus at Arizona State University, Tempe, where he served as a faculty member in counselor education for 29 years. His professional work history includes public school
teaching, counseling, and administration. He is currently retired and
living in Three Rivers, Michigan. He has been president of the Arizona
Counselors Association, president of the Western Association for Counselor Education and Supervision, chairperson of the Western Regional
Branch Assembly of the American Counseling Association (ACA), president of the Association for Humanistic Education and Development,
and treasurer and parliamentarian of the ACA.

    Dr. Gross has contributed chapters to seven texts: *Counseling and
Psychotherapy: Theories and Interventions* (1995, 1999, 2003); *Youth at Risk:
A Resource for Counselors, Teachers, and Parents* (1989, 1996, 2000); *Founda-
tions of Mental Health Counseling* (1986, 1996); *Counseling: Theory, Process
and Practice* (1977); *The Counselor's Handbook* (1974); *Introduction to the
Counseling Profession* (1991, 1997, 2001); and *Introduction to Group Counsel-
ing* (1992, 1998, 2002). His research has appeared in the *Journal of
Counseling Psychology; Journal of Counseling & Development; Association for
Counselor Education and Supervision Journal; Journal of Educational Research,
Counseling and Human Development; Arizona Counselors Journal; Texas Coun-
seling Journal;* and *AMHCA Journal.*

    Dr. Gross provides national training for certification in the areas of
bereavement, grief, and loss.

Melinda Haley, MS, is a doctoral student at New Mexico State University in Las
Cruces. She is currently working on her dissertation regarding the effects of ethnicity on attitudes of punitiveness or leniency toward inmates.
She is a published author in the areas of group counseling, counseling
theory, and youth at risk. Her current research interests are personality
disorders and personality development, multicultural issues in counseling, and counseling offenders and other populations at risk.

Fred J. Hanna, PhD, is a professor in the Department of Counseling and
Human Services at Johns Hopkins University. He has served on the

editorial boards of six scholarly journals and has published a wide variety of scholarly and professional articles. In addition to many years of counseling practice, he gives training seminars across the United States on the subject of difficult clients and adolescents. He also serves as a consultant to community agencies and school systems. Much of his research is devoted to developing innovative clinical strategies and techniques aimed at positive change in the area of suicide, victimization, criminal personalities, spirituality, addictive behaviors, and defiant, aggressive adolescents. His book, *Therapy With Difficult Clients: Using the Precursors Model to Awaken Change,* presents a new model of how to achieve therapeutic change and is published by the American Psychological Association.

Barbara Richter Herlihy, PhD, is a professor in the Counselor Education Program at the University of New Orleans. She has worked as a counselor and supervisor in schools, community agencies, and private practice. Her primary focus in teaching and research is counselor ethics. Her books include *Ethical, Legal, and Professional Issues in Counseling* (with Ted Remley) and *Boundary Issues in Counseling* and *ACA Ethical Standards Casebook* (5th ed.; both with Gerald Corey). She has presented workshops and seminars on ethics across the United States and internationally. She combines her work in ethics with her other research interests in feminist therapy, multicultural counseling, and counselor supervision.

Dale Elizabeth Pehrsson, EdD, is a counselor educator and faculty-in-residence at Oregon State University. She has many years of experience working with families in mental health, schools, university counseling, and agency settings. Her areas of research include diversity competency, trauma impact, and play and art therapy. She is a clinical licensed professional counselor in Idaho, a nationally certified counselor and approved clinical supervisor, and a registered play therapy supervisor. Additionally, Dr. Pehrsson is a registered professional nurse with expertise working with families, trauma, and organizational consulting.

Theodore P. Remley, Jr., PhD, is a former executive director of the American Counseling Association. He is a national certified counselor and a licensed professional counselor (LPC) in Louisiana, Mississippi, and Virginia. He is a member of the Florida and Virginia bars. He has been appointed to four state counselor licensure boards, currently is a member of the Louisiana LPC Board, and has been an active leader in the counseling profession. Dr. Remley has served as a counselor in a high school, community colleges, universities, community mental health centers, and private practice. He practiced law for 7 years and currently serves as an expert witness in counselor malpractice cases.

Suzanne R. S. Simon, MEd, is a doctoral student in the Special Education and Counseling Program at Portland State University. She has a master's degree in adult education with a concentration in gerontology from San Francisco State University. She has teaching and research interests in the areas of lifelong learning, memory, meta-cognition, dementia, and social change/justice issues related to long-term care.

Mark D. Stauffer is a master's student in the Counselor Education Program at Portland State University where he serves as a research assistant. He was a 2003 Chi Sigma Iota International fellow. He plans to pursue a doctorate in counselor education upon the completion of his master's degree. He has worked in crisis centers in the Portland Metropolitan Area. His areas of professional interest are death and dying, spirituality, and couples, marriage, and family counseling.

Zarus E. P. Watson, PhD, is an associate professor in the Counselor Education Program at the University of New Orleans (UNO). He is the co-founder, research director, and principal investigator of the UNO Research Center for Multiculturalism and Counseling. He has served as a research coordinator and counselor for the student Support Services Project at Our Lady of Holy Cross College and as pediatric researcher for the Louisiana State University Health Services Center. He conducts organizational workshops and consults with K–12 schools and in business and industry. His teaching and research interests include macrosystemic conditioning; cultural competence issues in counseling and consultation; and sociorace, class, and gender identity development within and between groups.

1
Background

The chapters in this section of the book are intended to provide professionals with the foundation on which the subsequent sections of this text are based. Chapter 1, From Seneca to Suicidology: A History of Suicide, was written by Mark D. Stauffer to provide readers with an understanding of how voluntary death has been conceptualized over time. The chapter begins with a history of suicide, highlighting pertinent values expressed through time that influence current views of suicide. This chapter also addresses how concepts of death relate to suicide and how early suicidologists attempted to classify suicide. This chapter places special emphasis on broadening the counselor's understanding of suicide as a phenomenon.

Jonathan W. Carrier and Kay Ennis's chapter, Depression and Suicide (chap. 2), discusses the relationship between depression and suicide and includes invaluable information and guidelines for diagnosing depression and developing counseling/treatment plans for clients who are depressed. Some outstanding aspects of this chapter include case study material; a discussion of depression and suicide as related to children, adolescents, adults, and the elderly; and an excellent summary chart.

Chapter 3, Hope and Suicide: Establishing the Will to Live, was written by Fred J. Hanna and Alan G. Green of Johns Hopkins University. The chapter provides evidence that hope is correlated with coping and with therapeutic change processes, and it thus sheds light on a practical path of approach for counseling clients with suicidal ideation. Ways of assessing the presence or absence of hope and a variety of counseling approaches that illustrate the use of hope with clients who are contemplating suicide are also included. Readers will find this chapter interesting, philosophical, practical, and inspirational and pertinent to their own self-assessment and professional development.

Chapter 1

From Seneca to Suicidology
A History of Suicide

Mark D. Stauffer

"Suicide." This word has been used for a girl found dead on the floor with toxic blood levels of prescriptions, an African slave looking to escape the unbearable aboard a slave-trading vessel, an elder asking for death with dignity, a dishonored warrior fallen upon his own sword, and the clinically depressed man who pulled a trigger killing the one he hated. Such images fill our minds, conjuring a mix of emotion and thought. Suicide is one of the most profoundly personal actions and socially disturbing events. Across the life span and around the world, suicide is a reality.

For the counselor, the suicide of a client can be an emotionally difficult experience, making it tough to leave "work" at work, let alone to leave home for work. It is our job as counselors to help those who find life in its present condition unsatisfactory, if not intolerable. Knowledge cannot protect a counselor from pain nor provide a perfect solution for such life-and-death crises, but it can better prepare a counselor to provide the best level of care for all involved.

This chapter provides introduction and background pertinent to a study of suicide across the life span. Some key issues covered in this chapter are how ideas about suicide are shaped by history, how sociocultural views of life and death affect one's relationship to suicide, and how a person's ability to understand death and suicide is influenced by development. Although suicide and voluntary death are further defined in depth throughout this book, this chapter gives basic definitions, classifications, and perspectives on the topic. Finally, implications for counseling are discussed.

History

To better understand suicide across the life span, I provide a historical background detailing the precedent values and ideas that influence us today. A history of suicide can help us understand the origins of many of our values. Peering into our own conscious beliefs about suicide, we find social and cultural representations of suicide, because those who have come before shape our current belief. It is important to be aware of majority cultural values if counselors are to be culturally competent and remain open to the possibilities presented by the client. Throughout this book and in subsequent chapters, adaptations for diversity will help counselors see the breadth of possible relationships to suicide that appear in counseling those of various cultures. Because *Suicide Across the Life Span* is primarily used by counselors in North America, this section focuses on the history that most affects current dilemmas in the assessment, treatment, and prevention of suicide.

Studying suicide from a historical standpoint is limited. The factual information that one might use in research today is not available. As Minois (1999) pointed out, historical statistical data on rates of suicide are not available as they might be for diseases or plagues, making the task of delineation a challenge for historians. For example, suicides were not recorded through church organizations because the bodies of the suicidal deceased were not given Christian burial; one can find incomplete data from criminal records because suicide was at times treated as a crime. Nonetheless, historians and suicidologists must draw from literary sources and subsequent psychological autopsies rather than a wide range of factual information available in current cases of suicide. However, historical writings and psychological autopsies can give us a glimpse into past notions and values surrounding suicide.

Antiquity

The "sanctity of life" is a Western value. The sanctity of life as a value does not belong to any one culture but is shared by all, for life itself is one of society's underlying motives. Sanctity of life is a value heavily influenced by Jewish law, which held that suicide was morally wrong with few exceptions; in certain circumstances it was acceptable to kill oneself, such as in the case of capture or torture. The mass suicide of Jews at Masada left 960 dead in the first century CE (Common Era—corresponds to AD, Anno Domini). They took their lives rather than suffer capture and torture by the Roman Army (Droge & Tabor, 1992). The Judaic tradition has held the notion that life is sacred. Grollman (1993) wrote, "There is but one statement to which all Jewish scholars would agree, Judaism has one major prejudism—a prejudice toward life. This tradition has always said to do everything possible to preserve life" (p. 22). Life is God's gift; one should not heedlessly dispose of it. The pantheistic Greeks also held the belief that life was a gift of the Gods.

Other beliefs about suicide were observed in antiquity: First, the highest value is the quality of life rather than life itself, and, second, the autonomy of the self gives a free individual the right to choose voluntary death (Battin, 1998). The "Stoics," a school of philosophy that originated in Greece around 400 BCE and remained influential in the Roman Empire, believed that suicide was a right of the individual in many situations. Suicide was often seen as heroic. For example, Cato, a Roman statesman, chose self-inflicted death rather than to find defeat in battle and compromise of his cause (Fedden, 1938/1972). Taking life into one's own hands was lawful, whether one was mentally ill, struck by poverty, altruistic self-sacrificing, escaping a perpetrator, or in pain of illness (Jamison, 1999; Retterstol, 1993). Seneca, perhaps the most commonly referenced Stoic on suicide, stated,

> Life has carried some men with the greatest rapidity to the harbor, the harbor they were bound to reach even if they tarried on the way, while others it has fretted and harassed. To such a life, as you are aware, one should not always cling. For mere living is not a good, but living well. (as cited in Gumere, 1998, p. 35)

Other Roman schools of thought reproached suicide on several grounds. One reason Epicurean and Cynical schools objected to suicide was due to economic concerns. The Roman Empire for centuries had unchallenged success in battle. One of the rewards of victorious military campaigns abroad was the acquisition of slaves and servants. Suicide was condemned because it had economic effects on others, namely the free and enfranchised masters. Roman legislature ruled that only free citizens, which did not include slaves and servants, had the right to voluntarily choose death. Wives and children were the property of men, falling into the same category as many other possessions such as cattle. Soldiers were likewise the possessions of the Empire. A soldier committing suicide was thought to weaken the Roman Army; it was a crime of desertion (Retterstol, 1993).

Some traditions held that suicide was a detriment to family, the community, and the village. This was true for the Pythagoreans and Neoplatonists, who were the only philosophical schools of antiquity that entirely condemned voluntary death. Plato and Aristotle felt that one of the major problems with suicide was that it was an abandonment of one's duty to others, including duty to state. For example, suicide to escape civil trial was prohibited across philosophical traditions because such an evasion of responsibility would undermine Roman law. There were exceptions to this, when it benefited or was instituted by the state (Droge & Tabor, 1992). A much cited example is Socrates, who drank hemlock under order; without resistance he obliged. The influence of the Greco-Roman era is important in that intellectuals throughout the following ages referenced and drew upon their examples.

Early Christian Period

Voluntary death and altruistic suicide for a noble or divine cause were acceptable if not heralded. Some point to the story and life of Jesus Christ (Alvarez, 1972; Fedden, 1938/1972; Lieberman, 2003; Stern-Gillet, 1998). According to the Bible, he was both man and God, innocent of wrong, able to prevent his death, and yet he intentionally proceeded with actions to end his physical life. Jesus chose to die for others. Stern-Gillet (1998) commented, "Is it only piety that prevents us from viewing Jesus' death as a suicide? Indeed, if we read the gospels with the question, 'Did Jesus intend his own death?' a positive answer appears almost inevitable" (p. 120). The point here is not to label the God of one of the world's major religions or to advocate for suicide but rather to point out that voluntary death, whether or not it is classified as an altruistic voluntary death, has found an acceptable place in Western society. Many scenarios of this exist today: the scenario of the spy who takes poison hidden in a shirt button to avoid divulging a nation's top secrets or the soldier who jumps on a live hand grenade to save his fellow comrades in arms (Tolhurst, 1998).

Altruistic suicide and martyrdom is often a sensitive subject, because those qualifying are often dearly honored figures from history. Nonetheless, some of our most notable figures in history have died voluntarily under auspices to save others. A question arises, where is the drawing line between martyrdom and suicide? Stern-Gillett (1998) in commenting on the rhetoric of suicide gave this formula:

> To call X a suicide amounts, amongst other things, to ascribing to X the moral responsibility (and sometimes, but not always, the blame) for X's death. To call X a martyr amounts, amongst other things, to ascribing the moral responsibility (and, usually, the blame) for X's death to someone else (usually a government, an institution, or an organization). (p. 123)

The established and powerful often determine whether a death is suicide or martyrdom. At present, one need not look too far past any news article on tragedies in the Middle East to see this rhetoric of sides come into play. Who is responsible for death? Blame and incrimination are often a component of suicide.

Early Christian history was heavily marked by acts of martyrdom that were more or less intentional suicides, for it was believed that the body trapped the soul, keeping the faithful from a rewarding afterlife. Droge and Tabor (1992) commented,

> The martyrs are portrayed as going to their death in one of three ways: either as a result of being sought out, by deliberately volunteering, or by actually taking their own lives. On the basis of the evidence that has survived, it would appear that the majority of Christian martyrs chose death by the second and third means. (p. 156)

The focal figure of Christianity had after all volunteered to die. Many sought out Baechler's transfiguration style of suicide, in which a person ends his of her life to achieve a more valued state (Alvarez, 1972; Baechler, 1979; Retterstol, 1993). This trend would soon change with the fall of the Roman Empire.

Fall of Rome and St. Augustine

After a reported vision from God, Constantine officially converted the Roman Empire to Christianity, starting with the Roman Legions (Bullough, 1970). A blending of the Christian faith and Rome meant that the church now carried the proclivity of the empire. "For the Church the fact that voluntary martyrdom, the only honorable form of suicide, disappeared with the conversion of the Roman Empire to Christianity, meant that no religious motivation remained to commit suicide" (Minois, 1999, p. 30). By the early fifth century, Roman rule was failing, Constantine's heirs had pulled out of Britton, and Visigoths had sacked Rome (Bullough, 1970).

During this great transition of power, Augustine, one of the Christian church's prominent theologians, wrote *The City of God* in which suicide was denounced as a sin against God. This early patriarch's stance still influences how suicide is viewed today. Droge and Tabor (1992) believed his strong stance against suicide was in response to Christendom being blamed for the fall of Rome. When Rome was sacked, many were raped and many committed suicide. Pagan Rome blamed Christianity for weakening cultural ties to Roman Gods, thus causing disaster and downfall. Augustine's objections removed blame placed on Christianity by implicating the individuals who took their own lives. Others speculate that it was the rash of earlier martyr suicides that brought about this strong stance (Alvarez, 1972; Gibbon, as cited in Szasz, 1999).

During the same period, Augustine forwarded several lasting notions: Suicide was caused by a lack of fortitude; it was a sin, self-murder, and an act that damned the soul. St. Augustine assumed that one should bear it all. Biblical figures like Job were examples of saints who proved themselves to God, for it was God who was testing them with life's afflictions. It was unacceptable to commit suicide to escape from rape, murder, and torturous situations (Aquinas, 1925/1998).

Saint Augustine maintained that murder was a sin; this included self-murder. Alvarez (1972) pointed out that the Bible does not directly state a ban on suicide and provided examples of suicide in which the figures were mostly held in neutral light, if not honored. He suggested that Augustine was more influenced by Plato's *Pheado,* which promoted the Greek stance that the Gods owned human life. Augustine argued that the Old Testament commandment "Thou shalt not kill" applied to killing oneself, implying that God alone had the right to take a person's life. Augustine in short said that life is God's gift to man, and though a man have free will during his life, his passing is the right of God's to decide (Fedden, 1938/

1972; Retterstol, 1993; Szasz, 1998). Who owns this very human (you and I) is still up for debate today.

Augustine declared that the very act of suicide damned the soul, making it part of the eternally lost. Only those commanded by God or the Holy Spirit were exceptions (Lieberman, 2003). Those in history who had been martyred were exempted for the reason that the Holy Spirit had directed such church saints to fulfill higher mandates. Suicide soon became a wrong punishable with the greatest severity, to be shunned from God to a realm of torture. Some theologians even held that Judas' suicide was a greater sin than his betrayal of Christ (Fletcher, 1998; Jamison, 1999).

Into the Middle Ages

Suicide and attempted suicide eventually became a crime against God and church (Jamison, 1999; Retterstol, 1993). Augustine's condemnations became the official stance of the church, becoming more severe as culture moved toward the Middle Ages. In 452 CE the Church Council in Arles rejected suicide for *famuli* (servants and slaves). The Council of Braga in 563 AD and the Council of Auxerre in 578 CE established that there should be no religious ceremonies after a suicide, which Minois (1999) claimed was a greater punishment than was for murder, which was punishable by payment of a fine. Retterstol (1993) noted that at this time in practice three reasons were acceptable for committing suicide: to preserve chastity of a virgin or married woman, voluntary death through asceticism, and voluntary martyrdom. In 590 AD the Council of Antisidor codified restrictions on suicide. Later the Council in Nimes decided that the corpse of the suicide victim would be buried outside of church grounds and would not receive a burial service, thus the soul of the person who commits suicide was sealed out of the holy community (Fedden, 1938/1972). Echelbarger (1993), a Lutheran minister, expressed the impact of this history: "More than once a family member has responded by saying, 'you will?,' when I have agreed to conduct a funeral for someone who has taken their life. Old attitudes die hard" (p. 218).

Prohibitions on suicide enforced the rule of earthly powers. The change in severity during the Middle Ages allowed for power over slaves and servants. Minois (1999) commented,

> The severity of the civil and religious authorities regarding self-murder might strike us as odd in the general climate of the bloodthirsty violence and scorn for human life that reigned from the fifth to the tenth century. The seeming contradiction needs to be set between God and Humankind that reflected other changing relations between masters and dependents. Ties of dependency multiplied in the late Roman Empire, and God's interests reflected those of the property owners: Taking one's own life was an offense against the rights of both God and the master. (p. 31)

Nobles had other means of voluntary death (Minois, 1999), but for the poorest of the poor, suicide was punishable and costly; one could lose his or her eternal soul. Individuals were emotionally stripped of the freedom to end the most intolerable conditions of oppression (Fedden, 1938/1972).

Families were threatened with punishment if there was a suicide within the family. Civil law reflected this; confiscation of a person's estate was punishment. Families had to defend their dead relative's innocence in court after a member's suicide. In certain regions of France, the family of the suicide victim forfeited their house and dwellings. In one region the roof was left intact while the house walls were knocked down and their family fields were set on fire (Minois, 1999).

Suicide was seen as diabolical. It was believed that Satan directly influenced such deaths; these suicides were the result of demonic possession. "Barbaric" Europe and Christian Rome had blended along with customary ways of dealing with suicides. Corpses of suicides were desecrated. They were dragged to the gallows, burned, hung by chains, and left to rot. Many rituals were done in hopes of preventing the spirit of the suicide victim from haunting the living. For this reason, some corpses were staked through the heart to the ground at a crossroad so that the evil spirit would not arise and find its way to haunt the living (Alvarez, 1972; Fedden, 1938/1972). In France, some corpses were thrown into sewers or onto the city dump (Jamison, 1999). Minois (1999) provided this case from 1257:

> A Parisian jumped into the Seine. When he was rescued, he took communion before he died. His family claimed the body, arguing that he had died in a state of grace, but because he had attempted suicide and had been in his right mind, as shown by his repentance, the court sentenced his corpse to torture. (p. 7)

Social pressure on families and communities created by public desecration of corpses and the damnation of their kinsmen's soul would not fall out of practice until social movements changed the sociopolitical landscape.

The Renaissance and Enlightenment

In the early 16th century, freedom to think and write about subjects like suicide flowered as early humanists challenged the earlier Dark Ages by ushering in the age of Renaissance. There was a "fundamental shift from absolutism and obedience, to personal inquiry and the formation of reasonable personal judgments" (Fedden, 1938/1972, p. 156). The use of movable type printing was making access to scholarship more possible, not to mention literacy, a skill previously held by a mere minority. This scholarship caused sweeping changes in how life was viewed (Bullough, 1970). Shakespeare reflected a new dilemma for the humanist: "To be or not to be?" His tragedies were often sympathetic to self-inflicted death. As with

9

Shakespeare, intellectuals of the time were addressing issues of life and death philosophically, looking at human limits and life conditions. Individualism was on the rise along with mercantilist economy. An admiration for the writings of antiquity flourished (Minois, 1999).

The Protestant Reformation was under way when Martin Luther proclaimed in 1517 that the pope could not remit guilt or the sin of an individual, that each was accountable to God (Bullough, 1970). It ended religious unity in Europe. Though the Reformation had lasting effects on spiritual freedom, early Protestants held a limited view of suicide. Luther believed it was the work of the devil. This stance continued over the next few centuries; noted figures like John Wesley felt the corpses should be "gibbeted and . . . left to rot" (as cited in Jamison, 1999, p. 16). A gibbet is a stake from which one is executed by hanging. An open challenge of Protestant or Catholic churches may not have aired; however, writers, under the guise of fictions about utopian societies, indirectly proclaimed that rational death could be freely chosen. Books with affirmative notions of voluntary death were often published posthumously for fear of punishment. Traditionalists feared that such secular means of delving into suicide would provoke a rash of suicides.

In the 16th century, religion, philosophy, and science began to share a piece of the debate on self-inflicted death. This break challenged a preceding notion about suicide: Only the Church's view should be proclaimed. Intellectual venturing about suicide went beyond what was morally acceptable to religious mandates. Fedden (1938/1972) stated, "Throughout the Middle Ages philosophy and scholarship were the eager servants of religious authority. . . . With the renaissance there came a change" (p. 185). Systematic studies emerged, listing pros and cons of suicide. Notably, French essayist Montaigne wanted to study suicide without prejudice, for he reasoned such a subject should be viewed rationally. Empirical study was at its early stages, a methodology that is still prominent in suicidology today.

Philosophical questions emerged, such as, was suicide a rational act? Graber (1998) stated one side of the issue succinctly: "It is rationally justified to kill oneself when a reasonable appraisal of the situation reveals that one is really better off dead" (p. 157). When it came to suicide, if one was deemed irrational, others had the right to determine affairs. But what happens if the act of suicide in all cases is considered irrational? Do the mentally ill lose their freedom to choose?

Often suicide was posited as a result of madness. In this way, the impulsive quality of many suicides was seen less as frenzied demon possession and more as madness. In the Middle Ages, to claim that the disparaged soul could flee life was taken to mean that divine power to save people from misery was negligible, whereas in the Renaissance, *melancholia* became one of the stated causes of suicide. The word melancholia was first used by Hippocrates to describe an affective state that would later be called depression (Goodwin & Guze, 1992). But where did melancholia come from?

A medical interpretation of what caused such depressive states soon secularized ideas about suicide. Robert Burton's *Anatomy of Melancholy* (1652/1988) was a monumental work claiming suicide was not a satanic sin but rather an illness. It was supposed that excess black bile caused this dysfunction. Psychological-type treatments such as fresh air, good food, family relationships, sex, and wine would cure this illness that caused suicide (as cited in Minois, 1999). Although medicine provided a more natural view of suicide, some have felt that overreliance on medical explanations led to common misbeliefs. Fairbairn (1995) wrote of this influence today:

> The pervasive influence of medicine is partly, and perhaps largely, responsible for what is arguably the most common belief about suicide—that anyone who kills or tries to kill himself must be mad, because no one who is sane would want to end his life. Those who have ended or want to end their lives or who seem to want to do so are often assumed to be depressed in the sense of being mentally ill. (p. 28)

Nonetheless, a medical view was a fresh view that brought with it less incrimination and more compassion.

Compassion for those who committed suicide began to appear in policy and writing. William Ramesey, in 1672, wrote *The Gentlemen's Companion*, which called for compassion for the victims of suicide. Matthew Beuvelet's manual for priests on dealing with suicides in the field of their parish called for tolerance (as cited in Minois, 1999). If suicide was truly caused by irrational thought, a medical problem, or insanity, such a person deserved leniency. Toward the end of this era, old traditions were dying and the view of suicide as a crime was waning. Medical perspectives of the body made it seem unnecessary for magistrates to drag a corpse around, thus humiliating the family.

The age of Enlightenment marked a growth in the printed press. This brought stories of suicide into closer reach of the commoner. Stories related to suicide, found in coroner's sections of papers, were frequently neutral and descriptive in tone. The press made the topic a secular one. The birth of demographics and the use of statistics in papers offered a new way to look at suicide. This new vantage produced initial shock and attention to suicide. English readers in the late 17th century were struck by what appeared to be an epidemic of suicide. The same was true in France (Lieberman, 2003). They were not the first in history to worry about epidemics and waves of suicide. Some believed these epidemics were the result of rampant secular movements. In reaction to secular movements, religious movements like the Casuist attacked acts of suicide by providing concrete legal-like condemnation of specific acts of suicide (Minois, 1999).

"Was suicide natural?" became a matter of philosophical debate. Montesquieu, a French philosopher and politician, maintained that as part of nature an individual is able to modify nature, including that part of nature that concerns his or her own life. He, along with writers and philosophers Rousseau and Voltaire, criticized the official view of suicide (Fedden, 1938/1972). Hume, a Scottish philosopher and historian, reasoned that it is the individual's right to choose death when life is unbearable, whether it is due to illness, poverty, or the result of social ills (Retterstol, 1993). Hume argued that at times it was natural, "that suicide is not contrary to love of self, of neighbor, or of God." Hume claimed that "even assuming the truth of Aquinas's theism, one need not preclude suicide from being rational and moral" (Donelly, 1998, p. 12). If suicide is seen as unnatural, it becomes viewed as pathological or criminal. For example, viewing preservation of life as the only natural inclination led to suicides being legally categorized under one of two titles: *non compos mentis* (uncontrolled mind, mad) or *felo de se* (crime against oneself; Szasz, 1999).

Ideas such as a right to property and inalienable personal liberties had an impact on societal views of suicide (Battin, 1998). Similar to Stoic claims, a group of intellectuals called the *philosophes* believed in personal ownership of one's life. The *philosophes* were not dependent economically on the church or kings and so voiced their opposition to absolute monarchies (Bullough, 1970). Such monarchies were no better at recognizing personal ownership of life than the religious establishment. The movement for inalienable personal liberty would in years to come produce worldwide manifestos declaring that there were natural rights belonging to all humans: the American Bill of Rights, Communist Manifesto, French Declaration of the Rights of Man, and U.N. Declaration of Human Rights (Battin, 1998). The old ways of confiscating land and harming the honor of families was not just to "individuals," namely the wife and children of a suicide. Often, canonical and civil law, which remained conservative, were not in harmony with the sentiments of commoners (Fedden, 1938/1972). Szasz (1999) depicted the dilemma thus

> One result was men sitting on coroner's juries found it increasingly more difficult to deprive innocent wives and children of their dead husbands' possessions. But the jurors were in a bind. Repealing the laws against self-murder was politically unthinkable, yet punishing the deed as prescribed by law was morally unacceptable. (p. 33)

During revolutionary movements, political suicides and patriotic suicide were prevalent. Revolutionary movements often eradicated legal precedent along with the outgoing rulers. After the French Revolution, the penal code of 1790 made no mention of suicide (Fedden, 1938/1972). Nationalism and the requirements of a social contract between government and the individual replaced duty to king and church. Though this was true, suicide was at times seen as an aversion of one's duty to country. The idea of a social contract existing between government and the individual for the sake of welfare may not have changed notions that suicide was selfish. Minois (1999) wrote,

Whatever its nature, power seeks to prevent and conceal suicide. The subject must dedicate his life to the king; the citizen must conserve his life for the homeland. Desertion is out of the question. The social contract requires everyone's participation in maintaining the state, which, in exchange, watches over everyone's well being. (p. 302)

In contemporary culture, governments are seen as responsible for solving problems like suicide. Societal solutions and interventions are supported and funded by tax dollars collected from the citizenry. Society was asked to prevent the suicidal person not only from doing harm to him- or herself but also from doing harm to others (Szasz, 1999).

Modern Times

Humanitarianism has had lasting effects on the way the public views suicide. Humanitarian movements set out to lessen the suffering of society. Institutions for addictions, mental illness, and the poor were operated out of a wish to conquer the ills of society. Humanitarianism has had a sweeping impact with its notion that suffering should be lessened. Bullough (1970) wrote, "The role of the nineteenth century humanitarians in lessening suffering can hardly be overestimated—on the battlefield, in hospitals, asylums, prisons, factories, the military service, schools and in their general concern for the welfare of human beings and animals" (p. 349). One critique is often that such institutions set on improving life were carried out with a monocultural myopia.

The pursuits of science birthed the study of suicide as an entity; suicidology emerged (Shneidman, 1985). Emile Durkheim's (1897/1951) work, *Le Suicide*, was the first systematic study of suicide. It was important in that it promoted future in-depth studies of suicide. Durkheim maintained that suicide was the result of a conflict between the individual and society. He focused on the ills of the new industrialized societies that had come into being in the 19th century; ills that disconnected people from family, community, and society at large.

At its onset, suicidology focused on psychological autopsies and was interested in suicide trends drawn from statistical measures. Later in the 1950s, the study shifted emphasis toward problem-oriented issues. These studies found statistically significant correlates between mental illness and suicide (Sourbrier, 1997/1998).

Psychological ideas of humanity blossomed, placing suicide in the context of a more systematic and in-depth examination of the nature of mind and human development. Sigmund Freud drew on his theory that intrapsychic tensions, as with an ego's loss of a love object, caused maladies such as suicide. Learning theorists believed that inadequate reinforcement and learned helplessness were possible reasons for self-inflicted death. Cognitive–behaviorists noted a sequence of unhealthy thoughts leading to unhealthy behaviors. Adlerians blamed lack of social interest and personal feelings of inferiority. Rogerians were concerned with internal incongruency between an ideal self and the real self. Regardless of theoretical orientation, these helpers sought to provide therapy in pursuit of curing mental ills (Lester, 1988).

A modern medical view became a predominant understanding of suicide (Szasz, 1998). Psychiatry with its emphasis on biochemistry has shifted focus from primarily psychological notions of mental illness toward problems with the material self. Depression and mood disorders caused by chemical imbalances are often the attributed causes of suicide. The medical model is often ascribed as a "disease model." In this way, the patient presents an ill and a cure is given. Life and health are the core values of the Hippocratic oath that doctors take, not death and disease. Is suicide inherently a disease, a maladaptation, or some type of a correctable problem? In cases where "yes" has been the answer, suicide prevention has been the guiding force.

Mental illness and resultant suicide have gained a sympathetic eye in comparison with past centuries, often necessitating social acts of compassion such as prevention. In 1958, Edwin Shneidman and Norman Farberow received a U.S. Public Health grant for the Suicide Prevention Center in Los Angeles, the first of its kind (Farberow & Shneidman, 1961). Later they, along with others such as Edwin Ringel, formed the International Association for Suicide Prevention (Goldney, 1998). A suicide hotline was instituted; to these pioneers' credit, hotlines now abound in nations all over the world, giving callers a chance to seek help. Over the past several decades, suicide prevention increased exponentially as is evidenced by the initiation of suicide protocols throughout most human services.

Among helping professionals, a tendency exists to view suicide from medical and psychological models that call for preventative interventions. Currently, suicide is commonly addressed as a multidimensional phenomenon but often seen through the lens of the statistical research. The following is an example of a how a book might convey the numerical quality and quantity of suicide:

> The World Health Organization (2002b) estimated that in 2000, approximately 1 million people died from suicide; the "global" mortality rate was 16 per 100,000 persons. Completed suicides are said to have occurred about one every 40 seconds and attempted suicide once every 3 seconds. The World Health Organization is calling global suicide an epidemic, stating that suicide rates have climbed 60% over the last 45 years. Illustrating its view, an organizational letter states that suicide is "1.8% of the total global disease burden" (World Health Organization, 2002a). Past trends have placed the elderly as the most at-risk group for suicide; however, over the last two decades a trend shows an increase in worldwide youth suicides. Around the world men complete suicides more often than women. Arab and Latin American countries report low rates of suicide;

European countries and countries populated with European descent report higher rates of suicide (Diekstra, 1993). The World Health Organization (2002a) estimates that 90% of suicides worldwide are the result of mental illness (e.g., depression and schizophrenia).

The above are all facts, albeit limited by the vast complexity of the world. Although it calls suicide a disorder, the World Health Organization (2002a) rightly established that "suicide is a multidimensional disorder which results from a complex interaction between biological, genetic, physiological, sociological and environmental factors" (p. 1).

In the 19th and 20th centuries, suicide has become more of a shame or disgrace than a sin or crime (Barraclough, 1987). "Most European countries formally decriminalized suicide in the eighteenth and nineteenth centuries, although it remained a crime in England and Wales until 1961 and in Ireland until 1993" (Jamison, 1999, p. 18). Suicide itself is not a crime, but assisting a suicide is a crime in most parts of the United States. In 1994, voters in the State of Oregon passed a Death With Dignity Act, calling for physician-assisted voluntary death. It was taken to higher courts, denied further hearings by the U.S. Supreme Court, and finally passed again by Oregon voters with an even greater margin in 1997. Last year, the state of Oregon allowed a few dozen of its residents to choose death with the aid of a physician (Oregon Death With Dignity Center, 2003). This legislation is provoking internal debate, not just for the various branches of government but also within individuals, because it challenges the notion of what our own life and death mean.

Suicide and Death

To look clearly into the subject of suicide, one must start by examining the social and cultural significance of death. There is a fair amount of debate in the United States around life and death issues. Abortion and euthanasia are not what many would call "polite conversation" topics. How we experience and perceive life and death shape how we view suicide (Kral, 1994; Orbach, Gross, & Glaubman, 1981; Payne & Range, 1995). How we feel about death often makes us think about what it means to be human, to be living ("Is Death the Spice of Life," 2003). Because of space limitations, I will not delve into such a monumental topic; rather I touch on the significant aspects of death to reveal how we are all personally involved. Consideration of suicide as seen through history has seldom been devoid of opinion, emotion, and conflict; it is personal to us because it challenges our deepest emotions and beliefs about our existence.

Death is universal. What is death, exactly? Most cultures recognize the physical death of an individual: the cessation of observable human behavior. After which bereavement and ritual follow. Western science is adamant about the clarity with which it certifies the biological scope of this process. The

15

Harvard Medical School in 1968 presented a standard for biological death, which has since been widely accepted (Monaghan & Guterman, 2002). In short, total death of the brain is death of the person (Swinburn, Ali, Banerjee, & Khan, 1999). Having ruled out a reversible coma, if a body is unresponsive to stimuli, fails to breathe for 3 minutes, lacks movement for 1 hour, has lost all reflexes, and an electroencephalogram (EEG) shows no sign of electrical activity in the brain, death is proclaimed (Sigelman, 1999). Obviously not all deaths in the world are certified by expensive equipment like an EEG. Many countries, industrialized or not, do not see brain death as death (C. B. Becker, 1990; Monaghan & Guterman, 2002), for that would suggest a most Western notion, "I think therefore I am" (Watson, 2002).

The process of death shapes and affects our lives to an unknown degree. Sigmund Freud fostered the idea that there is an inherent instinct for life and one for death (Jones, 1963). Whether there is such an instinct or not, one could argue that many of our everyday actions are deeply rooted in survival, the survival of self. Like an iceberg with 90% of its mass below, the deeper motives that drive a person's thoughts and behavior are not in conscious light. How we experience our lives directly relates to our feelings about death (Kral, 1994; Payne & Range, 1995). Accumulated loss from death experiences may mold our perceptions, but rarely do such experiences of others' deaths give us full insight into our own. We cannot see into the obscure future let alone into what is beyond.

What happens after we die? One uniform view would not emerge from an array of answers. A person's concepts of death indicate what cultures, ethnicities, philosophies, and religions have been influential in making up a personal worldview. There are as many cultural variations as there are individual differences in human beliefs about death. In many cultures, there is a demarcation between the dead and the living. Those who are dead are gone. For others, the dead may linger or may have to be ushered into a new realm or form (Becker, 1990; Monaghan & Guterman, 2002).

Acceptance of Death

Avoidance and acceptance are two primary ways the fact of biological death is addressed. Yudhishthira, an ancient Indian ruler, was asked, "What is the greatest wonder in the whole world?" and he replied, "That we see people dying all around us and never think that we too will die" (Brahmaprana, 2001). Owing to the multidimensional nature of death, it is best to look at avoidance and acceptance along a continuum, changing with time and circumstance.

Many have argued that much of Western culture, as evidenced by its medical philosophy and practice, has increasingly moved away from an acceptance of death (Connelly, 2003). Karasu (1985) held that a transformation has occurred in Western attitudes about death over the last 400 years. Moreover, the last century has been marked by less acceptance of death and a viewpoint of death as a disease to be overcome by a cure. Davies (1996) made this point in relation to funerary ritual: "Major changes have taken place in the way that the remains of the dead are disposed of. These distance the living from decay, dissolution and indeed death itself" (p. 60). Regardless of such speculation, a cultural wish to prevent death and prolong life is prevalent.

Although death is disruptive and entails loss, it can be seen as natural. In some cultures death is something in which the whole community should take part. For example, in traditional Hmong communities, where youth must learn death ritual, children take part in many aspects of a typical funeral. Some are keepers of death ritual, some act as counselors, whereas others learn instruments or direct funerals for the community (Bliatout, 1993). What may make death more acceptable is that it is seen as a part of life. Whether death is viewed positively or negatively, such constructs directly affect how counselors work with clients. Many have turned toward human development as a background for understanding the complexities behind the constructs.

Development and Concepts of Death

When looking at suicide across the life span, it is important to note developmental effects on ideation and behavior about death. A young child, a midlife woman, and the oldest of old may experience life differently because of how perception changes as life progresses. Many parents readily know that their child does not understand death the way an adult does. Sometimes it is surprising when children have a curiosity or even an obsession with death. Often in a grieving family, different ideas of death and what it means arise. The sister of a woman who had just died wrote this letter:

> I am inquiring to you today on behalf of my 2½ year old niece. Her mother died of cancer (Leimayo Sarcoma). . . . She is now beginning to comment often on the fact that her mom died and went to heaven to be with Jesus. What do you say? What do you do? We love her so. She lives with her Daddy. They are more existing than living. Daddy is having a hard time dealing with himself and the loss of his long-time best friend. My niece is not happy. She is only comfortable at my mother-in-law's house. There she has Grandma and Grandpa and her young aunt. They are dealing with the loss also, but not dwelling on it. My niece was not allowed to go to the funeral. I had mixed feelings on this. I feel that she needs some kind of closure. We tell her that her mommy went to heaven. Where is that? A two year old doesn't understand. I felt that she needed to see where mommy's body is, not just her soul. Maybe I am wrong; maybe in God's way she does understand. I would like to know how to deal with her, what to say when she inquires about her mom. I don't feel that Daddy is in the mental state to deal with this without bias and without putting himself first. I don't know if my niece is comfortable asking him. Please help. Thank You. (Sims, 2003)

One can sense the grief and confusion affecting this family after the loss of a loved and valued family member. Even though these individuals are related and share the same cultural background, it is evident that no one's understanding or grief is exactly the same. A person's ability to cognitively process death and suicide greatly depends on where the person is along the developmental life span (Gothelf et al., 1998; Stallion & Papadatou, 2002; Stanley, 2000).

Theorists hold that a concept of self emerges with human development; a child starts to understand that it is a "self" within the first few years after birth (Burton & Mitchell, 2003; Kochanska, Gross, Lin, & Nichols, 2002; Sigelman, 1999). From a certain standpoint, existence brings about death; only a self can die. Death as a concept is something that children begin to formulate just as they develop a sense of self (Gothelf et al., 1998). One study looking at children's understanding of the death of plants suggested that between the ages of 4 and 6, significant development in the understanding of death becomes salient (Nguyen & Gelman, 2002). Kane (1979) suggested that concepts of death develop in stages directly relating to the preoperational, concrete operations, and formal operations stages proposed by Piaget. These stages mark mental development as symbolic, logical, and abstract thinking emerge. Thus, as a human's mental development grows in complexity, so too does the potential for their view of death to take on a multifaceted quality.

A Western sense of a "developed" view of death has in the past held four qualities: universality, finality, irreversibility, and biological causality. Universality implies that it happens to all living beings. Finality means that it is the end of life and living processes, such that the dead in the coffin is not still listening or hearing. This departs from many cultures that recognize the presence, spirit, or soul inhabiting space after death. Irreversibility implies that death cannot be undone. For example, preschool children sometimes believe a dead person is gone as if "on a trip" and will return. The biological causality of death means that death is a result of an internal biological process even when this internal process is initiated by external factors (Sigelman, 1999). For example, total brain death is facilitated by a car accident, drowning, old age, small pox, and so on. Despite developmental stages, whether the circumstances of death are viewed in a positive or negative light directly affects how counselors work with clients.

What Makes a "Good Death"?

"What would it look like if you died well? What hopes, wishes, and aversions would emerge? What would be the components of a 'bad' death?" When asked to respond to these questions, a person's answer would take us to the heart of internalized social and cultural ideas of death. Bradbury (1996) posited that such "social representations of death are temporally and culturally specific" (p. 94); in other words, ideas of a good or bad death are not consistent through time and across cultures.

Death holds the potential for the loss of everything dear and valued. A good death embodies control over transience or assurance in the midst of disruption and the unknown. At other times, death is a way out of despairing times. Jung (1958) commented, "Historically, it is chiefly in times of physical, political, economic and spiritual distress that men's eyes turn with anxious hope to the future, and when anticipations, utopias and apocalyptic visions multiply" (p. 11)

A "good death" is an emerging term as hospice workers and other medical care providers have begun to "manage" death and dying (Connelly, 2003). The remnants of a good death are not new and can be seen in writings throughout various periods of history (Short, Hart, & Sainsbury, 1998). Others find it is more accurate to use the term "good enough death" (Masson, 2002). Notions of good or bad deaths can affect the decision to take one's life and how survivors bereave and deal with loss.

Consider these two scenarios as they relate to good and bad death: (a) Grandmother died after living a full and long life. She died of natural causes with her large family at her side in the comfort of her own home. Grandma died with clarity of mind and little physical pain; she sensed it was time to go on and so started to prepare. The local minister, a longtime friend of the family, provided last rites before her death and presided over her funeral attended by what seemed like the whole community. Grandma and the whole family had time to prepare for death, everyone had time to say goodbye. All legal work was settled, and her considerable estate was divided fairly among members of the family. (b) John, in a violent intoxicated rage, killed his wife, son, daughter, and an intervening neighbor before turning the gun on himself. He had suffered for many years from depression, drug addiction, and problems with the law. He became increasingly at risk after another failed job attempt. John had broken ties with his family. Having been in debt, state funds were used to take care of John's remains. His wife's family suffered financial difficulty giving the rest of the family a burial. Moreover, the deaths have left many unresolved feelings, and several communities are shocked and disrupted by the news of this horrific crisis. From these two stories one can glean the qualities and components of a good and bad death.

There are many definitions proposed for a good death (Mak, 2002; Short et al., 1998). In a qualitative study (Mak, 2002), terminally ill Chinese hospice patients were interviewed about dying. Seven components of a good death surfaced: death awareness, hope, comfort (freedom from pain), personal control, connectedness (maintenance of social relationships), preparation, and completion (acceptance of the timing of death). Mak further explained that to these patients timing was a central issue. Some elements emerged about the timing of death: the completion of social roles, death being perceived as good and natural, in accord with faith and the experience of life as meaningful leading to an optimistic view of the future. Short et al. (1998) looked at various definitions of a good death and arrived at the following features: dying with dignity, awareness, peacefulness, preparedness, acceptance, and adjustment.

One could say that the qualities of what one looks for in a good death are what are sought after in life. Suicide attempts are often made from a state of ambivalence; many completed suicides are impulsive and marred by lack of clarity. With other suicides, there is a balancing mechanism at work. An unvoiced question drives action: Are these current conditions of life more difficult than some unknown future potential held in death?

Afterlife

Is it paradoxical that individuals are concerned with the preservation of self while in the midst of choosing death? Suicidal behavior is often surrounded by ambivalence. Stone (1999) suggested that the physical act of killing oneself is not difficult; thus suicide is in a person's own hands. Orbach et al. (1981) proposed that suicidality was influenced by the interaction of four attitudes: attraction to life, attraction to death, repulsion for life, and repulsion for death (as cited in Payne & Range, 1995). For many, they are escaping the intolerable aspects of life. Formed beliefs about a potential beyond death can play a significant role in the decision to end life (Gothelf et al., 1998; Payne & Range, 1995).

A commonly held belief in many cultures is that physical death is not the entire death of the person; afterlife in some form exists. Harley and Firebaugh (1993) estimated from a general social survey taken between 1973 and 1991 that Americans in general believe in an afterlife and that rates have not declined across generations. Globally, afterlife constructs give context to meanings of life and death.

Afterlife beliefs can affect how a person gives context to his or her own death and that of others (Irion, 1993; Kamal & Lowenthal, 2002). Cultures and systems of belief provide the circumstances and parameters in which voluntary death is personally and socially acceptable. These mores become embedded, and the story of afterlife determines the meaning behind self-inflicted death.

Spirituality issues have a heightened presence during periods of death. Belief can be a remedy for the difficulties that one is facing. Often it is the primary coping mechanism that one has; belief systems and those representing traditions of belief can provide hope in the midst of despair. They can also provide closure to a seemingly unfinished story. Here is an example of a minister who provided context and a sense of completeness by presenting a eulogy adapted from a wife's story about her husband's seemingly rational suicide.

> For many years now, Mark has been suffering. Life has declined, just the simple things that you and I take for granted have become a burden. There was the stroke, which made it difficult for him to control his moods. The very part of ourselves that we cherish the most, the ability to direct

our actions and emotions, had faded for Mark. He had said that he couldn't cope with the prospects of facing still more surgery. Today we struggle to understand how illness contributed to his death. (Echelbarger, 1993, p. 221)

In this story afterlife was not mentioned, but the sheer presence of a minister presiding over the funeral was important.

Belief systems and how they are ritualized can have a negative effect as well (Rose & O'Sullivan, 2003), leading to isolation, anxiety, guilt, and incrimination. Abdel-Khalek (2002) studied 1,046 college students from Egypt, Kuwait, Lebanon, and Saudi Arabia who were mostly Arabic and Muslim. This study found that fear of pain and punishment, and religious transgressions and failures, were significant reasons why the students feared death. This study may not be generalizable to all groups in North America; however, such reasons for fearing death extend beyond Arab culture and Muslim religion. Abdel-Khalek's (2002) research is important because it delved into the reasons that people fear death. Most research until now has focused on death anxiety in various forms as well as meanings attributed to death. Although many avoid suicide because of potential afterlife consequences, intolerable conditions can marginalize the role of belief.

Sometimes pain is unbearable, thinking becomes constricted, and action is taken regardless of belief systems (Shneidman, 1985). When counseling someone who is grappling with the possibility of voluntary death, chronic and acute pain is a key factor shaping the desirability of life. For some clients it is best to use the prevention method of delay, giving "life" a chance to improve. As is discussed in chapter 3, hopelessness is a factor in voluntary death. To many, an afterlife might seem more advantageous. This section categorizes several different types of afterlife belief: rewarding, continuation on earth, punishment, extinction/sleep, imaginary, and in-between realms.

A Rewarding Afterlife. In many afterlife belief systems, a glorious heaven awaits the faithful or "good" departed. This place is often a place shared with a creator and gods, departed loved ones are there, and those things that make life unpleasant are minimized or absent. In some traditions, this reward realm becomes the eternal home of the deceased (Early, 1992), for others it is only temporary. This realm is often procured through faith and good merits.

Continuation of Life on Earth. Many afterlife beliefs hold the notion that the self remains closely connected to or returns to life on earth. For example, a traditional view of Dogon people in Mali is that humans are composed of various components. Some but not all of the components stay in contact and reside among the related living here on earth (Griaule, 1994). Ancestors who remain after death help and guide the living. In such a manner, death releases life to the earth.

Here is a story that exemplifies how this belief played a role in suicide. Slave ships were tightly packed in American colonial times, conditions were inhumane, individuals were often chained to the recently dead, and severe illness was only one of the unbearable aspects of this vicious transport (Cowley & Mannix, 1994). Slaves had to be watched on the deck because they would commit suicide to return to life where they were from, thus returning to families. A ship's surgeon wrote the following about the intentional deaths of enslaved Iboos:

> [They] wished to die on an idea that they should then get back to their own country. The captain in order to obviate this idea, thought of an expedient viz. to cut off the heads of those who died intimating to them that if determined to go, they must return without heads. The slaves were accordingly brought up to witness the operation. One of them by a violent exertion got loose and flying to the place where the nettings had been unloosed in order to empty the tubs, he darted overboard. . . . [He] made signs which words cannot express expressive happiness in escaping. He then went down and was seen no more. (as cited in Cowley & Mannix,1994, p. 108)

Punishment in the Afterlife. While some fear intolerable conditions on earth, others fear it in afterlife. Rose and O'Sullivan (2003) found that belief in an afterlife is not necessarily comforting, especially for those who believe in a judgment/punishment-based afterlife. Often there is a punishment realm whether temporary or eternal for those who erred, transgressed, or committed punishable sins. The notion is that one's actions during life will transfer into the next life. In cultures where Buddhism is present, the act of voluntary death may not be viewed negatively depending on a person's state of mind at the time of death (C. B. Becker, 1990). Sects of Christianity and Islam have for a long time propagated the belief that one might find eternal hell or "tortures of the grave" for transgressions in this life (Abdel-Khalek, 2002; Minois, 1999). There is no consistent view of afterlife in Judaism because of an emphasis placed on the present life; however, orthodoxy holds that there is a judgment in the afterlife (Grollman, 1993). Suicide is in general condemned by those beliefs that have a punishment-based afterlife.

Extinction/Sleep. For some, death is final, and the phenomenal world is the only real world. In this way the uniqueness or entity of a person does not continue. Extinction of a self after death is at times likened to the state of sleep in which there is rest but no consciousness. Consciousness fades in death in the same manner that it fades when one goes to bed each night. If extinction is true, all is equal in death to the deceased regardless of the manner in which they went.

Imaginary. For those of nonconventional beliefs, images of death are not formulated by but may be influenced by traditional beliefs. These images can serve as a means of coping. This may take the form of a metaphysical belief that fulfills a basic spiritual need. Such a belief may have been drawn from experience or from one's grounding in science. It may simply reflect the great mystery of death and the unknowable hereafter. Personally derived imaginations and theories of afterlife should not be considered delusional as if nonconvention implies erroneous thinking (Irion, 1993).

In-Between Realms. In many afterlife belief structures, there are several potential realms that one might go to upon death. Some of these are contingent on a merit system. For example, Catholics often believe that the dead are sent to purgatory. Purgatory is a place where the deceased can work to improve their merit and purify the soul; the living can pray for the dead to be purified and thus delivered from this realm (Miller, 1993). Tibetan Buddhists believe in a Bardo realm where a spirit goes in transition between one life and another (Evans-Wentz, 1974). In some traditions ghosts and spirits linger.

Classifying Suicide

> In times such as ours there is a great pressure to come up with concepts that help men understand their dilemma; there is an urge toward vital ideas, toward a simplification of needless intellectual complexities. Sometimes this makes for big lies that resolve tensions and make it easy for actions to move forward with just the rationalizations people need. But it also makes for the slow disengagement of truths that help men get a grip on what is happening to them, that tell them where their problems are. (E. Becker, 1973, p. 1)

It is clear that classifications of suicide are limited without a specific purpose. A counselor who rigidly conceptualizes the reality of the client's situation misses the true experience of the individual. For the counselor, it is important to try on different lenses when looking at this issue and to challenge current thinking and held assumptions. For this reason, examination of these attempts to make sense of and understand the multidimensional topic of voluntary death is presented.

Over the last several centuries, science and its methods have become part of the way that industrialized cultures have come to understand the world. Historians mark the origins of modern science to be around the 16th and 17th centuries (Mason, 1962). It brought the scientific method and an emphasis on finding truth in nature by using logic, empirical methods, deconstruction, and rational thought; it emphasized observable truth found outside of the biases of dogmatic religion and the untested postulations of philosophy. A guidepost that the scientific community held was objectivity, removing self and thus one's opinions, to provide a clear view of the subject. Modern theorists note that there is not a completely neutral way of observing, because the observer and the observed are not separable.

Classification embodied modern science's meticulous effort to find clarity and sort out the facts. Cartesian thought stipulated that to observe the universe one should observe the parts to understand the whole. Humans, and animals for that matter, were not much different than a machine. Mechanization of reality has become a common mental task and professional tool across disciplines (Durant & Durant, 1965/1992).

23

Some early scientists, whether they were sociologist or biologists, attempted to understand suicide by using classification. Many classifications of suicide have been put forward, but none are ever sufficient to capture the nature of such a multidimensional human phenomenon. Shneidman (1985) stated, "I submit that all these classifications, taken singly or together, have either an arbitrary, esoteric or ad hoc quality to them. They do not seem impressively definitive" (p. 29). Zubin (1974) had another point to offer: "The classification of human behavior presents a major problem because no single criterion for classification exists" (p. 3). Our world is so complex that our mental formulations are limited in constructing a full representation of life. Although one need not confuse thought with reality, it is essential that theoretical models be used for a better understanding of one's world.

One of the earliest and most used schema for looking at suicide through a scientific lens was proposed by Emile Durkheim, a sociologist who presented a social theory that he applied to suicide in his work *Le Suicide*, which was published in 1897. As a theoretical work it continues to be a critical reference point. However, Durkheim's classification of suicide as well as many other early models did not translate easily into applicable clinical use. Eventually those who followed expanded on earlier classifications, making them more useful for a clinician handling suicidal behavior (Shneidman, 1985).

Durkheim (1897/1951) proposed four basic types of suicides: egotistic, altruistic, anomic, and fatalistic. Those who have lost connection with the world, the lonely, best typify egotistic suicide. "Egotistical" in this sense is not selfishness, but rather a state of isolation and aloneness. Isolation puts one at a greater risk for suicide. Durkheim elaborated that one cause of this stems from education. In this way education expands possibilities of thought and behavior, separating an individual from traditional life. Durkheim cautioned that knowledge is not the culprit, but the by-product of education is often alienation. Suicide stems from the lack of integration into religious, domestic, familial, and political society. It is the strength of society that prevents egotistical suicide.

Altruistic suicide occurs as a result of enmeshed relationship to society. Durkheim (1897/1951) stated, "Excessive individuation leads to suicide, insufficient individuation has the same effects" (p. 217). A classic example of altruistic suicide would be the Hindu practice of *suttee*. In some levels of the caste system in India, when a husband died the wife would throw herself upon the funeral pyre. It was not for a dispassion for life or an avoidance of life that brought about these deaths; rather it was brought upon by institutional values and pressures.

Anomic comes from *anomia* in Greek, which means lawless (Merriam Webster, 1993). In short, situational crises and chaos lead to suicide. Dire financial straits, death, and divorce cause crises and shock. Increased stressors and trauma precede suicide. This alludes to the impulsive quality of some suicidal behavior—the events of life can be overwhelming. Often some fail to adjust (Durkheim, 1897/1951).

Fatalistic suicide occurs when personal freedom seems to be hampered such that the person takes a fatal position toward life and thus ends it. Individual suppression by societal forces leads to pessimistic speculation about life. A person filled with this constricted view kills him- or herself (Durkheim, 1897/1951). One historical example of this was the fate of "witches" in Europe and the British Isles. Those found to be witches had little choice; "suicide or the stake were often the last alternatives that remained for her" (Fedden, 1938/1972, p. 150).

In 1968 Shneidman promoted another system for looking at suicide. Three categories were used to classify suicides: egotic, dyadic, and ageneratic. The egotic suicide stems from "intrapsychic" machinations of a person. In such a case external factors influencing the person are secondary and the decision to die is meted out by the ego. "This is what one sees in the extremely narrowed focus of attention, self-denigrating depression, and other situations where the suicide occurs without regard for anyone else including loved ones and significant others" (Shneidman, 1985, p. 25).

Dyadic suicide refers to suicide caused because of problems or issues related to a primary dyad; suicide occurs from the failure or dissolution of an important interpersonal relationship. Shneidman (1985) clarified, "Although suicide is always the act of a person and, in this sense, stems from within his mind, the dyadic suicide is essentially an interpersonal event" (p. 25). Japanese *shinju* or love-pact suicides are a good example of this. An attributed cause of this style of self-inflicted death is a conflict between "obligation and love" and "love without parental approval" (Iga, 1986, p. 149).

Ageneratic suicide results from a lost sense of identity related to personal lineage, or how one's life affects the future. Such a person "falls out" and does not see him- or herself as being part of a historical line, cut off from the process of ancestry and progeny. Shneidman (1985) commented, "to have no sense of serial belonging or to be an 'isolate' is truly a lonely and comfortless position, for then one may, in that perspective, truly have little to live for" (p. 26).

Farberow (1975) proposed that one could classify suicides into two specific categories: (a) personal or individual and (b) social or institutional. He pointed out that in various cases there is a blend of the two. He commented on psychological autopsies that fit this typology,

> Personal suicide was an individual act of protest or declaration against either interpersonal hurts or transgressions against society. The motives were preservation of honor and dignity, expiation of pusillanimity or cowardice, avoidance of pain and ignominy by old age and/or disease, preservation of chastity, escape from personal disgrace by falling into the hands of the enemy, unwillingness to bear the hurt of separation or the loss of a love, and others. (Farberow, 1975, p. 2)

Farberow pointed out that most social and institutional mandated suicides normally give an occasion and a form for how it is to take place.

Baechler (1979) had four categories of suicides: escapist, aggressive, oblative, and ludic suicides. Not all are distinct categories of completed suicides; many incorporate gestures and other suicidal behavior. This is particularly the case with the aggressive category.

Baechler's first category, escapist, has three subtypes. First, escape by flight is when a person takes his or her life so as to escape the intolerable. The second type is escaping from grief or sudden "loss of a central element of his personality or way of life" (Baechler, 1979, p. 84). The last subtype of escape occurs when an individual is killing him- or herself to atone for some perceived or real fault. Here the inability to deal with the shame of committing a crime or a heinous act is the reason for this subtype of suicidal escape; one might think of Judas Iscariot, Jesus' disciple and betrayer, who hung himself out of grief and guilt.

Baechler's (1979) second category, aggressive suicide, has four subtypes: crime, vengeance, blackmail, and appeal. Crime refers to the aggressive suicide that often ends in suicide when the individual and others end up dead. Domestic violence and the slew of high school suicide-homicides in the United Stated come to mind. Vengeance is meant to "provoke another's remorse or to inflict the opprobrium of the community on him" (Baechler, 1979, p. 120). Suicide as blackmail is using suicidal behavior to threaten in order to obtain or deprive something from someone. Baechler presents a case example in which a prisoner threatened suicide until his request for release was reviewed. After three such attempts, he was released. "A suicide whose meaning is appeal involves an attempt on one's life with the intention of informing one's friends and family that the subject is in danger" (Baechler, 1979, p. 146). This is often seen in cases in which a person has serious mental distress and is making a fatal gesture to get help from others.

Oblative suicides are those suicides that entail sacrifice or transfiguration. It is for higher purpose that Baechler stated these come about. Sacrifice is one subclass of oblative suicide in which a person attempts or commits suicide to save or acquire a perceived merit greater than the value of his or her personal life. Baechler illustrated this category with the notorious example of kamakazi pilots in World War II. He also provides a story in which a boy stole and drank a glass of rat poison prepared by and meant for his suicidal father. Transfiguration is another subclass of oblative suicide. In such an instance, a suicidal person seeks a higher state felt to be more valuable than the present. Many martyrs and hopeful religious adherents of historical record fall into this category (Baechler, 1979).

Finally, ludic suicides involve self-challenge or self-induced personal ordeal. Dueling, proving oneself by challenging death, entering games of chance that are life threatening, and other such ordeals are part of this classification of suicide. Here life is risked to test personal metal and challenge existential notions.

Thomas Hill Jr. looked at four other types of suicide: impulsive, apathetic, self-abasing, and hedonistic calculations (see Shneidman, 1985).

Impulsive suicides are prompted by sudden and abnormally intense emotions to commit suicide; they are committed without much forethought, implying irrationality. Apathetic suicide is juxtaposed to an impulsive suicide; intentional lack of action causes the death of an individual. The loss of a passion for life is Hill's stated reason for apathetic suicide. Self-abasing suicides are suicides that are the result of despair and hopelessness. Here self-rejection and hate are the driving motives for ending life. Hill's final category, hedonistic calculated suicide, has an economic quality to it; life is evaluated, with pleasure and pain on opposite ends of a decision scale.

Maris placed suicides into five categories: escape, revenge, altruistic, risk-taking, and mixed type (see O'Carroll et al., 1998). Mixed type alludes to events that have "mixed" classification. Suicide-homicides are prime example of this type.

Groups of professionals and experts began to draw up classifications of suicide. The American Medical Association and the American Psychiatric Association performed a study of suicides committed by physicians. An extensive questionnaire was given to discover the nature of these suicides. The examiner was asked to classify the suicide as rational, reactionary, vengeful (as in to punish someone), manipulative, psychotic, or accidental (Shneidman, 1985, p. 29). Of note is the category of rational suicide; it assumes that the only reason is judgment. An example of a rational suicide might be the Hindu practice of *prayopavesa*, death by fasting. This form of voluntary death is performed slowly to maintain a clear mind and give ample time to prepare oneself and others for death. It is performed under strict community guidelines, and so is done when the timing is right and duties have been taken care of. Mahatma Gandhi's associate, Vinod Bhave, chose death this way (Rajan, 1999).

Although these types of classifications describe the fundamental reasons for suicides, they do little to inform us of the entire realm of suicidal thinking and behavior. Other issues such as the severity of intention, method, lethality of method, and mitigating circumstances (confusion, intoxication, etc.) are other valuable aspects not highlighted by many early classifications. Others have addressed these items and more in their classification systems. Aaron Beck chaired a committee put together by the National Institute of Mental Health and the Center for Studies of Suicide Prevention in 1972–1973. Jobes and Ellis are credited with another classification system, which was produced by a panel of experts from a dozen prominent health related organizations (Maris, 1992). Maris also provided a multiaxial approach to suicide. Moreover, he implicated self-destructive behaviors such as alcoholism, drug use, anorexia or bulimia, sexual promiscuity, accident proneness, and even stress as "indirect suicides."

In the *Diagnostic and Statistical Manual of Mental Disorders—Test Revision* (*DSM–IV–TR*; American Psychiatric Association, 2000), there is no subject entry for suicide in the index. Suicide is discussed in the manual as a by-product of mental and physical disorder, not as a disorder itself. Suicidal ideation and destructive behaviors are symptoms of disorders. Such ideation and behavior mark impaired functioning and distress caused by mental illness (e.g., Bipolar II, schizophrenia, adjustment disorder). Referring primarily to the International Classification of Diseases (ICD) and *DSM* systems, Maris (1992) stated, "Usually psychiatric classification schemes view suicide as a possible complication, symptom, or consequence of mood disorders" (p. 77).

Kazarian and Persad (2001) noted that too much emphasis behind understanding suicidal behavior has to do with the reason for dying at the exclusion of a "reason for living" approach. Moreover, Kezarian and Persad advocated for an atheoretical cultural model for understanding suicide. Shea (2002) suggested that suicide and suicidal behavior must be seen as a matrix in which a co-occurrence of issues is present.

Defining Suicide

The word *suicide* started to appear in writings around the mid-17th century. As Shneidman (1985) pointed out, a person could not technically "commit suicide" because such a nomenclature had not been used as of then and so the basic unifying idea of suicide was nonexistent. A person could take poison, kill herself by hanging, or fall upon his knife. Before then, terms like *self-murder* and *self-destruction* were used (Alvarez, 1972).

The Oxford English Dictionary cites the first written use of the word suicide in 1651, and others point to the text *Religio Medici* written by Sir Thomas Brown in 1635 (as cited in Alvarez, 1972; see also Shneidman, 1985). Although the word emerges at this time, it did not come into popular use for another 200 years.

Counselors are required to be specific and yet unburdened by overly complicated terminology. For this reason, classification and nomenclature have been debated in the study of suicide. The words *classification* and *nomenclature* are at times used interchangeably; however, others use them distinctly. Classifications are detailed and specific, and nomenclatures are more functional words with logical definition. For example, the ICD might have a classification like malignant neoplasm of the lower-outer quadrant of the female breast instead of the nomenclature, breast cancer, used by professionals when long technical classifications are inappropriate (see O'Carroll et al., 1998). Sometimes classifications can help us put an act or behavior into a conceptual framework. On the other hand, it is often limited in its application in a clinic. Pokorney (1974) in conjunction with this stated,

> Essential to this research (suicide) is the adoption of a common nomenclature, which must be simple, short, readily acceptable, codable, and adaptable to variable sized programs of study. It should aid in the diagnosis and should serve the clinician as well as the researcher. (p. 29)

Counselors and other helping professionals need consistent nomenclature to communicate effectively around this issue (Maris, 1992; O'Carroll et. al., 1998; Shneidman, 1985).

O'Carroll et al. (1998) provided an excellent scenario in which lack of clarity can affect treatment of a client:

> A liaison psychiatrist is called to the hospital emergency room to interview a newly admitted patient. The patient, a 44 year old, married female with diagnosis of Dysthymic Disorder (Axis I) and Borderline Personality Disorder (Axis II), had been brought to the hospital confused and dissociative, after taking an overdose (estimated eight pills) of her prescribed antidepressants on the evening her therapist was to leave for vacation. Her chart noted the following: (a) "patient admitted to ER following suicide attempt by overdose . . . " (ER psychiatric nurse), (b) "patient referred to ER following suicide gesture . . . " (patient's psychopharmacologist), and (c) "patient engaged in manipulative self-harm behavior . . ." (patient's therapist). Since none of the clinicians explicitly stated what they meant by the terms they used, the liaison cannot determine whether or not the patient did in fact try to end her life. He prepares to start his interview from scratch, essentially disregarding the input of the three clinicians who proceeded him. (p. 21)

It is obvious that one word cannot catch the gestalt or complex phenomenon. Pokorney (1974) wrote, "The overall term suicide has been applied so broadly that it has lost precise meaning. Should we discard the word? In lay and legal circles, the term suicide is firmly established, and to laymen it seems simple and definite" (p. 29). Across professional disciplines, there is not an agreed upon set of terms for use. This can pose problems. Even so, as counselors, we must familiarize ourselves with and use words that capture the meaning of what is essential.

Some Definitions

Completed Suicide

Completed suicide is a self-inflicted lethal act resulting from intentional life-threatening action. In conjunction with this, the Centers for Disease Control and Prevention provided an Operational Criteria for the Classification of Suicides that listed three essential elements of a completed suicide: death, self-infliction, and intentionality (O'Carroll et al., 1998).

Retterstol (1993) provided a definition with a broader sense of the reason for suicide:

> An act with a fatal outcome, that is deliberately initiated and performed by the deceased him- or herself, in the knowledge or expectation of its final outcome, the outcome being considered by the actor as instrumental in bringing about desired changes in consciousness and/or social conditions. (p. 2)

Between these two definitions a couple of elements affecting suicide become apparent: undesirability of the present condition and desirability of a potentially better future. Many acts fulfill the above definitions of suicide but would not publicly be labeled suicide by many, because suicide often connotes wrongdoing and mental illness.

A horrible tragedy that has had a ripple effect around the globe was the destruction of the World Trade Center towers in New York City. As was the case in other tall building fires, victims jumped from entirely lethal heights. It is assumed that the pain caused by the fires was unbearable; jumping was the best alternative and, in fact, may have been an instinct or impulse to evade such a torturous situation. "Suicide" fails to capture the essence of these events because it implies wrongdoing or mental illness. However, in such cases, of key importance is when and why an individual says, "It is finished." These were Christ's last words before physical death by torturous execution (John 19:30; *New American Standard Bible*, 2001).

Other terms such as *death with dignity* and *voluntary death* have been used instead of *suicide* to remove stigmatization. The use of the word suicide as rhetoric is not uncommon. For example, an opposing political group might call the other group's martyr's act a suicide. For this reason, throughout this chapter descriptive words are used interchangeably to challenge rhetoric.

Suicide Attempt or Parasuicide (With or Without Injury)

A suicide attempt is a suicidal act that has a nonfatal outcome in which the person has some level of intention to die. According to Stone (1999), a major problem for many who attempt suicide is that they do not understand the lethality of the method chosen for killing themselves. Sometimes this results in permanent disabilities that further complicate one's life. The lethality of the attempt has become an area of concern for counselors to examine. Attempt also includes when a person intends to kill him- or herself and does not plan for others to intervene or attempt when intervention is predictable. Parasuicide suggests the notion that it is an act "short" of completed suicide.

Suicidal Behavior

Suicidal behaviors are all behaviors that clearly represent a person's intent to commit suicide or his or her desire to appear as if suicide was intended.

Suicide Gesture

Suicide gesture is a gesture meant to portray an appearance of suicide and self-harm but lacks any real intention to kill oneself to accomplish an ulterior motive. In some completed suicides, it is impossible to clarify whether the suicide attempt carried intention to die or was actually a call for help in the form of a suicidal gesture. Often a suicide gesture is made, but unfortunately the outcome is death. Such scenarios present challenges to researchers; research may be less valid when obtaining ex post facto information in an attempt to classify suicide by ideation occurring a priori.

Suicide Threat

A suicide threat is any behavior in the form of interpersonal communication, verbal or nonverbal, without physical harm, that implies that the person has intentions at some level to behave in a suicidal manner.

Suicidal Ideation

Suicidal ideation is thinking about future or fantasized suicidal action. Shea (2002) believes that less that 1% of those who have suicidal ideation go on to commit a completed suicide, suggesting that one does not lead to the other and that such ideation may be transient.

Assisted Suicide

Although relevant terms and definitions are elaborated on in the following chapter on assisted suicide, a brief definition is placed here for inclusion. Roughly, assisted suicides are those completed suicides in which a person intended to die and relies on the assistance of another person who becomes the agent of the suicide.

Implications for Counselors

This chapter has focused on conceptual understandings. This is meant to inform one's procedural knowledge (the how-to) and one's conditional knowledge (the when and where to apply knowledge). Concepts of suicide and death change over time; there are differences among groups and practical problems are always present (e.g., words do not transliterate well). For these reasons it is necessary to clarify with clients exactly what their perspective and worldview of death and suicide are. Suspending one's own assumptions until further information arises is a skill that will help inform the counselor of the complex background of an individual.

Developmental stages may be another variable to take into account in dealing with suicide. Especially for children, a 1- or 2-year age difference may mean quite a difference in how a child cognitively processes death. It may be very different than an adult's understanding, potentially causing anxiety for families who do not know how to help a grieving child. Interventions catered to age should be implemented in such clinical situations.

To be culturally competent, one must know one's own biases and have an ongoing practice of understanding other worldviews and ways of being. Furthermore, it is important for counselors to understand the limits of their abilities (Sue & Sue, 2003). This chapter is limited; there are many histories not represented in regards to how various cultures have traditionally felt about suicide. Many of our current ideas are informed by past sociocultural history. To provide the best possible care for clients, counselors have a responsibility to be informed and enriched by ongoing education. Such exploration encourages one to remain open-minded and to explore personal biases and blind spots as well as to fill the gap between one's knowledge and experience of other cultures. Counselors would do well to avoid monocultural assumptions:

> An Arizona physician friend recounted recently in conversation how a colleague who was not very patient-centered proceeded to explain in considerable detail numerous technical procedures that would be used to extend the life of dying Tohono O'odhan (Papago Indian). When the doctor finished, the patients response was, "But Indians don't care for life support!" (Irish, Lundquist, & Nelsen, 1993, p. 4)

It is also important to understand the terminology that we use to describe suicide and be consistent with those we work with. If communication lacks clarity, it is essential for the counselor to elaborate on and make clear problems to avoid poor care of clients. Many of the words, including the word *suicide*, may have pejorative implications. A professional counselor is sensitive in how words are used.

It is necessary to conceptualize the dilemmas that face clients. Counselors are challenged to look through different lenses of understanding to fully grasp the possibilities that may emerge in counseling those affected by suicide. At the same time, the counselor should refrain from rigidly adhering to a story of reality by conceptualizing dilemmas or disorders. Simply stated, thought is not reality but a part of it.

In many cultures, suicide is met with antagonism. It is never far from the center of moral and ethical dilemma. No doubt, suicide is rarely a passing event, and often it is a most grievous circumstance for survivors. A thorough understanding of grief, loss, bereavement, and cultural mores regarding death and suicide makes the counselor a resource for clients. One major area that counselors can assist the survivors of suicide is to bring context, healing, and closure to a suicide. Many feel isolated and alienated after a family suicide. Helping to minimize guilt and incrimination is essential.

The World Health Organization (2002a) stated, "Worldwide, the prevention of suicide has not been adequately addressed due to basically a lack of awareness of suicide as a major problem and the taboo in many societies to discuss openly about it" (p. 1). It is important for a counselor to be part of a greater movement to provide psychological education to our clients and community about suicide.

Summary

Suicide and *suicidal* are modern words used to describe a host of actions, events, behaviors, and ideation relating to voluntary death. Across the human life span and in various cultures, suicide is a reality. It is one of the most profoundly personal actions and socially disturbing events. As suicidiologists have noted, there are many reasons and motives one might have for killing oneself. For some, voluntary death may be a viable solution. For others, it is ill conceived, impulsive, and tragic. Suicide is a "complex interaction between biological, genetic, physiological, sociological, and environmental factors" (World Health Organization, 2002a, p. 1).

Discussion of suicide often conjures a mix of emotion and thought because the process of self-inflicted death challenges our notions of human life and deeply touches what is most precious, our own life and death. Historical accounts of suicide reveal a landscape of different reactions to suicide. Cultures and societies have made laws about suicide by codifying morality and belief; these laws were influenced by religion, philosophy, politics, and science. Sometimes, the powerful, the advantaged, and the privileged created such laws for personal gain. Even in the absence of law relating to suicide, opinion and stigma have marked acts of voluntary death. Counselors who realize that current ideas of suicide are shaped by preceding sociocultural values and investigate how it affects their own values and biases may be better able to provide care for clients. Competent counselors are aware of their values and beliefs regarding suicide, especially those that could cause harm to a client. Blame, derogation, and incrimination manifesting in the present from the Western sociocultural history should not be a guide for counselor action. Moreover, because suicide is usually traumatic and viewed as a bad death, survivors need supportive counseling from a well-informed and open-minded counselor.

References

Abdel-Khalek, A. M. (2002). Why do we fear death?: The construction and validation of the Reasons for Death Fear Scale. *Death Studies, 26*, 669–680.

Alvarez, A. (1972). *The savage god: A study of suicide.* New York: Random House.

American Psychiatric Association. (2000). *Diagnostic and statistical manual of mental disorders* (4th ed., Text Revision). Washington, DC: Author.

Aquinas, T. (1998). The Catholic view. In J. Donelly (Ed.), *Suicide: Right or wrong* (2nd ed., pp. 40–42). Amherst, NY: Prometheus. (Reprinted from *Summa theological, Vol. II*, pp. 1225–1274, by T. Aquinas, 1925, New York: Benziger)

Baechler, J. (1979). *Suicides* (B. Cooper, Trans.). New York: Basic Books.

Barraclaugh, B. (1987). *Suicide: Clinical and epidemiological studies.* London: Croom Helm.

Battin, M. P. (1998). Suicide and rights. In J. Donelly (Ed.), *Suicide: Right or wrong* (2nd ed., pp. 283–300). Amherst, NY: Prometheus.

Becker, C. B. (1990). Buddhist views of suicide and euthanasia. *Philosophy East and West, 4,* 543–556. Retrieved from http://sino-sv3.sino.uni-heidelberg.de/FULLTEXT/JR-PHIL/becker.htm

Becker, E. (1973). *The denial of death.* New York: Free Press.

Bliatout, B. T. (1993). Hmong death customs: Traditional and acculturated. In D. P. Irish, K. F. Lundquist, & V. J. Nelsen (Eds.), *Variations in dying, death, and grief* (pp. 79–100). Washington, DC: Taylor & Francis.

Bradbury, M. (1996). Representations of "good" and "bad" death among deathworkers and the bereaved. In G. Howarth & P. C. Jupp (Eds.), *Contemporary issues in the sociology of death, dying and disposal* (pp. 84–95). New York: St. Martin's Press.

Brahmaprana, P. (2001, Fall). Vedanta and the art of dying. *Cross Currents, 51*(3), 337–346.

Bullough, V. L. (1970). *Man in Western civilization.* New York: Holt, Rinehart & Winston.

Burton, R. (1652/1988). *The anatomy of melancholia.* Cheapside, London: Thomas Tegg 1988 Reproduction Edition–Birmingham, AL: Gryphon Editions.

Burton, S., & Mitchell, P. (2003). Judging who knows best about yourself: Developmental change in citing the self across middle childhood. *Child Development, 74,* 426–444.

Connelly, R. (2003). Living with death: The meaning of acceptance. *Journal of Humanistic Psychology, 43,* 45–63.

Cowley, M., & Mannix, D. P. (1994). The middle passage. In D. Northrup (Ed.), *The Atlantic slave trade* (pp. 99–111). Lexington, MA: D. C. Heath.

Davies, C. (1996). Dirt, death, decay, and dissolution: American denial and British avoidance. In G. Howarth & P. C. Jupp (Eds.), *Contemporary issues in the sociology of death, dying and disposal* (pp. 60–71). New York: St. Martin's Press.

Diekstra, R. F. W. (1993). The epidemiology of suicide and parasuicide. *Acta Psychiatrica Scandinavica Supplement, 371,* 9–20.

Donelly, J. (1998). Introduction. In J. Donelly (Ed.), *Suicide: Right or wrong* (2nd ed., pp. 7–34). Amherst, NY: Prometheus.

Droge, A. J., & Tabor, J. D. (1992). *A noble death: Suicide and martyrdom amongst Christians and Jews in antiquity.* New York: Harper/Collins.

Durant, W., & Durant, A. (1992). *The story of civilization: The age of Voltaire.* New York: MJF Books. (Original work published 1965)

Durkheim, E. (1951). Suicide: A study in sociology (J. A. Spalding, Trans. & G. Simpson, Ed.). New York: Free Press. (Original work published 1897)

Early, K. E. (1992). *Religions and suicide in the African-American community.* Westport, CT: Greenwood Press.

Echelbarger, D. (1993). Spirituality and suicide. In K. J. Doka & J. D. Morgan (Eds.), *Death and spirituality* (pp. 217–226). Amityville, NY: Baywood.

Evans-Wentz, W. Y. (Trans. & Ed.). (1974). *The Tibetan book of the dead* (3rd ed.). Oxford, England: Oxford University Press.

Fairbairn, G. J. (1995). *Contemplating suicide: The language and ethics of self-harm.* New York: Routledge.

Farberow, N. L. (1975). Cultural history of suicide. In N. L. Farberow (Ed.), *Suicide in different cultures* (pp. 1–15). Baltimore: University Park Press.

Farberow, N. L., & Shneidman, E. S. (1961). *The cry for help.* New York: McGraw-Hill.

Fedden, H. R. (1972). *Suicide: A social and historical study.* New York: Benjamin Blom. (Original work published 1938)

Fletcher, J. (1998). Attitudes towards suicide. In J. Donelly (Ed.), *Suicide: Right or wrong* (2nd ed., pp. 57–66). Amherst, NY: Prometheus.

Goldney, R. D. (1998). Norman Farberow: A legend in suicide prevention. In R. J. Kosky, H. S. Eshkevari, R. D. Goldney, & R. Hassan (Eds.), *Suicide prevention: The global context* (pp. 13–16). New York: Plenum Press.

Goodwin, D. W., & Guze, S. B. (1992). *Psychiatric diagnosis* (2nd ed.). Oxford, England: Oxford University Press.

Gothelf, D., Apter, A., Brand-Gothelf, A., Offer, N., Ofek, H., Tyano, S., & Pfeffer, C. R. (1998). Death concepts in suicidal adolescents. *Journal of the American Academy of Child and Adolescent Psychiatry, 37,* 1279–1286.

Graber, G. C. (1998). Mastering the concept of suicide. In J. Donelly (Ed.), *Suicide: Right or wrong* (2nd ed., pp. 150–161). Amherst, NY: Prometheus.

Griaule, M. (1994). Systemic ethnophilosophy. In D. A. Masolo (Ed.), *African philosophy in search of identity* (pp. 68–83). Bloomington: Indiana University Press

Grollman, E. A. (1993). Death in Jewish thought. In K. J. Doka & J. D. Morgan (Eds.), *Death and spirituality* (pp. 21–32). Amityville, NY: Baywood.

Gumere, R. M. (Trans.). (1998). Seneca: The stoic view. In J. Donelly (Ed.), *Suicide: Right or wrong* (2nd ed., pp. 35–42). Amherst, NY: Prometheus.

Harley, B., & Firebaugh, G. (1993). Americans belief in the afterlife: Trends over the past two decades. *Journal for the Scientific Study of Religion, 32,* 269–278.

Iga, M. (1986). *The thorn and the chrysanthemum.* Berkeley: University of California Press.

Irion, P. E. (1993). Spiritual issues in death for those who do not have conventional religious beliefs. In K. J. Doka & J. D. Morgan (Eds.), *Death and spirituality* (pp. 93–112). Amityville, NY: Baywood.

Irish, D. P., Lundquist, K. F., & Nelsen, V. J., (1993). *Ethnic variations in dying, death, and grief: Diversity in universality.* Washington, DC: Taylor & Francis.

Is death the spice of life? (2003). *Illness, Crises and Loss, 11*(1), 74–89.

Jamison, K. R. (1999). *Night falls fast.* New York: Alfred A. Knopf.

Jones, E. (1963). *The life and work of Sigmund Freud.* New York: Anchor Books.

Jung C. G. (1958). *The undiscovered self* (R. F. C. Hull, Trans.). New York: New American Library.

Kamal, Z., & Lowenthal, K. M. (2002). Suicide beliefs and behaviors among young Muslims and Hindus in the U.K. *Mental Health, Religion and Culture, 5,* 111–118.

Kane, B. (1979). Children's concepts of death. *Journal of Genetic Psychology, 134,* 141–153.

Karasu, T. B. (1985). Idea of death. *Integrative Psychiatry, 3,* 280–283.

Kazarian, S. S., & Persad, E. (2001). Cultural issues in suicidal behavior. In S. S. Kazarian & D. R. Evans (Eds.), *Handbook of cultural health psychology* (pp. 267–302). Oxford, England: Oxford University Press.

Kochanska, G., Gross, J. N., Lin, M., & Nichols, K. E. (2002). Guilt in young children: Development, determinants, and relations with a broader system of standards. *Child Development, 73,* 461–472.

Kral, M. J. (1994). Suicide as social logic. *Suicide and Life-Threatening Behavior, 24,* 245–255.

Lester, D. (1988). *Suicide from a psychological perspective.* Springfield, IL: Charles C Thomas.

Lieberman, L. J. (2003). *Leaving you: The cultural meaning of suicide.* Chicago: Ivan R. Dee.

Mak, M. H. J. (2002). Accepting the timing of one's death: An experience of Chinese hospice patients. *Omega-Journal of Death and Dying, 45,* 245–260.

Maris, R. W. (1992). How are suicides different? In R. W. Maris, A. L. Berman, J. T. Maltsberger, & R. I. Yufit (Eds.), *Assessment and prediction of suicide* (pp. 65–87). New York: Guilford Press.

Mason, S. F. (1962). *A history of sciences.* New York: Collier Books

Masson, J. D. (2002). Non-professional perceptions of "good death": A study of the views of hospice care patients and relatives of deceased hospice care patients. *Mortality, 7,* 191–209.

Merriam-Webster. (1993). *Merriam-Webster's collegiate dictionary* (10th ed.). Springfield, MA: Author.

Miller, E. J. (1993). A Roman Catholic view of death. In K. J. Doka & J. D. Morgan (Eds.), *Death and spirituality* (pp. 33–50). Amityville, NY: Baywood.

Minois, G. (1999). *History of suicide: Voluntary death in Western culture* (L. G. Cochrane, Trans.). Baltimore: Johns Hopkins University Press.

Monaghan, P., & Guterman, L. (2002, February 22). The unsettled question of brain death. *Chronicle of Higher Education,* p. A14.

The New American Standard Bible. (Rev. ed.). (2001). Anaheim, CA: Foundation Publications.

Nguyen, S. P., & Gelman, S. A. (2002). Four and 6 year olds' biological concept of death: The case of plants. *British Journal of Developmental Psychology, 20,* 495–513.

O'Carroll, P. W., Berman, A. L., Maris, R., Moscicki, E., Tanney, B., & Silverman, M. (1998). Beyond the Tower of Babel: A nomenclature of suicidology. In R. J. Kosky, H. S. Eshkevari, R. D. Goldney, & R. Hassan (Eds.), *Suicide prevention: The global context* (pp. 23–40). New York: Plenum Press.

Orbach, I., Gross, Y., & Glaubman, H. (1981). Some common characteristics of latency age suicidal behavior: A tentative model based on case study analysis. *Suicide and Life-Threatening Behavior, 11,* 180–190.

Oregon Death With Dignity Center. (2003). *Brief history of the law.* Retrieved April, 25, 2003 from http://www.dwd.org/law

Payne B. J., & Range L. M. (1995). Attitudes toward life and death and suicidality in young adults. *Death Studies, 19,* 559–569.

Pokorney, M. D. (1974). A scheme for classifying suicidal behaviors. In A. T. Beck, H. L. P. Resnik, & D. J. Lettieri. (Eds.), *The prediction of suicide* (pp. 29–44). Bowie, MD: Charles Press.

Rajan, V. G. J. (1999). Better off dead?: How Hindus understand the euthanasia controversy and care of the terminally ill. *Hinduism Today.* Retrieved April 25, 2003 from http://www.hinduism-today.com/archives/1999/9/1999-9-07.shtml

Retterstol, N. (1993). *Suicide: A European perspective.* Cambridge, England: Cambridge University Press.

Rose, B. M., & O'Sullivan, M. J. (2003). Afterlife beliefs and death anxiety: An exploration of the relationship between afterlife expectations and fear of death in an undergraduate population. *Omega-Journal of Death and Dying, 45,* 229–243.

Shea, S. C. (2002). *The practical art of suicide assessment.* New York: Wiley.

Shneidman, E. S. (1985). *Definition of suicide.* New York: Wiley.

Short, S. B., Hart, B., & Sainsbury, P. (1998). Whose dying?: A sociological critique of the "good death." *Mortality, 3,* 65–67.

Sigelman, C. K. (1999). *Life-span human development* (3rd ed.). New York: Brooks/Cole.

Sims, D. (2003, March 26). *Ask the expert: A young child's grief.* Retrieved March 28, 2003, from http://www.beyondindigo.com/articles/article.php/artID/253

Soubrier, J. -P. (1998). Suicide prevention as a mission. In R. J. Kosky, H. S. Eshkevari, R. D. Goldney, & R. Hassan (Eds.), *Suicide prevention: The global context* (pp. 3–6). New York: Plenum Press. (Original work published 1997)

Stallion, J. M., & Papadatou, D. (2002). Suffer the children: An examination of psychosocial issues in children and adolescents with terminal illness. *American Behavioral Scientist, 46,* 299–215.

Stanley, L. (2000). Time to say goodbye. *Childhood Education, 76,* 170–171.

Stern-Gillett, S. (1998). The rhetoric of suicide. In J. Donelly (Ed.), *Suicide: Right or wrong* (2nd ed., pp. 118–126). Amherst, NY: Prometheus.

Stone, G. (1999). *Suicide and attempted suicide.* New York: Carroll & Graf.

Sue, D. W., & Sue, D. (2003). *Counseling the culturally diverse: Theory and practice* (4th ed.). New York: Wiley.

Swinburn, J. M. A., Ali, S. M., Banerjee, D. J., & Khan, Z. P., (1999). Ethical dilemma: Discontinuation of ventilation after brain stem death. To whom is our duty of care? *British Medical Journal, 318,* 1753–1755.

Szasz, T. (1998). The ethics of suicide. In J. Donelly (Ed.), *Suicide: Right or wrong* (2nd ed., pp. 186–195). Amherst, NY: Prometheus.

Szasz, T. (1999). *Fatal freedom: The ethics and politics of suicide.* Westport, CT: Praeger.

Tolhurst W. E. (1998). Suicide, self-sacrifice, and coercion. In J. Donelly (Ed.), *Suicide: Right or wrong* (2nd ed., pp. 105–117). Amherst, NY: Prometheus.

Watson, R. (2002). *Cogito ergo sum: A life of Rene Descartes.* Boston: David R. Godine.

World Health Organization. (2002a). *Background: Prevention of suicidal behaviors: A task for all.* Retrieved April 29, 2003, from http://www5.who.int/mental_health/main.cfm?p=0000000140

World Health Organization. (2002b). *Introduction.* Retrieved April 29, 2003 from http://www5.who.int/mental_health/download.cfm?id=0000000382

Zubin, J. (1974). Observations of nosological issues in the classification of suicidal behavior. In A. T. Beck, H. L. P. Resnik, & D. J. Lettieri (Eds.), *The prediction of suicide* (pp. 3–28). Bowie, MD: Charles Press.

Chapter 2
Depression and Suicide

Jonathan W. Carrier and Kay Ennis

Counselors face the complicated task of assessing individuals for suicidal risk on a daily basis (Shea, 1988). In an attempt to elucidate the causes of suicide, mental health professionals in all fields have published countless works on the risk factors that may eventually lead to suicidal behavior. Needless to say, with so many theorists and practitioners weighing in on the subject, hundreds of potential risk factors have been identified. Out of this abundance of factors described in the literature, counselors are faced with a great challenge in delineating which are the most important (Peruzzi & Bongar, 1999). This chapter discusses the one risk factor that is universally accepted in the field to be the most common and perhaps most important predictor of suicidal ideation and behavior: depression.

Depression has consistently been viewed by theorists and practitioners as the most common indicator and greatest predictor of suicide (Isometsa, Aro, Henriksson, Heikkinen, & Lonnqvist, 1994; Keller, 1994; Murphy, 1986; Rihmer, Barsi, Arato, & Demeter, 1990; Zweig & Hinrichsen, 1993). Although it is clear that not all individuals who engage in suicidal behavior are depressed, depressive symptoms have been implicated in approximately 54% to 85% of completed suicides (Robins, 1986). Researchers have found that the lifetime risk of suicide for patients with untreated depressive symptoms is 15% (Guze & Robins, 1970; Isometsa et al., 1994; Miles, 1977) and that the lifetime chances of someone committing suicide who has an untreated mood disorder may reach as high as 19% (Montano, 1994). Brown, Beck, Steer, and Grisham (2000) examined risk factors for suicide in psychiatric outpatients. They found that out of a sample of 49 individuals who had committed suicide, 47, or 96%, had a primary, secondary, or tertiary diagnosis of a mood disorder, with 34, or 69%, having a diagnosis of major depressive disorder.

Although this chapter seeks to deal primarily with the well-established link between depression and suicide, counselors should be watchful for individuals with both depressive and anxious symptomatology. Compared with individuals with depression or anxiety alone, those with a comorbid diagnosis of mood and anxiety disorders experience greater clinical morbidity, increased functional impairment, higher symptom severity, and worse overall prognosis (Hecht, von Zerssen, & Wittchen, 1990; Sherbourne & Wells, 1997). The poor prognosis associated with those who are comorbid for mood and anxiety disorders makes it unsurprising that some of the main features of this condition are increased suicidal ideation, suicide attempts, and completed suicide (Lewinsohn, Rohde, & Seeley, 1995). This is worth mentioning in any discussion on depression and suicide because the co-occurrence of mood and anxiety disorders is common. Approximately 57% of individuals with depression also experience an anxiety disorder, and 56% of individuals with an anxiety disorder also experience a depressive disorder (Kessler et al., 1996).

Other chapters in this volume explore the phenomenon of suicide and its assessment and prevention at length. Because depression is so often a precursor to suicide, this chapter provides population-specific (children, adolescents, adults, and elderly) indicators of depression through which counselors may make more accurate diagnoses of the disorder and discusses what treatment modality has been found most effective with these populations. A case study is presented, and adaptations for diversity are also discussed.

Case Scenario

The following is a case scenario of a potentially depressed client. This scenario is applied after the discussion on diagnosing depression to provide an example of how a comprehensive diagnosis of depression may look in an actual counseling situation.

> "James" is a 24-year-old Caucasian male student who has come to the university counseling center where you work because he is "so tired of not being able to leave his apartment." He further expresses a "total lack of motivation to do anything" and says that he has been sleeping up to 14 hours a day and still feels too tired to go out. He also says that he just doesn't feel hungry anymore and often eats only one meal per day, usually in the evening. He says that when he is able to drag himself out of his apartment he acts "like a jerk" to anyone who talks to him, which he feels guilty about but says "he cannot help it." He states that he has a difficult time concentrating on his schoolwork, because of looming thoughts of death and says he feels like "he has been beaten in the game of life."

Depression and the *DSM–IV*

Depression is found in the *Diagnostic and Statistical Manual of Mental Disorders* (4th ed., *DSM–IV*; American Psychiatric Association, 1994) within the framework of mood disorders, which includes major depressive disorder, dysthymic disorder, depressive disorder not otherwise specified, Bipolar I disorder, Bipolar II disorder, cyclothymic disorder, and bipolar disorder not otherwise specified, among others. Although any mood disorder significantly increases the risk of suicidal ideation and behavior, depression is the principal disorder associated with this risk (Maxmen & Ward, 1995). As the *DSM–IV* is the tool counselors will undoubtedly use to make a formal diagnosis of depression, an overview of the major kinds of depression outlined in it should be provided in any discussion on diagnosing depression. Below is a brief summary of the three major types of depression given in the *DSM–IV*.

Major Depressive Episode

(Note that major depressive episode is not a disorder or diagnosis in itself. It is instead used as a qualifier for major depressive disorder [discussed below], which is a diagnosable disorder.) A major depressive episode is a period of at least 2 weeks in which the individual exhibits either a depressed mood or the loss of interest or pleasure in most activities. In children and adolescents, this mood may be exhibited in irritability rather than depression or sadness. In order for an individual to meet the criteria for major depressive episode, he or she must exhibit at least five of the following nine symptoms: (a) depressed mood most of the day and nearly every day for adults or irritability most of the day and nearly every day for children and adolescents, (b) noticeably diminished interest in normal activities most of the day and nearly every day, (c) significant weight loss or weight gain or a noticeable increase or decrease in appetite nearly every day, (d) insomnia or hypersomnia nearly every day, (e) physical restlessness or agitation nearly every day, (f) apparent fatigue or energy loss nearly every day, (g) feelings of guilt and/or worthlessness nearly every day, (h) difficulty thinking or concentrating nearly every day, and/or (i) persistent thoughts of death or recurrent suicidal ideation, plan, or an actual suicide attempt.

Major Depressive Disorder

This is divided into two types: (a) major depressive disorder, single episode and (b) major depressive disorder, recurrent. Major depressive disorder, single episode requires the presence of a single major depressive episode, whereas major depressive disorder, recurrent requires the presence of two or more major depressive episodes. Both types of major depressive disorders must be differentiated from other disorders such as schizophrenia, schizoaffective disorder, or delusional disorder and cannot be inclusive of manic episodes, or the diagnosis of major depressive disorder would be incorrect. Major depressive disorder further requires six specifiers to describe the current major depressive episode: (a) severity, psychotic, and remission specifiers; (b) chronicity; (c) with catatonic features; (d) with melancholic features; (e) with atypical features; and (f) with postpartum onset. Refer to the *DSM–IV* (American Psychiatric Association, 1994) for more information regarding these specifiers.

Dysthymic Disorder

The individual exhibits a chronically depressed mood for most of the day and for more days than not for a period of at least 2 years. In children, dysthymic disorder may be manifested though irritability rather than depression and must occur for at least 1 year. To receive a diagnosis of dysthymic disorder, the individual must have, in addition to the depressed mood (irritable in children and adolescents) for 2 years (1 year in children and adolescents), at least two of the following six symptoms: (a) lack of appetite or overeating, (b) insomnia or hypersomnia, (c) lack of energy or fatigue, (d) poor self-esteem, (e) difficulty concentrating or making decisions, and/ or (f) feelings of hopelessness. Although major depressive disorder and dysthymic disorder are similar, they can be differentiated on the basis of severity, chronicity, and persistence. Major depressive disorder tends to have more severe symptoms but for a far shorter duration (at least 2 weeks), whereas dysthymic disorder tends to have less severe symptoms of a far more chronic nature (at least 2 years).

Depressive Disorder Not Otherwise Specified

This type of depression includes disorders with depressive features that do not meet the criteria for depressive disorder or dysthymic disorder. Examples of disorders in this category are (a) minor depressive disorder with episodes of at least 2 weeks of depressive symptoms but fewer than the required five items for major depressive disorder, (b) recurrent brief depressive disorder with episodes of depression lasting from 2 days to 2 weeks and occurring once a month for 12 months, and (c) any situation in which the counselor feels that a depressive disorder is present but is unable to determine if it is primary. Refer to the *DSM–IV* (American Psychiatric Association, 1994) for more examples of depressive disorder not otherwise specified.

It is important to note here that the above discussion on the major types of depression is only a brief summary of what is provided in the *DSM–IV* and is by no means meant as a substitute for it. Attempting to diagnose depression can be a daunting task because depression not only is a disorder in itself but also is a prominent and key feature of many other disorders. Thus, to avoid confusion, it is highly recommended here that counselors expecting to work with or diagnose individuals with depression become highly familiar with this section of the *DSM–IV* (American Psychiatric Association, 1994).

Diagnosing Depression

When attempting to evaluate depressive symptoms in clients, counselors would do well to use more than one assessment approach to weed out client answers colored by social desirability, lessen "human errors" caused by counselor misperception, and provide empirical backup for verbally gathered information (and vice versa). Chapter 5 (this volume) presents a three-part model of assessing imminent suicidal risk first introduced by Juhnke (1994). This model, comprising a clinical interview, empirical evaluation, and clinical consultation, is easily adapted for use in diagnosing depression. The following is a brief overview of this three-part model of assessment (presented at length in chap. 5), adapted for use when assessing individuals for depression:

1. *Clinical interview.* The clinical interview is the first part of a comprehensive diagnosis. It is a verbal, nonempirical method of assessing depression during a counseling session. It is essentially a list of questions or items designed to assess the symptoms of depression outlined in the *DSM–IV* (American Psychiatric Association, 1994) that are worked into the normal counseling milieu. These questions are not meant to be read as a list or fired one after the other at the client, but instead should be introduced into the counseling session as part of the normal flow of the session and facilitated through the use of such counseling cornerstones as empathy, genuineness, and authenticity (Kleespies, Deleppo, Mori, & Niles, 1998).

2. *Empirical evaluation.* Empirical evaluation, or psychological assessment, is the use of instruments, in a counselor-administered, self-report, or computerized form, designed to assess depressive symptoms in the client. Empirical evaluation, although highly important, is always the second part of a depression assessment and should never be used in place of or before the clinical interview. Empirical methods of screening or diagnosing depression are highly useful in validating what the counselor has found in the clinical interview and often provide information the clinical interview did not uncover. There are many depression screening instruments in use today, so the counselor should have little difficulty in finding one with suitable psychometric properties for use with the population he or she is working with.

3. *Clinical consultation.* Clinical consultation is the third part of a comprehensive assessment of depression. Consultation with a supervi-

sor or counseling team member can greatly reduce the chances of an inaccurate depression diagnosis. Clinical consultation can serve as a "checks and balances" system and can be of great use when there is a large discrepancy between the diagnosis found through the clinical interview and the diagnosis recommended by the empirical evaluation. Clinical consultation can also be indispensable when a counselor is faced with a resistant client or, for whatever reason, has reached an impasse in the diagnosing process.

Counselors should note that because of the well-established link between depression and suicide, in any assessment of depression, suicidal ideation or behavior may become apparent in the client. Counselors should remain mindful of this possibility and be prepared to switch the assessment of depressive symptomatology to an assessment of imminent suicidal risk. Refer to chapter 5 in this volume for information on how to carry out an assessment of suicidal risk.

Population-Specific Diagnosis of Depression

As useful and comprehensive as the *DSM–IV* (American Psychiatric Association, 1994) is for outlining the features and diagnostic requirements of mental disorders, it presents most of its information on depression in an umbrellalike and adult-biased format and provides little insight on population-specific subtleties the counselor should watch for. This section outlines population-specific signs and symptoms of depression and how psychological assessment can aid the counselor in the assessment of depression in each group. At the end of this section, a table presenting *DSM–IV* depressive symptomatology in addition to population-specific indicators of depression is provided as a reference tool.

Children

Much effort has been made to recognize that symptoms of depression may be manifested differently in children and adolescents than in adults (Birmaher et al., 1997; Kovacs, 1996). However, most often the criteria associated with adult depression have been applied to children, and developmental considerations that may affect the etiology, course, and outcome of depression in children and adolescents have been minimized or disregarded entirely (Cicchetti & Toth, 1998). There are several important differences between adult and child depression of which counselors working with children should remain mindful. Although the criteria for depression in the *DSM–IV* (American Psychiatric Association, 1994) must be met for any population member to receive a formal diagnosis, children may not manifest the required symptomatology in readily translatable ways. Researchers have found that indicators of depression in children more commonly revolve around symptoms of separation anxiety, phobias, somatic complaints, and behavioral problems than the more adult symptomatology found in the *DSM–IV* (Carlson & Kashani, 1988; Kolvin, Barrett, & Bhate, 1991; Mitchell, McCauley, Burle, & Moss, 1988). Fritz (1995) suggested that signs of child depression may include persistent sadness, a lack of interest in previously enjoyed activities, decreased performance in school, complaints of headaches or stomachaches, persistent boredom, and a change in eating or sleeping habits. Furthermore, children commonly do not use the same language as adults, and their articulations of sadness, hopelessness, and self-deprecation may not be easily identifiable as depression and may go unrecognized by professionals (Varley, 2002).

Although parents' mental health and familial instability are not symptoms of depression, counselors should remain aware that they can compound a child's depression and can even be the cause. Hammen, Burge, and Adrian (1991) studied the relationship between mother and child depression and found that there was a significant association between mother and child diagnoses, and most children in the study who experienced a major depressive episode did so in close proximity to maternal depression. Furthermore, the functional health and stability of the child's family and its effect on a child's mental health have been well documented in the literature. Research suggests that parental divorce increases the chances that a child will have difficulty with school, suffer depression, commit delinquent acts, and use illicit substances (McLanahan & Booth, 1989; McLanahan & Sandefur, 1994; Simons, 1996).

Because of the difficulty of verbally assessing depression in children, empirical evaluation may play a crucial role in screening and diagnosis. Many instruments have been designed for use in the assessment of child depression, but the Children's Depression Inventory (CDI; Kovacs, 1985), also available in a parent form, is by far "the most widely used and researched measure of childhood depression" (Kendall, Cantwell, & Kazdin, 1989, p. 121). The CDI is a 27-item scale that assesses affective, cognitive, and behavioral symptoms of childhood depression. For each item, the child or parent selects one of three statements, each representing different levels of symptomatology with scores ranging from *low* (0) to *high* (2). Several studies of the psychometric properties of the CDI have revealed high internal consistency, test–retest reliability, and construct validity (Mattison, Handford, Kales, Goodman, & McLaughlin, 1990; Smucker, Craighead, Craighead, & Green, 1986; Worchel, 1990) and provide evidence of cross-ethnic and cross-language equivalence (Knight & Hill, 1998; Knight, Virdin, & Roosa, 1994).

Children are often eager to please and can be highly influenced by social desirability, which can cause them to relay inaccurate information about their depression to the counselor. Because of this, some instruments have been designed to assess others' perceptions of an individual child's depressive symptomatology. For instance, the Peer Nomination Index of Depression (PNID; Lefkowitz & Tesiny, 1980) consists of 13 questions about depressive symptoms (e.g., "Who often looks sad?") through which class-mates nominate peers in their class. The PNID has been found to correlate significantly with self-reported depression, teacher-rated depression, and peer-nominated social status (Lefkowitz & Tesiny, 1984, 1985). Research on the PNID provides evidence of construct validity (Cole & Carpentieri, 1990), and the instrument has good internal consistency (Lefkowitz & Tesiny, 1985). The Teacher's Rating Index of Depression (TRID; Cole, Martin, Powers, & Truglio, 1996) is another instrument that assesses others' per-ceptions about a child's depression. The TRID was designed from the PNID and is used by teachers to answer items concerning depressive symptoms in their students. The TRID has demonstrated good convergent, discrimi-nant, and construct validity (Cole et al., 1996).

Overall, when assessing children for depression, counselors will have to remain mindful that children often do not have the verbal sophistication necessary to articulate depression in ways that are easily translatable into a cut-and-dried diagnostic format. For this reason, counselors may find them-selves more reliant on others' (such as teachers, parents, and peers) per-ceptions of a child's depressive symptomatology as well as on the results of psychological assessment than with other populations.

Adolescents

Much of the literature on adolescent depression is presented alongside information on child depression with little distinction made between the two groups. This is perhaps because there is no professional consensus on exactly what age childhood stops and adolescence begins or even at what age adolescence ends and adulthood begins. Therefore, counselors work-ing with adolescents should view the information listed for children as well as the information presented for adults as somewhat inclusive or overlap-ping and not mutually exclusive. Stanard (2000) stated that the diagnosis of depression in adolescents can be a difficult undertaking because of prob-lems differentiating among the normal, transient, and developmental diffi-culties that occur in this age group and depressive symptoms. Many symp-toms of adolescent depression, such as profound sadness, listlessness, di-minished ability to concentrate, dejection, pessimism, and low self-esteem (W. M. Reynolds, 1992), largely reflect what can be found in adult-oriented *DSM–IV* symptomatology, but as compared with adults, adolescents with depression demonstrate a more variable course, display more interpersonal difficulties, are more prone to overeat and undersleep, and are more likely to demonstrate suicidal ideation (Lamarine, 1995). Furthermore, depressed adolescents may describe themselves as socially inept, unliked, and stupid; and they often exhibit academic difficulty, trouble maintaining concentration, somatic complaints, nervousness, and substance abuse rather than a depressed mood (Rice & Leffert, 1997).

Empirical assessment may aid the counselor in differentiating depressive symptomatology from the developmental issues all adolescents experience (Stanard, 2000). The CDI (Kovacs, 1985), discussed earlier, is designed for use with both children and adolescents ages 7–17 and continues to be the most widely used assessment tool for this age group. The Center for Epidemiologic Studies–Depression Scale (CES-D; Radloff, 1977) and the Beck Depression Inventory (BDI; Beck, Ward, Mendelson, Mock, & Erbaugh, 1961, discussed later) are both well-established instruments with more than adequate psychometric properties and can be used with adolescents as well as adults and the elderly.

Overall, the challenge in diagnosing adolescents is the differentiation of depressive symptomatology from normal adolescent development and experimentation (Stanard, 2000). As with children, counselors are likely to rely more on psychological assessment and the perceptions of parents, teachers, and friends rather than self-report or clinical interviewing when diagnosing depression in adolescents.

Adults

Adults should be the easiest age group for counselors to assess for depression because most mainstream guidelines, including the *DSM–IV* (American Psychiatric Association, 1994), are designed primarily for use with the adult population. As with children and adolescents, counselors must remain aware that there is no consensus on when an adolescent becomes an adult or when an adult becomes elderly. Therefore, counselors working with adults should be mindful of the population-specific signs of depression for both adolescents and the elderly, as there is likely to be an overlap of symptomatology. For the most part, however, counselors will mainly use *DSM–IV* symptomatology as a guide for diagnosing adults, whereas when working with children, adolescents, and the elderly, the counselor will use the *DSM–IV* as well as supplemental guidelines found throughout the literature.

As with other populations, empirical assessment of depressive symptomatology will prove useful to counselors in coming to a comprehensive diagnosis of depression. Although there are many depression screening tools in use today, the CES-D (Radloff, 1977) and the BDI (Beck et al., 1961) are among the most respected and empirically supported instruments in the field. The CES-D (Radloff, 1977) is a 20-item self-report scale of depressive symptoms, designed for use with adults of all ages. In the CES-D, individuals rate the applicability of statements about depressive symptoms to themselves on a 0–3 scale (0 = *none at all* and 3 = *very much*) with respect to the past week. The 20 CES-D items have been found to be consistent across four factors of depression that are now commonly used as subscales on other inventories (Hertzog, Van Alstine, Usala, Hultsch, & Dixon, 1990). These subscales are depressed mood, psychomotor retardation, lack of well-being, and interpersonal isolation. The CES-D also has been found to have both discriminant and construct validity and is a reliable instrument (Radloff & Teri, 1986).

The BDI (Beck et al., 1961) is a self-report inventory that uses a symptom scale that assesses aspects of depression, including sleep and appetite problems, sadness, guilt and self-reproach, suicidal ideation, and loss of interest in everyday activities. There are 21 items, composed of four self-evaluative statements for each item, scored from 0 to 3. Responses are summed, yielding a range of scores from 0 to 63, with higher scores indicating greater depressive symptomatology. Both measures have demonstrated high validity and have been found to be reliable in psychiatric as well as nonpsychiatric populations (Beck, 1967; Beck, Steer, & Garbin, 1988; Dozois, Dobson, & Ahnberg, 1998; Lightfoot & Oliver, 1985).

Elderly

As adults get older, depressive symptomatology may begin to differ from those of younger adults. As with adolescence, aging is a transitional process that can complicate diagnosis and cause confusion as to which symptoms are merely transitional effects of aging and which are true indicators of depression. Furthermore, depression in the elderly often goes unrecognized, because symptoms may be mistaken for physical illness, dementia, or the effects of medications (Devons, 1996). Older adults are more likely to exhibit vegetative symptoms, such as sleep and appetite disturbances, and somatic complaints, as well as cognitive dysfunction in the forms of concentration difficulties and apathy (C. F. Reynolds, 1996). In contrast, young adults are more likely to complain of subjective dysphoria or a sad, "blue" feeling or loss of interest or pleasure in previously enjoyed activities (Brodaty, 1993). Elderly individuals may also exhibit greater signs of social withdrawal, isolation, and increased dependency than younger adults. Counselors should also remain mindful that the somatic symptoms of depression in the elderly often are attributed incorrectly to other medical problems.

As with any group, psychological assessment can be of great assistance in diagnosis. For the most part, two main instruments are used to assess depression in the elderly: the BDI (Beck et al., 1961, discussed above) and the Geriatric Depression Scale (GDS; Yesavage, Brink, Rose, & Adey, 1983). The GDS was designed specifically for use with the elderly and comprises 30 yes-or-no questions about depressive symptoms. Of the 30 items, 20 allude to the presence of depression when answered positively, whereas the remaining 10 indicate depression when answered negatively. Items are summed, and a score of 11 or higher indicates depression. The GDS has been tested and found to possess a high degree of internal consistency and reliability (Yesavage et al., 1983). The GDS has also demonstrated good convergent and discriminant validity in studies using multiple measures (Yesavage et al., 1983).

Overview of *DSM–IV* and Population-Specific Symptoms of Depression

Table 2.1 is meant to delineate what population-specific depressive symptomatology (taken from the population-specific discussions above) counselors may look for in addition to the standard symptoms presented in the *DSM–IV* (American Psychiatric Association, 1994). Note that information in the children, adolescents, adult, and elderly columns are not meant as a replacement for the information in the *DSM–IV* column. To make a formal diagnosis of a depressive disorder, *DSM–IV* criteria must be met. Refer to the *DSM–IV* for more information on formal diagnosis.

Table 2.1

Population-Specific Depressive Symptomatology

DSM–IV	Children	Adolescents	Adults	Elderly
Depressed mood, sadness, or emptiness	Irritability Separation anxiety	Irritability Substance abuse More prone to overeat and sleep	May overlap with adolescent symptoms	Significant appetite disturbances
Diminished interest in activities	Phobias Somatic complaints	Somatic complaints	May overlap with elderly symptoms	Somatic complaints Excessive sleep disturbances
Significant weight loss or weight gain	Behavioral problems Decreased school performance	Behavioral problems Academic difficulty	Generally reflects *DSM–IV* symptoms	Increased apathy
Insomnia or hypersomnia	Difficulties relating with other children	More interpersonal difficulties		Increased dependency on others
Psychomotor agitation or retardation	Persistent boredom	Persistent boredom		Greater difficulty concentrating
Fatigue or loss of energy		Depression presents in a more variable course		Increased social isolation and withdrawal
Feelings of worthlessness or excessive guilt				
Impaired concentration or indecisiveness				
Thoughts of death, suicide ideation, plan, or attempt				

Note. DSM–IV = Diagnostic and Statistical Manual of Mental Disorders (4th ed.; American Psychiatric Association, 1994).

Case Scenario Example of Depression Diagnosis

The following case example of "James," introduced earlier in the chapter, is intended to serve as an illustration of what the diagnosis of depression might look like in an actual counseling situation. It is intended only as a brief example, however, and is designed to be simple so the reader can easily recognize the basic aspects of a comprehensive diagnosis of depression. Actual counseling situations will almost invariably be more complex.

Diagnosis of Depression in "James"

Counselor: You said earlier that you are here today because you're tired of not being able to leave your apartment.

James: Yeah, that's right. I can't stand lying around anymore, but I'm so tired . . . you wouldn't believe the effort it took me to just come over here.

Counselor: I'm glad you were able to. You've made the first step; maybe together we can help you to make more.

James: I hope so.

Counselor: If you don't mind, I'm going to ask you some questions that might help us figure out what's going on with all this lying around which will make it easier to see how to help you.

James: I don't mind. I just want whatever is going on to change. I can't stand it. I've felt down before like everybody, but never like this.

Counselor: About how long has it been that you've been "lying around" and not able to go out?

James: I guess for about a month or so. I just started feeling bad and down and before I knew it, I was sleeping 14 hours a day, hardly eating, and never leaving my room; not even for class.

Counselor: And you feel "bad" and "down" just about every day?

James: Some days I feel a little better, but yeah most days I just feel bad.

Counselor: What does "bad" mean to you?

James: Well not bad like physically bad, but kind of empty.

Counselor: What do you do for fun, James?

James: I guess my favorite thing is to play chess. I'm in the chess club here and I play it a lot online. It's pretty much all I do though . . . lie around and play chess.

Counselor: It's good that you're still able to play chess, even if it is just in your room online.

James: Yeah, I used to go down to the square and play, but you're right, I know I still have some life in me if I can get out of bed to play, even if it is just on the computer in my room. Without that I'd probably be dead now . . . I think about it enough.

Counselor: I'm glad you have chess then! When you said you think about *it* enough, did you mean death?

James: Yeah I think about death, like how if I were dead I wouldn't feel so bad. I've been thinking about death a lot. Sometimes I can't really concentrate on things because it just kind of pops into my head, you know like gloom and doom stuff. Dark thoughts . . . stuff like that.

Counselor: When you're thinking of death, do you think of killing yourself?

James: No, it's not like that. I'm not suicidal or anything. I like being alive, I just think about death a lot. I don't know why.

Counselor: I'm starting to get a picture of what might be going on. Would you mind if I gave you a quick kind of questionnaire that you fill out yourself so I can see if the results match up with what I'm thinking?

James: Yeah, I'll take it. Whatever helps me get out of this funk.

Discussion of Diagnosis of Depression in "James"

The counselor in this situation was able to cover most of the items outlined in the *DSM–IV* for major depressive episode and would probably be thinking about a diagnosis of major depressive disorder. Of the nine criteria for depressive episode, James exhibited six, one more than is required for a major depressive episode. He specifically stated or alluded to a depressed mood almost every day, a decrease in appetite almost every day, hypersomnia, fatigue, trouble concentrating, and thoughts of death and experienced them for more than 2 weeks. On the basis of this clinical interview, James seems to meet the criteria for major depressive disorder, single episode. The counselor would next administer an empirical evaluation of depression, such as the BDI, to verify the preliminary finding of the clinical interview. If the results of the BDI concurred with the clinical interview, the counselor would likely make the diagnosis and begin treatment planning. If the results of the BDI did not match the findings of the clinical interview, the counselor would either interview James in more detail or seek feedback from a supervisor.

Counseling Clients With Depression

The management and treatment of depression generally involves counseling and psychotherapy, biotherapy (drug treatment), or both (Maxmen & Ward, 1995). Because this is a counseling text, the following discussion is limited to counseling approaches to working with clients with depression. Past reviews on the treatment of depression have suggested that counseling is reliably more effective than either no treatment or placebo control conditions but did not differentiate between the efficacy of different counseling models (Miller & Berman, 1983; Shapiro & Shapiro, 1982; Steinbrueck, Maxwell, & Howard, 1983). Cognitive-behavioral approaches are significantly effective in treating depression. Cognitive-behavioral approaches are based on a view of psychopathology that sees individuals' excessive affect and dysfunctional behavior as being due to excessive or irrational ways of interpreting their experiences and uses action or performance-based and cognitive interventions to produce changes in thinking, feeling, and behavior (Kendall, 1991; Weinrach, 1988). Dobson (1989) undertook a meta-analysis of the effectiveness of Beck's (1976) cognitive therapy for depression. He identified 28 studies that used the BDI (Beck et al., 1961) as a common outcome measure of depression and compared cognitive therapy against other therapeutic modalities. He found that clients who received cognitive therapy did 70% better than those receiving drug therapies, 67% better than clients receiving behavior therapy alone, and 70% better than clients receiving other forms of psychotherapy.

Normally, in discussions of counseling approaches to treating a particular mental disorder or client difficulty, numerous approaches would be presented. In this case, however, the literature on the treatment of depression is so heavily laden with studies touting the efficacy of cognitive-behavioral techniques across all population groups and over other forms of counseling and even drug therapy that there is little reason to go into great detail about other treatment paradigms. As an example of what can be found in the literature, presented below are several studies discussing treatment approaches (with a heavy cognitive-behavioral bias, reflecting what is in the literature) with different populations.

Children

Depressed children are more likely to view their lives pessimistically, to be less assertive in resolving interpersonal problems, to underestimate their own cognitive abilities, to harbor unreasonably high expectations of their own performance, and to perceive hostile intentions during neutral social interactions (Cole & Turner, 1993; Kaslow, Rehm, & Siegel, 1984; Quiggle, Garber, Panak, & Dodge, 1992). Because of this, it is no surprise that a cognitive-behavioral counseling approach with its emphasis on cognitive restructuring and behavioral change have overwhelmingly been proven in the literature to be most effective in treating child depression. Jaycox, Reivich, Gillham, and Seligman (1994) tested a program designed to reduce symptomatology in children displaying depressive symptoms. Cognitive-behavioral techniques were used to teach students coping strategies useful in dealing with stressful life events and to provide the children with a sense of competence in a variety of life situations. They found that after the introduction of these cognitive-behavioral techniques, depressive symptoms were significantly reduced and remained so in a 6-month follow-up.

In addition to cognitive-behavioral therapy, family therapy often is necessary because a depressed child will almost certainly produce a significant effect on the family unit. Whether or not the parents were initially suffering from mental illness, the stress of raising a depressed child can destabilize family dynamics (Roland, 1995). The inclusion of family therapy along with whatever treatment the child receives is crucial because (a) children are highly dependent on their parents, (b) research shows that depressed youth come from families with high rates of mood disorders and a high degree of conflicts, and (c) parent psychopathology and familial conflict can cause a poor outcome to treatment and increase risk for depressive relapses (Birmaher et al., 1997; Warner, Weissman, Fendrich, Wickramaratne, & Moreau, 1992).

Adolescents

As with children, cognitive-behavioral techniques have been supported in the literature to be the most effective treatment modality for adolescent depression. In fact, counseling interventions in general may be even more important in children and adolescents than with other populations because medications, although widely researched and used with depressed adults, have produced mixed or poor results in children and remain highly controversial for use with children and adolescents (Kazdin, 1990; Roland, 1995). As an example of the effectiveness of cognitive-behavior therapy over other forms of psychosocial treatments, a large study by Brent et al. (1997) compared cognitive-behavioral therapy with family and supportive therapy for major depression in adolescents. One hundred seven adolescents were divided into three different treatment groups using individual cognitive-behavior therapy, systemic behavior family therapy, or individual nondirective supportive therapy. The cognitive-behavioral therapy taught individuals to monitor and correct automatic thoughts and helped to develop problem-solving and social skills. Family therapy concentrated on problem solving, communication, and family interaction. Supportive treatment provided individuals with a chance to express feelings and discuss personal problems in a general manner. Of the individuals who completed the study, those receiving cognitive-behavioral therapy were found to most likely recover. They were also found to recover sooner and with a lower dropout rate.

Another treatment consideration counselors should remain mindful of for adolescents is family therapy. Adolescents, as with children, are vastly dependent on their parents. Thus, an examination of the adolescent's family environment and the possible institution of family therapy can prove highly effective in facilitating the treatment of depression (Fritz, 1995).

Adults

Adults, by and large, have received the most attention as to the treatment of depression, particularly the effectiveness of counseling (predominantly cognitive-behavioral approaches) and drug therapy, with many studies comparing the effectiveness of one against the other with counseling repeatedly performing at least as well as drug therapy (Hollon et al., 1992; Murphy, Simons, Wetzel, & Lustman, 1984; Rush, Beck, Kovacs, & Hollon, 1977). For example, a study by DeRubeis, Gelfand, Tang, and Simons (1999) compared acute outcomes of antidepressant medication and cognitive-behavior therapy in adult outpatients with severe depression. They found the overall comparison of antidepressant medication with cognitive-behavior therapy favored cognitive-behavior therapy. They concluded that cognitive-behavior therapy fared as well as antidepressant medication and that antidepressant medication should not be considered superior to cognitive-behavior therapy for the acute treatment of severely depressed outpatients.

Overall, the efficacy of cognitive and cognitive-behavioral therapy for treatment of depression in adults has been supported by the results of a number of well-known studies (Blackburn, Bishop, Glen, Whalley, & Christie, 1981; Elkin et al., 1989; Teasdale, Fennell, Hibbert, & Amies, 1984). Having noted this, however, it is important to state here that although cognitive therapy has been found to be overwhelmingly effective for use with depressed clients of all population groups, it should not be viewed as a panacea for depression (Dobson, 1989). Because of individual characteristics and differences, it is likely that some clients may not be appropriate for this form of counseling and may in fact benefit more from alternative interventions (Dobson, 1989). Counselors should discuss treatment options with their clients before deciding which modality to pursue in an effort to tailor counseling approaches to the specific needs of the individual.

Elderly

Counseling may have particular utility in treating older adults for depression because many receive drug treatment for various physical disabilities and maladies and cannot or will not tolerate additional medication for depression (Lebowitz et al., 1997). Furthermore, cognitive therapy can help modify and alleviate the negative thoughts entertained by an elderly individual faced with the challenges of a loss of physical ability or the consequences of a disabling illness or condition, such as a change in physical appearance and endurance (Plopper, 1990).

Research has proved that counseling is, as with younger adults, effective with older populations experiencing depression. Although most of the studies discussed in the adult section above that have compared the efficacy of drug treatment with cognitive-behavioral counseling for depression have incorporated older adults in their samples, making the results at least somewhat generalizable for use with the elderly population, there have also been numerous studies specifically targeting cognitive-behavioral approaches with elderly individuals. For example, Kemp, Gorgiat, and Gill (1992) examined the effects of brief cognitive-behavioral group therapy in older persons with and without disabling illness. The study comprised 41 participants with a diagnosis of major depression and living either at community homes or in retirement centers. Results showed a decrease in depression after a 12-week treatment period.

To delineate the use of nonpharmacological approaches with elderly individuals experiencing depression, Scogin and McElreath (1994) undertook a meta-analysis of 17 studies that examined the efficacy of psychosocial treatments, including cognitive-behavioral counseling, for depression among older adults. They found that counseling and psychotherapeutic approaches were highly warranted for use with the depressed elderly and often were at least as effective as drug therapy. Overall, it is clear that counseling, particularly a cognitive-behavioral approach, is effective with depressed elderly individuals as it is with all other age groups (Plopper, 1990).

Adaptations for Diversity

Despite the enormous volume of literature on depression, there are significant gaps of knowledge in depression research of ethnic minorities (Kim, 1996). Although study has been done in the area, the timeline of consistent studies in the area of cultural variations to depression is irregular at best. Without a greater regularity and larger volume of research in the area, it will prove difficult for counselors to infer any population-specific conclusions about how to approach depressed members of ethnic minorities or socioeconomic groups. Given this, the *DSM–IV* (American Psychiatric Association, 1994) suggests that counselors attempting to diagnose depression in members of other races or groups be mindful of variable and culture-specific expressions of depression. For example, some cultures express depression in largely somatic terms, and complaints of "nerves," "imbalance," "problems of the heart," and feeling "heartbroken" may reflect depression. Naturally, counselors who do not share the ethnicity of their client can and even are likely to be confronted by culture- or race-related behaviors that may be taken out of context or misunderstood (Turner & Hersen, 1994). Such misunderstandings can be of particular impact when attempting diagnosis. In such circumstances, it may be wise for the counselor to consult with another professional who shares the same race, ethnicity, socioeconomic group, or gender as the client so important behaviors are not overlooked (Kleepsies et al., 1998).

Summary

Depression has been consistently identified as the foremost precursor to suicidal behavior. The *DSM–IV* outlines three main types of depression: major depressive disorder, dysthymic disorder, and depressive disorder not otherwise specified. Although the *DSM–IV* provides guidelines for arriving at a formal diagnosis of depression, it approaches these guidelines from an umbrellalike and adult-oriented framework and does not go into great detail about population-specific indicators of depression. Children, adolescents, adults, and the elderly all exhibit some unique and overlapping characteristics of depression. Children may exhibit symptoms of depression through separation anxiety, phobias, somatic complaints, behavioral problems, decreased performance in school, complaints of headaches or stomachaches, persistent boredom, and a change in eating or sleeping habits. Adolescent symptomatology of depression may overlap somewhat with that of children and adults, but overall adolescents may display more interpersonal difficulties; be more prone to overeat and undersleep; can be more likely to demonstrate suicidal ideation; describe themselves as socially inept, unliked, and stupid; exhibit academic difficulty; and abuse drugs or alcohol. Adults should be the easiest group for counselors to diagnose with depression because the depressive symptomatology found in the *DSM–IV* is largely based on adult samples, but counselors should remain mindful that adult symptoms could overlap those of adolescents and the elderly. Elderly adults experience many of the same depressive symptoms as younger adults but may also exhibit vegetative symptoms, such as sleep and appetite disturbances, more somatic complaints, greater cognitive dysfunction, and may also exhibit greater signs of social withdrawal, isolation, and increased dependency.

Most forms of counseling have been found to be successful in the treatment of depression. However, the cognitive-behavioral counseling approach to treating depression has been demonstrated through an enormous amount of empirical support in the literature to have particular effectiveness for the treatment of depression in all age groups, over that of other counseling modalities, and, in many cases, even over drug therapy. Although it is certain that there are cultural variations to the experience of depression, there are significant gaps in the research in the area. Counselors working with ethnicities and population group members other than their own should remain mindful of cultural and group differences to expressing depression and should seek professional consultation whenever they are unsure of how to approach a diagnosis of depression with a specific population member.

References

American Psychiatric Association. (1994). *Diagnostic and statistical manual of mental disorders* (4th ed.). Washington, DC: Author.

Beck, A. T. (1967). *Depression: Clinical, experimental and theoretical aspects.* New York: Harper & Row.

Beck, A. T. (1976). *Cognitive therapy and the emotional disorders.* New York: International Universities Press.

Beck, A. T., Steer, R. A., & Garbin, M. G. (1988). Psychometric properties of the Beck Depression Inventory: Twenty-five years of evaluation. *Clinical Psychology Review, 8,* 77–100.

Beck, A. T., Ward, C. H., Mendelson, M., Mock, J. E., & Erbaugh, J. (1961). An inventory for measuring depression. *Archives of General Psychiatry, 4*, 561–571.

Birmaher, B., Kaufman, J., Brent, D., Dahl, R., Perel, J., Al-Shabbout, M., et al. (1997). Neuroendocrine response to 5-hydroxy-L-tryptophan in prepubertal children at high risk of major depressive disorder. *Archives of General Psychiatry, 54*, 1113–1119.

Blackburn, I. M., Bishop, S., Glen, A. I., Whalley, L. J., & Christie, J. E. (1981). The efficacy of cognitive therapy in depression: A treatment trial using cognitive therapy and pharmacotherapy, each alone and in combination. *British Journal of Psychiatry, 139*, 181–189.

Brent, D. A., Holder, D., Kolko, D., Birmaher, B., Baugher, M., Roth, C., et al. (1997). A clinical psychotherapy trial for adolescent depression comparing cognitive, family, and supportive therapy. *Archives of General Psychiatry, 54*, 877–885.

Brodaty, H. (1993). Think of depression: Atypical presentations in the elderly. *Australian Family Physician, 22*, 195–203.

Brown, G. K., Beck, A. T., Steer, R. A., & Grisham, J. R. (2000). Risk factors for suicide in psychiatric outpatients: A 20-year prospective study. *Journal of Consulting and Clinical Psychology, 68*, 371–377.

Carlson, G. A., & Kashani, J. H. (1988). Phenomenology of major depression from childhood through adulthood: Analysis of three studies. *American Journal of Psychiatry, 145*, 1222–1225.

Cicchetti, D., & Toth, S. L. (1998). The development of depression in children and adolescents. *American Psychologist, 53*, 221–242.

Cole, D. A., & Carpentieri, S. (1990). Social status and the comorbidity of child depression and conduct disorder. *Journal of Consulting and Clinical Psychology, 58*, 748–757.

Cole, D. A., Martin, J. M., Powers, B., & Truglio, R. (1996). Modeling causal relations between academic and social competence and depression: A multitrait–multimethod longitudinal study of children. *Journal of Abnormal Psychology, 105*, 258–270.

Cole, D. A., & Turner, J. E. (1993). Models of cognitive mediation and moderation in child depression. *Journal of Abnormal Psychology, 102*, 271–281.

DeRubeis, L. A., Gelfand, T. Z., Tang, A. D., & Simons, A. D. (1999). Medications versus cognitive behavior therapy for severely depressed outpatients: Mega-analysis of four randomized comparisons. *American Journal of Psychiatry, 156*, 1007–1014.

Devons, C. A. (1996). Suicide in the elderly: How to identify and treat patients at risk. *Geriatrics, 51*, 67–72.

Dobson, K. S. (1989). A meta-analysis of the efficacy of cognitive therapy for depression. *Journal of Consulting and Clinical Psychology, 57*, 414–419.

Dozois, D. J., Dobson, K. S., & Ahnberg, J. L. (1998). A psychometric evaluation of the Beck Depression Inventory–II. *Psychological Assessment, 10*, 83–89.

Elkin, I., Shea, M. T., Watkins, J. T., Imber, S. D., Sotsky, S. M., Collins, J. F., et al. (1989). National Institute of Mental Health Treatment of Depression Collaborative Research Program: General effectiveness of treatments. *Archives of General Psychiatry, 46,* 971–982.

Fritz, G. K. (1995). Child, adolescent depression distinct from adult version. *Brown University Child and Adolescent Behavior Letter, 11,* 4–7.

Guze, S. B., & Robins, E. (1970). Suicide and primary affective disorders. *British Journal of Psychiatry, 117,* 437–438.

Hammen, C., Burge, D., & Adrian, C. (1991). Timing of mother and child depression in a longitudinal study of children at risk. *Journal of Consulting and Clinical Psychology, 59,* 341–345.

Hecht, H., von Zerssen, D., & Wittchen, H. U. (1990). Anxiety and depression in a community sample: The influence of comorbidity on social functioning. *Journal of Affective Disorders, 18,* 137–144.

Hertzog, C., Van Alstine, J., Usala, P. D., Hultsch, D. F., & Dixon, R. (1990). Measurement properties of the Center for Epidemiological Studies Depression Scale (CES-D) in older populations. *Psychological Assessment, 2,* 64–72.

Hollon, S. D., DeRubeis, R. J., Evans, M. D., Wiemer, M. J., Garvey, M. J., Grove, W. M., & Tuason, V. B. (1992). Cognitive therapy and pharmacotherapy for depression: Singly and in combination. *Archives of General Psychiatry, 49,* 774–781.

Isometsa, E. T., Aro, H. M., Henriksson, M. M., Heikkinen, M. E., & Lonnqvist, J. K. (1994). Suicide in major depression in different treatment settings. *Journal of Clinical Psychiatry, 55,* 523–527.

Jaycox, L. H, Reivich, K. J., Gillham, J., & Seligman, M. E. (1994). Prevention of depressive symptoms in school children. *Behaviour Research and Therapy, 32,* 801–816.

Juhnke, G. A. (1994). Teaching suicide risk assessment to counselor education students. *Counselor Education and Supervision, 34,* 52–58.

Kaslow, N. J., Rehm, L. P., & Siegel, A. W. (1984). Social-cognitive and cognitive correlates of depression in children. *Journal of Abnormal Psychology, 12,* 605–620.

Kazdin, A. E. (1990). Childhood depression. *Journal of Child Psychiatry, 31,* 121–160.

Keller, M. (1994). Depression: A long-term illness. *British Journal of Psychiatry, 165,* 9–15.

Kemp, B. J., Corgiat, M., & Gill, L. (1992). Effects of brief cognitive-behavioral group psychotherapy on older persons with and without disabling illness. *Behavior, Health and Aging, 2,* 21–27.

Kendall, P. C. (1991). Guiding theory for treating children and adolescents. In P. C. Kendall (Ed.), *Child and adolescent therapy: Cognitive-behavioral procedures* (pp. 113–167). New York: Guilford Press.

Kendall, P. C., Cantwell, D. P., & Kazdin, A. E. (1989). Depression in children and adolescents: Assessment issues and recommendations. *Cognitive Therapy and Research, 13,* 109–146.

Kessler, R. C., Nelson, C. B., McGonagle, K. A., Liu, J., Swartz, M., & Blazer, D. G. (1996). Comorbidity of *DSM–III–R* major depressive disorder in the general population: Results from the U.S. National Comorbidity Survey. *British Journal of Psychiatry, 168,* 17–30.

Kim, M. T. (1996). Manifestations of depression in Korean- and Anglo-Americans. *Dissertation Abstracts International: Section B: Sciences & Engineering, 57,* 419–421.

Kleespies, P. M., Deleppo. J. D., Mori, D. L., & Niles, B. L. (1998). *Emergencies in mental health practice: Evaluation and management.* New York: Guilford Press.

Knight, G. P., & Hill, N. (1998). Measurement equivalence in research involving minority adolescents. In V. McLoyd & L. Steinberg (Eds.), *Research on minority adolescents: Conceptual, methodological and theoretical issues* (pp. 183–210). Hillsdale, NJ: Erlbaum.

Knight, G. P., Virdin, L., & Roosa, M. (1994). Socialization and family correlates of mental health outcomes among Hispanic and Anglo-American families. *Child Development, 65,* 212–224.

Kolvin, I., Barrett, M. L., & Bhate, S. R. (1991). The Newcastle Child Depression Project: Diagnosis and classification of depression. *British Journal of Psychiatry, 159,* 9–21.

Kovacs, M. (1985). The Children's Depression Inventory (CDI). *Psychopharmacology Bulletin, 21,* 995–999.

Kovacs, M. (1996). Presentation and course of major depressive disorder during childhood and later years of the life span. *Journal of the American Academy of Child and Adolescent Psychiatry, 35,* 705–715.

Lamarine, R. J. (1995). Child and adolescent depression. *Journal of School Health, 65,* 390–393.

Lebowitz, B. D., Pearson, J. L., Schneider, L. S., Reynolds, C. F., Alexopoulos, G. S., Bruce, M. L., et al. (1997). Diagnosis and treatment of depression in late life: Consensus statement update. *Journal of the American Medical Association, 278,* 1186–1191.

Lefkowitz, M. M., & Tesiny, E. P. (1980). Assessment of childhood depression. *Journal of Consulting and Clinical Psychology, 48,* 43–50.

Lefkowitz, M. M., & Tesiny, E. P. (1984). Rejection and depression: Prospective and contemporaneous analyses. *Developmental Psychology, 20,* 776–785.

Lefkowitz, M. M., & Tesiny, E. P. (1985). Depression in children: Prevalence and correlates. *Journal of Consulting and Clinical Psychology, 53,* 647–656.

Lewinsohn, P. M., Rohde, P., & Seeley, J. R. (1995). Adolescent psychopathology: III. The clinical consequences of comorbidity. *Journal of the American Academy of Child and Adolescent Psychiatry, 34,* 510–519.

Lightfoot, S. L., & Oliver, J. M. (1985). The Beck Inventory: Psychometric properties in university students. *Journal of Personality Assessment, 49,* 434–436.

Mattison, R. E., Handford, H. A., Kales, H. C., Goodman, A. L., & McLaughlin, R. E. (1990). Four-year predictive value of the Children's Depression Inventory. *Psychological Assessment: A Journal of Consulting and Clinical Psychology, 2,* 169–174.

Maxmen, J. S., & Ward, N. G. (1995). *Essential psychopathology and its treatment* (2nd ed.). New York: Norton.

McLanahan, S. S., & Booth, K. (1989). Mother-only families: Problems, prospects, and policies. *Journal of Marriage and the Family, 51,* 557–580.

McLanahan, S. S., & Sandefur, G. (1994). *Growing up with a single parent.* Cambridge, MA: Harvard University Press.

Miles, C. P. (1977). Conditions predisposing to suicide: A review. *Journal of Nervous and Mental Disease, 164,* 213–242.

Miller, R. C., & Berman, J. S. (1983). The efficacy of cognitive behavior therapies: A quantitative review of the research evidence. *Psychological Bulletin, 94,* 39–53.

Mitchell, J., McCauley, E., Burle, P. M., & Moss, S. J. (1988). Phenomenology of depression in children and adolescents. *Journal of the American Academy of Child and Adolescent Psychiatry, 27,* 12–20.

Montano, C. B. (1994). Recognition and treatment of depression in a primary care setting. *Journal of Clinical Psychiatry, 55,* 18–34.

Murphy, G. E. (1986). The physician's role in suicide prevention. In A. Roy (Ed.), *Suicide* (pp. 171–179). Baltimore: Williams & Wilkins.

Murphy, G. E., Simons, A. D., Wetzel, R. D., & Lustman, P. J. (1984). Cognitive therapy and pharmacotherapy: Singly, and together in the treatment of depression. *Archives of General Psychiatry, 41,* 3–41.

Peruzzi, N., & Bongar, B. (1999). Assessing risk for suicide in patients with major depression: Psychologist's views of critical factors. *Professional Psychology: Research and Practice, 30,* 576–580.

Plopper, M. (1990). Evaluation and treatment of depression. In B. Kemp, K. Brummel-Smith, & J. W. Ramsdell (Eds.), *Geriatric rehabilitation* (pp. 253–264). Boston: College-Hill.

Quiggle, N. K., Garber, J., Panak, W. F., & Dodge, K. A. (1992). Social information processing in aggressive and depressed children. *Child Development, 63,* 1305–1320.

Radloff, L. S. (1977). The CES–D scale: A self-report depression scale for research in the general population. *Applied Psychological Measurement, 1,* 385–401.

Radloff, L. S., & Teri, L. (1986). Use of the Center for Epidemiological Studies–Depression Scale with older adults. *Clinical Gerontologist, 5,* 119–135.

Reynolds, C. F. (1996). Depression: Making the diagnosis and using SSRIs in the older patient. *Geriatrics, 51,* 28–34.

Reynolds, W. M. (1992). Depression in children and adolescents. In W. M. Reynolds (Ed.), *Internalizing disorders in children and adolescents* (pp. 149–253). New York: Wiley.

Rice, K. G., & Leffert, N. (1997). Depression in adolescence: Implications for school counsellors. *Canadian Journal of Counselling, 31,* 18–34.

Rihmer, Z., Barsi, J., Arato, M., & Demeter, E. (1990). Suicide in subtypes of primary major depression. *Journal of Affective Disorders, 18,* 221–225.

Robins, E. (1986). Completed suicide. In A. Roy (Ed.), *Suicide* (pp. 123–133). Baltimore: Williams & Wilkins.

Roland, J. L. (1995). Child and adolescent depression. *Journal of School Health, 65,* 390–394.

Rush, A. J., Beck, A. T., Kovacs, M., & Hollon, S. D. (1977). Comparative efficacy of cognitive therapy and pharmacotherapy in the treatment of depressed outpatients. *Cognitive Therapy and Research, 1,* 17–37.

Scogin, F., & McElreath, L. (1994). Efficacy of psychosocial treatments for geriatric depression: A quantitative review. *Journal of Consulting and Clinical Psychology, 62,* 69–74.

Shapiro, D. A., & Shapiro, D. (1982). Meta-analysis of comparative therapy outcome studies: A replication and refinement. *Psychological Bulletin, 92,* 581–604.

Shea, S. C. (1988). *Psychiatric interviewing: The art of understanding.* Philadelphia: Saunders.

Sherbourne, C. D., & Wells, K. B. (1997). Course of depression in patients with comorbid anxiety disorders. *Journal of Affective Disorders, 43,* 245–250.

Simons, R. L. (1996). *Understanding differences between divorced and intact families: Stress, interaction, and child outcome.* Thousand Oaks, CA: Sage.

Smucker, M. R., Craighead, W. E., Craighead, L. W., & Green, B. J. (1986). Normative reliability data for the children's depression inventory. *Journal of Abnormal Child Psychology, 14,* 25–39.

Stanard, R. P. (2000). Assessment and treatment of adolescent depression and suicidality. *Journal of Mental Health Counseling, 22,* 204–217.

Steinbrueck, S. M., Maxwell, S. E., & Howard, G. S. (1983). A meta-analysis of psychotherapy and drug therapy in the treatment of unipolar depression in adults. *Journal of Consulting and Clinical Psychology, 51,* 856–863.

Teasdale, J. D., Fennell, M. J. V., Hibbert, G. A., & Amies, P. L. (1984). Cognitive therapy for major depressive disorder in primary care. *British Journal of Psychiatry, 144,* 400–406.

Turner, S. M., & Hersen, M. (1994). *The interviewing process: Diagnostic interviewing* (2nd ed.). New York: Plenum Press.

Varley, C. K. (2002). Don't overlook depression in youth. *Contemporary Pediatrics, 19,* 70–76.

Warner, V., Weissman, M., Fendrich, M., Wickramaratne, P., & Moreau, D. (1992). The course of major depression in the offspring of depressed parents. *Archives of General Psychiatry, 49,* 795–801.

Weinrach, S. G. (1988). Cognitive therapist: A dialogue with Aaron Beck. *Journal of Counseling & Development, 67,* 15–164.

Worchel, F. F. (1990). Evaluation of subclinical depression in children using self, peer, and teacher-report measures. *Journal of Abnormal Child Psychology, 18,* 271–282.

Yesavage, J. A., Brink, T. L., Rose, T. L., & Adey, M. (1983). The Geriatric Depression Rating Scale: Comparison with other self-report and psychiatric rating scales. In T. Crook, S. Ferris, & R. Bartus (Eds.), *Assessment in geriatric psychopharmacology* (pp. 153–167). New Canaan, CT: Mark Powley Associates.

Zweig, R. A., & Hinrichsen, G. A. (1993). Factors associated with suicide attempts by depressed older adults: A prospective study. *American Journal of Psychiatry, 150,* 1687–1692.

Chapter 3

Hope and Suicide
Establishing the Will to Live

Fred J. Hanna and Alan G. Green

Hope is one of the most fascinating concepts in the field of counseling. It is a powerful and global function in human beings that deserves far more recognition. Perhaps because of its ties to religion, it has not been considered to be an idea that is easily connected to scientific credibility. Thus, it has received too little attention by researchers, counselor educators, and practitioners. What we intend to show in this chapter is that hope is grounded in scientific research and has tremendous implications for counseling, especially for counseling of people contemplating suicide. We provide evidence that hope is correlated with coping and with therapeutic change processes, and thus sheds light on a useful and practical path of approach with people with suicidal ideation. We also discuss ways of assessing the presence or absence of hope for the purpose of counseling. Finally, we outline a variety of counseling approaches that illustrate the use of hope with clients who are contemplating suicide. Of course, it is first necessary to show the range and depth of hope, how it is related to suicide, and how fundamental it is to living a life of well-being and fulfillment.

The Nature of Hope

Hope is one of those common terms, like wisdom or love, that defies precise definition and understanding. It is a household term, and as such, it is sprinkled through the language of our culture in contexts ranging from religion to tragedy. It is present in phrases such as "Hope springs eternal,"

"Don't give up hope," "Where there is life there is hope," and a variety of others. The term is surrounded by vagueness, and yet it is so powerful as a phenomenon that ignoring it runs the risk of denying a valuable source of help to clients. For the purpose of professional counseling, it is necessary to separate the phenomenon of hope from the realm of cliché and folk wisdom. Thus, to add clarity to this discussion, we should mention at the outset what hope is not, and then proceed with a definition.

Hope is not wishing, desiring, yearning, or longing. It is not squinting one's eyes or gritting one's teeth in the depths of despair and "hoping beyond hope" that some miracle will take place that will save the day. Hope is not fantasizing about a situation or creating illusions that defy reality. In the context of this chapter, hope can be defined as the realistic expectation that a positive outcome or change can occur, and in a context in which the future is viewed as experienceable and acceptable, and indeed, even welcome (Hanna, 1991). This concept, while not ignored by researchers, has yet to gain the recognition that it deserves, even though there is a small body of literature that has been devoted to it. Let us follow that thread of attention given to it by researchers and counselors to get a sense of its development as a viable and valuable construct that can be a powerful asset in helping clients who contemplate suicide. We will see that hope, a concept that is probably as old as humanity itself, is still quite young in the sense of professional acceptance and recognition, and in terms of how much more there is to understand about it.

A Professional History of Hope

There were some classic studies done in the 1950s that indicated the power of hope as a human phenomenon. Nardini (1952), for example, studied American soldiers who were in Japanese prison camps during World War II. He found that prisoners who fared the best were those who maintained a sense of positive expectation that they would be eventually be freed and who could tolerate the miserable conditions of their environment. Similarly, Bettelheim (1960) noted the negative consequences of giving up, or the absence of hope, on the survival of the prisoners in Nazi concentration camps of World War II. A study of so-called "voodoo death" by Cannon (1957) in places such as Australia and Haiti found this phenomenon was related to nothing magical or supernatural at all. Cannon reported that people in these cultures died not because of spells or potions but by being deprived and denied of a sense of community and any hope for success within it. Richter (1957) speculated that the lack of hope is so powerful that it can cause sudden death in both humans and animals. Without hope, he noted, a human being will not respond to fundamental mechanisms such fight or flight. This was echoed in a behavioral context by Seligman (1975), who found that learned helplessness also nullifies fight-or-flight responses.

Learned helplessness may be nothing more than the absence of hope, and it is not uncommon in people contemplating suicide.

Mennigner (1959) and Erikson (1963) viewed hope as a vital aspect of human development. In other words, as a person achieves greater levels of personal growth, his or her level of hope would seem to increase as well. Korner (1970) observed that hope can equip a person to cope with states of despondency or despair, and that it is an aspect of healthy behavior and a remedy for some negative behaviors. He made it clear that hope should not be viewed as an emotion or feeling but as a method of coping. Frank's (1968, 1973; Frank & Frank, 1991) classic analyses of counseling and psychotherapy revealed hope to be a common factor present in any successful counseling. He also identified hope to be the primary cause of the placebo effect. It is the positive expectation that makes the placebo so powerful, he said. He also noted that the absence of hope in a person can hasten the process of death and serve as an obstacle to a healthy recovery from illness or injury.

Hope has also been associated with the ability to cope with adversity and difficult life situations. Stotland (1969) noted that hope mobilized a person's coping resources. Similarly, the research of Lazarus, Kanner, and Folkman (1980) referred to the function of hope as facilitating a person's coping abilities. Weisman (1979) referred to hope as a prerequisite for any coping to take place at all. In the medical field, Owen (1990) found that hope, along with social support, affected the seriousness of a person's perception of his or her cancer. Not surprisingly, she also found that hope tended to be higher when pain was at a lower level.

Another important aspect of hope is its relationship to expectation. Grencavage and Norcross (1990) mentioned that expectancy factors such as hope make up an important aspect of what helps a person improve in counseling, no matter what theory or approach is being applied. This is along the same lines as the work of Jerome Frank. Let us now look at the different ways in which hope is related to expectation.

Beck and colleagues (Beck, Weissman, Lester, & Trexler, 1974) were the first to actually measure hope in a clinical context. They based their perspective on the expectation aspect of hope as defined by Stotland (1969). From this perspective, hope was defined simply as the expectation of achieving a goal. The Hopelessness Scale, which is discussed in more detail later, was the result of this simple conception. But there is more to hope than this. Hope is a multifaceted phenomenon even if one short-sightedly limits it to the context of expectation and ignores coping aspects. Frank (1968) viewed hope as "desire accompanied by expectation" (p. 383), a definition that adds a dimension of need or want to the mix. Korner (1970) noted that the person's investment of energy, or dependence on outcome, was central to understanding hope. If the person has an expectation but is not personally invested in it, and the outcome does not come about, then there is little cause for concern. Korner was also careful to make sure that wishing was removed from the idea of hope, and noted that when hope is present, the expected outcome is viewed as occurring as a matter of likelihood. For him, hope was the key to activating a person's motivation. Without it, he said, a person would be unlikely to attempt a goal.

We find this aspect of hope to be closely related to Bandura's (1977) classic concept of self-efficacy (see also Grencavage & Norcross, 1990). Bandura found that if a person does not believe oneself capable of achieving a certain task or goal, the person will be unlikely to attempt it. We believe that hope subsumes Bandura's idea of self-efficacy under its own more global purview. We should also add that the concept of self-efficacy was not unique to Bandura. Adler (1956) had conceived of the idea decades before Bandura, and the philosopher Spinoza originally described it in the 17th century (Watson & Tharp, 1989).

Menninger, Maymon, and Pruyser (1963) pointed to an aspect of hope that was more ephemeral, more difficult to pin down. They said that hope is characterized by expectation that lies beyond visible facts. Although they did not identify or describe that elusive element, we suggest that there is an aspect of hope that involves an intuitive form of knowing, a strong hunch that things will turn out to be okay even if things look bleak in the moment. But this requires further analysis. For this task we resort to the domain of phenomenology, a branch of philosophy that specializes in describing the ineffable and pinning down elusive phenomena. Marcel (1987) made a highly potent and insightful observation when he related hope primarily to one's attitude toward the future itself, as an aspect of living in the process of the advance of time. For the hopeful person, he said, the attitude toward the future is open, extensive, and piercing. In the case of hopelessness, perception of the future is denied and closed, leading to a kind of imprisonment in time itself, specifically the past and a rigidly conceived present. Heidegger (1927/1962), who was also a phenomenologist, saw hope as a project that sought freedom from life's unpleasant burdens even while being tied up in them.

More recently, Snyder (1994) pointed out that increasing hope is a matter of rehabilitating a person's willpower, as well as what he called *waypower*, that aspect of coping in which a person will find a way to bring a difficult situation to a positive outcome. Research by Hanna and Ritchie (1995) revealed hope to be a vital common factor of positive, therapeutic change, in and out of counseling. They studied 20 significant moments of therapeutic change, and hope was reported to be present and active to some degree in 19 of those cases, or 95%. Their conclusion was that hope, among other factors they called *precursors of change*, may be a regulator of the change process in clients. Because these 20 cases of significant change each involved considerable stress and anxiety, it is probable that the presence of hope is what helped the clients through the difficulty. Hanna (2002) noted that hope has the capability of influencing other change factors by way of inspiring and stimulating their presence because of its aforementioned ability to activate coping responses (see also Snyder, 1994). Along these same lines, he noted that in working with difficult clients one of the goals of counseling would be to help increase a client's degree of hope. According to research, positive beneficial change will occur more quickly in the presence of hope. This is particularly significant for clients who are contemplating suicide, as we shall see. Let us now examine suicide.

A Professional History of Suicide

Suicide, unlike hope, is a dramatic and shocking phenomenon that immediately bends the mind toward seeking psychological explanations of the behavior. One of the earliest studies of suicide was done by the brilliant sociologist, Emile Durkheim. He pioneered the description and cataloging of suicide in the effort to further understand it. Durkheim's (1897/ 1951) book on the subject, titled simply *Suicide,* was published in 1897 and is still considered a classic. He observed that suicide manifests in many forms. Some of the types that he identified were referred to as fatalistic, anomic, altruistic, and egoistic. His chief and most important observation was actually in terms of a kind of prediction. To the degree the person is integrated with society, he said, especially in terms of religion, domestic, and political society, that person will be less likely to resort to suicide.

Freud's well-known notion of the death instinct posited that many of us have a drive toward death, to destroy ourselves, and suicide was a manifestation of this. Menninger (1938), however, extended Freud's ideas and made some of the most interesting categories concerning suicide that we have encountered. These were a part of his own psychodynamic perspective. For Menninger, suicide is a kind of self-murder. It could be quick, as with the use of a gun, or it could be slow, as in the case of alcoholism, or it could be somewhere in the middle, as in the case of slitting one's wrists. According to Menninger, suicidal impulses come in two major types. The first is the wish to kill, which he referred to as *suicide by aggression.* An example of this would be suicide by a self-inflicted gun wound. Menninger believed that this type of suicide is a response to anger or aggression toward another that becomes redirected toward oneself. Perls (1973) referred to this self-directed anger as *retroflection.*

The second type of suicide, according to Menninger, is more passive. He called it the wish to be killed, or *suicide by submission.* An example of this would be suicide by an overdose of sleeping pills or placing one's body in front of a train. An overarching feature of suicide, however, is what he called the *wish to die*, and he used Freud's term of *death instinct* to describe this. Menninger believed that no suicide will be successful unless the actual wish to die is present in the person. As for the two types, Menninger believed that each of these can be regarded separately. This has clinical implications, as we shall see. Menninger (1938) also believed that unsuccessful suicides are often the result of the wish to kill oneself without the necessary wish or intent to actually die. The wish to die is distinguished from the aggressive act of killing or murdering oneself and consists primarily of a surrendering or giving up of one's life and all desire for potential satisfaction or fulfillment.

Along the lines of our present work, Farber (1968) held that suicide is a function of hope. He actually referred to suicide as a disease of hope. He noted, as we do now, that the best short-term means of predicting suicide is the measurement of a person's level of hope. In some pioneering research in this area, Beck (1963) isolated hopelessness from the more general phenomenon of depression. Until that time, no one had thought to differentiate between the two, and many practitioners still neglect this important distinction. The significant discovery was that a person who is without hope will be inclined toward suicide, and that depression that has hope still present will not be characterized by suicidal content. Eventually, in 1974, Beck and his associates published the Hopelessness Scale (Beck et al., 1974), which was designed to reveal the likelihood of a client's potential for suicide. The hypothesis that hopelessness is highly correlated with suicide and less so with depression has been confirmed by Kazdin, French, Unis, Esveldt-Dawson, and Sherick (1983), Petrie and Chamberlain (1983), and Snyder (1994).

It is important to note that suicide is often associated with a state of panic or fear (Frankl, 1967). This is a state of crisis wherein a person experiences what is called *disequilibrium.* This can be understood as a state of reduced coping ability brought about by the shock of sudden stress (Janosik, 1986). Paradoxically, a person who is contemplating suicide can be experiencing both the wish to die and the horror and fear of dying, at one and the same time. The feelings that accompany suicidal ideation can be highly complex, but it is important to note that these variations of affect may well revolve around the absence of hope.

Some, such as Menninger (1938), have described the urge toward suicide as an attempt to escape. Farber (1968) referred to this as a *no-exit condition* whereby the only real option for the person appears to be suicide. We believe that when Marcel (1951/1987) wrote about the phenomenon of *imprisonment in time,* he was referring to this state. Accompanying the state of hopelessness can be a variety of feelings such as self-pity, helplessness, self-loathing, acute apathy, extreme sadness, and self-deprecation. Durkheim (1897/1951) summed it up well, saying that the suicidal person "sees everything as through a dark cloud" (p. 64).

A slightly different way of viewing suicide is not so much as a means of escape but as a solution to a problem, especially when all other solutions have been considered and rejected or failed (Glasser, 1984a). An intriguing perspective on this aspect of suicide is that suicidal ideation is more likely for a person who has problem-solving deficits (Schotte & Clum, 1987). It stands to reason that if a person is not skilled at solving problems, then living will likely be highly discouraging, and the person will not have much hope for positive outcomes in difficult situations. On the other hand, if a person does have considerable problem-solving skills, that person will tend to see a host of options for given situations and experience a greater amount of freedom in the world as a result.

Yet another aspect of this is related to an individual's desire for power. Much is made of the desire for power, but the truth is that without a reasonable measure of it, life would be nearly impossible to live. We are not speaking of power in the sense of absolute control or destruction but a reasonable degree of control over the forces in the world that would deprive us of basic needs. Without some power or control, we do not eat, find shelter, or earn a living. Relevant to our earlier discussion, without a degree of power, we will also not be able to solve problems. When a person is powerless, it is only logical to suppose that the person may also be to some degree hopeless, and thus, suicide may begin to appear as a potent and compelling solution. The need for power of the nonpathological sort may well be one of the most primary drives of human beings. Bertrand Russell, the great philosopher of the early 20th century, called power the primary motivation of humankind. He defined it as the "production of intended effects" (Russell, 1938, p. 25). Jerome Frank (1973) identified the concept of mastery as a common goal of all counseling theories and schools. Mastery is, of course, a variant of power and a vital aspect of healthy functioning. However, for the person who is considering suicide, the act of taking one's own life may be the ultimate exercise of power. If the world will not respond to the person's wishes or will, the act of suicide will, phenomenologically at least, destroy the world utterly, as part of destroying one's own life. In the act of suicide, the entire universe will disappear, and along with it any and all of the problems that the world contains. If a problem cannot be solved it may be possible, through suicide, to annihilate it. In the depths of despair, such an option is tempting indeed.

From Double Negative to Positive

Research makes it clear that there is a relationship between hopelessness and suicide. In other words, the more hopeless the person, the more likely the prospect of suicide. In a remarkable 10-year study, Beck, Steer, Kovacs, and Garrison (1985) showed that the Hopelessness Scale has tremendous capacity to predict suicide, as much as 90% predictive. This would seem to make it clear that the absence of hope in a human being has some powerful and disturbing consequences in terms of a person's will to live.

For years, because of such powerful evidence, the field focused on the reduction of hopelessness in cases of suicidal ideation. This tendency remains and is quite unfortunate, for it considers only the negative aspect of a powerful dynamic. If hopelessness is predictive of suicide, then it is probable that the opposite is true as well. Specifically, if a person is filled with hope then he or she may be quite psychologically healthy, has attained a high degree of fulfillment in life, and is possessed of a powerful will to live (Hanna, 2002). The field may do well to devote more study to the phenomenon of hope itself, and not merely to its absence.

Reducing hopelessness is a double negative. Why not concentrate on simply building hope? Hope now has research support in its own right (Hanna & Ritchie, 1995). If a person who does not want to live is characterized by a lack of hope, perhaps the person who has the most zest for life is the person who is overflowing with it. Miller (1986) noted that the hopeful person has attained a satisfying and successful existence. We would add that a person who is filled with hope would also demonstrate high problem-solving ability in terms of resolving life's dilemmas and conundrums. This is supported by the research by Schotte and Clum (1987), which found that the suicidal person has problem-solving deficits. The results of this study show that a person highly adept at problem solving would be less suicidal, and therefore, we have observed, would tend to have a higher degree of hope.

In clinical settings, when counseling suicidal individuals, we have noted that a common characteristic of these individuals is an indefinable or vital aspect or element that is "missing" or not present. Part of this is a sense of valuing death over life in the suicidal person, often compounded by alienation, loss, or failure (Lester, 1983). Do we view this as a high degree of hopelessness or as a low degree of hope? We prefer the latter characterization. In the person who is determined, aware, and dedicated to solving a problem, or getting through a difficult situation, we observe that there is no such missing element. Hope is the great motivator, and the lack of motivation may also be what is missing in so many of these clients. Thus, to rehabilitate hope is to rehabilitate problem-solving ability, motivation to resolve problems, and indeed, the will to embrace life itself.

If we are to take seriously what we have learned from research, the phenomenon of hope may well reveal to us the nature of phrases often found in literature, such as "the joy of being alive" or the "zest for life" or "the love of life." We believe that hope building should be an integral part of counseling in almost any context. If hope is indeed closely related to motivation, building hope in a client may well pave the way to faster, more efficient use of time in counseling. Motivation has often been shown to be vital to the therapeutic change process, and hope may well be at its source (Hanna, 2002; Snyder, 1994). It would seem to us that any suicide intervention program worth its salt would take such factors into account and move a client from the crisis stage to toward a stage at which hope is rehabilitated, with the end result of a person displaying a renewed degree of enthusiasm about life and living. In this sense, hope could be the focus of an entire approach to counseling, and almost any client could enter such a program at some stage and find considerable benefit.

Hope and Suicide: The Existential Encounter With Time

Hope and suicide have one area that brings them together onto the same phenomenological playing field: They are both fundamentally concerned with the passage of time, specifically, the perceived future. Although how each of them view the future is radically different, if we consider that the perceived future is the crucial pivot, we can then better understand how to focus interventions so as to build and increase levels of hope. Perhaps the best way to approach our analysis of hope, suicide, and the perceived future is through phenomenology, once again. Let us start at the fundamental level and work our way to clinical interventions.

The passage of time is so fundamental to human beings that the philosopher and phenomenologist Martin Heidegger (1927/1962) identified it as one of the primary aspects of human existence. Husserl (1964) noted in his brilliant analysis of how we perceive time that we are constantly adjusting and calculating the future in our minds based on each passing event. As time and its events present themselves to our awareness, we are constantly constructing and deconstructing possible events that the future may offer. Hope itself may rise or fall precisely at this fundamental level of perception and being. Curiously, Rychlak (1982) referred to mental illness in general as "sickness in the future" (p. 264), because of the poor outlook and expectations that mentally ill people tend to have. If correct, this would tend to orient the subject of psychopathology around the notion of hope.

The idea of death, or nonbeing, represents a future, bleak and abruptly final, that no longer has any content at least so far as this world is concerned. In the case of life and hope, the future is seen as extensive and infinite with all manner of desired possibilities and events perceived as yet to occur. When the future is missing, as in the case of suicide, expectations become fantasies and are placed in an imagined, fantasized, or deluded future, totally divorced and separate from what is perceived as a cruel and heartless world.

Hope, with its positive and realistic expectations, welcomes the future, recognizing its offerings of life satisfaction, personal fulfillment, and enhanced meaning and growth. Hopelessness and suicide, on the other hand, involve abandoning the future as having nothing to offer or to pursue, lacking meaning and satisfaction. Simply stated, hope invites the "march of time," whereas suicide is an attempt to inhibit it, stop it, or elude it. Thus, it is the domain of the perceived future where hope and suicide meet, but with opposing attitudes toward it. The person contemplating suicide, and shunning the future, sees a "viable" alternative in seeking to avoid a bleak future and the painful passage of time. The beginning counselor is often puzzled by how calm, resigned, and even comfortable a person can sometimes be with the prospect of suicide. This option of stepping out of time as a last resort may be a reason.

Let us look at suicide and hope and their stance toward the future a bit more deeply. In an ontological sense, at the level of being, hope can be seen as the psychological intention that existence itself continues to be, whereas hopelessness represents the decision that the future should cease entirely. Phenomenologically, hope is the spontaneous psychological act of creating or positing a future, whereas complete hopelessness is the intention to deconstruct, undo, or annihilate the future. Hope is extending the future out before oneself, whereas hopelessness is seeking to obliterate it, passively or violently as the case may be. Hope is the willingness to experience the future, whereas hopelessness is an attempt to evade the inexorable and unstoppable approach of the future. Why would one do such a thing? Simply, to avoid pain, anguish, suffering, shame, or anything deemed unexperienceable. The remarkable and moving paradox here is that, in the state of hopelessness, the only hope for change and improvement lies in the prospect of death. Thus, in a twisted sort of way, suicide, the act of greatest despair, is seen as a means of change.

The sense of mastery or ability to problem solve alluded to earlier in this chapter is worthy of revisiting here. Mastery over one's life, and solving problems that one encounters, are essential to being able to posit or create a real and desired future. When this act of the vision and creation of the future is sabotaged or severely threatened, the environment begins to take over the person's future. Take the example of a childless wife who is being stalked by an abusive, violent husband. Her environment is at odds with her security and safety, and her mastery of her own life becomes diminished. Because of her husband's harassment, threats, and violence, her future becomes dictated by painful circumstances over which she has little or no mastery.

As a result, her mind becomes filled with frightening thoughts about her survival in the future and terrible but possible events that the future may hold, due to his threats and intimidation. These thoughts intrude and impose themselves into her mental or life space (Lewin, 1936) and affect how she perceives her future, even though this may be against her will. After a while, she sees nothing positive in her future and moves toward a sense of hopelessness. As she loses mastery over her life, the future becomes more grim and undesirable, and circumstances spin out of her control. Options become severely limited as he isolates her from social support and shows her that he can harm her at any moment. Future possibilities for escape or fulfillment are denied. Hopelessness deepens and dominates her mindset. Crisis conditions manifest. Suicide is now perceived as a viable option to solve the problem from this no-exit condition. Remarkably, it is the status of the perceived future that is centerpoint around which this entire scenario revolves. The question now becomes how to assess the level of hope in a person who presents in counseling.

Assessing the Level of Hope

When it comes to assessing suicide potential in a client, we believe that attending to both hope and hopelessness is important. With that said, probably the most important measure ever devised is the Hopelessness Scale introduced by Beck et al. (1974). In that classic article, they describe the scale showing clear supporting evidence that has withstood the tests of decades, that hopelessness is an indicator of suicidal intent. The scale itself focuses questions on how likely the person is to commit suicide based on the perception of how much the future has to offer. Once one understands concepts such as hope and hopelessness, it is not difficult to understand the test itself. When a client agrees with statements that express the future in a grim, dispirited, almost oppressive manner, hope building would seem to be in order.

It is not at all uncommon for clients to express views about the future that parallel statements in the Hopelessness Scale, and thus indicate the lack of hope. It is important for the counselor to hear the cues. We present some examples below, from actual clients.

"This world has nothing to offer me."
"I really don't have anything to live for."
"Life has passed me by and left me in the dust."
"There is nothing to gain by living."
"The world is a cruel, cold place, that cuts you no slack."
"No matter what I try, I f—— it all up anyway so why bother?"

It is clear that some of these statements are more indicative of a suicidal tone than others. But each such statement is worthy of pursuing with the client to determine suicidal ideation or intent.

We have addressed the lack of hope. What about its presence? Because hope is a multifaceted phenomenon, Miller (1986) noted that it should be measured from a variety of perspectives and not just from a one-dimensional view. Miller's assessment of hope addresses areas ranging from self-esteem to identity, and such existential factors as meaning and freedom, as well as items dealing with expectation. Thus, if a counselor were to assess factors such as self-esteem, the strength of the person's identity, how free they believe themselves to be, and how much meaning they have in their life, the person's level of hope would become more clear from a variety of perspectives. In other words, the reason a person may not be able to see a positive future may be precisely because he or she has low self-esteem and poor ego strength and sees few options in his or her life.

Snyder (1994) devised an accurate and efficient measure of a person's level of hope that he called the Hope Scale. It is based on eight points that measure the degree of a person's will and the degree of a person's resourcefulness. Snyder referred to these two modalities as *willpower* and *waypower*, respectively. The eight points can be summarized as follows:

1. Person energetically pursues goals.
2. Person can come up with many ways to get out of a difficult situation.
3. Person's past has provided good preparation to meet the future.

73

4. Person sees many ways to get around any problem.
5. Person has been reasonably successful in life.
6. Person sees many ways to acquire things that are important.
7. Person achieves goals set for oneself.
8. Person is confident about solving a problem even when others get discouraged.

According to Snyder, the willpower indicators of hope are the four odd-numbered points in the Hope Scale, and the even-numbered items are indicative of waypower. For the purpose of counseling, this scale covers the important aspects of hope. It is uncomplicated, easily done, and represents a workable, efficient, and clinical heuristic device. It can be done orally with clients, directly asking them their view of each point with regard to themselves. It can also be done with clients who are absent. In these cases, the counselor can rate the client by answering the questions for them. For counselors interested in fully utilizing this approach, we recommend reading the source of this material in Snyder's (1994) book, *The Psychology of Hope.*

These instruments can be used to monitor the progress of hope, counseling process, and even outcome. The scales of Snyder (1994), Beck et al. (1985), and Miller (1986) can also be used to follow the progress of hope from the crisis stage to termination stage. Termination would occur when hope is evident in cognition, affect, and behavior.

In summary, although hope is difficult to define because of its multifaceted cognitive and existential aspects, it does possess a practical and operational aspect that lends itself to measurement. Counselors working with clients who lack hope and are in need of interventions to address suicide can take advantage of this aspect. Once it is determined that a client does indeed lack hope, hope building can begin in earnest. The next section outlines a host of strategies and case examples.

Therapeutic Applications: The Rehabilitation of Hope

From what we have learned about suicide, orienting counseling around the client's perception of the future would seem to be a worthy goal indeed. This would involve three primary objectives: to establish a viable and highly empathic relationship; to focus on removing obstacles that prevent the client from comfortably being in the future; and to help the client posit or create a future that is interesting, pleasurable, and meaningful. The overall goal is to help the client see his or her future as experienceable and fulfilling, and to see obstacles and problems as situations with solutions from which valuable lessons can be learned. This, in essence, is at the core of the rehabilitation of hope. In this section we examine a variety of different approaches from the perspective of establishing and maintaining hope, but it must begin with the counseling relationship, which is vital to any form of counseling (Cornelius-White, 2002; Garfield & Bergin, 1994; Goldfried, Greenberg, & Marmar, 1990).

Empathy and Establishing the Relationship

We have found that the counselor's level of empathy has a profound effect on whether a client who is contemplating suicide will trust the counselor. The importance of the therapeutic relationship and empathy in particular is a highly significant aspect of counseling, and any discussion of techniques is premature without it (Mahoney, 1991; Wampold, 2001). What is important here is for the counselor to show the client that he or she amply understands why this particular client would want to take his or her own life. If the client believes that the counselor is only trying to prevent a suicide, it will immediately tell the client that he or she is not of primary concern.

The counselor must understand the "private logic" of the client's conclusion that suicide is a viable option. And the counselor needs to be able to reflect the feelings and the meanings of a client caught in this dangerous dilemma. An effective counselor can, through reflecting meanings and feelings, help focus and clarify issues that the client "had been approaching hazily and hesitantly" (Rogers, 1961, p. 43). We have observed that in many cases a client who is contemplating suicide prefers to approach life problems, as Rogers said, hazily and hesitantly, precisely because clarity will sometimes present a solution or path that is actually far more difficult than the relatively easy act of suicide. Thus, in this somewhat apathetic state, death is easier for some clients to contemplate than a complex solution. But here is precisely where change can begin to manifest, for the clearer the situation gets, the more easily a client can confront it (Hanna, 2002). However, without empathy, and the support and compassion of the counselor, such a desirable state will probably not arrive.

In the context of hope, the counseling relationship has much more to offer. Hatton and Valente (1984) stressed the importance of a counselor passing a genuine message of hope to the client. This must be real and genuine, and sometimes a client will get the message without the counselor having to say it explicitly. It is also true that the client can sometimes perceive the counselor's sense of hope for the client, even when there is little hope in the client. In other words, the message of hope can be transmitted not only verbally but also through the counselor's warmth and caring that is perceived by the client in an empathic relationship. If a client can perceive a counselor's compassion and empathy, knowing that the counselor understands, still cares, and is positive, hope can dawn through a wonderful kind of "interpersonal osmosis." This is sometimes referred to in literature as the *contagion of hope*. We have observed it with many clients, when the counselor is genuine and authentic.

Sometimes the only interest the client has in his or her future is seeing the counselor in the next session. Clients may say that it is the only thing that keeps them going. To maintain the relationship, the counselor should remember that trying to talk a client out of suicide without showing empathy and understanding can actually harm the therapeutic relationship. This has been known for decades (see Beck, Rush, Shaw, & Enery, 1979). Such "clever polemics" lead far astray from building hope and can lead into a competition with the client, with the counselor coming up with a brilliant argument to stay alive. Unfortunately, if empathy and compassion are absent, the counselor may win the argument but lose the client. A possible result is that the client may actually view counseling as just another failure.

Managing the Counselor's Own Issues Concerning Death and Loss of Life

The counselor's countertransference can be a major obstacle to successful counseling with people considering suicide. *Countertransference* is defined generally as a counselor's emotional reactions to the client, both conscious and unconscious (Walrond-Skinner, 1986). However, many have questioned the value of this term in describing the phenomenon in question. Strean's (1993) alternative term was *counterresistance.* The point here is that it is perfectly fine to experience reactions and feelings toward clients in counseling but the counselor gets into trouble when he or she acts on those feelings in the session. In other words, although it is quite natural for a counselor to experience impatience, irritation, or extreme sadness with a client, to express the anger or sympathy is probably a mistake. The difference between an effective counselor and an ineffective counselor, aside from relationship skills, is the ability to manage one's own issues in counseling (Van Wagoner, Gelso, Hayes, & Diemer, 1991). When a counselor does act out his or her own issues in a session, we prefer to call it *counselor interference* with the counseling process (see Hanna, 2002) because of its negative consequences.

An issue that would need to be kept in check when working with these clients is the issue of death. If the counselor has not to some degree resolved his or her own death issues, it is likely that he or she may have difficulty helping clients with it. We believe that a counselor familiar with existential philosophy and who has confronted death anxiety (see Yalom, 1980) would be far more comfortable with the idea of death. This would allow the relationship to develop much more deeply because of the counselor's tolerance of the uncertainties and imperfections of existence.

In the paragraphs that follow, we present a variety of techniques and strategies for working with this population. We emphasize again that in the absence of a working relationship between counselor and client, techniques are likely to fail. In addition, no one technique is successful with all clients and thus should not be forced on a client when it appears to be a dead end. We believe that the key is to know as many techniques as possible so that if one fails, another may turn out to be an appropriate match for that client at that time. All of what we present in the following paragraphs are empirically informed approaches to counseling (see Beutler, 2000).

Crisis Counseling and Suicide

In addition to establishing the relationship, crisis work (Aguilera & Messick, 1982; Janosik, 1986; Whitlock, 1978) is an important aspect of counseling. Reality therapy (Glasser, 1965, 1984b) is also well suited to crisis work because of its practical problem-solving approach. Crisis counseling is done when a person is experiencing the disequilibrium typical of having experienced some kind of shock or trauma. The disequilibrium results in the person's coping ability being reduced because of the shock and disorientation. Crisis work exists to get the person back to normal functioning, with a return to his or her former level of coping ability.

Of course, if a client mentions suicide it is important for the counselor to ascertain if the client has a plan with a specific time in mind. If there is a plan and if the client will not withdraw from commitment to it, it may be necessary to hospitalize the client and to get him or her as much help as possible. Counseling can resume during and after his or her release. If there is no plan, suicidal ideation should become the focus of counseling. If appropriate, the counselor should also consider sending the client to a psychiatrist for medication to augment the counseling process. The counselor would be well advised to check for alcohol or drug abuse as well, and if any of this is present, substance abuse counseling (Perkinson, 2002) should also be used.

From the viewpoint of hope building, both crisis counseling and reality therapy utilize concrete principles to removing behavioral and environmental obstacles that stand in the way of developing hope. Crisis counseling and reality therapy are of great value during those moments in counseling when the client slips back into crisis mode, and his or her behavior may be out of control or prone to irrational acts. This occurs when a person fails to solve urgent problems by conventional and customary means and then begins to desperately and impulsively generate irrational and dangerous alternative solutions (Glasser, 1984a). Family therapy is also a valuable approach to the building of hope by opening avenues to the future blocked by family-of-origin and other systemic influences.

Cognitive Approaches to Suicide

Cognitive approaches (Beck, 1976; Beck et al., 1979; Meichenbaum & Cameron, 1974) to suicide have been used for over 25 years with considerable success. From the perspective of hope and hopelessness, it is helpful to understand some of the core beliefs or irrational beliefs that prevent the formation of hope. Many of these beliefs are so much a part of the personality structure of the individual that they have been referred to as *implicit learning*

(Dowd & Courchaine, 1996). These are conclusions about the world and self that were formed before the person had developed language to express them. Getting a client to articulate them is difficult indeed. These have also been referred to as *ontological core beliefs* (Ottens & Hanna, 1998) and as beliefs formed at a preverbal level (see Cashdan, 1988). Some of the core beliefs that prevent hope from manifesting are listed below (see Hanna, 2002).

> "Only bad things are in store for me."
> "The world is a cruel place."
> "No matter what you do, things never really get better."
> "The future holds only what others want for me."
> "I am afraid of what will happen to me."
> "The future provides nothing but anxiety."
> "The future is filled with unforeseen catastrophes."
> "I cannot do anything about my future."
> "Nobody has any idea of the future."

Recall that these are beliefs articulated here but may be fuzzy and obscure for the client. It is up to the counselor to help the client clarify these beliefs and bring their affective and behavioral consequences to awareness. This is done by helping the client articulate the belief. Sometimes, considerable probing is necessary to give the client hope to the degree that he or she becomes motivated to work. The following case example illustrates the process.

Case Example

Bruce was an introverted, soft-spoken, 25-year-old, highly intelligent male. He was of European descent, and both of his parents worked and were good providers. He had difficulty holding a job and seemed to have a way of angering his employers. He thus had established a work pattern that often resulted in his quitting jobs before his supervisors had a chance to fire him. He worked mostly part-time jobs as a waitperson or in retail shops in malls. He had not had any romantic relationships for several years and thought that he had nothing to offer women, as there was nothing interesting about him or his lifestyle. Although he was interested in philosophy and history, there were no religious or spiritual pursuits in his life.

Bruce had suffered from moderate depression for many years but had refused to take any form of medication, saying any sort of good feeling from medication was "unnatural and fake." After two sessions, a rapport had developed between Bruce and his counselor, and in a moment of complete honesty he declared simply, "I probably should tell you that I hate the world and everything about it. When I get bored I think about the ways that I can kill myself and get out of here once and for all." Bruce said all this with a tone of melancholy and despair, but also curiously mixed with pride. When asked, he said that he had no plans for suicide, but after discussing feelings connected with this attitude, the counselor decided to pursue his core beliefs.

Counselor: You say that you hate the world and everything in it, Bruce. Do you believe that the world is cruel place?

Client: It's more than that. I think it is downright cold and evil. Look at how vicious nature is. Killing is what nature is all about. I just don't want any part of it but I can't escape it unless through dying.

Counselor: I see what you mean. Animals, including humans, kill other animals as food. Trees in the forest compete for life-giving sunlight and block other trees' access to it. Nature can be very bleak.

Client: Exactly.

Counselor: So for you, the world is cold, unfeeling, and evil.

Client: Yeah. I am glad you see that. Most people don't have the guts to see it like it is.

Counselor: Was there a time when all this began to sink in?

Client: It was always there with me. I just sort of, like, always knew it.

Counselor: Can I ask you a difficult question?

Client: Sure, go ahead.

Counselor: Do you have this same belief about your family as well?

Client: Well, yeah, now that you mention it. My father was always beating my sisters and me. He never quit yelling. All he did was scream and yell and tell us how he was going to kick our asses if we did this or that, and he would do it even if we obeyed him.

Counselor: Is it okay if I ask you more about this?

Client: Yeah. I kinda thought you might get to this stuff anyway.

Counselor: I see. It sounds to me like what you say about the world being cold and evil, actually describes your father and your experience with your family. Am I close on this?

Client: Sounds about right (sighing).

Counselor: Would it be fair to say that because of that experience with your father, you have judged the world only according to what you see as negative, and that maybe you have developed a habit of ignoring the positive aspects of life?

Client: Could be that's true.

Counselor: Do you think this focusing on the negative and ignoring the positive might have something to do with your depression?

Client: What do you mean?

Counselor: Well, please tell me if I am wrong, but if the world is cold and evil, it doesn't give you much to look forward to in life. That could lead to a pretty depressed way of life. What do you think?

Client: That is probably true.

Counselor: I would think that if you expanded your viewpoint to include the positive, you might have a more balanced view of things and a bit less depression.

Client: Makes sense.

Counselor: Would you want to work on achieving this balance? It would probably involve getting more into your family and your father . . .

Client: But, you know, I really don't feel like talking about all that stuff.

Counselor: I see. Sounds like there is a lot of hurt there, is that right?

Client: Yeah. A lot.

Counselor: I am going to say something to you. Tell me if I'm wrong, okay?

Client: [nods]

Counselor: In a way, your father is still hurting you, because you are still carrying the pain in your mind that he caused you and your sisters. Does this seem true to you?

Client: [nods slowly and seriously]

Counselor: Is it time to be free of your father and the evil, cold world that he handed down to you?

Client: [a bit brighter and more energetic] Yeah. Let's try it.

This was the point when Bruce began to reduce his depression and hopelessness by, in essence, agreeing to develop hope. He eventually saw that his despondent core belief about the world being cold and evil resulted from painful experiences with his father and had caused him to place a needlessly negative interpretation on almost everything he perceived.

Hopelessness often involves a high degree of dichotomous—all or nothing—thinking patterns, and people with this simplistic way of thinking tend to exaggerate the difficulty of their problems, not because of any deviousness but because this kind of thinking precludes the formulation of efficient solutions (Beck, 1976). Getting a client to see shades of gray is often helpful for this kind of difficulty. Another approach is to examine the more realistic positions that lie between the dichotomous extremes. Beck and his associates recommended a *forced fantasy technique* that involves a three-step cognitive rehearsal. The first step asks the person to imagine being in a desperate situation. The second step is to ask the client to report on the despair, suicidal ideation, and any impulses generated. Once these are reported, the person is asked, in the third step, to come up with solutions to the situation without giving in to the anxiety or the distractions caused by the suicidal impulses and ideations. This technique need not be a fantasy. The technique can also be done on painful moments in the past that the person has survived. Alternative therapy (Beck, 1976; Beck et al., 1979) is also valuable and useful in finding alternative solutions to situations in a search for options to suicide. This technique explores options for currently difficult situations and problems, thus building hope from the freedom angle.

In the section on Adaptations for Diversity in this chapter, we introduce another cognitive approach that has not, to our knowledge, been previously discussed in the context of suicide. It has to do with counseling victims of oppression. We have found that in highly difficult cases of suicidal ideation and intent, this approach can be of great utility, and we encourage the reader to explore that section.

Existential Counseling Approaches

Existential philosophy entered the realm of counseling approximately 50 years ago. This philosophy provides a workable framework for hope building. Although existentialism is not a cohesive school of philosophy and there are conflicts among the major figures (Kaufmann, 1975), we focus on the work of Heidegger (1927/1962) and Sartre (1953). Existential counseling is concerned with themes such as anxiety, authenticity, being, nonbeing, death, freedom, isolation, meaninglessness, and the human condition. Existential counseling seeks to enhance a person's capacity for awareness, experiencing, and freedom. This experiential approach is in contrast to counseling theories that seek to explain human life according to principles and concepts.

Along the lines of this chapter, existential counseling is unique in that it focuses directly on death (Yalom, 1980), not in terms of grieving but with regard to being able to accept it as an inevitable phenomenon that affects us all. Thus, the predicament of a person who is seeking his or her own death, or nonbeing, as an escape from existence itself would be easily accommodated by an existential approach. Yalom (1980) went as far as to say that many suicides occur because of a fear or abhorrence of death. Paradoxically, he said, this causes such people to produce their own death so that the experience is now on their own terms and under their own control in the act of suicide.

As strange as it may seem, we have found that some people contemplating suicide often ask the same questions about the nature of death as do philosophers and counselors. These are questions that pertain to the meaning of life and the value of one's own life, and whether and how it is worth pursuing (Frankl, 1967). In some cases, a counselor can use this as an opportunity for a reframe. Specifically, a person's preoccupation with the nature or function of death need not be viewed as morbid or morose. As a philosophical or psychological phenomenon, death is a subject that has fascinated many great minds. Reframing it in this way can serve to remove some of the stigma that often accompanies the entertainment of suicidal ideation, almost normalizing it. Of course, the counselor can then make it clear that, as far as we know, the mysteries of death and nonbeing can only be explored consciously, while alive, and that existentialists tell us that death is most appreciated and understood by the person who has embraced life and being.

Existential counseling also provides an avenue for the compulsive contemplation of death as an opportunity for growth (Van Dusen, 1962; Yalom, 1980). The key is focusing not so much on death as an escape but as a teacher about how we live and how we do everything we can, in this culture, to avoid the thought of death. Many wonderful points along these lines are made in the classic, Pulitzer prize winning book, *The Denial of Death* (Becker, 1974), which addressed the need of human beings to avoid their mortality

81

at all costs. This approach places counseling people contemplating suicide in a context that enhances a person's ability to simply be-in-the-world, complete with a high level of acceptance of the twists, cruelties, and uncertainties of life. This high level of tolerance of uncertainty and ambiguity, and of undesirable circumstances, can be developed through the process "letting-be" described by Heidegger (1965, p. 305) as a key to understanding the nature of freedom. It also helps us to tolerate events and circumstances that lie beyond one's control. Letting-be is not a passive, apathetic helplessness but quite the contrary. It is an active interest and acceptance of what is and what exists. For Heidegger, we cannot truly achieve any measure of authenticity and genuineness as a human being until we can accept existence as it is, and only then can we seek to change it. From Heidegger's (1965) perspective, "freedom reveals itself as the letting-be of what is" (p. 305).

We submit that a person contemplating suicide is in a dilemma of freedom, a loss of freedom, or a lamenting of freedom never realized. Freedom is a major existential theme. Weiss (1958) long ago categorized several aspects of freedom, three of which are relevant to this discussion: *freedom-from, freedom-to,* and *freedom-with.* In freedom-from, there is the aspect of release or liberation from limiting circumstances, whether environmental such as oppression, or psychological such as harmful beliefs. In freedom-to, we see freedom manifesting as a wide range of choices and options for actions in the present and future. In freedom-with, the person can coexist with others, respecting their freedom without seeking to inhibit it.

From an existential perspective, suicide can be seen as a move toward freedom in one or all three of these modalities; as a release from suffering, shame, or pain; as a powerful choice when there is no exit; and as a way of finally being accepted by one's peers. A counselor may be helpful in reframing suicide as a move to freedom, however misguided it may be. If the client expresses a desire to be free, or is willing to explore the possibility of freedom, existential counseling can be an appropriate avenue of approach, and the result may be a powerful growth experience. When freedom is realized, hope seems to rise to that degree. Another application of the notion of freedom can be found in Sartre's (1953) treatise in a section that he called existential psychoanalysis. Rather than constantly running through painful moments of the past, it is of far greater therapeutic benefit, he said, to instead examine the choices that one made in that past, and the influences and incidents that led to those choices.

Still another use of existential counseling would be to map out a person's meaning system. This involves exploring a person's values and authentic goals. Although this may sound like a distinctly cognitive procedure, cognitive and existential approaches are easily integrated (Ottens & Hanna, 1998). A goal of counseling would be to positively reconstruct a person's meaning system, free of any other person's influence or dictates. The more elaborate, realistic, flexible, balanced, and richly detailed this meaning system becomes, the more hopeful the person is likely to be. The person's meaning system can then be expanded so that it can encompass and integrate a host of life experiences, positive and negative.

Addressing Subpersonalities

A technique that we highly recommend is a relatively new way of approaching a phenomenon that has been in the literature for over a hundred years. It addresses different parts, or sides, of the personality with a degree of therapeutic precision. This technique also has the advantage of bypassing resistance in some clients. The phenomenon itself was noted by such major historical figures as William James (1890/1981) and Carl Jung (1934/1969), and more recently by Goulding and Schwartz (1995) and Hanna, Hanna, and Keys (1999). Assagioli (1965) was the first to use the aptly descriptive term of *subpersonalities* (see also Rowan, 1990). Note that this technique is not about multiple personalities, which is quite a different phenomenon (see Ornstein, 1986).

Regardless of the source of the phenomenon, the technique itself is our focus here. If a client is particularly hesitant and even difficult with regard to responding to counseling, we recommend this technique as an alternative. When the client makes it clear that suicide is the only solution or exit from a difficult situation, the counselor can fully acknowledge it and empathize, saying something to the effect of, "You have made it very clear that this is the only way. Can I ask you a question about this?" And after the client agrees, the counselor can say, "Is there a part of you that wants to stay alive?" The chances are the client will respond with a positive answer. After all, the client is still alive for some reason. If the client admits to this the counselor can then ask, "Can I talk to that part of you?"

At this point, it often happens that the counselor will encounter a different side, or subpersonality of that client. The client's mood, tone, or attitude can soften or become more emotional as the case may be. At this point it is quite possible that the counselor has now engaged the client at a level closer to the client's authentic or genuine self. More fruitful and responsive counseling can often take place as a result of this simple but at times dramatic procedure.

Other Approaches

The Reasons for Living Inventory (Lineham, Goodstein, Nielsen, & Chiles, 1983) was developed to work with suicidal clients to motivate them to want to stay alive. The hope-building potential here is obvious and of great value, and can delay suicide until more stable changes can be made. Bonner (1990) suggested addressing three key domains while working with clients contemplating suicide. He referred to this as M.A.P., or Mental state, Affective state, and Psychosocial context.

We also recommend the enhancement of social support during the troubled times in which a client contemplates suicide. Social support is so powerful that it can alleviate depression all by itself (Arkowitz, 1992) and be a source of spontaneous improvement (Lambert, 1992). The support of loved ones and friends can also give a person a sense of hope through the contagion of hope mentioned earlier. Social support is also an active ingredient in therapeutic change (e.g., Beutler & Clarkin, 1990). Empathy is at the heart of social support (Arkowitz, 1992), and a relationship is supportive to the degree that empathy is present. In terms of counseling, we recommend that the client be taught the nature of empathy, so as to be able to recognize empathy when it is present and absent in his or her relationships. The goal is to enhance and encourage those relationships in which empathy is present and to question the value of relationships in which it is absent (see Hanna, 2002).

Because the enhancement of hope is an implicit goal for many schools of counseling, a wide variety of theories of counseling can be handily combined, converted, and aligned toward the rehabilitation of hope in suicidal clients. Existentialism (Heidegger, 1927/1962; Sartre, 1953), which has its roots in phenomenology (Husserl, 1913/1931, 1964, 1936/1970), and cognitive and other approaches outlined here pave a path from the depths of despondency to the heights of the creative, realistic vision that is hope. All of these closely related approaches provide a platform that supports range and depth of understanding, and diversity and flexibility of technique in almost any counseling context (Hanna & Puhakka, 1991).

Adaptations for Diversity

Counseling Victims of Oppression

The American Counseling Association has made important advances in raising consciousness concerning issues of diversity in the helping professions (see, e.g., Robinson & Ginter, 1999). It has been well established that any mental health practitioner needs to be familiar with the culture and background context of the client with whom he or she is working. This is also true with clients contemplating suicide, of course, given the fact that issues of race, sexual orientation, gender, and ability may play a role in the client's condition.

However, there is an aspect of diversity that is so important that we believe it is the underlying condition that makes attention to the subject so vitally necessary. We are speaking of the issue of oppression. Oppression is generally defined as putting down and keeping down an individual or group through the use of unjust force or authority. Although this is generally thought of in the context of politics, oppression is a common phenomenon in relationships, families, and the workplace. Oppression comes in two modalities: force and deprivation (Hanna, Talley, & Guindon, 2000).

Oppression by force is literally imposing something harmful on a person that the person does not desire or need. This can be a bullet or a set of beliefs. Oppression by deprivation is a harmful taking away of something that the person does need or want. This can also include neglect. Oppression by deprivation includes denying an individual or group of education, opportunity, or self-determination. Issues commonly and routinely encountered while counseling clients largely involve oppression in one or both modes. This can include such classic issues as anxiety, depression, and abuse in all forms.

Jacobs (1994) went so far as to say that oppression can be seen as the source of all psychopathology that is not genetic or disease based. We submit that the reason there is so much emphasis on issues such as multiculturalism, homophobia, sexism, racism, and so forth is precisely because there is oppression that is perpetrated on the members of these groups. Controversial issues such as multiculturalism or sexual orientation would be much more benign if not for the oppression that commonly accompanies them in a society.

So the question becomes, how does this relate to clients contemplating suicide? In our experience people who see suicide as a viable option, regardless of race, culture, gender, age, or sexual orientation, have often been victims of severe oppression. Thus, we can suggest an approach to suicide that directly takes oppression into account. It is primarily cognitive but adds a new dimension to standard cognitive counseling. This approach addresses the source of the cognitive dysfunction or irrational belief in the person's past or current environment. This approach, unlike some cognitive approaches, does not blame the victim for generating irrational and destructive beliefs (Hanna, 2002). We have found that most of the time, irrational beliefs are inflicted on people by oppressors, with the result of the victim helplessly or ignorantly agreeing. Rather than indirectly accusing the client of originating the harmful belief, the counselor asks the client to stop agreeing with these destructive messages. Because the technique does not blame the victim, in this case the client, it also allows the counselor not only to dispute the irrational belief but to *discredit its original source*.

Therefore, if a client gives voice to an irrational belief concerning his or her own self-worth, or echoing one of the negative core beliefs about hope listed above, the counselor can ask if there was someone in the client's past or present environment from whom these beliefs were received. Or if clients mention someone who hurt them in the past or present, the counselor can ask what that person wanted them to believe about themselves. The following case example illustrates how this approach is utilized in a case of a person whose victimization as a woman played a role in her suicidal ideation.

Case Example

Patrisha was 42 years old and presented with marital problems. Patrisha's self-esteem was quite low, and she appeared to have little faith in herself.

She reported that she had no life, and now that her two kids were pretty much on their own, her "purpose was carried out." When the counselor inquired into this statement, she said, cautiously, that her purpose in life was to raise children, and now it was completed and there was no more reason to live. The counselor asked if she was considering hurting herself and she said "I think about it a lot," and added that maybe it was "time to end it all." The counselor asked if any of this was related to her marriage. She became cynical and said that marriage was "overrated." She reported that her husband of 23 years had an extremely critical view of women and constantly harassed her about being fat, overly emotional, and "incapable of having a logical thought." Her husband was a union truck driver in his early 50s who worked a great deal of overtime and had an income of around $100,000 per year. He said it was alright for her to be seeking counseling "as long as it was with a man."

The counselor eventually asked Patrisha, "Do you think that being with your husband has affected the way you think about yourself and life?" She nodded slowly and sadly. The counselor then asked, "What do you think he wants you to believe about yourself?" After a bit of clarification of the question, the counselor listed the beliefs that Patrisha mentioned.

"I am dumb."
"I never do anything right."
"I am worthless."
"All I am good for is sex."

The counselor then asked Patrisha, with each belief, if she bought into it or had come to believe it. The degree of agreement was measured on a verbal scale of 1 to 10. The first belief she rated as a 5. The next three she rated as 8. The counselor asked if these three were not true would she still feel like killing herself. She brightened a bit and said no. Then, in an effort to discredit the source of these negative beliefs, the counselor asked if her husband was an expert on human nature or human behavior. She laughed mirthlessly and said, "No way." The counselor then asked if she thought her husband "really and truly" understood her. She laughed again in the same way and said, "Hell no. All he cares about is himself."

At this point the counselor ventured the question that is designed to disengage the client from the oppressive beliefs. "Well, if your husband doesn't know anything about human nature and doesn't understand you at all, then anything he says about you is probably dead wrong." This dislodged her agreement with the oppressive beliefs, and she soon began to actively disagree with and drop these beliefs. From then on her counseling was focused on finding out more about herself and how she could come to enjoy life being her own guide to what is true about her. With this single action, her hope began to be restored, and suicide became less and less of an issue in her counseling sessions.

This same approach to oppression can be done with racial/ethnic minorities, for example, asking African Americans, "What does the White society want Black people to believe about themselves?" and inquiring into the degree of agreement with those beliefs. Gay and lesbian clients can be asked, "What does the dominant heterosexual society want gay or lesbian (as the case may be) people to believe about themselves?"

An alternative question can be, "When you are around [a group or individual] what do you tend to believe about yourself?" By ending the agreement, discrediting the source, and disputing the belief, we have found that this approach to oppression opens a new dimension to cognitive counseling that can be effective when the standard approaches fail (see Hanna, 2002; Hanna et al., 2000).

Recalling the work of Menninger (1938) referred to earlier in this chapter, it may well be oppression that leads to the phenomenon of turning one's anger inward upon oneself. Asking clients how they might carry out the act of suicide can reveal whether the suicide is aggressive or passive toward oneself. If their suicidal ideation is by an act of aggression in the sense of, say stabbing oneself or shooting oneself with a gun, the anger could actually be toward a specific person whom they believe they are helpless to change. Thus, the anger is turned inward, displaced toward changing the self instead of the oppressive other. It is that other person that could be a major oppressor in the client's life, and if so, this person could be approached in the manner and mode of the cognitive counseling of oppression outlined above. It is quite a healthy turnaround for a client to see that his or her self-loathing is not actually toward the self and can be defused and redirected toward its true source. This brings about a sense of freedom and hope.

Summary

The goal of building hope is more constructive, positive, and functional than concentrating on the doubly negative goal of reducing hopelessness. From what we have learned from both research and practice, we can conclude that there may be some truth to at least one of those sayings about hope. Instead of "where there is life there is hope," we propose that there may be more truth in its reversal. "Where there is hope there is life" sounds more appropriate, and there is research to back the reversal of the cliché. We can also add one of our own, namely that "Where hope is failing, life is faltering." Hope is so powerful that we still have much to learn about it, especially in terms of what causes it to increase and what causes it to diminish.

In the case of clients suffering from a lack of hope, various measures can be used to assess the degree to which this has occurred. Beck et al.'s (1974) Hopelessness Scale is valuable, as well as Snyder's (1994) Scale of Hope. As far as counseling is concerned, the counselor's level and degree of empathy is crucial to working with people with this problem, as well as the counselor's ability to manage his or her own issues, or countertransference. The crisis approach is important and usually a necessity to some degree for such clients, and goes well with a reality therapy approach. Cognitive approaches are of great utility, including examining core beliefs and alternative therapy.

Existential approaches such as rebuilding the client's authentic meaning system and helping the client realize his or her true freedom are helpful, as well as emphasizing choice. The subpersonality technique is of use for more difficult clients, and the Reasons for Living Inventory can be inspiring in some cases. In cases in which there is clear evidence of oppression, the cognitive counseling of oppression directly addresses harm done to client and seeks to free the client of the lingering oppressive beliefs that are usually part and parcel of the lack of hope. This approach to oppression, we believe, should be a standard aspect of any counselor working with victims of racism, sexism, homophobia, and so forth. In fact we believe that those who perpetrate such oppression are themselves deserving of a diagnosis that could be called intolerant personality disorder (Guindon, Green & Hanna, 2003).

It appears that hope compels a person to contemplate life and its living in the future. The lack of hope, in contrast, leads one to abandon life and to seek to stop the passing of time itself. Clients contemplating suicide can only benefit from a counseling program oriented toward hope. It would also appear that clients at any level would benefit from an enhancement of hope, and by so doing would have that much more life to contemplate.

References

Adler, A. (1956). *The individual psychology of Alfred Adler* (H. L. Ansbacher & R. R. Ansbacher, Eds.). New York: Harper & Row.

Aguilera, D. C., & Messick, J. M. (1982). *Crisis intervention: Theory and methodology.* (4th ed.). St. Louis, MO: Mosby.

Arkowitz, H. (1992). A common factors therapy for depression. In J. C. Norcross & M. R. Goldfried (Eds.), *Handbook of psychotherapy integration* (pp. 402–432). New York: Basic Books.

Assagioli, R. (1965). *Psychosynthesis: A manual of principles and techniques.* New York: Penguin.

Bandura, A. (1977). Self-efficacy: Toward a unifying theory of behavioral change. *Psychological Review, 84,* 191–215.

Beck, A. T. (1963). Thinking and depression. *Archives of General Psychiatry, 9,* 324–333.

Beck, A. T. (1976). *Cognitive therapy and the emotional disorders.* New York: New American Library.

Beck, A. T., Rush, A. J., Shaw, B. F., & Emery, G. (1979). *Cognitive therapy of depression.* New York: Guilford Press.

Beck, A. T., Steer, R. A., Kovacs, M., & Garrison, B. (1985). Hopelessness and eventual suicide: A 10-year prospective study of patients hospitalized with suicidal ideation. *American Journal of Psychiatry, 142,* 559–563.

Beck, A. T., Weissman, A., Lester, D., & Trexler, L. (1974). The measurement of pessimism: The Hopelessness Scale. *Journal of Consulting and Clinical Psychology, 42,* 861–865.

Becker, E. (1974). *The denial of death.* New York: Touchstone Books.

Bettelheim, B. (1960). *The informed heart.* Glencoe, IL: Free Press.

Beutler, L. E. (2000). David and Goliath: When empirical and clinical standards of practice meet. *American Psychologist, 55,* 997–1007.

Beutler, L. E., & Clarkin, J. F. (1990). *Systematic treatment selection: Toward targeted therapeutic interventions.* New York: Brunner/Mazel.

Bonner, R. L. (1990). A "M.A.P." to the clinical assessment of suicide risk. *Journal of Mental Health Counseling, 12,* 232–236.

Cashdan, S. (1988). *Object relations therapy: Using the relationship.* New York: Norton.

Cannon, W. B. (1957). Voodoo death. *Psychosomatic Medicine, 19,* 182–190.

Cornelius-White, J. H. D. (2002). The phoenix of empirically supported therapy relationships: The overlooked person-centered basis. *Psychotherapy, 39,* 219–222.

Dowd, E. T., & Courchaine, K. E. (1996). Implicit learning, tacit knowledge, and implications for stasis and change in cognitive psychotherapy. *Journal of Cognitive Psychotherapy, 10,* 163–180.

Durkheim, E. (1951). *Suicide.* New York: Free Press. (Original work published 1897)

Erikson, E. (1963). *Childhood and society* (2nd ed.). New York: Norton.

Farber, M. (1968). *Theory of suicide.* New York: Funk & Wagnalls.

Frank, J. (1968). The role of hope in psychotherapy. *International Journal of Psychiatry, 5,* 383–395.

Frank, J. (1973). *Persuasion and healing: A comparative study of psychotherapy.* New York: Schocken Books.

Frank, J. D., & Frank, J. B. (1991). *Persuasion and healing: A comparative study of psychotherapy* (3rd ed.). Baltimore: Johns Hopkins University Press.

Frankl, V. E. (1967). *Psychotherapy and existentialism.* New York: Washington Square Press.

Garfield, S. L., & Bergin, A. E. (Eds.). (1994). *Handbook of psychotherapy and behavior change: An empirical analysis.* New York: Wiley.

Glasser, W. (1965). *Reality therapy: A new approach to psychiatry.* New York: Harper & Row.

Glasser, W. (1984a). *Control theory: A new explanation of how we control our lives.* New York: Harper & Row.

Glasser, W. (1984b). Reality therapy. In R. J. Corsini & D. Wedding (Eds.), *Current psychotherapies* (3rd ed., pp. 320–353). Itasca, IL: Peacock.

Goldfried, M. R., Greenberg, L. S., & Marmar, C. (1990). Individual psychotherapy: Process and outcome. *Annual Review of Psychology, 41,* 659–688.

Goulding, R. A., & Schwartz. R. C. (1995). *The mosaic mind: Empowering the tormented selves of child abuse survivors.* New York: Norton.

Grencavage, L. M., & Norcross, J. C. (1990). Where are the commonalities among the therapeutic common factors? *Professional Psychology: Research and Practice, 21,* 372–378.

Guindon, M. H, Green, A. G., & Hanna, F. J. (2003). Intolerance and psychopathology: Toward a general diagnosis for racism, sexism, and homophobia. *American Journal of Orthopsychiatry, 73,* 167–176.

Hanna, F. J. (1991). Suicide and hope: The common ground. *Journal of Mental Health Counseling, 13,* 459–472.

Hanna, F. J. (2002). *Therapy with difficult clients: Using the precursors model to awaken change.* Washington, DC: American Psychological Association.

Hanna, F. J., Hanna, C. A., & Keys, S. G. (1999). Fifty strategies for counseling defiant and aggressive adolescents: Reaching, accepting, and relating. *Journal of Counseling & Development, 77,* 395–404.

Hanna, F. J., & Puhakka, K. (1991). When psychotherapy works: Pinpointing an element of change. *Psychotherapy, 28,* 598–607.

Hanna, F. J., & Ritchie, M. H. (1995). Seeking the active ingredients of psychotherapeutic change: Within and outside the context of therapy. *Professional Psychology: Research and Practice, 26,* 176–183.

Hanna, F. J., Talley, W. B., & Guindon, M. H. (2000). The power of perception: Toward a model of cultural oppression and liberation. *Journal of Counseling & Development, 78,* 430–441.

Hatton, C. L., & Valente, S. M. (1984). *Suicide: Assessment and intervention.* Norwalk, CT: Appleton-Century-Crofts

Heidegger, M. (1962). *Being and time.* New York: Harper & Row. (Original work published 1927)

Heidegger, M. (1965). *Existence and being.* Chicago: Henry Regnery.

Husserl, E. (1931). *Ideas: A general introduction to pure phenomenology.* New York: Collier Books. (Original work published 1913)

Husserl, E. (1964). *The phenomenology of internal time-consciousness.* Bloomington: Indiana University Press. (Original lectures given 1905 to 1910)

Husserl, E. (1970). *The crisis of European sciences and transcendental phenomenology.* Evanston, IL: Northwestern University Press. (Original work published 1936)

Jacobs, D. H. (1994). Environmental failure: Oppression is the only cause of psychopathology. *Journal of Mind and Behavior, 15*(1–2), 1–18.

James, W. (1981). *The principles of psychology.* Cambridge, MA: Harvard University Press. (Original work published 1890)

Janosik, E. H. (1986). *Crisis counseling: A contemporary approach.* Monterey, CA: Jones & Bartlett.

Jung, C. G. (1969). *The structure and dynamics of the psyche: Collected works* (Vol. VIII). Princeton, NJ: Princeton University Press. (Original work published 1934)

Kaufmann, W. (1975). *Existentialism: From Dostoevsky to Sartre*. New York: New American Library.

Kazdin, A. E., French, N. H., Unis, A. S., Esveldt-Dawson, K., & Sherick, R. B. (1983). Hopelessness, depression, and suicidal intent among psychiatrically disturbed inpatient children. *Journal of Consulting and Clinical Psychology, 51*, 504–510.

Korner, I. N. (1970). Hope as a method of coping. *Journal of Consulting and Clinical Psychology, 34*, 134–139.

Lambert, M. J. (1992). Psychotherapy outcome research: Implications for integrative and eclectic therapists. In J. C. Norcross & M. R. Goldfried (Eds.), *Handbook of psychotherapy integration* (pp. 94–129). New York: Basic Books.

Lazarus, R. S., Kanner, A. D., & Folkman, S. (1980). Emotions: A cognitive-phenomenological analysis. In R. Plutchik & H. Kellerman (Eds.), *Emotion: Theory, research and experience* (pp. 189–217). New York: Academic Press.

Lester, D. (1983). *Why people kill themselves: A 1980's summary of research findings on suicidal behavior*. Springfield, IL: Charles C Thomas.

Lewin, K. (1936). *Principles of topological psychology*. New York: McGraw-Hill.

Lineham, M. M., Goodstein, J. L., Nielsen, S. L., & Chiles, J. A. (1983). Reasons for staying alive when you are thinking of killing yourself: The Reasons for Living Inventory. *Journal of Consulting and Clinical Psychology, 51*, 276–286.

Mahoney, M. J. (1991). *Human change processes: The scientific foundations of psychotherapy*. New York: Basic Books.

Marcel, G. (1987). Sketch of a phenomenology and metaphysic of hope. In T. Busch (Ed.), *The participant perspective: A Gabriel Marcel reader* (pp. 197–243). Lanham, MD: University Press of America. (Original work published 1951)

Meichenbaum, D., & Cameron, R. (1974). The clinical potential of modifying what clients say to themselves. *Psychotherapy: Theory, Research and Practice, 2*, 103–117.

Menninger, K. (1938). *Man against himself*. New York: Harcourt, Brace & World.

Menninger, K. (1959). Hope. *American Journal of Psychiatry, 116*, 481–491.

Menninger, K., Maymon, M., & Pruyser, P. (1963). *The vital balance: The life process in mental health and illness*. New York: Viking Press.

Miller, J. F. (1986). Development of an instrument to measure hope (Doctoral dissertation, Health Sciences Center, University of Chicago, 1986). *Dissertation Abstracts International, 47*. (University Microfilms No. DA8705572)

Nardini, J. E. (1952). Survival factors in American prisoners of war of the Japanese. *American Journal of Psychiatry, 109*, 242–248.

Ornstein, R. (1986). *Multimind: A new way of looking at human behavior*. London: MacMillan.

Ottens, A. J., & Hanna, F. J. (1998). Cognitive and existential therapies: Toward an integration. *Psychotherapy, 35*, 312–324.

Owen, C. (1990). *The relationship of selected variables to level of hope in women with breast cancer.* Unpublished doctoral dissertation, University of Toledo, Toledo, OH.

Perkinson, R. R. (2002). *Chemical dependency counseling: A practical guide.* Thousand Oaks, CA: Sage.

Perls, F. S. (1973). *The gestalt approach and eyewitness to therapy.* Palo Alto, CA: Science & Behavior Books.

Petrie, K., & Chamberlain, K. (1983). Hopelessness and social desirability as moderator variables in predicting suicidal behavior. *Journal of Consulting and Clinical Psychology, 51,* 485–487.

Richter, C. (1957). On the phenomenon of sudden death in animals and man. *Psychosomatic Medicine, 19,* 191–198.

Robinson, T. L., & Ginter, E. J. (1999). Racism: Healing its effects [Special issue]. *Journal of Counseling & Development, 77*(1).

Rogers, C. R. (1961). *On becoming a person: A therapist's view of psychotherapy.* Boston: Houghton Mifflin.

Rowan, J. (1990). *Subpersonalities: The people inside us.* London: Routledge.

Russell, B. (1938). *Power: A new social analysis.* London: Unwin Books.

Rychlak, J. F. (1982). Some psychotherapeutic implications of logical phenomenology. *Psychotherapy: Theory, Research and Practice, 19,* 259–265.

Sartre, J. (1953). *Being and nothingness.* New York: Washington Square Press.

Schotte, D. E., & Clum, G. A. (1987). Problem-solving skills in suicidal psychiatric patients. *Journal of Consulting and Clinical Psychology, 55,* 49–54.

Seligman, M. E. P. (1975). *Helplessness.* San Francisco: Freeman.

Snyder, C. R. (1994). *The psychology of hope.* New York: Free Press.

Stotland, E. (1969). *The psychology of hope.* San Francisco: Jossey-Bass.

Strean, H. S. (1993). *Resolving counterresistances in psychotherapy.* New York: Brunner/Mazel.

Van Dusen, W. (1962). The theory and practice of existential analysis. In H. M. Ruitenbeek (Ed.), *Psychoanalysis and existential philosophy* (pp. 24–40). New York: Dutton.

Van Wagoner, S. L., Gelso, C. L., Hayes, J. A., & Diemer, R. A. (1991). Countertransference and the reputedly excellent therapist. *Psychotherapy, 28,* 411–421.

Walrond-Skinner, S. (1986). *Dictionary of psychotherapy.* New York: Routledge & Kegan-Paul.

Wampold, B. E. (2001). *The great psychotherapy debate: Models, methods, and findings.* Mahwah, NJ: Erlbaum.

Watson, D. L., & Tharp, R. G. (1989). *Self-directed behavior: Self-modification for personal adjustment.* Pacific Grove, CA: Brooks/Cole.

Weisman, A. D. (1979). *Coping with cancer.* New York: McGraw-Hill.

Weiss, P. (1958). Common sense and beyond. In S. Hook (Ed.), *Determinism and freedom: In the age of modern science* (pp. 231–236). New York: Collier Books.

Whitlock, G. E. (1978). *Understanding and coping with real-life crises.* Monterey, CA: Brooks/Cole.

Yalom, I. D. (1980) *Existential psychotherapy.* New York: Basic Books.

2

Examining the Issues
Counselors Must
Address

The chapters in this section of the book extend the content of the three foundational chapters in Part One. Chapter 4, Risk and Protective Factors, written by Melinda Haley, a doctoral candidate at New Mexico State University, points out the risk and protective factors that counselors need to look for in the lives of suicidal clients. In her thorough and expertly written and researched discussion of these factors, she considers a number of predisposing and potentiating risk factors. Because, quite often, it is not possible to eliminate or reduce many of the risk factors that may be part of the life of a particular client, the discussion of risk factors is followed by an overview of what the research tells members of the profession about protective factors. (Although a client may have several risk factors, having just three protective factors can often reduce the risk of a suicide attempt by 70%–80%). Increasing the protective factors in the life of a client has been effective in cases in which the risk factors cannot be eliminated or are ill defined. Counselors will find the content of this chapter essential to their desire to follow the best and most competent of practices with their clients.

Jonathan Carrier's chapter, Assessing Suicidal Risk (chap. 5), is essential to the assessment, management, and treatment of a suicidal client. He presents a tripartite paradigm for assessment: the clinical interview, empirical evaluation, and clinical consultation. Readers will find the practical guidelines inherent in each of the three parts of the paradigm, as well as the case study material, extremely helpful and applicable to working with clients. As is the case in conjunction with each chapter, adaptations for diversity are also included in the discussion of assessment.

Because assisted suicide is an issue that challenges the core values and assumptions that counselors bring to their work with clients, readers will find chapter 6, Assisted Suicide: Ethical Issues, written by Barbara

Richter Herlihy and Zarus E. P. Watson of the University of New Orleans, essential reading. The chapter includes the following: an overview of the various means by which a person can achieve hastened death, a brief history of how society's views on assisted suicide have fluctuated from the beginning of the 20th century into the new millennium, the role of mental health professionals in the assisted suicide decision making, and positions taken by professional associations. The chapter continues with discussion of ethical issues, adaptations for counseling culturally diverse clients, and guidelines for practice with clients who are considering requesting a hastened death through assisted suicide.

This section of the book concludes with Ted Remley's, also of the University of New Orleans, chapter Suicide and the Law (chap. 7). Remley does an excellent job of providing counselors with guidelines for avoiding malpractice claims related to clients who have attempted or completed suicide. In addition, the discussion of approaches to managing clients who may be at risk for suicide provides information pertinent to the role responsibilities of counselors in all settings. The chapter concludes with a brief overview of diversity issues.

Chapter 4

Risk and Protective Factors

Melinda Haley

Currently, according to statistics, about 55,000 people in the United States intentionally kill themselves each year, a rate that has remained stable over the recent decade (Yaniv, 2001). Researches have been working diligently to identify factors that can indicate who is at risk for suicide to aid counselors and other mental health professionals in working with those people. Historically, the best indicator of whether an individual was in active crisis and was at immediate risk for suicide has been *ideation, plan, intent,* and *means.* If a client expressed suicidal ideation, had made a plan, had the intent to carry out the plan, and had the means (e.g., the gun or poison), then that client was considered in extreme risk for making a suicide attempt and the counselor needed to make an immediate intervention.

Another indicator that has been helpful in determining risk is the number and lethality of previous attempts; a higher number and degree of lethality exponentially increases the risk for suicide (Borowsky, Ireland, & Resnick, 2001; Gust-Brey & Cross, 1999). In fact, having made a past suicide attempt is touted as the strongest predictor of both future suicide attempts and completions (Lewinsohn, Rohde, Seeley, & Baldwin, 2001). However, this may be more salient for females. Suicidal behavior (past attempts and ideation) during childhood is highly predictive for females making another attempt in young adulthood, but it is not as predictive for males (Lewinsohn et al., 2001).

It should be noted that not all risk and protective factors are universal. Many different variables come into play when discussing suicidal risk and protective factors, such as age, developmental level, socioeconomic factors, ethnicity, gender, sexual orientation, and so forth; these variables affect which risk and protective factors are salient for each group. Following is a discussion regarding general risk and protective factors that can affect an individual regardless of the aforementioned variables, although each are pertinent to varying degrees. In the section Adaptations for Diversity, the reader will find a more in-depth discussion relating to risk and protective factors for specific groups such as adolescents, senior citizens, different minority groups, and gays, lesbians, bisexuals, and transgendered individuals.

Risk Factors

The method outlined earlier—ideation, plan, intent, and means—is currently the best practice when working with a client who is actively in crisis. Nevertheless, what if the client is not in crisis while he or she is in the counselor's office? How can counselors assess a client's risk for potential suicide if the client is not currently experiencing or admitting to suicidal ideation? The single best method for ascertaining who is at risk has not been fully determined yet (Gray et al., 2002). Research is still needed to make that determination conclusively.

However, researchers have been focusing on everything that could be predictive to help aid counselors in making an assessment. These studies have looked at everything from as broad a range as predisposing genetic factors to specific, isolated factors such as tone of voice (Sample, 2000). Even though counselors still cannot accurately or conclusively predict who will attempt suicide, research over the last 10 years has enabled counselors to identify specific factors that can assess risk. More specifically, it is now possible to foresee certain normative events of crises that may make suicide a more likely choice for any individual. Generally, the more risk factors a client has, the greater the risk that individual will make an attempt (Jacobs, 2000).

Risk factors for suicide fall into two basic categories: predisposing (distal/chronic/trait) factors and potentiating (proximal/acute/state) factors (Fernquist, 2000; Jacobs, 2000; Maris, 2002). The predisposing risk factors include the major psychiatric disorders, especially affective disorders such as major depression or bipolar disorder, but also disorders such as schizophrenia, panic, anxiety, and personality disorders, substance abuse, and genetic influences (Fernquist, 2000; Jacobs, 2000).

Potentiating risk factors include situational stressors. When these situational stressors interact with a predisposing risk factor such as a mental illness, they increase the risk potential for that individual. Potentiating (proximal) risk factors may include such things as physical illness, a dysfunctional unsupportive family environment, physical illness, access to a firearm, or being under the influence of a substance (Jacobs, 2000).

Predisposing Factors

Psychiatric Disorders. Many studies indicate there is a high percentage of suicide completers who have a history of a psychiatric disorder (Bailey et al.,

1997; Fernquist, 2000; Gust-Brey & Cross, 1999; Hiroeh, Appleby, Mortensen, & Dunn, 2001). Psychological autopsies conducted after completed suicides indicate that 90% of adults and adolescents have one or more diagnosed mental illnesses (Glowinski et al., 2001; Harris & Barraclough, 1994; Maris, 2002). There is controversy regarding which mental disorders have the highest suicide rates, but the affective disorders, such as major depression and bipolar disorder, have the greatest validation. Studies indicate that affective disorders carry a 10%–15% lifetime risk of suicide (Maris, 2002).

When an affective disorder is combined with a personality disorder and/ or substance abuse, it is especially lethal (Foster, 2001; Gray et al., 2002; Gust-Brey & Cross, 1999). Personality disorders, specifically impulsive-dramatic and avoidant-dependent types, were found to be associated with a higher degree of suicide (Brent, Johnson, et al., 1994). In the United States and abroad, psychological autopsies show that as high as 56% of suicide completers had a history of a substance abuse disorder, and lifetime risk of suicide for alcohol dependence is 7% (Foster, 2001). In addition, 70% to 80% of people who commit suicide had at least one mental disorder that was comorbid with substance abuse (Maris, 2002). Other disorders that carry a high risk for suicide attempt include chronic insomnia; schizophrenia, especially in the postpsychotic stages; borderline personality; and antisocial personality disorders (Maris, 2002).

Depression/Hopelessness. As noted earlier, affective disorders carry a high risk for suicide attempt (Maris, 2002). The risk of suicide among people with depression of all ages is 30 times higher than for those in the general population (Brown & Blanton, 2002). There are many theoretical explanations for why depression occurs, but regardless of its theoretical cause, depression often carries with it feelings of hopelessness, helplessness, or worthlessness and an inability to cope with life's problems. When depressed, clients experience lowered mood and perhaps a view that life is meaningless, that he or she is worthless as a person, and that his or her future is minimal or nonexistent. These feelings are closely related to making a suicide attempt (Malone et al., 2000; Pinto & Whisman, 1996).

Everyone feels the blues at times, but depression is more oppressing than the blues and has greater consequences. Studies show that major depressive disorder significantly increases the risk of suicidal ideation, suicide attempt, and suicide completion. Glowinski et al. (2001) stated that at least 50% of adults and 22% of adolescents who reported a suicide attempt met the criteria for major depressive disorder. In adolescents, major depressive disorder was found to be the mental disorder that carried the highest rate of persistent suicidal ideation (Glowinski et al., 2001; Wichstrom, 2000).

Malone et al. (2000) postulated that when a person becomes depressed, the associated feelings of hopelessness color that person's perspective and he or she becomes more susceptible to life's stressors. Gust-Brey and Cross (1999) believed when a person lacks critical problem-solving skills and has

97

experienced repeated failures, it leads to depression and hopelessness and compounds stress. Often, these individuals see suicide as their only viable option.

The hopelessness associated with depression can be debilitating in itself, and many find it a significant risk factor outside of depression. A study conducted by Beck, Steer, Kovacs, and Garrison (1985) seemed to confirm the role hopelessness plays in suicide. They measured a group of inpatients with the Beck Hopelessness Scale and later examined the suicide rate among those individuals. Of the 14 patients who later committed suicide, 13 had scored 10 or greater on the Hopelessness Scale.

Malone et al. (2000) also conducted a study using major depressive inpatients and found of those who had already attempted suicide, their scores on a hopelessness scale, subjective depression scale, and suicidal ideation were significantly higher than for those who had not made an attempt. Maris (2002) went so far as to assert that *state hopelessness* is more prognostic of suicide than even depression because *suicidal hopelessness* is indicative of cognitive rigidity and this can cause an individual to believe there are no nonsuicidal alternatives.

Substance Abuse. The comorbidity of suicide and substance abuse (alcohol and other drugs) is well established (Borowsky, Resnick, Ireland, & Blum, 1999; Crumley, 1990; Morgan, 1993; Wichstrom, 2000). Up to 50% of people who commit suicide are intoxicated at the time they take their life, and 18% of people with alcohol use disorders end up committing suicide (Crumley, 1990). However, this seems more prevalent for males than for females as almost 90% of these cases are men (Maris, 2002). As mentioned before, this risk is amplified when substance abuse has comorbidity with another mental disorder (Foster, 2001). Furthermore, it has been reported in the studies by Foster (2001) and Maris (2002) that alcohol abuse was the strongest single predictor of completed suicide in people who initially made nonfatal suicide attempts, and Glowinski et al. (2001) stated that lifetime abstinence from alcohol is significantly correlated to never having made a suicide attempt.

The role of substance abuse is associated with suicidal risk even if the individual is not personally abusing. Bailey et al. (1997) found risk of suicide increased if any other member of the household was abusing substances. Glowinski et al. (2001) found that, for adolescents, parental alcoholism increased the risk for suicide attempt in their children. Their findings showed that for 46.1% of the participants who had reported a suicide attempt, at least one parent was alcohol dependent. Substance abuse as a risk factor also seems to defy cultural differences. Studies show the risk is equally prevalent among all ethnicities (Borowsky et al., 2001; Crumley, 1990).

While it cannot be said that substance abuse causes suicide, it does appear that there is a correlational relationship (Crumley, 1990; "Report: Three Million Youths," 2002). A study conducted by Borowsky et al. (1999)

indicated that alcohol, marijuana, and other drug use remained a significant factor in suicide attempt even when they controlled for other factors such as emotional well-being. Forman and Kalafat (1998) believed the correlation between substance abuse and suicide risk is because the environmental factors that play a role in increasing the probability of substance abuse are the same environmental factors that increase the probability for suicide. In addition, substance abuse may increase the effects of depression, anxiety, isolation, and loneliness and may affect the thought processes in ways that increase the risk for suicide (Loos, 2002).

Those who abuse alcohol may be trying to self-medicate their distress, and this may work in the short term. However, long-term alcohol use further depresses the system, as ethanol is a depressant. Long-term use of alcohol is also correlated with reduced impulse control, which may be the catalyst the suicidal person needs to attempt or complete the act (Maris, 2002). It has been found that alcohol has an effect on serotonin neurosis in the brain stem and may reduce the amount of serotonin in the prefrontal cortex. This is thought to decrease protection against suicidal impulses ("A Serotonin Marker," 1996).

Concerning psychoactive substance abuse, there appears to be a correlation between greater frequency of use and repetitive suicide attempts, as well as more lethal attempts with greater use (Crumley, 1990). In addition, when comparing the known statistics regarding the use of these substances over the last 20 years, a noticeable comparison is seen in a similar rise in suicide rates, especially among adolescents (Crumley, 1990). This does not, however, connote causality but only that there is similarity.

Other substances such as tobacco, which may seem to be more benign than either alcohol or psychoactive substances, are still externally linked to suicidal risk. This link may simply be because smoking causes illness and illness increases risk for suicide, or it may be that people who smoke engage in other risky behavior (Bower, 1993; Hemenway, Solnick, & Colditz, 1993). Smith, Phillips, and Neaton (1992) attributed the connection to other factors that predispose individuals to be attracted to smoking as well as factors that increase the risk of suicide. They did not consider smoking itself to be a causal factor of suicide.

However, Hemenway et al. (1993) stated that there is a strong link between tobacco use and depression. They cited an interesting study whereby 103,602 women were followed for 12 years concerning their smoking habits and suicide rates. One hundred and thirty six of these women ended up committing suicide. Statistics showed that women who smoked between 1 and 24 cigarettes per day had twice the suicide rate than those women who had never smoked, and women who smoked over 25 cigarettes per day were four times more likely to commit suicide.

Although no studies have shown conclusively that substance use is a direct cause of suicide, many studies have shown that increased uses of substances, even tobacco, is correlated with high risk of suicide. More studies are needed to ascertain why this may be the case.

Genetics. Closing the discussion on predisposing risk factors for suicide, there appears to be some genetic links to risk of suicide ("The Suicide Gene," 2000). Maris (2002) stipulated that suicide "tends to run in families" and that approximately 11% of suicide attempters have had at least one other family member who had attempted or completed suicide. When looking at twins, Maris found that monozygotic twins showed greater concordance than did dizygotic twins in attempted as well as completed suicides.

Another analysis conducted for suicidality in Australian adult male and female twins ($N = 5,995$) found that genetic factors accounted for 45% of the variance in lifetime suicide rates. Breaking the data down further, other studies found a familial liability for suicide between shared genetics and environmental features that accounted for 33%–73% of the variance in risk (Glowinski et al., 2001).

When looking at individuals who were adopted, a case for environment can be made. In one study, 4%–5% of adoptive parents of children who committed suicide also ended up taking their own lives, whereas only 0.07% of the control group who were parents of nonsuicides did so (Maris, 2002). Although these studies are not conclusive, environmental factors in conjunction with genetic factors seem to increase the risk of suicide attempts and completions.

Potentiating Factors

Suicide of Family Member. As noted in the above discussion, risk for suicide increases when there has been another suicide in the family (Borowsky et al., 2001; "Suicide Risk Factors," 1985; Wichstrom, 2000). Relatives and friends of a person who commits suicide are considered a vulnerable population at high risk for suffering disturbances in physical and mental functioning and can experience significant changes in emotional, physical, cognitive, and psychosocial functioning (Van Dongen, 1991).

Borowsky et al. (1999) stated that the most powerful risk factor for a suicide attempt is having a close friend or family member who either attempted or completed a suicide. This seems especially true for both male and female adolescents. One hypothesis for this includes the role of imitative behavior especially among adolescents (Mercy, Kresnow, & O'Carroll, 2001; Metha, Chen, Mulvenon, & Dode, 1998). This imitation may also account for the outcropping of "cluster suicides" found periodically in the schools and Native American reservations.

Another rationale for why having a friend or family member commit suicide is such a potent risk factor may be the resulting bereavement, associated depression, and perhaps self-blame that accompany these types of deaths. Brent, Moritz, Bridge, Perper, and Canobbio (1996) reported adolescents who had a sibling commit suicide were seven times more at risk for developing major depression and making a suicide attempt. Research also shows high proportions of suicide attempters and completers have a family history of suicidal behavior (Metha et al., 1998).

Major Injury or Illness. There is an increase in suicidal risk in people dealing with a serious injury or illness, but the increase in risk differs among types of afflictions (Harris & Barraclough, 1994; McHugh, 1994). For example, people with HIV/AIDS have an elevated risk of suicide by as much as 7 to 36 times higher than the general public, especially for males (Dannenberg, McNeil, Brundage, & Brookmeyer, 1996; Kirchner, 1996; "Men With AIDS," 1993; Valente & Sunders, 1997). In addition, the suicide rate for general hospital patients is almost 3 times higher than the general population (Dhossche, Ulusarac, & Syed, 2001).

However, the illnesses that carry the most risk are those associated with mental disorders or substance abuse (McHugh, 1994). This is not surprising given the previous discussion regarding the role of mental disorders and substance abuse in suicide. The presence of comorbidity between any medical disorder and substance abuse increased suicide rates regardless of the diagnostic group (Teasdale & Enberg, 2001).

Studies that examine specific risk for particular diseases or illnesses are scarce, but increased risk has been found for Huntington's disease, Parkinson's disease, multiple sclerosis, systemic lupus erythematosus, spinal cord injury, neoplasms (particularly head and neck cancers), peptic ulcers, traumatic head injury, and renal dialysis (Druss & Pincus, 2000; Feinstein, 1997; Lewis, 2001; McHugh, 1994; Teasdale & Engberg, 2001). For example, individuals suffering from a spinal cord injury have four times the risk for suicide than the general population, whereas in a study of individuals with Huntington's disease, 20% of the participants ended up attempting suicide (Harris & Barraclough, 1994). Teasdale and Engberg (2001) reported that for traumatic brain injury, suicide risk increased according to length of hospital stay. However, it was also found that individuals with simple concussions, who spent no more than 1 day in the hospital, also had an increase in suicide rates. More research is needed to ascertain why.

One reason that serious illness or injury might cause an increase in risk is because both are associated with depression (McHugh, 1994). A person with a major illness or injury can often experience devastating and enduring changes in all aspects of life, including employment, family, and social relationships. Profound emotional responses of anxiety, and in particular major depression, are not uncommon (Teasdale & Engberg, 2001). People who have serious, incapacitating, or oppressive medical conditions are susceptible to austere assumptions about both their future and their worth. These feelings of worthlessness, or loss in quality of life post illness or injury, may increase feelings of helplessness and depression and contribute to the increase in risk.

It is difficult to get too precise regarding specific risk given the multitude of medical possibilities. It would be advised that whenever doing an assessment for suicidal ideation, counselors should note if the individual has had a major medical problem or debilitating injury.

Social Isolation. There are two components to social isolation. On the one hand, individuals may become suicidal from being isolated from society. On the other hand, individuals who are already suicidal may seek isolation in the throes of their despair (Forman & Kalafat, 1998; Hazler & Denham, 2002). In the former, whether it is because of poor social networks, lack of support, or extreme social introversion, some individuals find themselves isolated or marginalized from society (Bailey et al., 1997; Hazler & Denham, 2002; Wichstrom, 2000).

Support networks are essential for human emotional and mental well-being. One study conducted in Chicago found 50% of the people who committed suicide did not have even one close friend. However, when someone had even one other person in his or her life, even if it was only the counselor, risk was decreased (Maris, 2002). Today, one fourth of all U.S. households consist of a single person, and many neighbors do not know each other (Wright, 1995). This may indicate that more and more people are going to be affected by isolation at times. It would be prudent for counselors to assess for social networks routinely and provide interventions that provide connection to others for clients who are feeling lonely and isolated.

Access to Firearms. Obviously, access to a firearm provides a quick and lethal method to end one's life if one is so inclined. While guns do not cause suicide or even the ideation behind wanting to take one's life, having a gun in the home increases the chances that when an individual is vulnerable and within easy access to a lethal means, suicide is more likely to occur (Christoffel, 2000; "Mortality Among Recent Purchasers," 2000; Sacks, Mercy, Ryan, & Parrish, 1994). A study of suicide conducted over 3 years found that 66.4% of the 60,786 suicides were conducted within the home and 43.2% of these homes had handguns (Sacks et al., 1994).

The risk of having easy access to firearms cuts across gender and ethnic lines. Many studies show that regardless of the age, gender, or ethnicity, firearms were used in 57% of all suicide deaths (Bailey et al., 1997; Kellermann et al., 1992; Maris, 2002). Contrary to expectation and stereotype, some studies show that female gun owners were 49 times more likely to commit suicide than females who did not own guns, and women were also five times more likely to attempt suicide if there was a gun in the home in which they were living (Bailey et al., 1997; "Mortality Among Recent Purchasers," 2000). For adults also, there is a strong association between substance abuse and firearm use in suicide, and firearms were used in 62% of the suicides completed by adult males (Forman & Kalafat, 1998).

The same is true for adolescents. Adolescents with guns in the home have between 4 to 10 times the suicide rate than do adolescents without guns in the home (Kellermann et al., 1992; Maris, 2002; Sacks et al., 1994); this is especially true for Hispanic and Black males (Rollins, 2001). Forman and Kalafat (1998) found that among adolescents ages 15–19, guns accounted for 81% of the increase in the overall suicide rate between 1980 and 1992, and weapon-carrying at school was predictive of suicide attempt for all adolescent boys (Borowsky et al., 2001; Rollins, 2001).

Studies have also shown the increased risk for suicide attempt and the risks associated with the purchase of a handgun persist for more than 5 years after the purchase (Cummings & Koepsell, 1998; Cummings, Koepsell, Grossman, Savarino, & Thompson, 1997). One study that followed a cohort of individuals for 6 years who had recently purchased handguns found that suicide was the leading cause of death during the initial 12 months following those purchases ("Mortality Among Recent Purchasers," 2000). Therefore, assessing for firearm ownership or access and removing firearms from an individual's home who is at risk for suicide is a good first step toward prevention.

Low Self-Esteem. Low self-esteem is often found among suicide attempters. While low self-esteem is correlated with depression and substance abuse, both of which are major risk factors for suicide, self-esteem does play an individual role in suicide risk (Wichstrom, 2000; Winters, Myers, & Proud, 2002). In studies with adolescents, findings showed that students who had more suicidal ideation were more likely to have lower self-esteem (Groholt, Ekeberg, & Wichstrom, 2000; Roberts, Roberts, & Chen, 1998). In addition, low self-esteem is associated with youth involvement in alcohol, tobacco, and other drug use; depression; violence; early sexual activity; teenage pregnancy; and poor peer relationships, all of which can contribute to suicidal ideation (King, Vidourek, & Davis, 2002).

In one study by Overholser, Adams, Lehnert, and Brinkman (1995), the direct relationship between self-esteem and suicidal tendencies in adolescents was examined by assessing suicidal ideation and history of suicide attempts in relationship to self-esteem. They also looked at an indirect relationship between self-esteem and suicidality by assessing depression and hopelessness. The findings were that low self-esteem was related to higher levels of depression, hopelessness, suicidal ideation, and an increased likelihood of having previously attempted suicide.

Even though many studies show that low self-esteem is a correlate of other disorders such as major depression and substance abuse, studies on adolescents identify low self-esteem as a risk factor by itself. Counselors should assess for level of self-esteem as a possible risk factor for suicide especially within the adolescent population.

History of Abuse. History of abuse is another risk factor that cuts across all ethnic groups (Borowsky et al., 2001; Vermeiren, Ruchkin, Leckman, Deboutte, & Schwab-Stone, 2002). For adolescents and children, the abuse may be vicariously induced. The child does not have to be the intended victim; the victim can be another family member. In a study conducted between 1979 and 1983, 61 suicidal children between the ages of 5 and 13 in a psychiatry unit were evaluated for analogous risk factors and histories in comparison with a control group who were not suicidal ("Suicide Risk Factors," 1985). Even though these children had not been victims of abuse directly, the suicidal children were more likely than the control group children to have a mother who was being abused by the father.

Silverman, Raj, Mucci, and Hathaway (2001) found that teenage girls who have been abused by their boyfriends were also at risk for suicidal ideation and suicide attempt by as much as six to nine times more than the general population. These girls were also found to be at greater risk for eating disorders, substance abuse, and engaging in unhealthy sexual behaviors, all of which can contribute to suicidal ideation. These risks were compounded for the adolescents who had experienced both physical and sexual abuse. Silverman et al. (2001) also found through extensive surveys that as high as 20% of teenage girls had been abused by a boyfriend. Therefore, dating history becomes important when doing an assessment.

Garcia, Adams, Friedman, and East (2002) concurred with the above study. They also found when children were directly subjected to physical and sexual abuse, it caused a long-term effect on their emotional, behavioral, and physical development. Some of the emotional/behavioral effects noted include "fear, depression, suicide ideation, suicide attempts, anger, truancy, running away, aggressive behavior, low self-esteem, increased substance abuse, eating disorders, criminal behavior, and risky sexual behavior" (p. 9).

In another study with 2,918 participants who were part of an epidemiological study of mental health, 29% stated that they had been sexually assaulted at some point in their lives. Individuals who reported a history of sexual assault were significantly more likely to have made a suicide attempt (14.9%) than those who did not (1.4%). When other risk factors or variables known to be related to suicide attempts were controlled for, those who had experienced a sexual assault were still six times more likely to have made a serious suicide attempt than those who were not ("Risk of Suicide," 1996). Therefore, history of abuse is pertinent even if an individual was not abused directly, and if abused directly, the abuse did not have to occur at the hands of a family member nor did the individual have to be a child at the time abuse occurred. Counselors need to assess abuse in clients not only to ascertain risk for suicide but also to help with emotional, behavioral, and developmental issues that come with the abuse. Even if the client is an adult and the abuse occurred during childhood, the ramifications can create risk when compounded by daily life events, especially if the client has never dealt with the trauma of the abuse. It is essential that counselors assess for this risk factor.

Inability to Cope With Stress. Stress is an important mitigating factor in the life of a suicidal client. Often, when a person is barely coping, the addition of stress to other concurrent risk factors is enough to push that person over the edge (Fernquist, 2000). Kaslow et al. (2002) suggested that every individual has a "pain threshold" beyond which he or she cannot cope. When the suicidal person's threshold is surmounted, that individual begins to see suicide as a viable option to end the pain he or she is experiencing.

Gust-Brey and Cross (1999) examined family factors associated with high suicide risk, and among those identified, stress was an important component. They acknowledged that exposure to family stress at an early age can cause many rebound effects that increase the propensity for suicide risk. They identified such stressors as the loss of social support through the death of a parent, parental separation or divorce, change in school or neighborhood, and having difficulty with peer relationships. If an individual does not learn a way to deal with stress, he or she can be at increased risk for suicide when his or her pain threshold is breached (Kaslow et al., 2002).

Stress comes in a lot of forms, and every individual's stress and stress levels can be different. However, stress is debilitating, and even high-functioning people who perhaps handle stress well can be overwhelmed when working in high-stress occupations. Individuals working in such occupations have a higher risk for suicide than those working in nonstress occupations. One study conducted with individuals in the medical profession found that doctors had twice the expected suicide rate as the general public ("Suicide in Doctors," 2002). In a similar study conducted in England and Wales, annual suicide rates in both male and female doctors were 19.2 and 18.8 per 100,000 (Hawton, 2001). Stress within the profession was attributed to these higher rates (Feskanich et al., 2002; Sonneck & Wagner, 1996).

It appears that while stress alone may not be a potent risk factor for suicide, risk factors tend to interact and exponentially compound each other. When an individual has more than one suicidal risk factor, the addition of stress may be too much for that individual to handle and may be the catalyst that pushes him or her over the edge (Kaslow et al., 2002).

Family Relational Problem. As indicated previously, family environment is influential in the lives of each family member. The following factors are found to be particularly relevant in increasing suicide risk: profound economic problems, dependent personalities, genetically linked depressive or affective disorders, substance abuse, imitative behavior patterns or other family psychopathology, problems with social or personal interaction, styles of child rearing (authoritarian vs. authoritative), and family disorganization or an absent parent (e.g., single-parent household with working parent; see Glowinski et al., 2001; Gust-Brey & Cross, 1999; Wichstrom, 2000).

Family integration, as measured by family social support and amount and extent of parental monitoring, shows an inverse relationship to suicide: The less social support and parental monitoring, the higher the rates of suicide in adolescents. However, too much integration has also been found to increase risk (Fernquist, 2000). Further, in a meta-analysis of 85 different studies spanning 20 years, significance was found regarding the level of attachment between parents and teen suicide rates. Parental partners who were more diffuse and individuated and who did not spend much quality time interacting together increased the risk of suicidality for adolescents (Fernquist, 2000).

If a family is diffuse and does not spend much quality time together, then individual family members are lacking an important source of support. It may be important for counselors to assess the degree or amount of family cohesion when determining risk for clients. This may be especially relevant for adolescents or children but also applies for adults.

Minority Status. Risk factors applicable to specific minority groups are covered in more detail under the section Adaptations for Diversity. However, minority status seems to be "the one exceptional demographic discriminator that is independent of age and sex contributions to the risk of suicide attempt" (p. 6) at least for children (Peterson, Zhang, Lucia, King, & Lewis, 1996). When studying discriminating factors that differentiated between suicide ideators and suicide attempters with children in an emergency medical center, Peterson et al. found that minority status played a significant role.

The underlying assumption behind why minority status elevates one's risk for suicide is that people of minority status inherently encounter more stressors such as lower socioeconomic status and racism than the majority culture and may internalize negative messages as children. This can place them at higher risk when other risk factors are considered (Peterson et al., 1996). As minority status seems to contribute an additive, independent risk for a suicide attempt, counselor interventions and prevention efforts should be intensified for minority children who are having suicidal thoughts. However, it should also be noted that Peterson's et al.'s study assessed children in emergency room situations.

Epidemiological studies indicate this increased risk does not necessarily lead to increased suicide completions in adults. In a study on suicide rates for the years 1990–1999, the rate for overall minority suicide completions was 7 per 100,000. In contrast, White rates were 13.2 per 100,000. Other studies report that White people commit 90% of suicides in the United States, with 72% of those committed by White men (Bloch, 1999; Kaslow et al., 2002). Given the controversial nature of these studies, more research is needed to ascertain exactly what role minority status plays in the risk for suicide. Currently, it seems that for children the risk is increased but that may not hold true for adults.

Sexual Orientation. Many studies have shown that gay, lesbian, bisexual, and transgendered teens and young adults are at higher risk for both suicidal ideation and attempts than heterosexual youth. Same-sex attraction was predictive of suicidal attempt in all boys, and lesbian/bisexual women report more suicidal ideation than their heterosexual counterparts (Faulkner & Cranston, 2000; Fergusson, 2000; Lock & Steiner, 1999).

One study conducted in New Zealand with 1,000 individuals who identified as gay, lesbian, and bisexual indicated this population was 6.2 times more likely to have a suicide attempt in their history ("Gays, Bisexuals," 1999). More specific information regarding risk and protective factors for those who identify as gay, lesbian, bisexual, or transgendered can be found in the section Adaptations for Diversity.

Gender. Studies have identified gender-specific risks for suicidal ideation that are evident as early as preschool. These studies described children whose behaviors ran counter to typical gender norms, such as an aggressive female or a dependent or effeminate male. These children were found to be more at risk in adulthood in comparison with those children whose behaviors fell within the continuum of accepted gender-typed behavior (Iribarren, Reed, Wergowske, Burchfiel, & Dwyer, 1995; Reinherz et al., 1995).

In addition, there are gender differences between suicidal ideation and suicide completions. Many studies and various statistics show that females are three to nine times more likely to make an attempt than are males, and just being female is seen as an additive risk factor for suicide attempt (Borowsky et al., 1999; Lacourse, Clases, & Villeneuve, 2001; Peterson et al., 1996; "Women Less Likely," 2001). However, females also have higher rates of major depressive disorder, which may also account for this discrepancy (Peterson et al., 1996).

It may also be that risk factors are not specifically different for males and females but are weighted differently (Glowinski et al., 2001). For example, greater developmental complexity has been postulated to transmit attribution of sources of unhappiness from an external to an internal locus, resulting in increased self-destructive tendencies more so for females than for males, and women are socialized differently regarding culturally acceptable forms of self-destructive behavior (Lewinsohn et al., 2001; Peterson et al., 1996).

The discrepancy between males and females seems especially pronounced at the adolescent level (Glowinski et al., 2001; Wichstrom, 2000). Many authors attribute this to the effects of puberty and the increased stress and self-consciousness that come with it. Pubertal timing affects both males and females, and being on either end of the spectrum (late or early) can bring psychological difficulty (Wichstrom, 2000). Specifically, late-maturing girls and early-maturing boys have more difficulty than do their peers who develop in the mid-range. However, pubertal timing seems to affect girls more strongly than it does boys, and early pubertal timing has been identified as a risk factor for both internalizing and externalizing behavior among girls (Wichstrom, 2000). Many adolescents who are either early or late bloomers receive increased peer attention, which may be perceived as negative. This can lead to poor self-esteem or an increase in bullying or peer rejection (Wichstrom, 2000).

In relationship to this discussion, suicide rates in women tend to peak at menopause, whereas male suicide rates peak only in very old age. Some might

107

speculate that loss of sexual reproductivity causes similar stressors and emotions between both genders as does puberty. Women lose sexual reproductivity many years earlier than men, and the suicide rates seem to correspond with this trend. As men become less biologically fit and less able to reproduce, their suicide rate increases correspondingly (Kaslow et al., 2002).

Although females attempt suicide more frequently, statistically males complete it five times more often (Bailey et al., 1997; Borowsky et al., 2001; Brent, Baugher, Bridge, Chen, & Chiappetta, 1999). Reasons attributed to this discrepancy are that males choose methods more lethal when they attempt, such as firearms or hanging. Therefore, when an attempt is made usually a completion is achieved, whereas females choose less lethal methods such as chemical poisoning (e.g., sleeping pills or tranquilizers) and are not successful completers (Bailey et al., 1997; Iribarren et al., 1995; Kaslow et al., 2002). However, this statistic may be changing as the number of women committing suicide with a gun is increasing ("Mortality Among Recent Purchasers," 2000).

George E. Murphy, emeritus professor of psychiatry at Washington University School of Medicine in St. Louis (Missouri), noted another difference. He believes that even though women attempt suicide twice as often as men, their attempts are usually ploys to call attention to their emotional anguish and not expressly a solemn attempt to take their lives ("Women Less Likely," 2001). Another difference noted by Metha et al. (1998) in their model of adolescent suicide risk is that males progress from depression to substance abuse and then on to suicidality, whereas females go straight from depression to suicide attempt.

Biological. Biological factors can also play a role in suicide risk. Serotonin, one of the neurotransmitters in the brain, has long been associated with depression. New studies are pointing to evidence that a low level of serotonin is also a risk for suicide ("A Serotonin Marker," 1996). Maris (2002) even boldly proclaimed that "the most common biological marker of suicide is reduced concentrations of the serotonin metabolite 5-hydroxyindoleacetic acid" (p. 319).

Maris (2002) cited studies that indicate people who commit suicide, especially violent and nonpremeditated types of suicide, tend to have these lower concentrations of the serotonin metabolite 5-hydroxyindoleacetic acid. In one powerful study conducted at the University of Illinois, 23 living suicidal clients, 15 depressed clients, and 40 normal clients who had neither been depressed nor suicidal were examined for 5HT2-A receptors in their blood. Clients who had recently made a suicide attempt, or had merely even thought about suicide, had an unusually high density of these receptors. This abnormality did not exist in normal controls, nonsuicidal depressed clients, or even in the depressed clients who had been suicidal in the past ("A Serotonin Marker," 1996).

Studies have linked suicidal behavior with a deficit in the transmission of serotonin, and metabolite reduction is correlated with the lethality of the

suicide attempt. People who commit suicide have fewer serotonin transporter sites, smaller serotonin neurons, and less functional neurons than
those people who have not committed suicide. Suicidal individuals also
seem to have higher levels of norepinephrine and tyrosine hydroxylase and
reduced numbers of postsynaptic b-receptors, locus coeruleus neurons,
and norepinephrine transporters (Maris, 2002). In addition, it appears that
there may be an alcohol effect on serotonin neurons in the brain stem and
reduction of serotonin transporter function in the prefrontal cortex, both
of which are thought to play a role in the decreased protection against
suicidal impulsivity (Foster, 2001).

In relationship to the above discussion, it has also been found that levels
of homovanillic acid and MHPG (3-methoxy-4-hydroyphenylglycol) are much
higher in people who commit a violent suicide than those who commit
nonviolent suicide. Results of some studies also suggest that the stress system associated with the hypothalamic-pituitary-adrenal cortex axis is overac-
tive in individuals at risk of suicide (Maris, 2002).

Increasingly, researchers are also finding a link between cholesterol
levels and suicidality in men (Ellison & Morrison, 2001; Iribarren et al.,
1995; "Is Cholesterol," 1996; Law, 1996; Zureik, Courbon, & Ducimetiere,
1996). This appears to be especially relevant if the men are also suffering
from a psychiatric disorder ("Low Cholesterol Linked," 1995). Many researchers hypothesize low cholesterol creates a suicide risk by slowing the
transmission of serotonin, which decreases impulse control (Iribarren et
al., 1995). Many of these studies are contradictory, but in Europe, a morato-
rium on drugs that lower cholesterol has been established based on findings that low serum cholesterol levels in men increase risk of suicide. Some
studies have found that men with low cholesterol have three times more risk
for suicide than men with high cholesterol ("Low Serum Cholesterol," 1993;
Muldoon, Manuck, Mendelsohn, Kaplan, & Belle, 2001). This was found to
be true even when age, weight, race, income, alcohol use, and depression
were controlled ("Low Cholesterol Linked," 1995).

Conversely, some studies show it is not low cholesterol levels but rather
high levels that increase risk for men. In one longitudinal study of 7,309
middle-aged Japanese American men, a positive correlation was found between high serum cholesterol level and risk of suicide (Iribarren et al.,
1995). It is clear that more research is needed to ascertain what effect, if any,
cholesterol levels play in suicide risk for men.

Increase in Age. Epidemiological studies have found that increased age is a
predictor for both attempted suicide and completed suicide. This seems to
be the case for children, adolescents, and adults (Brent et al., 1999; Peterson
et al., 1996). In one study conducted with children and adolescents in emergency rooms, those presenting with a suicide attempt augmented significantly with increase in age. One distinguishing factor found between suicide
ideators and suicide attempters was that attempters were older and com-

pleted suicide at nearly 10 times the rate than did their younger counterparts (Peterson et al., 1996). In addition, many risk factors have been found, which when combined cause substantially greater risk in older adolescents than in younger adolescents or children (Brent et al., 1999). Both older age (within adolescence) and being male increased risk of suicide as much as five times than for younger male or female adolescents (Brent et al., 1999). It is not yet clearly understood why this might be the case.

Maris (2002) summarized data reported in deaths per 100,000 from suicide during 1990 to 1999 that show a direct increase in the number of suicides as age increases. According to the data, for the ages of 5–14, the rate of suicide is less than 1 in 100,000. The rate of completed suicides steadily climbs, with numbers reported in the teens for ages 15 through age 64. However, after age 65, rates increase significantly with 18.1% per 100,000 after age 65; 20.7 per 100,000 after age 75; and finally 21.6 per 100,000 after age 85 (Binder, 2002).

Some possible explanations for the sharp increase in completed suicides after age 65 are that living alone and being isolated can cause nutritional deficiencies and associated health problems ("Living Alone," 1992). Isolation can in turn induce despondency and perhaps suicidal thoughts. More is written about the older population in the section Adaptations for Diversity.

Sociological/Environmental Stressors. Stress can take its toll on both the body and the mind. Many studies show that suicide risk increases when individuals are subjected to chronic amounts of environmental and psychosocial stress (Borowsky et al., 2001; Forman & Kalafat, 1998; Glowinski et al., 2001; Maris, 2002). Poor economic conditions, low socioeconomic status, and poverty carry increased suicide risk for those individuals who suffer from these circumstances. In fact, the abject conditions that have occurred in the former Soviet Union since the 1990s have caused male suicide rates to climb substantially in Russia, Belarus, the Ukraine, and the Baltic countries. These countries are now considered to have the highest suicide rates in the world specifically because of these poor economic factors (Brainerd, 2001). Poverty, lack of opportunity, and not having enough of the essentials of life to make living pleasant can lead to depression and desperation, which in turn can lead to increased suicidal ideation and completion.

However, other studies show that stress can be situational, and in some cases, having wealth may represent a risk factor. A report by Agerbo et al. (2001) found wealthy people who are hospitalized for mental illness commit suicide more often than poor people under the same conditions. It is thought that the stigma for mental illness is greater among the rich and may account for the higher rates under these conditions.

Information-Processing Deficits. Many individuals, especially those who are depressed, make cognitive errors in their information processing. These individuals often minimize the positive and accentuate the negative (Goldston, Daniel, & Reboussin, 2001). This narrow view can lead to problem-solving deficits whereby eventually the individual believes he or she has no other way to solve the problem except by suicide (Forman & Kalafat, 1998). Individuals considering suicide may then incorporate information that confirms their negative expectations for the future, thereby setting up self-fulfilling prophecies that are predictive of later suicidal behavior (Goldston et al., 2001). People who use negative connotations about the world and life can be acknowledged as making cognitive errors in their thinking and should be considered at risk.

When evaluating a client, counselors should consider what risk factors may be present in his or her life regardless of whether the client is actively in crisis. These risk factors can identify which client may be at risk for a suicide attempt in the future or indicate the level of risk for a client in crisis. The general rule of thumb is the more risk factors an individual has, the greater his or her risk. However, risk factors have differing levels of potency, and in individuals with poor coping skills, it may take fewer factors to substantially increase risk. In addition, risk factors in combination can have an additive effect; therefore, several factors that might be considered small in risk, when presented together, can exponentially increase the risk for that individual. Therefore, all of these risk areas should be explored.

Protective Factors

While there is a plethora of research on risk factors for suicide, there is not so much on protective factors. One might assume of course with any of the risk factors discussed, not having that factor would be considered protective. This is true in many cases and may be why there is not as much research for this aspect of suicidality. One important fact that has come out of the research within the last 10 years is that it may be more effective to increase the protective factors in a suicidal client's life than it is to try to reduce the number of risk factors. Whereas a client may have several risk factors, having just three protective factors reduced the risk of a suicide attempt by 70%–80%. This was found to be true for both gender and racial/ethnic groups (Borowsky et al., 2001). Increasing protective factors has been effective even for cases in which one cannot eliminate the risk or the risk is ill defined (Forman & Kalafat, 1998). In a perusal of the literature, these protective factors were found to be essential and important.

Social Network/External Support

Protective factors such as having a strong social support can minimize conditions of suicidality. Having people to turn to, to discuss problems, and get feedback regarding the reality of a situation can be immensely helpful. Having others in one's life to share burdens or vent frustrations can lead to increased emotional health (Borowsky et al., 1999; Kaslow et al., 2002).

Some researchers theorize that social networking underlies why fewer women than men actually commit suicide even though women suffer from major depression at significantly higher rates than men ("Women Less Likely," 2001). Women are much more apt to talk about and process their problems with others. Women take their social network into consideration when contemplating suicide and ask themselves questions such as "How would my loved ones feel?" and "What might happen to them when I am gone?" whereas men are much less likely to process pain in this manner ("Women Less Likely," 2001).

Having a social network is also seen as protective for adolescents and youth; those adolescents who are connected to their families and have a good network of friends are less likely to make an attempt at suicide. This finding seems to transcend both gender and ethnicity (Borowsky et al., 2001; Forman & Kalafat, 1998; Kaslow et al., 2002; Thompson, Eggert, & Randell, 2001). In a study using 13,000 student participants ages 10 to 19 years, level of parental and family connectedness was seen as one of the most common factors that provided protection against suicide (Rollins, 2001).

The implication for counselors is that it is imperative to assess for a client's connectedness with others. Just as social isolation is a risk factor, social connectedness is a protective factor. One intervention in a suicidal client's life might be to encourage him or her to become more connected with others. Counselors should also understand that the therapeutic relationship becomes even more important as a means of social connectedness when a client is suicidal.

Reasons for Living

This protective factor seems obvious. If one has no sense of purpose or feels there is no future, one is much more likely to make a suicide attempt. Most research conducted on this subject has dealt with the population of adolescents and young adults (Larzelere, Smith, Batenhorst, & Kelly, 1996; Pinto, Whisman, & Conwell, 1998; Roehrig & Range, 1995; Scheel & Westefeld, 1999; Thompson et al., 2001). More research is needed to ascertain if this generalizes to other populations, but it seems reasonable that if a person has a strong reason for living, he or she would be less likely to attempt suicide. If a counselor can help a client explore the client's reasons for living, this intervention may increase this protective factor (Fernquist, 2000).

Reasons-for-living assessments have emerged as a powerful strength-based tool for assessing suicide risk. This approach also seems to merge well with other cultures as it allows clients to use their own worldview in their reasons for living (Crofoot-Graham, 2002). In a study of 84 clients with major depression, measures were given to two groups to ascertain the differences between those who attempted suicide ($n = 45$) and those who had not ($n = 39$). Participants were given scales on hopelessness, subjective depression, and suicidal ideation; as expected, those who had attempted suicide had significantly higher scores on these scales than those who did not. However, when participants were assessed on reasons for living, an inverse relationship was found between having reasons for living and suicide attempt. The depressed clients who scored highest on this scale scored lowest on the combined scores on the other three scales, and subsequently had not made a suicide attempt. It is important to note that neither the objective severity of depression nor quantity of recent life events differed between the two groups (Malone et al., 2000). Both groups perceived their depression similarly. The difference was one group had reasons for living and the other group did not. Therefore, it is important that reasons for living are assessed along with suicidal ideation when making an evaluation.

Self-Efficacy/Self-Esteem

Minimal studies have been done looking at self-efficacy as a protective factor. Those that have been done showed that having a sense of personal control over the events of one's life is seen as an important protective factor. Self-efficacy can be defined as a perceived ability in coping with problems and influencing positive outcomes (Forman & Kalafat, 1998; Thompson et al., 2001). So, rather than feeling hopeless, an individual has a sense of empowerment that things will work out. This individual has confidence he or she can resolve problems, can make things happen for himself or herself, can learn to adjust or cope with difficult situations, and that it will get better eventually. This fundamental attitude, in contrast with the hopelessness described by many depressed and suicidal individuals, minimizes that individual's risk that he or she may eventually attempt a suicide (Thompson et al., 2001).

Self-efficacy can also be related to high self-esteem, which can also serve as a protective factor. High self-esteem is protective in all age groups but especially so with adolescents and children. High self-esteem is associated with high academic achievement, involvement in sport and physical activity, and development of effective coping and peer pressure resistance skills, all of which can reduce risk (King et al., 2002).

Goldston et al. (1997) suggested that clients with low self-efficacy and low self-esteem probably will not believe that anything can change, will have low opinions of self, and will more likely be noncompliant with treatment. Therefore, it may be a good idea to assess a client's belief system regarding change. Does the client believe in his or her ability to make things happen and change his or her own circumstances? Does the client believe things can get better, or is he or she entrenched with the belief that nothing will ever change? This latter attitude can lead to the hopelessness so prevalent in the suicide and depression literature.

Emotional Well-Being

Emotional well-being is another protective factor that seems obvious; however, not much research has been done in this area either. For the research that has been conducted, strong associations have been found between emotional well-being and protection from suicide. This is particularly true for adolescent girls in the racial/ethnic groups studied (Borowsky et al., 1999; Rollins, 2001).

As suicide is highly correlated with loneliness, depression, and anger, not having these aversive emotions serves as a protective factor (Field, Miguel, & Sanders, 2001). Emotional well-being has typically been measured using depression scales. A study by Field, Miguel, and Sanders (2001) found that even moderate unhappiness was predictive of suicidal ideation at least within the adolescent population studied. Eighty-eight high school seniors were given a questionnaire that assessed relationship quality and intimacy with parents, siblings, and peers. The students were also assessed for overall emotional well-being (which included anger, happiness, and depression), drug use, and grade point average. These variables were compared with levels of suicidal ideation. Field et al. found that happiness (or emotional well-being) accounted for 46% of the variance between the students who had experienced suicidal ideation and those who had not. It is therefore important to assess level of emotional well-being even in clients who are not severely depressed.

Problem-Solving Skills

The ability to effectively solve life's problems may serve as a protective factor (Forman & Kalafat, 1998). This sense of being "able" may also tie in with issues of self-esteem and self-efficacy. For example, a review of research on resiliency in children and adolescents showed that resilient children have four broad attributes: social competence, problem-solving skills, autonomy, and a sense of purpose and future (Benard, 1993).

Thompson et al. (2001) found interventions that focused on teaching problem-solving skills, which included the development of coping and help-seeking behavior, were more likely to produce significant reductions in suicide risk. They also found being able to cope and solve problems effectively had an impact on reducing emotionality and distress while increasing feelings of personal competency. In turn, this led to protection against stress, depression, and suicide.

Therefore, problem-solving deficits in clients can lead to low self-esteem, low self-efficacy, increased stress, depression, and suicidal ideation. It is important when doing assessments with clients to ascertain their problem-solving ability. Counselors can offer interventions that can increase these skills, which will serve as a protective factor in the lives of clients.

Gender

As was noted in the earlier discussion on risk factors, there are gender differences when it comes to suicide. Current research shows that more females attempt suicide but more males complete it (Lacourse et al., 2001). There are many postulations as to why this may be so. However, in general, it appears there are different risk factors for males and females, or risk factors and protective factors affect both genders in different ways. In general, being female is more protective than being male, at least statistically (Kaslow et al., 2002; Maris, 2002). It may be, as also discussed earlier in this chapter, that women are more socially connected, tend to process their problems and affect more often, and choose less lethal methods (Kaslow et al., 2002).

Ethnicity

Not being White can also be seen as an element of protection (Kaslow et al., 2002). Non-White ethnic minority adults have approximately half the rate of completed suicides as White individuals (Maris, 2002). The exception to this may be Mexican Americans. A study by Tortolero and Roberts (2001) found that Mexican Americans were 1.8 times more likely to have engaged in suicidal ideation than European Americans. This risk for suicide remained unchanged even when the authors controlled for gender, age, family structure, depression, low social support, and self-esteem.

Similar findings were reported by Rew, Thomas, Homer, Resnick, and Beuhring (2001). They looked at a population base of over 10,000 students for suicidal ideation and found the percentage of suicide attempts was significantly higher among Latina girls (19.3%) than in any other ethnic-gender group. So, although the overall rate of suicide attempt is lower in ethnic minorities as compared with Whites, this may not hold true for all genders in all ethnicities. In addition, it was noted under the Risk Factors section that minority children may have an increased risk as compared with Whites.

Religiosity

Several authors mention the role religion plays as a protective factor (Ellison, Burr, & McCall, 1997; Fernquist, 2000; Forman & Kalafat, 1998; Foster, 2001; Maris, 2002). However, not much is extrapolated from these studies as to why religion plays such a role other than that most religions do not condone the taking of one's life. It could be when a person is staunchly religious, his or her faith precludes him or her from engaging in activities that could be considered risk factors for suicide. For example, in a study of nearly 3,000 North Carolina residents ages 18–97, results showed that recent and lifetime alcohol disorders were a third less common among weekly churchgoers and recent alcohol disorders were 42% less common among those who frequently read the Bible or prayed privately (Foster, 2001). As substance abuse is highly correlated with suicidality, this may be one factor that plays a role in why religion is seen as a protective factor.

Another prospective reason is churchgoers usually have a greater amount of fellowship with a support network. They are less isolated because presumably they attend church at least once per week, if not attending other church activities throughout the week. Generally, too, people with faith have a belief system that God will take care of it. They "let God and let go" and have a faith either that all will work out or that it was meant to be as a will of God. Whatever the reason, being religious has been found to be a protective factor against suicide (Forman & Kalafat, 1998; Foster, 2001; Maris, 2002).

Miscellaneous

Included in this category are protective factors that came up often in the literature but not enough information was given to discuss the topic thoroughly. Among these are a socioeconomic status above the poverty line, adequate social skills, a behavioral disturbance, high literacy, and good physical health (Kaslow et al., 2002).

It is important when assessing clients for risk that counselors also take into consideration protective factors that may mitigate those risks. Interventions that increase the protective factors in a client's life are more effective than those that simply attempt to reduce risk factors. For many populations such as those living in poverty and in areas in which there is a lot of community violence, reducing risk factors may be impossible. Therefore, with these individuals, increasing protective factors is crucial to reduce risk.

Adaptations for Diversity

Not all clients will have the same pertinent constellation of risk factors because of differences in diversity. There will be relevant risk factors for older individuals that will not be as germane to adolescents. In addition, there will be risk factors for White individuals that will not be as applicable to a person of a different ethnic or cultural background. The following discussion attempts to bring to the fore risk and protective factors that are more salient to specific groups and give counselors guidance as to what types of issues may need to be assessed.

Adolescents

Research into risk and protective factors has centered on the population of adolescents to a large degree. A plethora of studies exist, more so than could be read for this chapter, as teen suicide is considered a major social problem in most countries of the world. In the United States between 1950 and 1990, suicide rates for adolescents have risen over 300%. Today, suicide is ranked the third most frequent cause of death for adolescents (Beautrais, Joyce, & Mulder, 1996; Grossman, Milligan, & Deyo, 1991; Lacourse et al., 2001; Thatcher, Reininger, & Drane, 2002).

One study conducted in 2000 found of the 3 million adolescents ages 12–17 who expressed suicidal ideation, over one third (37%) actually made an attempt ("Report: Three Million Youths," 2002). This study found the risk equally prevalent for Hispanic, White, Black, and Asian youth. It did not matter whether these adolescents lived in a large metropolitan city or in the suburbs. However, attempted suicide rates were found to be higher in Western countries than in Eastern ones. In the United States, adolescent suicide rates are higher in most intermountain states and Alaska as compared with the rest of the United States, although there are no clear answers as to why that is the case (Gray et al., 2002; "Report: Three Million Youths," 2002; Wichstrom, 2000).

For the adolescent population, it is still true that males complete suicide more often but females attempt more often. Again, it is hypothesized that males use more lethal means (gun or hanging) than do females, and this accounts for the higher male success rate (Gray et al., 2002). Statistics also show for every adolescent suicide completion there are 100–200 attempts (Agerbo, Nordentoft, & Mortensen, 2002; Maris, 2002; Swedo et al., 1991).

Adolescents, like other populations, are susceptible to many of the same risk factors such as mental illness and substance abuse, and approximately 90% of adolescents who commit suicide have at least one mental disorder (Agerbo et al., 2002; Gray et al., 2002). Risks of serious suicide attempt among adolescents increase with extent of exposure to childhood adversity, social disadvantage, and psychiatric morbidity, with each of these factors making independent contributions to risk of serious suicide (Beautrais et al., 1996; Garber, Little, Hilsman, & Weaver, 1998; Gould, 1977). General risk factors found to be associated with increased additive risk in adolescents include increasing age (younger teens have less attempts that older teens), being female, and racial minority membership (Peterson et al., 1996). The following are some factors that appear to be specific to this population.

Aggression. Aggression is strongly correlated with suicide risk (Garrison, McKeown, Valois, & Vincent, 1993). Approximately 7%–48% of people with a history of violent acts have also made a suicide attempt. This has been found true for young children as well as older teens and adults (Apter et al., 1995). Many studies have found that adolescents with externalizing behaviors, conduct disorder, and oppositional defiant disorders are more at risk, particularly for males (Peterson et al., 1996). One study, using a large sample of students from all ethnicities in Grades 9–12, found a strong correlation between suicidal ideation/attempt and committing aggressive acts such as carrying weapons and fighting. This remained true even after the researchers statistically controlled for extraneous variables such as alcohol and illicit drug use, race, and gender (Bower, 1993). Some researchers go so far as to suggest that aggression is every bit as important a risk factor as depression (Apter et al., 1995). Regardless, aggression as a risk factor is exponentially compounded when aggression is paired with depression (Borst & Noam, 1993).

It has been suggested that programs in schools that are designed to prevent suicide among high school students should also address the coexisting factors of aggression and substance abuse (Garrison et al., 1993). See chapter 9 (this volume) for specific methods and interventions for use with this population.

Contact With the Justice System. There may be an association between adolescents who are exposed to the juvenile justice system and an increased suicide rate (Feldman & Wilson, 1997; Sanislow, Grilo, Fehon, Axelrod, & McGlashan, 2003). A study conducted in Utah found 63% of youth who completed suicide had contact with the juvenile justice system (Gray et al., 2002). The researchers found a direct correlation between number of referrals and increased suicide risk. The data showed that whereas there was little if any increased risk for those with one to three referrals, the risk increased exponentially with each additional referral.

However, Gray et al. (2002) noted that behaviors that are indicative of suicide risk might also put these teens into contact with the criminal justice system. For example, it was found that 24% of these adolescents also had substance use/abuse issues as well (Gray et al., 2002). It has also been noted that those adolescents that have attempted suicide more than once may be more prone to violence (Stein, Apter, Ratzoni, Har-Even, & Avidan, 1998). More research needs to be done in this area to make any firm conclusions. All that can be said currently is that there seems to be a correlation between contact with the juvenile justice system and increased rates of suicide. Counselors would be advised to evaluate level of aggressive behavior in the history of an adolescent, especially if that adolescent is a multiple attempter. Suggestions have been made that it may be helpful to examine aggression, impulsivity, and history of drug abuse when assessing suicide risk for detained adolescents (Sanislow et al., 2003).

Gifted Student/Poor Student. Many studies seem to indicate that adolescents with higher rates of attempts and completions also have a higher IQs than their peers (Gust-Brey & Cross, 1999; Sargent, 1984). A survey of 382 students attending a special high school for the gifted found that 9% of these students reported making at least one suicide attempt (Gust-Brey & Cross, 1999). Dixon and Scheckel (1996) suggested the factors that cause gifted students to be more at risk are unusual sensitivity and perfectionism, extreme introversion that may cause the student to self-isolate, and emotional excitabilities. Some hypotheses as to why gifted students are more at risk are that gifted students may often feel they are worthless unless they are the best, have the highest grades and test scores, and rank the highest in their class. Therefore, a lot of pressure may be placed on these students to achieve "great things" (Gust-Brey & Cross, 1999).

In relationship to this discussion, some studies show a link between school performance and suicide risk (Rollins, 2001; "Suicide Risk Factors," 1985). A study conducted by Adkins and Parker (1996) found that students who were "passive perfectionists" were at increased risk. They defined passive perfectionists as those students whose perfectionism creates impediments such as fear of making mistakes and procrastination. These authors contended that perfectionism may lead to depression and suicidal intention.

There is a lot of controversy regarding gifted students and suicide risk. More research is needed to ascertain what factors play a role. Some alternative studies have shown that high grades (not necessarily giftedness) and strong parental expectations that their child do well in school can also be a protective factor, especially for boys (Borowsky et al., 2001; Rollins, 2001). As a preventative measure, school counselors should evaluate the level of perfectionism, fear of making mistakes, and pressure to succeed and how it is affecting mentally and emotionally those students who are either gifted or have higher IQs than their peers.

On the other end of the spectrum, those students at greatest risk of flunking out or dropping out of school are also are at higher risk for suicide attempt. Many factors are thought to play a role in why the adolescent at risk for failing school also has a higher risk for suicide. These include low self-esteem, a high degree of psychosocial distress, problems with drug involvement, pessimism about ability to achieve in school, and disrupted family relations (Thompson & Eggert, 1994). Thompson et al. (2001) suggested that behaviors linked to suicide are correlated to school performance factors and suicidal ideation is associated with feeble academic orientation and that actual attempts are related to deficits in school performance. They also suggested that suicides follow long absences from school.

It may be important to keep these students in school to reduce risk, as there seems to be evidence of an inverse relationship between education and suicide. The more education an adolescent or young adult has, the less likely he or she is to attempt a suicide (Agerbo et al., 2002), although why this might be the case has not been well defined in the literature.

Access to Firearms. As with other populations, access to firearms is problematic for teenagers. Current estimates are that suicide rates increase 4 to 10 times for adolescents who have guns in their home and among adolescents ages 15 to 19, firearm-related suicides accounted for 81% of the increase in the overall rate from 1980 to 1992 (Forman & Kalafat, 1998; Maris, 2002). Therefore, adolescent access to guns is a salient risk factor. Parents with at-risk children should be encouraged to lock up or get rid of firearms in the home.

Disruptive Family Life. Teenagers have increased sensitivity to changes in their routine. A disruptive family life can increase risk for adolescents. Types of disruptions can include such things as parental divorce or death of a parent, mental or medical illness in the family, a family move, parental unemployment, living in poverty, or low income (Adams, Overholser, & Lehnert, 1994; Agerbo et al., 2002; Maris, 2002; Yaniv, 2001).

Poor parent–child relationships also seem to play a role in increased risk. Perceived family functioning and mother–adolescent relationships were significantly correlated with levels of depression, hopelessness, and self-esteem (Adams et al., 1994; Wichstrom, 2000). Adolescents with suicidal ideation perceive their families as having high levels of conflict, reduced communication, discouraging of independence and achievement, and lacking in organization (Adams et al., 1994). Studies also show that when an adolescent perceives he or she is connected to his or her family, that connectedness is a significant protective factor (Borowsky et al., 1999).

Counselors need to be aware of all the risk factors associated with this population so that appropriate interventions can be planned. Current methods of prevention, such as school education programs and teen hotlines, have not been shown to be effective (Gray et al., 2002). Research indicates for some adolescent populations that increasing protective factors is more effective than reducing risk factors. According to the probability model presented by Borowsky et al. (1999), 81% of girls and 75% of boys with three risk factors and no protective factors would be expected to commit suicide. However, these numbers are reduced to 1% for each gender when adolescents have at least three protective factors.

One protective factor that seems more salient to adolescents and young adults than other populations is amount of exercise. Exercise is known to reduce depressive symptoms, and this may be why it plays a role in reducing suicidal ideation among the young (Brown & Blanton, 2002). A study conducted by Simon and Powell (1999) found among people 13 to 34 years old, lethal suicide attempts were correlated with lack of exercise within 1 month before the attempt. Exercise and participation in sports seems to provide a protective factor against suicide not only for adolescent males but even in older males who were not currently exercising or participating in sports and yet were athletic when younger. However, this protective factor does not seem to extend to females. An inverse relationship appears to exist with women; the more active the woman, the more the risk for suicide (Brown & Blanton, 2002).

Senior Citizens

Suicide is the third leading cause of death for seniors (Devons, 1996; "Suicide Among Older Persons," 1996). Suicide rates for men and women above age 65 are among the highest for all populations and accounts for 19% of all suicides (Binder, 2002). Partial explanation may be because older adults constitute the largest percentage of the population. It is estimated that by the year 2050 there will be 2 billion people over the age of 60, which means there will be more people over age 60 than under (Binder, 2002).

The suicide rate has increased steadily among this population since the 1980s and has increased by 36% during 1980–1992, with 84% of those suicides occurring among men. White men over age 85 in particular have the highest suicide rate in this population, and suicide rates for women over age 75 are increasing steadily (Bennett & Collins, 2001; Devons, 1996;

Kirchner, 1997). Divorcees, widows, and widowers had the highest rates, and the method of choice for both genders was firearms ("Suicide Among Older Persons," 1996).

One method used by older individuals that is not often found in other groups is suicide by passivity. The older individual may simply lose the will to live and stop caring for himself or herself. This may be done by refusing to take medication or obtain medical care, or ceasing to eat or drink until he or she dies (Cicirelli, 1998; Devons, 1996). Salient risk factors for this age group include depression, bereavement, a history of alcohol abuse, being male, being White, a history of a mental or emotional disorder, having cancer or another pervasive medical problem, expression of suicidal ideation, and social isolation (Kirchner, 1997; "Suicide Among Older Persons," 1996; Waern, Beskow, Runeson, & Skoog, 1999).

Depression. Affective disorders play a strong role in suicide for seniors (Kirchner, 1997; Waern, Beskow, Runeson, & Skoog, 1996). Depression afflicts 20% of people over the age of 65 and is considered the most common emotional disorder of late life and the biggest influential factor when an older individual takes his or her own life (Butler & Lewis, 1995; Devons, 1996; "Suicide and the Elderly," 1996). One myth that should be negated regarding depression in the older population is that depression is a normal part of the aging process. This myth is not true, and it is essential that depression is recognized and treated to reduce the suicide rate among seniors (Devons, 1996; "Late-Life Depression," 1998; Lebowitz et al., 1997).

Depression is seen as a complicating or additive factor with other diseases that strike during this time and significantly compounds suicidal risk (Devons, 1996). It is important for counselors as well as medical doctors to assess routinely for depression and suicide (Waern et al., 1999). Unfortunately, medical doctors and not mental health counselors are on the front line in battling suicide among older individuals. As high as 20% of older people visit a primary care physician within 4 weeks of committing suicide (Devons, 1996; "Late-Life Depression," 1998; Lebowitz et al., 1997; Sherman, 2002; "Suicide Among Older Persons," 1996).

Yet, depression may be difficult to diagnose in this population because older individuals may express their depressed symptoms differently from younger individuals. Symptoms may include more somatic complaints, social withdrawal, and memory disturbances than in clients who are younger (Butler & Lewis, 1995). For example, instead of talking about depression, an older person may complain to the doctor that his or her stomach is upset or complain of aches and pains or loss of energy (Devons, 1996; Lebowitz et al., 1997). More complete and thorough examinations and assessments relating to depression in an older individual must be made to properly diagnose this important risk factor for suicide within this population.

One assessment tool that is talked about frequently in the literature is the Geriatric Depression Scale, which was designed specifically for use with the older population and is composed of 30 yes/no questions about depressive symptoms (Devons, 1996; "Suicide Among Older Persons," 1996). Devons (1996) also outlined what is called a stepwise approach to interviewing older individuals regarding suicidal ideation. This approach is known as the *suicide ladder*. The first step is to ask whether they feel as if they are becoming a burden to their family. The second step is to ask whether they feel as though their family would be better off without them. The final steps are then to concretely explore thoughts of suicidal ideation.

Bereavement. Bereavement as an issue should be assessed. After age 65, individuals may begin to suffer many losses. These can be as obvious as the death or loss of a loved one but can also include less obvious losses, such as loss of job or declining socioeconomic status, loss of social role, loss of independence and privacy, loss of a home, and deteriorating physical health (Devons, 1996).

At times, it may be difficult to distinguish the difference between bereavement and depression, as depression is often a subsidiary symptom of bereavement. In fact, bereavement reactions can lead to major depressive disorder, which is a potent risk for suicide (Brent, Peters, & Weller, 1994; Rebecca et al., 1993). The distinguishing factor between bereavement and depression is level of impairment. Accordingly, major depression cannot be diagnosed within a few months of a death of a loved one unless there is a significant impairment in functioning or morbid preoccupation with worthlessness, suicidal ideation, psychotic symptoms, or psychomotor retardation (Brent, Peters, & Weller, 1994). Therefore in general, grief and loss issues must be a focus of counseling for this population, and it must be ascertained whether symptoms are a result of a bereavement reaction to a loss or whether the individual is also suffering from an accompanying depression. Both need to be treated for increased emotional health of the individual.

Health Problems. Issues of deteriorating health can affect an older individual profoundly. Often, one complication of a health problem is depression. Illnesses found particularly prone to induce depression in seniors include hypertension, myocardial infarction, coronary artery bypass surgery, congestive heart failure, stroke, Alzheimer's disease, Parkinson's disease, diabetes, thyroid disorders, cancer, chronic obstructive pulmonary disease, rheumatoid arthritis, deafness, chronic pain, renal dialysis, anxiety, chronic constipation, and sexual dysfunction (Butler & Lewis, 1995; Juurlink, Hermann, Szalai, & Redelmeier, 2001). Individuals with multiple illnesses were 3.3 times as likely to commit suicide than those with a single illness, and those with a single illness were 4.0 times more likely to commit suicide than those with no illness (Juurlink et al., 2001).

Social Isolation. Whether it is because an older person's social network begins to deteriorate through the deaths of friends or loved ones or because they cannot travel and ambulate like they used to, many seniors are left with feelings of emptiness and loneliness. They often feel lonely and their self-esteem suffers. Society places an emphasis on youth and dexterity, and many seniors may begin to feel useless, insignificant, and dehumanized, which can feed depression and suicidal ideation (Devons, 1996). In addition, living or feeling alone after age 65 can cause nutritional deficiencies and increase risk of heart problems, cancer, and suicide ("Living Alone," 1992). Therefore, counselors need to assess degree of connectedness for older clients. Interventions that strengthen social support can lessen isolation and the accompanying psychological symptoms that accompany it.

Alcohol Abuse. Substance abuse is a risk factor for many populations and is especially so for seniors. Older individuals who abuse alcohol are nine times more likely to commit suicide than their peers who do not (Kirchner, 1997). Many seniors may try to self-medicate in response to late-life stressors such as a declining socioeconomic status, deteriorating health, loss of support network, loss of autonomy, and so forth. Assessment for alcohol and other substances should be routine when doing an intake for any population but becomes particularly relevant because of the high rate of suicide for substance abusers in this population.

Current strategies for reducing suicide rates among seniors include senior peer counseling programs, improving mental health services through suicide-prevention centers, efforts that target high-risk persons, and programs that increase awareness of risk factors among those who have frequent contact with seniors ("Suicide Among Older Persons," 1996). One effective mode of psychotherapy appears to be reminiscence and life review because it helps the senior analyze his or her own life and put things into perspective. It has also been found helpful to increase the social network of seniors through support groups (Devons, 1996).

Ethnicity

Just as there are differences in potency and salience of risk factors between young and old, there are also differences between ethnicities. Many things may account for these disparities, such as differences in socioeconomic status, level of education, place of residence, worldview, acculturation level, or ethnic identity development, to name a few. More research needs to be done in this area to ascertain why there are differences.

One note of caution when reading the following sections on ethnicity is that in order to confine the discussion to one chapter, individual and within-group differences are not discussed. The intent is not to stereotype and assume all ethnic individuals are alike. However, space constraints limit the ability to discuss the differences within ethnic groups. For example, the terms Hispanic and Latino are umbrella terms that represent many different cultural groups such as Cubans, Mexicans, Puerto Ricans, San Salvadorians, Guatemalans, and so forth. Counselors need to be aware of the vast differences within groups as well as between them. For the purposes of this chapter, only broad differences between ethnic groups are discussed.

African Americans or Blacks. Historically, African American suicide rates have been lower than Caucasian suicide rates (Gibbs, 1997). However, recent trends indicate this may be changing because the rates of completed suicides have risen significantly, especially for African American male adolescents. Suicide rates among Blacks of both sexes rose more than 36% between 1960 and 1985. The rate among Black adult males rose 45% to 63% between 1980 and 1993, whereas Black teenage male suicide rates rose between 75% and 165% depending on geographical area (Bloch, 1999; Burr, Hartman, & Matteson, 1999; "Why Suicide," 1996). It is expected that the suicide rates for this newest Black male generation will be similar to that of Whites (Glowinski et al., 2001).

Hypotheses given for the rise in suicide rates among the African American population are that despite civil rights, Blacks are still underrepresented in many areas of status. For example, Blacks still have lower occupational positions, lower educational achievement, and higher unemployment and poverty rates (Burr et al., 1999). This often causes feelings of disfranchisement and disenchantment that in turn can cause feelings of "hopelessness, alienation, and despair associated with entrenched and extreme poverty, generated and maintained in part by rigid and persistent spatial isolation" and "creates an atmosphere ripe for social dislocation, social disorganization, and, ultimately, lethal violence" (Burr et al., 1999, p. 4). Black leaders in the community hypothesize that easy access to guns, a lack of effective coping mechanisms, and drug-related problems contribute to the growing rate of Black male suicide. They also cite the breakdown of the African American family that leaves children without male role models. Currently, in impoverished Black communities, the divorce rate is 50%, whereas the rate of out-of-wedlock births approximates 75% ("Why Suicide," 1996).

Generally, risk factors that apply to African Americans are being male, being a young adult, engaging in substance abuse, having one or more psychiatric disorders, conflictual family or interpersonal relationships, antisocial behavior, living in poverty, and homosexuality. In addition, protective factors for this population are religious faith, being an older adult, living in a southern state, and having social support (Griffith & Bell, 1989; Glowinski et al., 2001).

African American women have lower rates of suicide in comparison with African American men and other ethnic groups. African American female risk declines even further during midlife (Griffith & Bell, 1989; Kaslow et al., 2002). Risk factors affecting African American females appear to be exposure to severe negative life events, having a history of child maltreatment, having high levels of psychological distress and depression, feeling hopeless about the future, and having substance abuse issues (Kaslow et al., 2002). Protective factors include feeling hopeful about life and the future; having self-efficacy, coping skills, and social support; and being successful in obtaining material resources (Kaslow et al., 2002).

Native Americans. American Indians and Alaska Natives have the highest suicide rates of all ethnic groups in the United States, and suicide is the second leading cause of death for this population (Cameron, 1999; Crofoot-Graham, 2002; Grossman et al., 1991; Manson, Beals, Dick, & Duclos, 1989). During the 1980s, the Native American suicide completion rate increased by 200%–300%, and the attempt rate rose by 1000% ("Indian Suicides Rising," 1984). Suicide rates for Native American teens and young adults is nearly three times the national average for the general population, and often different parts of the country have been hit with the "cluster suicides" of young Native teens (Bloch, 1999; Manson et al., 1989). Generally, a common factor among those Native Americans who take their lives is membership in a tribe with loose social integration that is undergoing rapid socioeconomic change (Manson et al., 1989).

One study with 11,666 Native American and Alaskan Native youth from reservation schools found 22% of Native American or Alaskan Native girls and 12% of the boys have attempted suicide at least once and for every suicide completion, there were approximately 13 suicide attempts (Borowsky et al., 1999). In this population, it is again apparent that females have a higher rate of attempt. Yet, the low attempt/completion ratio suggests that these adolescents are using methods that are more lethal.

Hypotheses explaining Native American suicide rates relate to several historical events, including the mass extinction of the Native peoples during European colonization, the massacre of family and way of life, and the ensuing fallout from the Termination Era between 1946 and 1968 when the U.S. government sought to terminate its responsibility toward the Native people and began terminating tribes. During this time, many Native Americans and Alaskans were forcibly removed from their homes and relocated to large cities with little means to support themselves (Crofoot-Graham, 2002; Sullivan & Brems, 1997). Historical trauma and disenfranchisement is thought to play a significant role in the suicide of today's Native Americans.

Salient risk factors for this population include illness; access to firearms; physical or sexual abuse; being female; engaging in substance abuse; gang involvement; having been in a special education class; having emotional problems, depression, or long-term unresolved grief; feeling alienated from family, community, and culture; poverty; internalized oppression; and negative self concept from believing in Native stereotypes (Crofoot-Graham, 2002; Manson et al., 1989; Potthoff et al., 1998).

Cultural conflict and associated problems in identity formation are believed to produce a persistent dysphoria and anomie, which render Native American and Alaskan Native youth vulnerable to suicidal behavior during periods of heightened stress (Manson et al., 1989). However, the most powerful risk factor was having a friend or family member who attempted or completed a suicide. Protective factors included having a strong family relationship, being able to discuss problems with others, and being in good mental/emotional health (Borowsky et al, 1999).

It has been found especially relevant within this population that increasing the number of protective factors was more effective than reducing the number of risk factors. In some populations, it is difficult to remove risk factors such as poverty, exposure to violence, poor family relationships, and so forth. It is more effective in these cases to increase the number of protective factors (Borowsky et al., 1999).

Counselors need to consider approaches other than the traditional Western psychotherapeutic methods when working with this population. These methods do not work as well with Native Americans (Crofoot-Graham, 2002). It has been suggested by those who work with this population that interventions should incorporate the native culture, worldview, and traditional healing practices. American Indian child welfare workers and American Indian community leaders strongly emphasize the importance of spiritual connections as a primary focus for suicide assessment, prevention, and intervention (Crofoot-Graham, 2002). Therefore, it is especially important for counselors to assess areas concerning the *spirit* (spiritual practices and teaching, dreams, symbols, stories, gifts, intuition, grace, protecting forces, and negative forces), *context* (family, work, culture, community history, climate, and weather), *mind* (intellect, emotion, memory, judgment, and experience), and *body* (chemistry, genetics, nutrition, substance use and abuse, sleep and rest, age, and condition). The native relational worldview perceives wellness as a balance among these four areas (Crofoot-Graham, 2002). However, it is also important to recognize the diversity within the umbrella term "Native American" because there is much diversity between the native peoples, and the above descriptors may not apply to all cultural groups.

Hispanic or Latino. Research on the Hispanic groups is sparse. What little has been done has shown that Hispanics have lower suicide rates than most other ethnicities, although this is not true for Mexicans, who have almost twice the rate of suicidal ideation as White Anglo Americans. Why this might be remains unclear (Tortolero & Roberts, 2001).

Salient risk factors identified in the literature for Hispanics in general include previous suicide attempt, violence victimization, violence perpetration, substance use/abuse, acculturation stress, and school problems (Borowsky et al., 2001). For Hispanic adolescent girls, risk factors also include somatic complaints, a friend's suicide attempt or completion, having to repeat a grade at school, substance use/abuse, and a history of mental health treatment (Borowsky et al., 2001). For boys, risk factors include weapon-carrying at school, easy access to guns at home, and same-sex romantic attraction (Borowsky et al., 2001). Pertinent protective factors that have been identified include perceived family connectedness, and specifically for adolescent boys, high grade point average. In addition, for adolescent girls emotional well-being and access to counseling were found to be protective (Borowsky et al., 2001).

Given the above risk factors, at least for adolescents, it would be important for counselors to ask about family interactions and connectedness, school achievement, history of fighting and injury from fighting, signs of depression, suicidal behaviors by the adolescent or someone they know, use of alcohol and illicit drugs, and access to firearms (Borowsky et al., 2001).

Asian/Pacific Islander. There is not much research on Asian Americans either. In general, the most germane suicidal risk factors for Asians appear to be severe depression, a previous suicide attempt, chronic and pervasive stress, low quality of life, severe interpersonal conflict; and a relative, friend, or acquaintance with previous suicidal behavior. Risk factors for Asians are particularly additive in nature. For example, an Asian individual who has two to three risk factors has an increased suicide risk of 30%, whereas an individual with four to five risk factors has an increased risk of 85%, and someone with six or more risk factors has an increased risk of 96% (Eddleston et al., 2002; Phillips et al., 2002).

Asian women, especially among the Chinese and Japanese, appear to have much higher suicide rates than men, which sharply contrasts the norm for other ethnic or cultural groups (Bloch, 1999). No research was found that discussed why this may be the case. One speculation may be that women are more subservient in these cultures, and exposure to Western traditions may cause conflict within these women.

Sexual Orientation

Controversy surrounds the issues of sexual orientation as a risk factor for suicide. Some studies have shown gay and lesbian youth are much more likely to attempt suicide than their heterosexual peers and may account for as many as 30% of completed youth suicides and 20%-42% of attempted suicides. This may be especially prevalent for gay and bisexual males, ages 13 to 18, who are seven times more likely to attempt suicide than heterosexual males (Borowsky et al., 2001; "Gays, Bisexuals," 1999; Lee, 2000; Pohan & Bailey, 1998; Remafedi, 1999; "Youth At Risk," 1997).

Homosexual adult males are six times more likely to attempt suicide than their heterosexual counterparts, lesbians are twice as likely to attempt suicide as heterosexual women, and suicide attempts by gay men are more severe than those of their heterosexual counterparts (Borowsky et al., 2001; "Gays, Bisexuals," 1999; Lee, 2000; Pohan & Bailey, 1998; Remafedi, 1999; "Youth At Risk," 1997). However, other studies find that lesbians have lower rates of risk in comparison with their heterosexual and bisexual peers (Lee, 2000).

It appears the controversy only extends to the rate of risk for lesbians as most of the studies agree that male homosexuals, whether adolescent or adult, have increased lifetime risk of suicidal behaviors (Friedman, 1999). One study using twins, with one twin being heterosexual and the other homosexual, found the homosexual twin was 6.5 times more likely to have made a suicide attempt than the heterosexual twin. These findings were found after controlling for psychiatric disorders, substance abuse disorders, and other confounding variables ("Gays, Bisexuals," 1999; "Health," 1999; Remafedi, 1999).

Many factors may play a role as to why suicide risk is heightened in males but not so much for females. One hypothesis relating to gay men who are effeminate and lesbian women who are masculine is that society is more punitive toward effeminate males than masculine females (Friedman, 1999; "Youth At Risk," 1997). It is also hypothesized that parental disapproval for atypical sex role behaviors in childhood may be more severe for males than females. As a result, it has been found that childhood atypical sex role conduct has been linked with depression, anxiety, and suicidality in men but not in women (Friedman, 1999).

Salient risk factors for homosexual individuals include gender nonconformity; early awareness or early self-identification as gay, lesbian, or bisexual; first homosexual experience at an early age; history of sexual or physical abuse; homosexual-related stress; victimization by violence; lack of social support; dropping out of school; family problems; suicide attempts by friends or relatives; substance abuse; and homelessness (Lee, 2000; Remafedi, 1999). Issues to be aware of concerning gay, lesbian, bisexual, or transgendered individuals include the following.

Homophobia. For all populations of gay, lesbian, bisexuals, and transgendered individuals, there may be a constant wearing down from homophobic members of society. Even though homosexuality is becoming more accepted, there are many pockets of society whereby nothing has really changed. Constant harassment by heterosexuals may cause negative internalizations within gay, lesbian, bisexual, and transgendered individuals, which may adversely influence self-esteem and a sense of security (Friedman, 1999). A sense of isolation may be especially keen for this population as many with a nonheterosexual orientation go through a stage in which they feel they have no one to turn to, not even family (Rotello, 2001). They may so fear a homophobic reaction and rejection that suicide is preferable to having family or friends find out.

Social Isolation. More than 95% of lesbian, gay, bisexual, and transgender youth feel alienated and emotionally isolated from their peers because they feel different or are not accepted (Borowsky et al., 2001; "Gays, Bisexuals," 1999; Lee, 2000; Pohan & Bailey, 1998; Remafedi, 1999; "Youth At Risk," 1997). Unless these individuals live in larger communities whereby they can find support among their homosexual peers or nonhomophobic individuals, isolation may play a key role. This may be especially salient in smaller, rural communities. Counselors need to assess for feelings of isolation within these individuals and plan interventions that can increase support.

Victimization. Almost half of gay youth and 20% of lesbians are verbally or physically assaulted in school. Lesbian, gay, bisexual, and transgendered youth are four times more likely to be endangered or threatened with a weapon on school property than their straight peers. Lesbian, gay, bisexual, and transgendered youth are five times more likely to miss school for fear of their personal safety, and 28% of these students drop out of high school (Borowsky et al., 2001; "Gays, Bisexuals," 1999; Lee, 2000; Pohan & Bailey, 1998; Remafedi, 1999; "Youth At Risk," 1997).

Substance Abuse. Perhaps as a result of living in a homophobic society and an attempt to dull the pain of internal conflicts, gay, lesbian, bisexual, and transgendered youth are three times more likely than their heterosexual peers to abuse substances. These youth are also nine times more likely to use intravenous drugs, as well as engage in sexual activity, use cocaine, and smoke marijuana and tobacco before age 13 (Lee, 2000; Pohan & Bailey, 1998).

Homelessness. Studies show that as many as 6%–40% of homeless youth self-identify as homosexual (Pohan & Bailey, 1998). One reason for these high rates may be because as much as 26% of those who "come out" to their families are thrown out of their homes because of conflicts with moral and religious values (Pohan & Bailey, 1998). The associated stressors that come with homelessness, feelings of despair, loneliness and isolation, concern about safety, where to sleep, when a next meal may be forthcoming, and victimization for being homosexual exponentially increase the risk that homeless homosexual youth will commit suicide (Borowsky et al., 2001; "Gays, Bisexuals," 1999; Lee, 2000; Pohan & Bailey, 1998; Remafedi, 1999; "Youth At Risk," 1997).

It is important for counselors to ask clients about their sexual orientation so that the specific risk factors germane to this population can be identified within the individual. Several factors are unique to this population and may be missed if sexual orientation is not discussed.

Summary

There are no precise answers as to who will or who will not commit suicide. However, with the current research counselors are able to understand pertinent risk and protective factors and how they might apply to various groups and individuals. Generally, the more risk factors an individual has, the more risk that person has of eventually committing suicide. However, a counselor cannot accurately predict from those risk factors which client will finally succumb to suicide because protective factors as well as other variables also mitigate the effects. The most pertinent and efficacious way of ascertaining "imminent" risk is still ideation, plan, intent, and means.

Nonetheless, counselors, with the growing knowledge of various risk factors, can understand long-term risk and plan interventions and strategies that can be most effective in helping individuals reduce their risk for suicide. It is now possible to predict certain normative events or crises that may make suicide a more likely choice for any individual. However, many factors must be considered when planning appropriate interventions, such as developmental level, age, socioeconomic status, sexual orientation, ethnicity, and gender. Each of these groups and subgroups has various and differing risk factors that are germane to each as well as general factors that will pertain to all.

References

Adams, D. M., Overholser, J. C., & Lehnert, K. L. (1994). Perceived family functioning and adolescent suicidal behavior. *Journal of the American Academy of Child and Adolescent Psychiatry, 33*, 498–508.

Adkins, K. K., & Parker, W. (1996). Perfectionism and suicidal preoccupation. *Journal of Personality, 62*, 529–543.

Agerbo, E., Mortensen, P. B., Eriksson, T., Qin, P., Westergaard-Nielsen, N., & Gunnell, D. (2001). Risk of suicide in relation to income level in people admitted to hospital with mental illness: Nested case-control study. *British Medical Journal, 322*, 334–335.

Agerbo, E., Nordentoft, M., & Mortensen, P. B. (2002). Familial, psychiatric and socioeconomic risk factors for suicide in young people: Nested case-control study. *British Medical Journal, 325*, 74–78.

Apter, A., Gothelf, D., Orbach, I., Weizman, R., Ratzoni, G., Har-Even, D., & Tyano, S. (1995). Correlation of suicidal and violent behavior in different diagnostic categories in hospitalized adolescent patients. *Journal of the American Academy of Child and Adolescent Psychiatry, 34*, 912–919.

A serotonin marker for suicide. (1996, March 12). *Harvard Mental Health Letter*, 6–8.

Bailey, J. E., Kellerman, A. L., Somes, G. W., Banton, J. G., Rivara, F. P., & Rushforth, N. P. (1997). Risk factors for violent death of women in the home. *Archives of Internal Medicine, 157*, 777–783.

Beautrais, A. L., Joyce, P. R., & Mulder, R. T. (1996). Risk factors for serious suicide attempts among youths aged 13 through 24 years. *Journal of the American Academy of Child and Adolescent Psychiatry, 35*, 1174–1183.

Beck, A. T., Steer, R., Kovacs, M., & Garrison, B. (1985). Hopelessness and eventual suicide: A 10-year prospective study of patients hospitalized with suicidal ideation. *American Journal of Psychiatry, 142*, 559–563.

Benard, B. (1993, November). Fostering resiliency in kids. *Educational Leadership*, 44–48.

Bennett, A. T., & Collins, K. A. (2001). Elderly suicide: A 10-year retrospective. *Journal of the American Medical Association, 286*, 1293.

Binder, S. (2002). Injuries among older adults: The challenge of optimizing safety and minimizing unintended consequences. *Injury Prevention, 8*(4), 2–5.

Bloch, D. S. (1999). Adolescent suicide as a public health threat. *Journal of Child and Adolescent Psychiatric Nursing, 12*(1), 26–38.

Borowsky, I. W., Ireland, M., & Resnick, M. D. (2001). Adolescent suicide attempts: Risk and protectors. *Pediatrics, 107*, 485–493.

Borowsky, I. W., Resnick, M. D., Ireland, M., & Blum, R. W. (1999). Suicide attempts among American Indian and Alaska Native youth: Risk and protective factors. *Archives of Pediatrics and Adolescent Medicine, 153*, 573–580.

Borst, S. R., & Noam, G. G. (1993). Developmental psychopathology in suicidal and nonsuicidal adolescent girls. *Journal of the American Academy of Child and Adolescent Psychiatry, 32*, 501–509.

Bower, B. (1993, February 13). Suicide signs loom in pair of surveys. *Science News*, 101–103.

Brainerd, E. (2001, May). Economic reform and mortality in the former Soviet Union: A study of the suicide epidemic in the 1990s. *European Economic Review*, 1007.

Brent, D. A., Baugher, M., Bridge, J., Chen, T., & Chiappetta, L. (1999). Age and sex related risk factors for adolescent suicide. *Journal of the American Academy of Child and Adolescent Psychiatry, 38*, 1497–1505.

Brent, D. A., Johnson, B. A., Perper, J., Connolly, J., Bridge, J., Bartle, S., & Rather, C. (1994). Personality disorder, personality traits, impulsive violence, and completed suicide in adolescents. *Journal of the American Academy of Child and Adolescent Psychiatry, 33*, 1080–1087.

Brent, D. A., Moritz, G., Bridge, J., Perper, J., & Canobbio, R. (1996). The impact of adolescent suicide on siblings and parents: A longitudinal follow-up. *Suicide Life Threat Behavior, 26*, 253–259.

Brent, D. A., Peters, J. J., & Weller, E. (1994). Resolved: Several weeks of depressive symptoms after exposure to a friend's suicide is "major depressive disorder." *Journal of the American Academy of Child and Adolescent Psychiatry, 33*, 582–590.

Brown, D. R., & Blanton, C. J. (2002). Physical activity, sports participation, and suicidal behavior among college students. *Medicine and Science in Sports and Exercise, 34*, 1087–1096.

Burr, J. A., Hartman, J. T., & Matteson, D. W. (1999). Black suicide in U.S. metropolitan areas: An examination of the racial inequality and social integration-regulation hypotheses. *Social Forces, 77*, 1049–1051.

Butler, R. N., & Lewis, M. I. (1995). Late-life depression: When and how to intervene. *Geriatrics, 50*(8), 44–51.

Cameron, L. A. (1999). Understanding alcohol abuse in American Indian/ Alaskan Native youth. *Pediatric Nursing, 25*, 297–300.

Christoffel, K. K. (2000). Commentary: When counseling parents on guns doesn't work: Why don't they get it? *Journal of the American Academy of Child and Adolescent Psychiatry, 39*, 1226–1228.

Cicirelli, V. G. (1998). Views of elderly people concerning end-of-life decisions. *Journal of Applied Gerontology, 17*, 186–204.

Crofoot-Graham, T. L. (2002). Using reasons for living to connect to American Indian healing traditions. *Journal of Sociology and Social Welfare, 29*, 55–77.

Crumley, F. E. (1990). Substance abuse and adolescent suicidal behavior. *Journal of the American Medical Association, 263,* 3051–3057.

Cummings, P., & Koepsell, T. D. (1998). Does owning a firearm increase or decrease the risk of death? *Journal of the American Medical Association, 280,* 471–472.

Cummings, P., Koepsell, T. D., Grossman, D. C., Savarino, J., & Thompson, R. S. (1997). The association between the purchase of a handgun and homicide or suicide. *American Journal of Public Health, 87,* 974–979.

Dannenberg, A. L., McNeil, J. G., Brundage, J. F., & Brookmeyer, R. (1996). Suicide and HIV infection: Mortality follow-up of 4147 HIV-seropositive military service applicants. *Journal of the American Medical Association, 276,* 1743–1747.

Devons, C. A. J. (1996). Suicide in the elderly: How to identify and treat patients at risk. *Geriatrics, 51*(3), 67–72.

Dhossche, D. M., Ulusarac, A., & Syed, W. (2001). A retrospective study of general hospital patients who commit suicide shortly after being discharged from the hospital. *Archives of Internal Medicine, 161,* 991–994.

Dixon, D. N., & Scheckel, J. R. (1996). Gifted adolescent suicide: The empirical base. *Journal of Secondary Gifted Education, 7,* 386–392.

Druss, B., & Pincus, H. (2000). Suicidal ideation and suicide attempts in general medical illnesses. *Archives of Internal Medicine, 160,* 1522–1526.

Eddleston, M., Zhang, Y., Li, X., Phillips, M. R., Fleischmann, A., Bertolote, J. M., & Reardon, D. C. (2002). Suicide rates in China. *The Lancet, 359,* 2274–2279.

Ellison, C. G., Burr, J. A., & McCall, P. L. (1997). Religious homogeneity and metropolitan suicide rates. *Social Forces, 76,* 273–299.

Ellison, L., & Morrison, H. I. (2001). Serum cholesterol concentration and risk of suicide. *Journal of the American Medical Association, 285,* 2694.

Faulkner, A. H., & Cranston, K. (2000). Correlates of same-sex sexual behavior in a random sample of Massachusetts high school students. *American Journal of Public Health, 88,* 262–267.

Feinstein, A. (1997). Multiple sclerosis, depression and suicide. *British Medical Journal, 315,* 691–693.

Feldman, M., & Wilson, A. (1997). Adolescent suicidality in urban minorities and its relationship to conduct disorders, depression, and separation anxiety. *Journal of the American Academy of Child and Adolescent Psychiatry, 36,* 75–85.

Fergusson, D. M. (2000). Is sexual orientation related to mental health problems and suicidality in young people? *Journal of the American Medical Association, 283,* 183.

Fernquist, R. M. (2000). Problem drinking in the family and youth suicide. *Adolescence, 35,* 551–558.

Feskanich, D., Hastrup, J. L., Marshall, J. R., Colditz, G. A., Stampfer, M. J., Willet, W. C., & Kawachi, I. (2002). Stress and suicide in the nurses' health study. *Journal of Epidemiology and Community Health, 56,* 95–99.

Field, T., Miguel, D., & Sanders, C. E. (2001). Adolescent suicidal ideation. *Adolescence, 36*, 241–249.

Forman, S. G., & Kalafat, J. (1998). Substance abuse and suicide: Promoting resilience against self-destructive behavior in youth. *School Psychology Review, 27*, 398–406.

Foster, T. (2001). Dying for a drink: Global suicide prevention should focus more on alcohol use disorders. *British Medical Journal, 323*, 817–818.

Friedman, R. C. (1999). Homosexuality, psychopathology and suicidality. *Archives of General Psychiatry, 56*, 887–888.

Garber, J., Little, S., Hilsman, R., & Weaver, K. R. (1998). Family predictors of suicidal symptoms in young adolescents. *Journal of Adolescence, 21*, 445–458.

Garcia, J., Adams, J., Friedman, L., & East, P. (2002). Links between past abuse, suicide ideation and sexual orientation. *Journal of American College Health, 51*, 9–15.

Garrison, C. Z., McKeown, R. E., Valois, R. F., & Vincent, M. L. (1993). Aggression, substance use and suicidal behaviors in high school students. *American Journal of Public Health, 83*, 179–185.

Gays, bisexuals have greater suicide risk. (1999, November 1). *Mental Health Weekly*, 8.

Gibbs, J. T. (1997). African-American suicide: A cultural paradox. *Suicide and Life-Threatening Behavior, 27*, 68–80.

Glowinski, A. L., Bucholz, K. K., Nelson, E. C., Qiang Fu, P., Madden, A. F., Reich W., & Heath, A. C. (2001). Suicide attempts in an adolescent female twin sample. *Journal of the American Academy of Child and Adolescent Psychiatry, 40*, 1300–1308.

Goldston, D. B., Daniel, S. S., & Reboussin, B. A. (2001). Cognitive risk factors and suicide attempts among formerly hospitalized adolescents: A prospective naturalistic study. *Journal of the American Academy of Child and Adolescent Psychiatry, 40*, 91–101.

Goldston, D. B., Kelley, A. E., Reboussin, D. M., Daniel, S. S., Smith, J. A., Schwartz, R. P., et al. (1997). Suicidal ideation and behavior and noncompliance with the medical regimen among diabetic adolescents. *Journal of the American Academy of Child and Adolescent Psychiatry, 36*, 1528–1537.

Gould, M. S. (1977). Psychosocial risk factors of child and adolescent completed suicide. *Journal of the American Medical Association, 277*, 688F.

Gray, D., Achilles, J., Keller, T., Tate, D., Haggard, L., Rolfs, R., et al. (2002). Utah youth suicide study: Phase I. Government agency contact before death. *Journal of the American Academy of Child and Adolescent Psychiatry, 41*, 427–435.

Griffith, E. H., & Bell, C. C. (1989). Recent trends in suicide and homicide among blacks. *Journal of the American Medical Association, 262*, 2265–2279.

Groholt, B., Ekeberg, O., & Wichstrom, L. (2000). Young suicide attempters: A comparison between a clinical and an epidemiological sample. *Journal of the American Academy of Child and Adolescent Psychiatry, 39*, 868–875.

Grossman, D. C., Milligan, C., & Deyo, R. A. (1991). Risk factors for suicide attempts among Navajo adolescents. *American Journal of Public Health, 81,* 870–875.

Gust-Brey, K., & Cross, T. (1999). An examination of the literature base on the suicidal behaviors of gifted students. *Roeper Review, 22,* 28–35.

Harris, E. C., & Barraclough, B. M. (1994). Suicide as an outcome for medical disorders. *Medicine, 73,* 281–297.

Hawton, K. (2001). Suicide in doctors: A study of risk according to gender, seniority and specialty in medical practitioners in England and Wales, 1979–1995. *Journal of the American Medical Association, 285,* 2560–2571.

Hazler, R. J., & Denham, S. A. (2002). Social isolation of youth at risk: Conceptualizations and practical implications. *Journal of Counseling & Development, 80,* 403–409.

Health. (1999, December 7). *The Advocate,* 18.

Hemenway, D., Solnick, S. J., & Colditz, G. A. (1993). Smoking and suicide among nurses. *American Journal of Public Health, 83,* 249–251.

Hiroeh, U., Appleby, L., Mortensen, P. B., & Dunn, G. (2001). Death by homicide, suicide and other unnatural causes in people with mental illness: A population-based study. *Lancet, 358,* 2110–2112.

Indian suicides rising. (1984, July/August). *Children Today,* 4–5.

Iribarren, C., Reed, D. M., Wergowske, G., Burchfiel, C. M., & Dwyer, J. H. (1995). Serum cholesterol level and mortality due to suicide and trauma in the Honolulu Heart Program. *Archives of Internal Medicine, 155,* 695–701.

Is cholesterol a mood-altering lipid? (1996, September 21). *Science News,* 184.

Jacobs, D. G. (2000). A 52-year-old suicidal man. *Journal of the American Medical Association, 283,* 2693–2699.

Juurlink, D., Hermann, N., Szalai, J., & Redelmeier, D. (2001). Chronic illness and the risk of suicide in the elderly. *Journal of Toxicology: Clinical Toxicology, 39,* 530.

Kaslow, N. J., Thompston, M. P., Okun, A., Price, A., Young, S., Bender, M., et al. (2002). Risk and protective factors for suicidal behavior in abused African American Women. *Journal of Consulting and Clinical Psychology, 70,* 311–320.

Kellermann, A. L., Rivara, F. P., Grant, S., Reay, D. T., Francisco, J., Banton, G. J., et al. (1992). Suicide in the home in relation to gun ownership. *New England Journal of Medicine, 327,* 467–473.

King, K. A., Vidourek, R. A., & Davis, B. (2002). Increasing self-esteem and school connectedness through a multidimensional mentoring program. *Journal of School Health, 72,* 294–299.

Kirchner, J. T. (1996). AIDS and suicide. *Journal of the American Medical Association, 275,* 172D.

Kirchner, J. T. (1997). Health status and risk of suicide in elderly patients. *American Family Physician, 56,* 1188–1189.

Lacourse, E., Claes, M., & Villeneuve, M. (2001). Heavy metal music and adolescent suicidal risk. *Journal of Youth and Adolescence, 30,* 321–332.

Larzelere, R. E., Smith, G. L., Batenhorst, L. M., & Kelly, D. B. (1996). Predictive validity of the Suicide Probability Scale among adolescents in group home treatment. *Journal of the American Academy of Child and Adolescent Psychiatry, 35,* 166–173.

Late-life depression: An NIH consensus update. (1998). *Consultant, 38,* 954–957.

Law, M. (1996, September 14). Commentary: Having too much evidence (depression, suicide, and low serum cholesterol). *British Medical Journal, 313,* 651–653.

Lebowitz, B. D., Pearson, J. L., Schneider, L. S., Reynolds, C. F., III., Alexopoulos, G. S., Bruce, M. L., et al. (1997). Diagnosis and treatment of depression in late life: Consensus statement update. *Journal of the American Medical Association, 278,* 1186–1191.

Lee, R. (2000). Health care problems of lesbian, gay, bisexual, and transgender patients. *Western Journal of Medicine, 172,* 403–408.

Lewinsohn, P. M., Rohde, P., Seeley, J. R., & Baldwin, C. L. (2001). Gender differences in suicide attempts from adolescence to young adulthood. *Journal of the American Academy of Child and Adolescent Psychiatry, 40,* 427–434.

Lewis, G. (2001). Mental health after head injury. *Journal of Neurology, Neurosurgery and Psychiatry, 71,* 431.

Living alone: Can social isolation affect your health? (1992). *Mayo Clinic Health Letter, 10*(9), 4–6.

Lock, J., & Steiner, H. (1999). Gay, lesbian, and bisexual youth risks for emotional, physical, and social problems: Results from a community-based survey. *Journal of the American Academy of Child and Adolescent Psychiatry, 38,* 297–305.

Loos, M. D. (2002). The synergy of depravity and loneliness in alcoholism: A new conceptualization, an old problem. *Counseling and Values, 46,* 199–213.

Low cholesterol linked to suicide tries. (1995). *Science News, 147,* 157–158.

Low serum cholesterol levels and mortality from injuries. (1993). *American Family Physician, 47,* 484–485.

Malone, K. M., Oquendo, M. A., Haas, G. L., Ellis, S. P., Li, S., & Mann, J. J. (2000). Protective factors against suicidal acts in major depression: Reasons for living. *American Journal of Psychiatry, 157,* 1084–1089.

Manson, S. M., Beals, J., Dick, R. W., & Duclos, C. (1989). Risk factors for suicide among Indian adolescents at a boarding school. *Public Health Reports, 104,* 609–615.

Maris, R. W. (2002). Suicide. *The Lancet, 360,* 319–326.

McHugh, P. R. (1994). Suicide and medical afflictions. *Medicine, 73,* 297–299.

Men with AIDS have highest risk of suicide. (1993, February). *AIDS Alert, 31*–33.

Mercy, J. A., Kresnow, M., & O'Carroll, P. W. (2001). Is suicide contagious? *American Journal of Epidemiology, 154,* 120–127.

Metha, A., Chen, E., Mulvenon, S., & Dode, I. (1998). A theoretical model of adolescent suicide risk. *Archives of Suicide Research, 4,* 115–133.

Morgan, G. (1993). Long term risks after attempted suicide: Identifying risk factors should help to reduce subsequent suicide. *British Medical Journal, 306,* 1626–1628.

Mortality among recent purchasers of handguns. (2000, January). *OB/GYN Clinical Alert,* 65.

Muldoon, M. F., Manuck, S. B., Mendelsohn, A. B., Kaplan, J. R., & Belle, S. H. (2001). Cholesterol reduction and non-illness mortality: Meta-analysis of randomized clinical trials. *British Medical Journal, 322,* 11–15.

Overholser, J. C., Adams, D. M., Lehnert, K. L., & Brinkman, D. C. (1995). Self-esteem deficits and suicidal tendencies among adolescents. *Journal of the American Academy of Child and Adolescent Psychiatry, 34,* 919–929.

Peterson, B. S., Zhang, H., Lucia, R. S., King, R. A., & Lewis, M. (1996). Risk factors for presenting problems in child psychiatric emergencies. *Journal of the American Academy of Child and Adolescent Psychiatry, 35,* 1162–1174.

Phillips, M. R., Yang, G., Zhang, Y., Wang, L., Ji, H., & Zhou, M. (2002). Risk factors for suicide in China: A national case-control psychological autopsy study. *Lancet, 360,* 1728–1736.

Pinto, A., & Whisman, M. A. (1996). Negative affect and cognitive biases in suicidal and nonsuicidal hospitalized adolescents. *Journal of the American Academy of Child and Adolescent Psychiatry, 35,* 158–166.

Pinto, A., Whisman, M. A., & Conwell, Y. (1998). Reasons for living in a clinical sample of adolescents. *Journal of Adolescence, 21,* 397–406.

Pohan, C. A., & Bailey, N. J. (1998). Including gays in multiculturalism. *Education Digest, 63,* 52–56.

Potthoff, S. J., Bearinger, L. H., Skay, C. L., Cassuto, N., Blum, R. W., & Resnick, M. D. (1998). Dimensions of risk behaviors among American Indian youth. *Archives of Pediatrics and Adolescent Medicine, 152,* 157–164.

Rebecca. D. A., Canobbio, B., Perper, J., Moritz, G., Allman, C., Liotus, L., et al. (1993). Bereavement or depression? The impact of the loss of a friend to suicide. *Journal of the American Academy of Child and Adolescent Psychiatry, 32,* 1189–1198.

Reinherz, H. Z., Giaconia, R. M., Silverman, A. B., Friedman, A., Pakiz, B., Frost, A. K., & Cohen, E. (1995). Early psychosocial risks for adolescent suicidal ideation and attempts. *Journal of the American Academy of Child and Adolescent Psychiatry, 34,* 599–612.

Remafedi, G. (1999). Suicide and sexual orientation: Nearing the end of controversy? *Archives of General Psychiatry, 56,* 876–885.

Report: Three million youths considered suicide in 2000. (2002, July). *Alcoholism Drug Abuse Weekly, 14,* 7.

Rew, L., Thomas, N., Homer, S. D., Resnick, M. D., & Beuhring, T. (2001). Correlates of recent suicide attempts in a triethnic group of adolescents. *Journal of Nursing Scholarship, 33,* 361–368.

Risk of suicide and past history of sexual assault. (1996). *American Family Physician, 54,* 1756–1758.

Roberts, R. E., Roberts, C. R., & Chen, Y. R. (1998). Suicidal thinking among adolescents with a history of attempted suicide. *Journal of the American Academy of Child and Adolescent Psychiatry, 37,* 1294–1300.

Roehrig, H. R., & Range, L. M. (1995). Recklessness, depression, and reasons for living in predicting suicidality in college students. *Journal of Youth and Adolescence, 24,* 723–729.

Rollins, J. A. (2001). Item of interest. *Pediatric Nursing, 27,* 422.

Rotello, G. (2001, January 16). Calling all parents. *The Advocate,* 112.

Sacks, J. J., Mercy, J. A., Ryan, G. W., & Parrish, R. G. (1994). Guns in the home, homicide and suicide. *Journal of the American Medical Association, 272,* 847–879.

Sample, I. (2000). Voice from the grave. *New Scientist, 167,* 2252–2269.

Sanislow, C. A., Grilo, C. M., Fehon, D. C., Axelrod, S. R., & McGlashan, T. H. (2003). Correlates of suicide risk in juvenile detainees and adolescent inpatients. *Journal of the American Academy of Child and Adolescent Psychiatry, 42,* 234–241.

Sargent, M. (1984). Adolescent suicide. *Journal of Child and Adolescent Psychotherapy, 1*(2), 49–50.

Scheel, K. R., & Westefeld, J. S. (1999). Heavy metal music and adolescent suicidality: An empirical investigation. *Adolescence, 34,* 253–273.

Sherman, F. T. (2002). I want to die. *Geriatrics, 57*(10), 8–9.

Silverman, J. G., Raj, A., Mucci, L. A., & Hathaway, J. E. (2001). Dating violence against adolescent girls and associated substance use, unhealthy weight control, sexual risk behavior, pregnancy and suicidality. *Journal of the American Medical Association, 286,* 572–579.

Simon, T. R., & Powell, K. E. (1999). Involvement in physical activity and risk for nearly lethal suicide attempts. *Sports and Exercise, 31,* 271.

Smith, G. D., Phillips, A. N., & Neaton, J. D. (1992). Smoking as an "independent" risk factor for suicide: An illustration of an artifact from observational epidemiology? *Lancet, 340,* 709–713.

Sonneck, G., & Wagner, R. (1996). Suicide and burnout of physicians. *Omega–The Journal of Death and Dying, 33,* 255–264.

Stein, D., Apter, A., Ratzoni, G., Har-Even, D., & Avidan, G. (1998). Association between multiple suicide attempts and negative affects in adolescents. *Journal of the American Academy of Child and Adolescent Psychiatry, 37,* 488–495.

Suicide among older persons. (1996). *Journal of the American Medical Association, 275,* 509–510.

Suicide and the elderly. (1996). *Health Facts, 21,* 5.

Suicide in doctors. (2002). *Journal of Epidemiology and Community Health, 56,* 237.

Suicide risk factors. (1985). *Children Today, 14,* 6–2.

Sullivan, A., & Brems, C. (1997). The psychological repercussions of the sociocultural oppression of Alaska native peoples. *Genetic, Social, and General Psychology Monographs, 123,* 411–441.

Swedo, S. E., Rettew, D. C., Kuppenheimer, M., Lum, D., Dolan, S., & Goldberger, E. (1991). Can adolescent suicide attempters be distinguished from at-risk adolescents? *Pediatrics, 88,* 620–630.

Teasdale, T. W., & Engberg, A. W. (2001). Suicide after traumatic brain injury: A population study. *Journal of Neurology, Neurosurgery and Psychiatry, 71,* 436–440.

Thatcher, W. G., Reininger, B. M., & Drane, J. W. (2002). Using path analysis to examine adolescent suicide attempts, life satisfaction and health risk behavior. *Journal of School Health, 72*(2), 71–78.

The suicide gene. (2000, February 7). *Maclean's,* 20.

Thompson, E. A., & Eggert, L. L. (1994). Discriminating suicide ideation among high-risk youth. *Journal of School Health, 64,* 361–368.

Thompson, E. A., Eggert, L. L., & Randell, B P. (2001). Evaluation of indicated suicide risk prevention approaches for potential high school dropouts. *American Journal of Public Health, 91,* 742–794.

Tortolero, S. R., & Roberts, R. E. (2001). Differences in nonfatal suicide behaviors among Mexican and European American middle school children. *Suicide and Life-Threatening Behavior, 31,* 214–223.

Valente, S. M., & Sunders, J. M. (1997). Managing depression among people with HIV disease. *Journal of the Association of Nurses in AIDS Care, 8*(1), 51–68.

Van Dongen, C. J. (1991). Experiences of family members after a suicide. *Journal of Family Practice, 33,* 375–381.

Vermeiren, R., Ruchkin, V., Leckman, P. E., Deboutte, D., & Schwab-Stone, M. (2002). Exposure to violence and suicide risk in adolescents: A community study. *Journal of Abnormal Child Psychology, 30,* 529–538.

Waern, M., Beskow, J., Runeson, B., & Skoog, I. (1996). High rate of antidepressant treatment in elderly people who commit suicide. *British Medical Journal, 313,* 1118–1119.

Waern, M., Beskow, J., Runeson, B., & Skoog, I. (1999). Suicidal feelings in the last year of life in elderly people who commit suicide, *Lancet, 354,* 917–918.

Why suicide is increasing among young Black men. (1996, August 12). *Jet,* 12–16.

Wichstrom, L. (2000). Predictors of adolescent suicide attempts: A nationally representative longitudinal study of Norwegian adolescents. *Journal of the American Academy of Child and Adolescent Psychiatry, 39,* 603–610.

Winters, N. C., Myers, K., & Proud, L. (2002). Ten-year review of rating scales. III: Scales assessing suicidality, cognitive style, and self-esteem. *Journal of the American Academy of Child and Adolescent Psychiatry, 41,* 1150–1231.

Women less likely than men to commit suicide. (2001, April. *USA Today* (Magazine), p. 10.

Wright, R. (1995, August 28). The evolution of despair. *Time,* 50–54.

Yaniv, G. (2001). Suicide intention and suicide prevention: An economic perspective. *Journal of Socio-Economics, 30,* 453–469.

Youth at risk. (1997, October 14). *The Advocate,* p. 15.

Zureik, M., Courbon, D., & Ducimetiere, P. (1996). Serum cholesterol concentration and death from suicide in men: Paris prospective study I. *British Medical Journal, 313,* 649–652.

Chapter 5

Assessing Suicidal Risk

Jonathan W. Carrier

The assessment, management, and treatment of a suicidal client are some of the most difficult tasks a counselor can face (Deutsch, 1984; Jobes, 1995). Bonner (1990) stated that client suicide may be a counselor's "worst fear, often paralyzing the clinician emotionally and interfering with sound clinical judgment and effective crisis resolution" (p. 232). Rogers, Gueulette, Abbey-Hines, Carney, and Werth (2001) found that 71% of their sample of 241 counselors reported having worked with individuals who had attempted suicide, with 28% having a client die by suicide. Although there have been countless prevention and intervention efforts made by mental health professionals over the past 40 years, the U.S. suicide rate has remained relatively stable (Rogers, 2001) and continues to be the 11th leading cause of death to Americans (Minino, Arias, Kochanek, Murphy, & Smith, 2002).

According to Range and Knott (1997), suicide assessment is of critical importance for the following reasons: (a) Assessment can help counselors identify individuals who are most in need of mental health intervention, (b) assessment provides an initial screening so at-risk individuals can be identified, and (c) assessment instruments are essential for research into this vital area. Juhnke (1994) stated that the three components necessary for a comprehensive suicide assessment are the clinical interview, empirical evaluation, and clinical consultation. This chapter outlines these three components of suicide assessment and delineates the methods in which each may be used in a counseling situation. The first part of the chapter introduces each component, and the second part discusses how to establish suicide risk through the marriage of the three components. Brief guidelines for postassessment measures are also given.

An important thing to note at the beginning of any discussion on the assessment of suicidal risk is that all assessments of suicide risk are actually assessments of *imminent* suicidal risk. The major difficulty in assessing suicidality is correctly distinguishing those individuals who will ultimately commit suicide from those who will not (Bongar, 2002). There is currently no way to tell reliably if an individual will commit suicide in the long-term course of his or her life (Motto, 1980; Pokorny, 1983). This is because suicide completion occurs so infrequently, when the whole of the U.S. population is taken into account, one could predict that an individual would not commit suicide and be correct 98%–99% of the time (Callahan, 1993). Thus, counselors can only accurately assess imminent suicidal risk that may occur in the next hour, day, week, or possibly even month. For this reason, assessments of suicidal risk must be done frequently when working with individuals who have been identified as imminently at risk for suicide.

Case Scenarios

The following are two case scenarios of potentially suicidal clients. These scenarios are applied toward the end of the chapter to provide an example of how a comprehensive assessment of suicidality may look in an actual counseling situation.

Case Scenario I: "Frank"

"Frank" is a 22-year-old Caucasian male who has come to your counseling clinic because he "just can't take the loneliness of it all anymore." His intake information states that he has recently been honorably discharged from the Army and has been taking classes at the local community college but has not picked a major course of study yet. He is not currently employed. He says he hasn't been sleeping well at night since he left the Army and has difficulty concentrating on things for any length of time. He says that his grades have always been in the average range, but over the last month all he feels like doing is trying to catch up on his sleep and it has been successively more difficult to get up and go to class. Because of his poor attendance, his grades have suffered. He has never been married and does not have a girlfriend. You note that his affect is somewhat flattened although he does smile occasionally. Also, he seems to avoid eye contact.

Case Scenario II: "Claudia"

"Claudia" is a 30-year-old international student from Italy and has been accompanied to the university's counseling center where you work by two of her roommates. You notice that Claudia's right hand and wrist are bandaged. She is reticent to speak with you but you gather from her friends that she is about to graduate from the university and her application to graduate school has not been accepted. Furthermore, she has just been denied permission to stay and work in the United States and must return to Italy within the next 2 months. Her friends tell you that Claudia has been extremely angry since she found out she had to leave the country and recently had a physical confrontation with another roommate who moved out of the apartment after the altercation. They further tell you that Claudia has been spending hours at a time locked in the bathroom and has been heard to yell, "I'll kill myself if they try to make me go back!" Earlier today, they heard a crash from the bathroom and had to force the door open to see what happened. They tell you that Claudia punched the mirror and had cut herself fairly severely. After taking her to the campus health center, where Claudia told the nurse she cut her hand while cooking, they talked Claudia into coming to see a counselor. Claudia is flushed and still seems angry but agrees to stay and talk with you for a while.

Clinical Interview

The accurate identification of suicidal individuals is a complex and difficult task for even the most able and accomplished counselor (Kaplan et al., 1994). When addressing client suicidality, there may be no more effective assessment tool than a thorough face-to-face clinical interview (Maris, Berman, Maltsberger, & Yufit, 1992; Motto, 1991). A clinical interview is a verbal, nonempirical method of assessing suicidality during a counseling session. It is essentially a list of questions or items designed to assess suicidal risk that are worked into the normal counseling milieu. Generally, the clinical interview of suicidality begins soon after a client makes an allusion to suicide or otherwise acts or speaks in a manner that causes the counselor to become aware of suicidal risk or ideation. The clinical interview may also begin without a client's admission of suicide ideation but with the counselor's identification of risk factors for suicide present in the client's life or experience. These risk factors, such as presence of a mental disorder, gender, chronic physical illness, recent losses, and psychosocial stressors, are discussed at length in chapter 4 (this volume) and are not duplicated here. If the counselor becomes cognizant of several suicide risk factors within the client's life, he or she should ask about suicidal ideation regardless of whether the client has brought it up or not. A common fear of many counselors is that asking directly about suicide may put ideas into a client's head (Sommers-Flanagan & Sommers-Flanagan, 1995). There is no clinical or empirical evidence that this occurs (Pipes & Davenport, 1990). On the contrary, clients may be relieved at the opportunity to talk about suicidal thoughts (Sommers-Flanagan & Sommers-Flanagan, 1995).

The clinical interview differs from empirical measures of suicide assessment in that it is less structured than empirical measures, and the questions asked concerning suicide are worked into the session through the use of counseling techniques and as part of the counseling relationship. Empirical measures of suicide assessment generally cover similar questions and items as the clinical interview but are presented in a list form to be read or rated by the counselor or completed in a paper-and-pencil or computerized format by the client. It is important to note that although many counselors utilize only the clinical interview during an assessment of suicide risk, it is highly recommended here that it be only the first of a three-part process and should be followed with empirical assessment and clinical consultation whenever possible. When dealing with a potentially life-and-death situation such as suicide, it is far better for the counselor to err on the side of caution and slightly overassess suicidal risk than to miss important information that could potentially save a life.

On the basis of his review of the literature, Bonner (1990) suggested that counselors take a three-component approach to the assessment of suicidal risk during a clinical interview. Using the acronym "M.A.P." he suggested that counselors should assess the client's:

1. *Mental state:* Is the individual thinking about suicide? "If so, are the thoughts brief and fleeting or intense and pervasive?" (p. 233).
2. *Affective state:* Does the individual exhibit symptoms of a mood disorder, particularly major depression or bipolar disorder?
3. *Psychosocial context:* "Client's mental and affective states . . . are influenced by a psychosocial context and life condition" (p. 234). What life conditions, such as negative life stress, social isolation, and interpersonal losses, seem too overwhelming for the individual to continue living with?

From Bonner's (1990) M.A.P. framework and a review of the extensive literature on the subject (Beck, Shuyler, & Herman, 1974; Beck, Steer, Kovacs, & Garrison, 1985; Brent, Perper, & Allman, 1987; Cohen, Test, & Brown, 1990; Isometsa, Aro, Henriksson, Heikkinen, & Lonnqvist, 1994; Keller, 1994; Kleepsies, Deleppo, Gallagher, & Niles, 1999; Motto, Heilbron, & Juster, 1985; Peruzzi & Bongar, 1999; Rogers, Lewis, & Subich, 2002; Rosenberg, 1999; Shneidman, 1985), the following list of indicators of increased risk for suicide should be assessed when conducting a clinical interview, with the first four being the most important indicators of immediate suicidal risk:

1. *Suicidal ideation and frequency and intensity of ideation:* The more frequent and intense the ideation, the more likely a suicide attempt will be.
2. *Plan and specificity of plan:* The more specific the plan, the more at risk the individual may be.

3. *Means and opportunity to carry out plan:* If an individual has the means and opportunity to carry out the suicide plan, the chances of suicide are greatly increased.
4. *Previous suicide attempts:* Many individuals die in their first attempt, but previous unsuccessful attempts increase future risk. Also, lethality of previous attempts can be an indicator of lethality of future attempts.
5. *DSM–IV diagnosis:* Mood disorders, particularly depression and bipolar disorder (according to the fourth edition of the *Diagnostic and Statistical Manual of Mental Disorders,* or *DSM–IV;* American Psychiatric Association, 1994), are high indicators of increased suicide risk. Also, research suggests individuals with schizophrenia are at increased levels of risk for suicide.
6. *Drug and/or alcohol abuse:* Drug and/or alcohol abuse may inhibit an individual's judgment to the point at which he or she may carry out a suicide attempt while under the influence when otherwise he or she may not.
7. *Hopelessness:* Research suggests that hopelessness may be an even better predictor of suicide than depression.
8. *Social isolation:* Individuals who have no one to "talk them out" of the act or "talk down" their ideation are at an increased risk of carrying out a suicide attempt.
9. *Gender:* More women than men attempt suicide, but many more men than women complete a suicide attempt.
10. *Anger:* Anger may fuel the violence of a suicide attempt.
11. *Psychosocial stressors:* Stressful life events such as unemployment, financial difficulty, and relationship difficulties increase suicide risk.
12. *Family history of suicide:* Research has shown a familial link to suicide attempts and ideation.

Furthermore, the following items are associated with being protective factors against suicide and should also be assessed in the clinical interview. The counselor may use them as tools to diminish an individual's suicidal ideation:

1. *Marriage:* Marriage is considered to be a protective factor against suicide.
2. *Children:* Children can be a strong factor against suicide. The individual may not attempt suicide because of the guilt of leaving children without a parent.
3. *Social network:* Having a strong social network can be a protective factor against suicide. The guilt of hurting loved friends or family members may be enough to keep the individual from carrying out suicide. Also, having someone to talk to when the person experiences suicidal thoughts can significantly diminish ideation.

4. *Responsibilities:* Anything the individual may feel guilty about leaving behind without having sorted out first, such as pets, property, money, and financial obligations, can reduce the risk of suicide.

It should be noted that the above lists of items to be assessed during a clinical interview are not fully comprehensive of every item counselors in practice may ask suicidal clients; such a list could potentially be hundreds of items long. They are, however, empirically and anecdotally supported in the literature on suicidology to be the most common items that theorists and clinicians feel are important for counselors to address when attempting to assess suicidal risk in an at-risk individual.

Of equal importance to the clinical interview is the manner in which it is approached and carried out. The clinical interview of suicidality must not be viewed as a list of questions to be fired one after another at the client. Suicide assessment requires a special relationship marked by genuine caring and nonjudgmental response (Leenaars, 1994). Counselors should first attempt to develop a working alliance and establish a trusting relationship with the individual. This can be facilitated by using such counseling cornerstones as empathy, genuineness, and authenticity (Kleespies, Deleppo, Mori, & Niles, 1998). The items on the clinical interview should be worked rather than forced into the counseling session. All efforts should be made by the counselor to remain calm and reassuring to convey empathic understanding of the individual's distress. Also, when deemed appropriate, the counselor may choose to include the individual's family or friends in the interview to increase a sense of safety and to provide additional diagnostic information (Kleepsies et al., 1999). Naturally, when dealing with a potentially suicidal client, "clinicians face a variety of immediate legal, ethical, and pragmatic concerns related to the task of handling a potentially life-threatening situation" (Rosenberg, 1999, p. 84). Because of this, consultation with another counselor cannot be stressed enough.

Empirical Evaluation

Empirical evaluation should be the second part of a comprehensive suicide assessment (Eyman & Eyman, 1991; Juhnke, 1994; Motto, 1991; Yufit, 1991). Survey data suggest that relatively few mental health professionals use suicide-specific assessment instruments or psychological tests when assessing a potentially suicidal client, instead opting to rely solely on face-to-face clinical interviews (Jobes, Eyman, & Yufit, 1995). Relying on a single assessment method can be risky in any counseling situation but can be lethal when dealing with a life-and-death situation such as suicide. Some studies have shown that mental health professionals using just a clinical interview may overlook suicide risk or significantly misperceive a suicidal client's motivations (Coombs et al., 1992; Hawton, Cole, O'Grady, & Osborn, 1982).

Empirical evaluations can significantly decrease such human errors and provide a perspective untarnished by the interviewing counselor's theoretical approach, worldview, or attributes. Many clinicians advocate the use of suicide scales, checklists, and psychological instruments to augment the clinical interview and the counselor's clinical judgment (Jobes et al., 1995; Juhnke, 1994). Empirical evaluation instruments may also bolster confidence for less experienced counselors and provide an extra source of diagnostic information from clients who may be resistant to the verbal clinical interview. Many instruments provide clinical intervention guidelines and can provide a kind of "empirical consultation" when another professional is not immediately available. It should be stressed here that although the empirical evaluation can be a powerful tool in the assessment of suicide risk, it should only be used in support of the clinical interview and never as a stand-alone tool for suicide assessment. There can be no substitute for the establishment of a counseling relationship and working alliance when assessing suicidal risk.

Standardized assessment of suicide risk began with relatively simple checklists of demographic variables associated with higher risk and had little or no documented reliability (Range & Knott, 1997). Such tests as the Scale for Predicting Subsequent Suicidal Behavior (Buglass & Horton, 1974) and the Los Angeles Suicide Prevention Center Suicide Potential Scale (Farberow, Helig, & Litman, 1968) were very short and consisted of 6–10 yes/no questions revolving around prior suicidal and psychiatric history and demographic variables and, in retrospect, were of limited value for use with suicidal individuals. Fortunately, many suicide assessments have evolved into reliable instruments with high levels of psychometric validity, in part because of a recent increase of interest in the evaluation of empirical methods of suicide assessment (Bagge & Osman, 1998; Garrison, Lewinsohn, Marsteller, Langhinrichsen, & Lann, 1991; Hagstrom & Gutierrez, 1998; Osman, Gutierrez, Kopper, Barrios, & Chiros, 1998; Range & Knott, 1997; Rothberg & Greer-Williams, 1992).

Range and Knott (1997) completed a comprehensive review of 20 suicide assessment instruments. The following discussion is a description of some of the instruments they have found to have adequate psychometric properties for use with suicidal clients.

Clinician-Rated Suicide Instruments

Clinician-rated instruments are administered by the counselor in a "checklist" or direct questioning format and are not provided to the client to manually fill out. Examples of clinician-rated suicide instruments are as follow:

1. *Scale for Suicide Ideation (SSI; Beck, Kovacs, & Weissman, 1979):* The SSI is a 19-item rating scale that measures the intensity of an individual's attitudes, behaviors, and plans to commit suicide. It

has been found to be both highly reliable and valid (Beck et al., 1979; Clum & Yang, 1995) and is considered to be a strong instrument for the assessment of suicidal risk. The SSI takes 5–10 minutes to administer.

2. *Modified Scale for Suicide Ideation (SSI-M; Miller, Norman, Bishop, & Dow, 1986):* A revised version of the SSI (Beck et al., 1979), the SSI-M was designed with standardized prompt questions so that it can be administered by both professionals and paraprofessionals. It has 18 items: 13 from the original SSI and 5 new ones related to intensity of suicidal ideation, courage and competency to attempt, and talk and writing about death. It is a reliable instrument (Miller et al., 1986), and although it has had no formal measures of predictive validity applied to it (Clum & Yang, 1995), it is considered to be a strong instrument (Range & Knott, 1997). It takes about 10 minutes to administer.

Self-Rated Suicide Instruments

Self-rated suicide instruments rely on the self-reports of potentially suicidal clients and are administered in a paper-and-pencil or computerized format. Some theorists propose that self-rated instruments may more accurately assess suicide risk than a clinical interview or other types of suicide assessment because the individual is less constrained by social desirability (Range & Knott, 1997). The following are examples of self-rated suicide instruments:

1. *Self-Rated Scale for Suicide Ideation (SSI-SR; Beck, Steer, & Ranieri, 1988):* Basically, the SSI-SR is a self-rated version of the SSI described above. It is composed of 19 items and shares the active suicidal desire and preparation scales with the SSI as well as the same scoring. The SSI-SR is highly reliable (Beck et al., 1988) and has been found to have good short-term predictive validity (Rudd, Dahm, & Rajab, 1993). It takes 10–15 minutes for an individual to complete the SSI-SR.

2. *Reasons for Living Inventory (RFL; Linehan, Goodstein, Nielsen, & Chiles, 1983):* The RFL is a 48-item self-report measure that assesses an individual's potential reasons for not committing suicide should the thought occur. The RFL is made up of six subscales: survival and coping beliefs, responsibility to family, child concerns, fear of suicide, fear of social disapproval, and moral objections. The RFL is a reliable instrument and has been found to be relatively valid (Connell & Meyer, 1991; Linehan et al., 1983; Osman et al., 1993). The RFL takes about 20 minutes to complete.

3. *Suicide Behaviors Questionnaire (SBQ; Linehan, 1981):* The original SBQ was a lengthy seven-page questionnaire designed as a clinician-rated interview of suicidal ideation but was abbreviated by Cole

(1988) through factor analysis into four questions. The SBQ is a reliable instrument (Cotton, Peters, & Range, 1995) and has face validity. It is widely used because of its ease of administration and scoring, but because of its short length, it is of limited range for use as anything other than a brief screening instrument. The SBQ takes less than 5 minutes to complete.

Suicide Assessment Instruments for Adolescents and Children

Surprisingly, although there has been a dramatic increase in child and adolescent suicide in recent years (Centers for Disease Control and Prevention, 2000), very few psychometrically sound instruments have been designed for use with this population. The following instruments were found by Range and Knott's (1997) review to be appropriate for use with children and adolescents:

1. *Suicidal Ideation Questionnaire (SIQ; Reynolds, 1987):* This questionnaire assesses an individual's thoughts about suicide in the past month. As well as an adult form, the SIQ has a junior high form of 15 items designed for use with 12- to 14-year-olds. It has been found to be both reliable and valid (Range & Antonelli, 1990; Reynolds, 1987). The SIQ takes about 15 minutes to administer.
2. *Suicidal Behaviors Questionnaire for Children (SBQ-C; Cotton & Range, 1993):* This is a simplified version of the SBQ described earlier. Because it consists of only four items and is written at a third-grade reading level, the SBQ-C is ideal for assessment of suicidal ideation in young children. It is a reliable (Cotton & Range, 1993) and valid instrument. Naturally, because of its similarity to the SBQ, it shares the same drawbacks and should only be used as a brief screening instrument. The SBQ-C takes less that 5 minutes to complete.

In selecting an empirical evaluation instrument for assessing suicidal risk, counselors should remain mindful that although there are potentially hundreds of questionnaires, scales, and checklists from which to choose, very few have had any type of formal studies to assess their psychometric properties applied to them. Empirical assessment of suicide risk is important, however, and should be a part of any comprehensive suicide assessment. Thus, it is recommended here that before selecting an instrument to use, counselors should take the time to make sure there are studies backing the instrument's reliability and validity for use with the counselor's desired population.

Clinical Consultation

Clinical consultation is the third and final part of a comprehensive suicide assessment. As important as consultation is in any counseling situation, it may be regarded as doubly so when dealing with a suicidal client. Consultation with a supervisor or a treatment team promotes a multifaceted approach and decreases the chance of an inaccurate assessment of a client's suicidality (Juhnke, 1994). Clinical consultation may also aid in insulating counselors from liability issues that may result from a faulty perception of client risk (Juhnke, 1994). Furthermore, dealing with suicidal clients is one of the most stressful of all clinical activities, and for the sake of their own mental and emotional health, suicide assessors should not work in isolation (Sommers-Flanagan & Sommers-Flanagan, 1995).

Ideally, a team of counselors could work with every client and consultation would be readily available at every instance it is needed. Sadly, this is not the case, and face-to-face clinical consultation is not always available. When a counselor feels there is need for clinical consultation regarding a potentially suicidal client but, for whatever reason, a supervisor or another counselor is not available, the counselor may be able to turn to a 24-hour emergency or crisis services number. This is not ideal, but it offers at least some measure of professional guidance when no other options are available. Naturally, in any situation in which there may be imminent danger to the counselor or client, law enforcement should immediately be contacted.

Establishing Suicide Risk

After the comprehensive assessment of suicidal risk has been completed, the next step is for the counselor to rate, based on all three parts of the assessment, the severity of suicidal risk. After the level of suicide risk has been determined, the counselor must then follow an appropriate course of action, which can range from establishing a no-suicide contract (Bongar, 1991) and an increase in counseling sessions (Joiner, Walker, Rudd, & Jobes, 1999) for low-to-moderate risk individuals to arranging psychiatric hospitalization on a voluntary or involuntary basis for individuals assessed to be in the severe and extreme risk categories.

Rating the Clinical Interview

As previously stated, the clinical interview is the most important aspect of a comprehensive suicide assessment and sets the initial risk level that may be added to during the empirical evaluation and clinical consultation. Although there are no uniformly accepted guidelines or scoring methods in the literature, Joiner, Walker, et al. (1999) provided the following continuum, adjusted for use with the model presented in this chapter, for suicide severity ratings that is of particular use for application gathered from the clinical interview:

1. *Nonexistent:* no identifiable suicidal symptoms, no past history of suicide attempts, and no or few other risk indicators.

2. *Mild:* (a) multiple suicide attempts with no other risk factors or (b) a nonmultiple attempter with suicide ideation of limited intensity and duration, no or vague plan, no or little means to carry out plan, and no or few other risk indicators.
3. *Moderate:* (a) multiple suicide attempts with vague plan, no or little means to carry out plan, and no or few other risk indicators; (b) nonmultiple attempter with moderate to severe ideation, moderate to definite plan, some to many means and opportunity to carry out plan, and few to some other risk indicators; or (c) nonmultiple attempter with severe ideation, vague plan, some means and opportunity to carry out plan, and few other risk indicators.
4. *Severe:* (a) multiple suicide attempts with moderate to severe ideation, little to moderate means and opportunity to carry out plan, and few to some other risk indicators or (b) nonmultiple attempter with severe ideation, moderate to definite plan, some to many means and opportunity to carry out plan, and some to many other risk indicators.
5. *Extreme:* (a) multiple suicide attempts with severe ideation, moderate to many means and opportunity to carry out plan, and few to many other risk indicators or (b) nonmultiple attempter with severe ideation, definite plan, many means and opportunity to carry out plan, and many other risk factors.

As can be seen from the above scale from Joiner, Walker, et al. (1999), counselors can obtain a good sense of client suicidality from the manner in which the client answers or addresses each item on the clinical interview, in particular the manner in which the client addresses the first four items on the clinical interview. For example, if a client thinks about suicide every now and then, has a vague plan and no means or opportunity to carry out the plan, and has never attempted suicide before, the counselor immediately knows that the client is at less initial risk of attempting suicide than an individual who considers suicide often, has a fairly specific plan with means and opportunity to carry out the plan, and has attempted suicide before. The next eight items on the clinical interview can be used by the counselor to obtain a clearer view of the picture painted by the first four questions. For instance, an individual with some ideation, a vague plan, no means or opportunity to carry out the plan, and no previous suicide attempts might initially be considered to have a mild risk of suicide. But, if the counselor finds through the next eight items on the clinical interview that the client meets the criteria for a mood disorder, abuses alcohol, exhibits hopelessness, has no social network, is male, is often angry, has recently lost a job, and has a family history of suicide, the counselor will immediately begin to consider this client in at least the moderate range for suicide risk and be aware that this could rapidly change to a high-risk situation.

Conversely, if the counselor finds that an individual is at extreme risk for suicide because the individual thinks about suicide frequently with a high level of intensity, has a well-defined plan with means and opportunity to carry out the plan, and has attempted suicide twice before, the assessment of extreme risk cannot be viewed as diminished even if the individual meets none of the next eight criteria. The first four indicators of suicide risk on the clinical interview set the initial standard of the comprehensive assessment and generally cannot be detracted from by the following eight.

Applying the Empirical Evaluation's Risk Assessment

After the counselor gets a sense of the individual's level of immediate suicidal risk through the use of the clinical interview, he or she must quantify this through the use of empirical evaluation. As has been previously stated, the counselor must be careful to choose an appropriate instrument of demonstrated worth for the population with whom he or she is working. For example, if a counselor were assessing an adolescent for suicidal risk, it would be inappropriate to use an instrument that, regardless of its psychometric merits for use with another population, was not designed for use with adolescents. As counselors who have worked with adolescents know, the difference between adolescents and other populations can be vastly different. Also, there are many instruments that possess wonderful face validity and contain lists of items or questions that seem extremely pertinent to the assessment of suicide risk but have had no or few studies supporting their psychometric properties applied to them. Without comprehensive studies supporting the instrument's reliability, validity, and scoring, an instrument should not be used in any counseling situation, let alone during an assessment of suicidal risk.

After the counselor has administered an appropriate instrument and scored it, he or she should compare the level of risk initially assessed in the clinical interview with the results of the empirical evaluation. Ideally, there would be a concordance between the clinical interview and the results of an empirical assessment of suicide risk (Joiner, Walker, et al., 1999). Unfortunately, this is not always the case. Joiner, Rudd, and Rajab (1999) studied this issue and discovered that discrepancies most often occurred because counselors took a better-safe-than-sorry approach and viewed clients more suicidal after the clinical interview than clients viewed themselves on self-report measures of suicide assessment. It is suggested here that taking such a better-safe-than-sorry approach in the clinical interview and initially assessing clients as more suicidal than they actually are is far better than being less cautious and assessing clients as less suicidal than they actually are. Discrepancies on the severity of suicide will occur between the clinical interview and empirical evaluation, but it is doubtful they will differ greatly (i.e., a clinical interview assessment of severe risk and an empirical evaluation assessment of mild risk). When discrepancies do occur, it is better for the counselor to treat the most severe risk assessment as the actual case. At any rate, discrepancies between the first two steps of a comprehensive suicide risk assessment can be cleared up a great deal by the third and final step of clinical consultation.

The Role of Clinical Consultation in Risk Assessment

Although consultation is important in any counseling situation, it becomes of dire significance during the risk assessment of a suicidal client. The clinical consultation serves the purpose of "tying" or "rethinking" the knot between the clinical interview and empirical evaluation. After the counselor has completed the clinical interview and empirical evaluation, he or she may wish to verify this finding with a supervisor or another counselor. This is not to say however, that if a client mentions the word suicide, the counselor should rush out and immediately obtain consultation. Provided below is a loose set of guidelines for when clinical consultation is most necessary and when it is not. It must be stated that these guidelines are not to be viewed as firm procedure and are only provided here as a recommendation. Anytime a counselor feels he or she needs support, consultation should be sought, regardless of what is recommended in the literature. Having said this, consultation is most likely needed when (a) the clinical interview or the empirical evaluation has resulted in a suicide risk severity level of moderate, severe, or extreme; (b) the clinical interview or empirical evaluation has resulted in a suicide risk severity level of nonexistent or mild but the counselor intuitively feels otherwise; or (c) there is a large discrepancy between the suicide risk severity rating of the clinical interview and the empirical assessment.

Post Assessment

Once the comprehensive assessment of suicidal risk has been completed and a risk level has been determined, what comes next? Other chapters in this volume deal with the actual counseling of suicidal clients, and it lies beyond the scope of this chapter to cover these extensive counseling interventions in any depth. However, the following sections do present a set of brief postassessment recommendations.

Moderate Risk

Joiner, Walker, et al. (1999) recommended the following interventions for an individual who has been assessed as being at moderate risk of suicide: (a) increase the frequency or duration of counseling sessions; (b) increase the client's involvement with family, friends, or other social supports; (c) frequently reevaluate suicidal ideation and risk indicators; (d) ensure 24-

hour availability of emergency crisis services; (e) consider referral for medication to treat mood disorder; and (f) establish a step-by-step emergency plan for the client to follow in case of an increase in suicidal thought or action.

Another highly effective suicide intervention for mild-to-moderate risk individuals is the *no-suicide contract*. Bongar (1991) described the no-suicide contract as a written or verbal statement in which the client agrees or promises not to make any kind of self-destructive gesture over a specified period of time on which the counselor and client both agree. Another part of the contract that should always be included is that the client agrees to call the counselor or a suicide crisis hotline if suicidal ideation increases or if the client feels that he or she is no longer able to contain suicidal impulses.

Severe and Extreme Risk

In the event that there is an assessment of severe or extreme suicidal risk and crisis intervention techniques do not work, there can be no other option but the immediate evaluation for psychiatric hospitalization (Joiner, Walker, et al. 1999; Peruzzi & Bongar, 1999). Ideally, the client can be convinced of voluntary hospitalization, but if this is not possible, procedures for involuntary hospitalization should immediately be pursued. Whenever possible, family members should be involved.

Case Applications for Assessing Suicidal Risk

The following case examples, introduced earlier, are intended to serve as illustrations of what the application of the material covered so far in this chapter might look like in an actual counseling situation. They are intended only as brief examples, however, and are designed to be simple so the reader can easily recognize the basic aspects of a comprehensive assessment of suicidal risk. Actual counseling situations will almost invariably be more complex. In the interest of brevity, the clinical interview in these cases does not cover all 12 items that should regularly be assessed but focuses on the all important first 4 items of suicide ideation, suicide plan, means and opportunity to carry out suicide plan, and prior suicide attempts.

Assessment of Suicidal Risk, Case I: "Frank"

Counselor: How long have you been feeling tired?

Frank: Pretty much since I got out of the Army 2 months ago, but it's been worse over the last few weeks. Lately it seems like I wake up four or five times a night and every time I wake up it's tough to fall back to sleep.

Counselor: Can you think of anything that would make you wake up at night? Maybe you have a lot on your mind?

Frank: No, that's part of the problem. I don't have anything on my mind. I don't do anything. I'm so lonely and bored sometimes I can't stand it.

Counselor: You've recently left the Army, where you probably knew a lot of people and had a lot of things to do. Now that you're out, you feel like there's nothing to do.

Frank: Yeah, my life has been pointless since I left the Army. When I was in, I was always going out, meeting my friends, having some drinks. Now I'm out and I don't know anybody and I can't seem to get anything going. I can't even get out of bed half the time. I'm not worth anything to anybody. Why bother going on anymore?

Counselor: Sounds like it has been hard adjusting to your new life.

Frank: What life? The only difference between me and a dead guy is I haven't gotten around to shooting myself yet.

Counselor: I'm glad you decided to come here before you did. Do you think of killing yourself often?

Frank: I don't know, sometimes I do when I'm laying in bed while class is going on and I can't get myself up to go. I think about getting a gun and putting an end to all this loneliness.

Counselor: Do you have a gun?

Frank: No, but I could always go buy one.

Counselor: Can you afford a gun?

Frank: Not really. The GI Bill covers my tuition and stuff, but doesn't leave a lot left over. Still, guns are pretty cheap.

Counselor: Did you ever think about how you would kill yourself if you had a gun?

Frank: I don't know. Just put it in my mouth and pull the trigger I guess. How hard can it be?

Counselor: Have you ever tried to kill yourself before?

Frank: No. I always thought it was the coward's way out. I'm not a coward.

Counselor: If suicide's the coward's way out and you're not a coward, do you think you would actually kill yourself, even if you had a gun?

Frank: Probably not. I only think about it when I'm alone and feeling so damn low I can't get out of bed.

Counselor: If you weren't alone, and had some friends to do things with, you probably wouldn't think about killing yourself at all.

Frank: Yeah, I'd be having too much fun to think about something like that. But the way things are now, just about anything would be better than this. I mean, who wants to be alone all the time?

Counselor: If you killed yourself, wouldn't you be leaving some people who cared about you all alone?

Frank: Yeah. It'd hurt my mom real bad. And my brother. He's about to graduate from high school and he was thinking about coming to school here and rooming with me for a while. Yeah I forgot about that. If I was gone it'd be worse on them than when my dad got cancer.

Counselor: Maybe if you started coming to see me every week, we could think of some ways to help you get moving again so your family wouldn't have to go through anything else.

Frank: Yeah, I could do that. Anything would be better than laying in bed all day.

Counselor: Before we start working together, you'll have to promise me that you wouldn't go and buy a gun or try to kill yourself. And if you felt like you were going to, you'd have to promise to call me or an emergency number first.

Frank: Yeah, I promise. I'm not seriously suicidal or anything, I just think about it every now and then when I'm real down.

Counselor: I know you've said that you wouldn't kill yourself and only think about it every now and then when you're feeling low, but anytime someone says they think about suicide, even if it's not often, I like to double check with this suicide questionnaire that I'd like you to fill out. Would you mind taking a couple of minutes to do it?

Frank: Yeah, I guess. I don't think I really need to, but if you want to be sure, I will.

The counselor in this situation covered several areas of the clinical interview, including the four most important, and was able to assess that Frank was at a mild risk for suicide. Although Frank had some suicidal ideation, he had only a vague plan and no immediate means to carry out his plan. Frank had no prior suicide attempts, and although he was socially isolated, the counselor was able to remind him of his family members, which was enough to make Frank take stock of the situation. It is important to note that although the counselor determined that Frank was not at a high level of suicide risk, he still followed up the discussion with a suicide contract. After the clinical interview, even though Frank and the counselor had established a verbal no-suicide contract, it would still be important for the counselor to administer an empirical evaluation of suicide risk to verify his initial risk assessment, which he did. Because of an assessment of only mild suicidal risk, which we will assume was also reflected in the empirical evaluation, it may not be crucial for the counselor to seek clinical consultation in this case.

Assessment of Suicidal Risk, Case II: "Claudia"

Counselor: From what you and your roommates have told me, it sounds like you're in a pretty rough situation.

Claudia: Yeah? Is that what it sounds like to you? I wouldn't call it rough. I'd call it the end of my life.

Counselor: Is there no life for you in Italy?

Claudia: Not as far as I'm concerned. The day they come to take me back is the day I'm out the window.

Counselor: When you say "out the window" do you mean you're thinking of committing suicide?

Claudia: I'm not thinking about doing it. I am doing it. I am not going back there. I've been here for 5 years. This is my home now. They can't just make me go like that.

Counselor: Do you have a plan worked out for killing yourself when they come to get you?

Claudia: Not that you'd care, but the moment they knock on the door, I'm taking as many pills as I can and going out the window. If for some reason a seven-story fall doesn't kill me, I'm sure the pills will.

Counselor: You've thought this through a great deal and it sounds like you're very serious about it, which concerns me greatly.

Claudia: Yeah I'm serious. I was serious the last time.

Counselor: You've tried to kill yourself before?

Claudia: Yeah, so? Why do you want to know all this? I suppose you're going to do the counselor thing and try to talk me out of it. They couldn't talk me out of it last time, I don't think you can now. Tell you what, counsel them into letting me stay and I won't do it. How's that?

Counselor: You're so angry right now. It's one of the worst things in the world to feel like there's nothing you can do to change your situation.

Claudia: Yeah, it is . . . when I came here, I had nothing, but I worked so hard to be able to afford and complete my degree and get into graduate school. They're going to win because I can't stop them from sending me back.

Counselor: No one wins if you kill yourself. Let's assume for the moment that what you say is true and there's no way you can appeal the decision long enough to get into graduate school and you have to go back to Italy for a while. Don't you have family there who would want to see you?

Claudia: Yeah, I have family there, but I will be a failure if I go back now. They said I wouldn't make it. When I left, I promised myself I wouldn't go back until I went as far as I could. I was going to show them that I made it.

Counselor: Isn't graduating from college showing them that you made it? Not only did you go to an entirely new country with nothing, you completed college and have a degree to prove it. Your family might be proud of you.

Claudia: Maybe . . . I just don't know what to do. I'm so overwhelmed right now.

Counselor: Perhaps together we might explore some options for things you could do. You said you had 2 months to leave the country. Two months is a long time. Do you agree that killing yourself right now will give us zero options?

Claudia: Yeah, I guess. I just got so angry when I found out I had to leave, I didn't know what to do. Two months is a long time. I won't kill myself yet.

Counselor: If we're going to try to work out some ideas together, it's important to me that you give me your promise that you won't kill or hurt yourself and sign a no-suicide contract that says won't kill or hurt yourself and if you feel like it, you'll call me or an emergency number first.

Claudia: Yeah, I'll sign it. I promise I won't do anything for at least 2 months.

> *Counselor:* Also, I would like it very much if you would complete a question-
> naire that will help me keep track of how suicidal you're feeling. We'll
> go over it together when you're done and talk about it.
> *Claudia:* Yeah, I'll fill it out. I just want to work all this out.

In this situation, the counselor was faced with a very angry client who felt that she had no other option but suicide. The counselor was quickly able to assess from the first four items on the clinical interview that the situation was serious. Initially, Claudia appeared at severe risk for suicide with a previous attempt, intense ideation, a clear plan, and opportunity to carry out the plan. Fortunately, the counselor was able to calm Claudia down and get her to sign a no-suicide contract. The counselor then administered an empirical evaluation of suicide risk, which we will assume reflected a moderate suicide risk. At this point, the counselor would obtain professional consultation from his or her supervisor. The supervisor would then help the counselor decide if inpatient treatment would be needed or if Claudia may be seen on a weekly or biweekly outpatient basis. Because Claudia's ideation and plan was linked to a particular event 2 months away (being forced to leave the country) and agreed to the no-suicide contract, the counselor and supervisor would probably agree to assess Claudia at a moderate level of suicide risk but monitor her ideation closely and be prepared to initiate inpatient psychiatric treatment quickly, especially as her departure date neared. Ideally, through counseling, Claudia would become reconciled with returning to Italy or find a legal way to stay in the United States, but the counselor would remain mindful and ready for any eventuality.

Adaptations for Diversity

Sensitivity to cultural differences between the counselor and the client is always important in any counseling relationship but may be especially so during an assessment of suicidality. Turner and Hersen (1994) stated that counselors assessing minority clients can be confronted by culture or race-related behaviors that may be taken out of context or misunderstood. In such circumstances, it may be prudent for the counselor to consult with another clinician who shares the same race, ethnicity, socioeconomic group, and gender as the client so important behaviors are not overlooked (Kleepsies et al., 1999). Although the literature covers some unique suicide risk factors (discussed in chap. 4, this volume) for different minority groups, it is practically devoid of information regarding assessment, particularly empirical evaluation, of imminent suicidal risk for these individuals. There is an obvious need for future research to address this dearth of information.

One population counselors may want to be especially mindful of during an assessment of imminent suicide risk are individuals who have a chronic or life-threatening illnesses or disability. The acceptance of death in terminally ill individuals may drastically increase suicidal ideation and cause them to take the "inevitable" into their own hands to shorten their suffering or relieve the burden they may feel they place on their loved ones. Assisted suicide, covered in chapter 6, relates directly to this. Individuals with chronic illnesses or disability may also be at an increased risk for suicide. It is generally thought that individuals with congenital (individuals born with illness or disability) illnesses or disabilities are not in as great a risk for suicide as are individuals with adventitious (acquired sometime after birth) illnesses or disabilities because they have never known any other kind of functioning. The dramatic change in functioning that one may experience after contracting a life-threatening illness or sustaining a serious injury that leads to a permanent disability can damage an individual's sense of self and well-being to such an extent that suicide seems the best possible option. For example, although suicide is the 11th leading cause of death for the general U.S. population, it is the 3rd leading cause of death for individuals with a spinal cord injury and the leading cause of death for individuals with paraplegia (Devivo, Black, Richards, & Stover, 1991; Devivo, Black, & Stover, 1993; Hartkopp, Bronnum-Hansen, Seidenschur, & Biering-Sorenson, 1997). Counselors working with this population who are unfamiliar with the assessment of adaptation to disability should immediately consult with a professional, such as a rehabilitation counselor, skilled in this area.

Summary

The assessment, management, and treatment of a suicidal client are some of the most difficult tasks a counselor can face. Counselors must realize that all assessments of suicidal risk are actually assessments of imminent suicidal risk, as it is impossible to accurately predict suicide beyond a few weeks. The three components necessary for a comprehensive suicide assessment are the clinical interview, empirical evaluation, and clinical consultation. The clinical interview consists of four crucial items (suicidal ideation, suicide plan, means to carry out suicide plan, and previous suicide attempts) and eight supporting items intended to add to or clarify the information gathered from the first four. Empirical evaluation is necessary to verify the initial risk level assessed during the clinical interview and may serve to, in the case of client-rated instruments, factor out answers colored by social desirability. Counselors must be careful to select only empirical evaluation instruments that have adequate psychometric properties for the population they are working with. Clinical consultation, the third and final step in a comprehensive suicide assessment, is necessary to provide support for counselors who need verification of a risk assessment or who otherwise require assistance with a potentially suicidal individual.

Establishment of suicide risk is a marriage of the three components of a comprehensive suicide assessment and can be broken down into risk categories of nonexistent, mild, moderate, severe, and extreme. Individuals in the moderate risk category can benefit from an intensification of counseling and social support services on an outpatient basis. Individuals in the severe and extreme risk categories who do not respond to crisis intervention techniques must be hospitalized on a voluntary or involuntary basis.

Counselors assessing minority clients for suicide may be confronted by culture or race-related behaviors that may be taken out of context or misunderstood. In such circumstances, counselors may wish to consult with another clinician who shares the same race, ethnicity, socioeconomic group, and gender as the client so important behaviors are not overlooked. Individuals with disabilities, particularly life-threatening and permanent disabilities, may be a population that at are greater risk for suicide because of the nature of hopelessness of terminal illness and the traumatic change in the individual's sense of self and well-being after sustaining a permanent disability. Counselors who are not trained in the assessment of adaptation to chronic illness and disability who are working with potentially suicidal clients with disabilities should immediately seek consultation with a professional skilled in working with this population, such as a rehabilitation counselor.

References

American Psychiatric Association. (1994). *Diagnostic and statistical manual of mental disorders* (4th ed.). Washington, DC: Author.

Bagge, C., & Osman, A. (1998). The suicide probability scale: Norms and factor structure. *Psychological Reports, 83*, 637–638.

Beck, A. T., Kovacs, M., & Weissman, A. (1979). Assessment of suicidal ideation: The Scale for Suicidal Ideation. *Journal of Consulting and Clinical Psychology, 47*, 343–352.

Beck, A. T., Schuyler, D., & Herman, I. (1974). Development of suicide intent scales. In A. T. Beck, H. L. P. Resnik, & D. J. Lettieri (Eds.), *The prediction of suicide* (pp. 45–46). Bowie, MD: Charles Press.

Beck, A. T., Steer, R. A., Kovacs, M., & Garrison, B. (1985). Hopelessness and eventual suicide: A 10-year prospective study of patients hospitalized with suicidal ideation. *American Journal of Psychiatry, 142*, 559–563.

Beck, A., Steer, R., & Ranieri, W. (1988). Scale for Suicide Ideation: Psychometric properties of a self-report version. *Journal of Clinical Psychology, 44*, 499–505.

Bongar, B. (1991). *The suicidal patient.* Washington, DC: American Psychological Association.

Bongar, B. (2002). *The suicidal patient: Clinical and legal standards of care* (2nd ed.). Washington, DC: American Psychological Association.

Bonner, R. L. (1990). A "M.A.P" to the clinical assessment of suicide risk. *Journal of Mental Health Counseling, 12*, 232–236.

Brent, D. A., Perper, J. A., & Allman, C. J. (1987). Alcohol, firearms, and suicide among youth. *Journal of the American Medical Association, 257*, 3369–3372.

Buglass, D., & Horton, J. (1974). A scale for predicting subsequent suicidal behavior. *British Journal of Psychiatry, 124,* 573–578.

Callahan, J. (1993). Blueprint for an adolescent suicidal crisis. *Psychiatric Annals, 23,* 263–270.

Centers for Disease Control and Prevention. (2000). *Suicide in the United States.* Atlanta, GA: National Center for Injury Prevention and Control.

Clum, G. A., & Yang, B. (1995). Additional support for the reliability and validity of the Modified Scale for Suicide Ideation. *Psychological Assessment, 7,* 122–125.

Cohen, L., Test, M., & Brown, R. (1990). Suicide and schizophrenia: Data from a prospective community treatment study. *American Journal of Psychiatry, 147,* 602–607.

Cole, D. A. (1988). Hopelessness, social desirability, depression, and parasuicide in two college student samples. *Journal of Consulting and Clinical Psychology, 56,* 131–136.

Connell, D. K., & Meyer, R. G. (1991). The Reasons for Living Inventory and a college population: Adolescent suicidal behaviors, beliefs, and coping skills. *Journal of Clinical Psychology, 47,* 485–489.

Coombs, D. W., Miller, H. L., Alarcon, R., Herlihy, C., Lee, J. M., & Morrison, D. P. (1992). Presuicide attempt communications between parasuicides and consulted caregivers. *Suicide and Life-Threatening Behavior, 22,* 289–302.

Cotton, C. R., Peters, D. K., & Range, L. M. (1995). Psychometric properties of the Suicidal Behaviors Questionnaire. *Death Studies, 19,* 391–397.

Cotton, C. R., & Range, L. M. (1993). Suicidality, hopelessness, and attitudes toward life and death in children. *Death Studies, 17,* 185–191.

Deutsch, C. J. (1984). Self-reported sources of stress among psychotherapists. *Professional Psychology: Research and Practice, 15,* 833–845.

Devivo, M. J., Black, K. J., Richards, J. S., & Stover, S. L. (1991). Suicide following spinal cord injury. *Paraplegia, 29,* 625–627.

Devivo, M. J., Black, K. J., & Stover, S. L. (1993). Causes of death during the first 12 years after spinal cord injury. *Archives of Physical Medicine and Rehabilitation, 74,* 248–254.

Eyman, J. R., & Eyman, S. K. (1991). Personality assessment in suicide prediction. *Suicide and Life-Threatening Behavior, 21,* 37–55.

Farberow, N., Helig, S., & Litman, R. (1968). *Techniques in crisis intervention: A training manual.* Los Angeles: Suicide Prevention Center.

Garrison, C. Z., Lewinsohn, P. M., Marsteller, F., Langhinrichesen, J., & Lann, I. (1991). The assessment of suicidal behavior in adolescents. *Suicide and Life-Threatening Behavior, 21,* 217–230.

Hagstrom, A. H., & Gutierrez, P. M. (1998). Confirmatory factor analysis of the Multi-Attitude Suicide Tendency Scale. *Journal of Psychopathology and Behavioral Assessment, 20,* 173–186.

Hartkopp, A., Bronnum-Hansen, H., Seidenschnur, A. M., & Biering-Sorenson, F. (1997). Survival and cause of death after traumatic spinal cord injury: A long-term epidemiological survey from Denmark. *Spinal Cord, 35*, 76–85.

Hawton, K., Cole, D., O'Grady, J., & Osborn, M. (1982). Motivational aspects of deliberate self-poisoning in adolescents. *British Journal of Psychiatry, 14*, 286–291.

Isometsa, E. T., Aro, H. M., Henriksson, M. M., Heikkinen, M. E., & Lonnqvist, J. K. (1994). Suicide in major depression in different treatment settings. *Journal of Clinical Psychiatry, 55*, 523–527.

Jobes, D. A. (1995). The challenge and promise of clinical suicidology. *Suicide and Life-Threatening Behavior, 25*, 437–449.

Jobes, D. A., Eyman, J. R., & Yufit, R. I. (1995). How clinicians assess suicide risk in adolescents and adults. *Crisis Intervention and Time-Limited Treatment, 2*, 1–12.

Joiner, T. E., Rudd, M. D., & Rajab, M. H. (1999). Agreement between self- and clinician-rated suicidal symptoms in a clinical sample of young adults: Explaining discrepancies. *Journal of Consulting and Clinical Psychology, 67*, 171–176.

Joiner, T. E., Walker, R. L., Rudd, M. D., & Jobes, D. A. (1999). Scientizing and routinizing the assessment of suicidality in outpatient practice. *Professional Psychology: Research and Practice, 30*, 447–453.

Juhnke, G. A. (1994). Teaching suicide risk assessment to counselor education students. *Counselor Education and Supervision, 34*, 52–58.

Kaplan, M. L., Asnis, G. M., Sanderson, W. C., Keswani, L., De Lecuona, J. M., & Joseph, S. (1994). Suicide assessment: Clinical interview vs. self-report. *Journal of Clinical Psychology, 50*, 294–298.

Keller, M. (1994). Depression: A long-term illness. *British Journal of Psychiatry, 165*, 9–15.

Kleespies, P. M., Deleppo, J. D., Gallagher, P. L., & Niles, B. L. (1999). Managing suicidal emergencies: Recommendations for the practitioner. *Professional Psychology: Research and Practice, 30*, 454–463.

Kleespies, P. M., Deleppo. J. D., Mori, D. L., & Niles, B. L. (1998). *Emergencies in mental health practice: Evaluation and management.* New York: Guilford Press.

Leenaars, A. A. (1994). Crisis intervention with highly lethal suicidal people. In A. A. Leenaars, J. T. Maltsberger, & R. A. Neimeyer (Eds.), *Treatment of suicidal people* (pp. 45–59). Washington, DC: Taylor & Francis.

Linehan, M. M. (1981). *Suicidal behaviors questionnaire.* Unpublished inventory, University of Washington, Seattle.

Linehan, M. M., Goodstein, J. L., Nielsen, S. L., & Chiles, J. A. (1983). Reasons for staying alive when you are thinking of killing yourself: The Reasons for Living Inventory. *Journal of Consulting and Clinical Psychology, 51*, 276–286.

Maris, R. W., Berman, A. L., Maltsberger, J. T., & Yufit, R. I. (1992). *Assessment and prediction of suicide.* New York: Guilford Press.

Miller, I. W., Norman, W. H., Bishop, S. B., & Dow, M. G. (1986). The Modified Scale for Suicide Ideation: Reliability and validity. *Journal of Consulting and Clinical Psychology, 54,* 724–725.

Minino, A. M., Arias, E., Kochanek, K. D., Murphy, S. I., & Smith, B. L. (2002). *Deaths: Final data for 2000* (National Vital Statistics Reports No. 50). Hyattsville, MD: National Center for Health Statistics.

Motto, J. A. (1980). Suicide risk factors in alcohol abuse. *Suicide and Life-Threatening Behavior, 10,* 230–238.

Motto, J. A. (1991). An integrated approach to estimating suicide risk. *Suicide and Life-Threatening Behaviors, 21,* 74–89.

Motto, J., Heilbron, D., & Juster, R. (1985). Suicide risk assessment: Development of a clinical risk instrument. *American Journal of Psychiatry, 142,* 680–686.

Osman, A., Gifford, J., Jones, T., Lickiss, L., Osman, J., & Wenzel, R. (1993) Psychometric evaluation of the Reasons for Living Inventory. *Psychological Assessment, 5,* 154–158.

Osman, A., Gutierrez, P. M., Kopper, B. A., Barrios, F. X., & Chiros, C. E. (1998). The Positive and Negative Suicide Ideation Inventory: Development and validation. *Psychological Reports, 82,* 783–793.

Peruzzi, N., & Bongar, B. (1999). Assessing risk for suicide in patients with major depression: Psychologist's views of critical factors. *Professional Psychology: Research and Practice, 30,* 576–580.

Pipes, R. B., & Davenport, D. S. (1990). *Introduction to psychotherapy: Common clinical wisdom.* Englewood Cliffs, NJ: Prentice Hall.

Pokorny, A. D. (1983). Prediction of suicide in psychiatric patients: Report of a prospective study. *Archives of General Psychiatry, 40,* 249–257.

Range, L. M., & Antonelli, K. B. (1990). A factor analysis of six commonly used instruments associated with suicide among college students. *Journal of Personality Assessment, 55,* 804–811.

Range, L. M., & Knott, E. C. (1997). Twenty suicide assessment instruments: Evaluation and recommendations. *Death Studies, 21,* 25–58.

Reynolds, W. M. (1987). *Suicide Ideation Questionnaire: Professional manual.* Odessa, FL: Psychological Assessment Resources.

Rogers, J. R. (2001). Psychological research into suicide: Past, present and future. In D. Lester (Ed.), *Suicide: Resources for the new millennium* (pp. 31–44). Philadelphia: Brunner-Routledge.

Rogers, J. R., Gueulette, C. M., Abbey-Hines, J., Carney, J. V., & Werth, J. L., Jr. (2001). Rational suicide: An empirical investigation of counselor attitudes. *Journal of Counseling & Development, 79,* 365–372.

Rogers, J. R., Lewis, M. M., & Subich, L. M. (2002). Validity of the suicide assessment checklist in an emergency crisis center. *Journal of Counseling & Development, 80,* 493–502.

Rosenberg, J. I. (1999). Suicide prevention: An integrated training model using affective and action-based interventions. *Professional Psychology: Research and Practice, 30*, 83–87.

Rothberg, J. M., & Greer-Williams, C. (1992). A comparison and review of suicide prevention scales. In R. W. Maris, A. L. Berman, J. T. Maltsberger, & R. T. Yufit (Eds.), *Assessment and prediction of suicide* (pp. 202–217). New York: Guilford Press.

Rudd, M. D., Dahm, P. F., & Rajab, M. H. (1993). Diagnostic comorbidity in persons with suicidal ideation and behavior. *American Journal of Psychiatry, 150*, 928–934.

Shneidman, E. S. (1985). *Definition of suicide.* New York: Wiley.

Sommers-Flanagan, J., & Sommers-Flanagan, R. (1995). Intake interviewing with suicidal patients: A systematic approach. *Professional Psychology: Research and Practice, 26*, 41–47.

Turner, S. M., & Hersen, M. (1994). *Diagnostic interviewing* (2nd ed.). New York: Plenum Press.

Yufit, R. I. (1991). American Association of Suicidology presidential address: Suicide assessment in the 1990's. *Suicide and Life-Threatening Behaviors, 21*, 152–163.

Chapter 6

Assisted Suicide
Ethical Issues

Barbara Richter Herlihy and Zarus E. P. Watson

Assisted suicide is an issue that challenges the core values and assumptions that counselors bring to their work with clients. As a rule, when clients reveal that they are contemplating suicide, the counselor's interventions are aimed at preventing these clients from harming themselves. Guiding assumptions for these interventions are that the desire to commit suicide is temporary and that clients can realize, through counseling, that there are better options than deliberately ending their lives. Clients who request aid in dying through assisted suicide, however, may be terminally ill or be suffering from a degenerative disease for which there is no cure. They may have no hope for improvement in their condition or quality of life. Thus, the assumptions that usually guide counselors in their work with suicidal clients are called into question here.

Over the past decade, a question that has been hotly debated is whether people who are terminally ill, have an incurable condition, or are in intolerable pain have a right to choose the time and the means of their own death by requesting aid in dying, or assisted suicide. The debate has been fueled by medical advances that have drastically reduced the occurrence rate of death at an early age caused by opportunistic infections. Due in large measure to the aging of American society and to ongoing developments in life-saving and life-sustaining medical technology, death in our society now more commonly occurs at an advanced age and as a result of chronic and degenerative diseases (Battin, 1994). As the issue of assisted suicide comes more to the forefront of medical practice, mental health care professionals, including counselors, will be called on more frequently to work with clients who are considering a request for aid in dying and with their families and significant others. To be effective as helpers, counselors need to be clear about their own beliefs and values regarding this issue. They also need to carefully consider the ethical issues involved.

We make no claim to having the answers to questions regarding the morality of assisted suicide or whether counselors have a role in clients' end-of-life decision making. We recognize that our own views have been influenced by our social conditioning—as a female and a male, as persons of Caucasian and of African American primary descent groups, and as persons raised in different religious traditions, among other factors—and that, as professional counselors, you may form conclusions that are very different from ours. Rather, we hope to present a balanced view of the issues surrounding assisted suicide and to stimulate your thinking regarding whether you want to work with clients who wish to hasten their own deaths, and if so, how you can provide counseling services that are ethically sound and clinically effective.

In the first section of this chapter, we identify the various means by which a person can achieve a hastened death, including assisted suicide, and we present a brief history that describes how our society's views on assisted suicide have fluctuated from the beginning of the 20th century into the new millennium. The focus of the chapter then turns to the role of mental health professionals in assisted suicide decision making of clients. Positions taken by professional associations, ethical issues that must be addressed, and adaptations for counseling culturally diverse clients are examined. The chapter concludes with guidelines for practice in working with clients who are considering a request for hastened death through assisted suicide.

Forms of Hastened Death

Various terms have been used to describe the process of assisting someone to achieve a hastened death. *Euthanasia* has become an emotionally charged term in the debate over assisted suicide. Although it is given varying definitions in the literature, its literal meaning as translated from the Greek is "a good death." It seems safe to assume that most people would want to have a good death, which might entail living in good health to a ripe old age and dying quietly in one's sleep. This ideal death will not be realized by everyone, however. Some individuals, such as those who are terminally ill, have an incurable and degenerative condition, or are in intolerable pain, might request a hastened death. Physician-assisted suicide is only one of a number of means by which an individual's death might be hastened. There is a continuum of what is demanded from others, ranging from acquiescence in a person's decision to performing an active intervention to cause death.

Refusal is a means of hastened death that requires little or no active intervention on the part of others. Refusal is a type of planned death in which a person dies because of declining to undergo medical or life-sustaining procedures (Lester & Leenaars, 1996). A person might voluntarily cease to consume food and water or might refuse to undergo surgery that might prolong life. *Passive euthanasia* is similar because it occurs when measures are not taken that might prolong a person's life. It differs from refusal, though, because it requires others to choose not to take life-saving measures (Albright & Hazler, 1995). An example might be a "do not resuscitate" order, a circumstance in which medical personnel "allow" a person's decision to be carried out by failing to take action to prevent death from occurring.

When a person is comatose or brain-dead, *withdrawal* of life support may hasten that person's death. In this circumstance, others make an affirmative decision to cease life-sustaining treatment for people who cannot decide for themselves (Lester & Leenaars, 1996). In the absence of advance directives made by the patient, this is considered to be *involuntary euthanasia* because the patient did not participate in the decision. A well-known example is the Karen Quinlan case, which involved a prolonged legal battle by a young woman's family for their daughter's "right to die" rather than live in a persistent vegetative state.

Assisted suicide, or *physician-assisted suicide* (PAS), is sometimes referred to as "aid in dying." This involves providing the means by which a person can end her or his life after a competent person has explicitly requested assistance in hastening death. It is not actually performed by a physician, although the physician would be the person providing the means for death to occur (Hendin, 1998).

Rational suicide is a term favored by proponents of the right of individuals to request aid in dying. These proponents believe that such a request can be a rational response to an incurable or terminal condition or to intolerable pain. Opponents of assisted death believe that the term "rational suicide" is an oxymoron, because no one who is thinking rationally would choose death (Jamison, 1997).

As a counselor, determining whether you believe that suicide can be a rational choice is only one of the questions you will need to answer for yourself in deciding whether you will work with clients who request assisted suicide. Assisted suicide is a controversial and emotionally charged issue, and regardless of what decision you make, you probably will have professional colleagues who applaud you and others who disapprove of the stance you have taken.

Historical Perspectives on Assisted Suicide

In most of the developed world, assisted suicide is held to be both illegal and a violation of social mores. Western culture, influenced by the Judeo-Christian tradition that affirms life as a gift from God even when it involves suffering, generally endorses the belief that life is preferable to death (Albright & Hazler, 1995). In the Western world, an exception is the Netherlands, where PAS has been traditionally practiced as a socially acceptable manner of ending life for over 30 years. Sanctioned by the Dutch legislature in 1993, assisted suicide can now be practiced there without legal ramifications as long as these criteria are observed: The individual must repeatedly and freely initiate the request and must be in a state of unrelenting pain and suffering from which no relief is possible, and the assisting physician must receive a concurring opinion from another consulting physician (Emmanuel, 1994).

In the United States, assisted suicide is illegal in most jurisdictions, although the practice has had its advocates since the 1870s. Interest in euthanasia developed around the beginning of the 20th century in conjunction with advances in medicine, increases in life expectancy, and the birth of the modern hospital as an institution that was able to provide curative medical and surgical treatment (Hendin, 1998). After initiatives to legalize PAS were introduced and defeated in Ohio in 1905 and in Iowa soon thereafter, no further proposals were made for three decades (Hendin). Public interest was revived in the 1930s when the first euthanasia society was formed but declined again in the 1940s in the wake of abuses of euthanasia in Nazi Germany during World War II.

It was not until the 1970s and 1980s that interest in PAS as an alternative to a painful and undignified death experienced a resurgence, fueled largely by the AIDS epidemic (Rogers & Britton, 1994; Werth, 1992) and an increase in the number of Americans who were living to an advanced age. Since that time, there have been continuing efforts to bring the issue before the public. One of the chief advocates of assisted suicide has been Derek Humphry, the founder of the Hemlock Society, an organization that supports the right of terminally ill individuals to determine their own course of action regarding death. Humphry's book, *Final Exit* (1993), describes in detail procedures for committing suicide and has generated considerable controversy. In addition, a great deal of publicity has attended the work of one physician, Dr. Jack Kervorkian, who has assisted numerous individuals to end their lives (Hendin, 1998; Kiser, 1996).

The question of the legality of assisted suicide was considered in 1997 by the U.S. Supreme Court, when it heard oral arguments on appeals to two Circuit Court decisions, *Vacco v. Quill* (1997) and *Washington v. Glucksberg* (1997). In these two cases, the Second and Ninth Circuit Courts had struck down criminal prohibitions against assisted suicide in the states of New York and Washington. Although the two circuit courts had used different reasoning, they both had affirmed that, within certain circumstances, individuals had the option to select the manner and hasten the time of a quickly and inevitably approaching death. In June 1997, the Supreme Court unanimously held in both cases that there is not a constitutional right to PAS, thus leaving it up to the individual states to determine whether or not to allow the practice (Werth & Gordon, 2002).

At the present time, Oregon is the only state that has legalized PAS. In 1994, the voters in that state approved the Oregon Death With Dignity Act (1995). Because of legal and legislative challenges, the Act was not implemented until 1997 when Oregon voters reaffirmed their approval of the right to physician-assisted aid in dying. Similar proposed legislation in other states has not been successful. Ballot initiatives were defeated in Washington state in 1991 (Callahan, 1994; Kiser, 1996) and in Maine in 2000 (Werth & Gordon, 2002), both by narrow margins. An attempt to legalize PAS in California in 1992 was also defeated. In several other states, the laws regarding PAS are ambiguous (Manetta & Wells, 2001).

Counselors who are willing to work with clients who request aid in dying will need to know the relevant laws in the state where they practice. In addition to legal considerations, PAS presents a host of ethical quandaries for mental health professionals. The next section of the chapter focuses on ethical issues that various mental health professionals face in counseling clients who are considering a request for PAS.

Mental Health Professional Associations' Positions on Assisted Suicide

It is increasingly likely that mental health professionals, including counselors, social workers, psychiatrists, and psychologists, will be called on to provide services to clients who want to explore options to hasten their deaths. The major professional associations of these mental health providers have taken differing positions on whether their members should be involved in PAS decisions of their clients. The positions of these associations are presented next, to provide readers with a sense of the spectrum of professional opinion.

Social Workers

The National Association of Social Workers (NASW) is the only one of the major mental health professions that has a policy statement on assisted suicide. In 1993 the NASW, in response to a request from the membership who felt a need for guidelines, published "Client Self-Determination in End-of-Life Decisions." Taking care to note that the association was not taking a position on the morality of end-of-life decisions, the statement affirmed the right of individuals to make their own choices regarding assisted suicide. In the document, the NASW took the stance that social workers may counsel terminally ill individuals regarding PAS and that they may even be present during an assisted suicide if the client so requests. As described in the policy statement, the social worker's role is to help clients who are considering PAS to "express their thoughts and feelings, to facilitate exploration of alternatives, to provide information to make an informed choice, and to deal with grief and loss issues" (National Association of Social Workers, 1993, p. 60). Alternatives that the social worker should explore with the client include pain management, counseling, hospice care, nursing home placement, and advance health care directives.

167

The NASW policy statement further describes the social worker's role as encouraging the involvement of the client's significant others in end-of-life decision making and providing them with support during their grieving process. Acknowledging that not all social workers would be comfortable dealing with PAS issues, the statement left association members free to participate or not, according to their own values and beliefs. Social workers who choose not to participate have an obligation to refer the client. The statement was also careful to include the caveat that social workers must perform their roles in PAS decisions with full knowledge of and compliance with the law. Because the laws on PAS differ from state to state, social workers who choose to participate in the end-of-life decisions of their clients would need to know the law in the state where they practice and would be wise to seek a legal opinion regarding their involvement.

Although the other major mental health professions have not issued policy statements regarding PAS, some insight into their positions can be gained by examining their decisions whether or not to join *amicus curiae* ("friend of the court") briefs submitted to the U.S. Supreme Court in 1997, and from other public statements they have issued.

Psychiatrists

When the U.S. Supreme Court agreed to deliberate the PAS cases in 1997, the American Psychiatric Association joined with the American Medical Association (AMA) in an *amicus curiae* brief opposing PAS. Because psychiatrists are physicians, this stance was in accord with the AMA's official position that its members must not participate in assisted deaths (Werth, 1999a). This decision was not unanimously endorsed by the psychiatric community, however. Six former presidents of the American Psychiatric Association issued a public statement expressing their disagreement (Werth & Gordon, 2002), and a number of prominent psychiatrists joined with a group of other mental health professionals in a coalition that submitted a brief supporting PAS (Werth, 1999a). The American Psychiatric Association Ethics Committee (1995), in its newsletter, noted the importance of the involvement of psychiatrists in end-of-life decisions, stating that to prevent psychiatrists from taking a role would be to "prevent the patient's access to the one specialist most suited to assess and intervene around a possible treatable condition" (p. 1). Nonetheless, given the official stance, the intervention would need to be aimed at persuading the patient to choose an alternative other than assisted suicide (Werth, 1999a).

Psychologists

The American Psychological Association (APA) did not sign on to an *amicus* brief related to the Supreme Court decision for a number of reasons, one of which was the lack of time to discuss the issue with the membership (Werth & Gordon, 2002). Instead, the association formed a task force that issued a public information paper stating that the APA "does not advocate for or against assisted suicide" (American Psychological Association, 1997). The document further advised that psychologists' personal beliefs should not influence the process of end-of-life decision making. The dual role of psychologists is to help ensure that the decision-making process includes a complete assessment of the patient's ability to rationally decide and to protect the patient's right to self-determination (Werth, 1999a).

Counselors

The American Counseling Association (ACA) was the only major mental health professional association to sign on to an *amicus* brief submitted to the Supreme Court in 1997 in support of the mental health provider's role in assisted suicide. Points to be considered in the brief were developed by an ad hoc coalition of mental health professionals that provided draft materials to three pro bono attorneys who prepared the final document. The Washington State Psychological Association and the Association for Gay, Lesbian, and Bisexual Issues in Counseling (AGLBIC) joined in signing the brief. The essential points of the brief were as follows:

- In certain circumstances, people are capable of choosing to control the manner and hasten the time of their own death. Such a choice is neither inherently irrational nor indicative of mental illness.
- Mental health professionals do not promote any particular resolution of end-of-life issues; rather, they are guided by their central values of autonomy and self-determination in helping clients come to their own decisions.
- Many mental health professionals have expertise in dealing with the crucial issues of competence, rationality, and voluntariness of end-of-life decisions.
- The role of mental health professionals in end-of-life decision making is to help clients or patients explore, ameliorate, cope with, or solve problems that interfere with their own control over their life and death.

Because the decision to join in the *amicus* brief was made by the ACA leadership, without a systematic polling of its members, the association experienced some negative feedback regarding its involvement (Werth & Gordon, 2002). A number of letters to the editor that criticized the decision appeared in *Counseling Today*, prompting the Executive Committee to publish a short explanatory response. There appears to be a lack of unanimity among counselors regarding their possible involvement in PAS.

Ethical Quandaries

In developing your own stance as a counselor working with clients who request PAS, a challenging question is how to balance the need to protect client rights to autonomy and self-determination with the need to fulfill your responsibilities to the legal system and society, while remaining true to your own moral values. The following are some of the ethical issues that arise from these sometimes-conflicting demands: (a) how to resolve the apparent conflicts among moral principles, (b) whether PAS constitutes an exception to the ethical "duty to warn," (c) how to maintain objectivity or neutrality in counseling clients who are considering a request for hastened death, and (d) whether accepting assisted suicide as an option to explore with clients could place mental health professionals on an ethical slippery slope that would lead to discrimination against vulnerable groups of people. We discuss each of these issues in turn in the following sections.

Competing Moral Principles

Moral principles are assumptions or beliefs about ideals that are shared by members of the helping professions. Three fundamental moral principles that guide the work of mental health professionals are respect for autonomy, nonmaleficence, and beneficence. *Respect for autonomy* means to foster self-determination; that is, to respect the rights of clients to choose their own directions, act in accordance with their own beliefs, and control their own lives. *Nonmaleficence* has its roots in medical ethics and means "do no harm." *Beneficence* is the responsibility to do good or actively promote client welfare (Remley & Herlihy, 2001; Welfel, 2002). Albright and Hazler (1995) noted that, in decisions regarding PAS, these three principles are embedded in the difficult issues of freedom of choice, defining harm, causing or preventing harm, and clarifying differences between "not harming" and "benefiting" another human being. Proponents and opponents of PAS alike have used the moral principles to support their positions.

Those who support PAS contend that counselors' commitment to respecting client autonomy is what justifies the involvement of counselors in helping clients explore whether to request PAS. Autonomy is what "enables us to live *and die* [italics added] according to our own values and beliefs about our own best interests" (Jamison, 1997, p. 224). Thus, to refuse a person's request for PAS would be disrespectful of that person's choice-making capacity. The ACA, in its *amicus curiae* brief to the Supreme Court, followed this line of reasoning when it advocated for the need to "protect a sphere of personal autonomy—specifically, an individual's right to choose the time and manner of ending the suffering caused by a terminal illness" (Werth & Gordon, 2002, p. 165). Thus, for a counselor to attempt to dissuade a client from assisted suicide or intervene with the intent of preventing the act would be practicing paternalism (the opposite of autonomy) by presuming to know what is best for the client.

Opponents of PAS believe that helping professionals are justified in violating a client's right to self-determination in some situations. Callahan (1994) advocated for mental health counselors to take the stance with clients that their lives are worth living and that most people can be helped to tolerate extremely difficult situations and hold on to life. Those who oppose PAS argue that there are limitations to self-determination, including instances when the consequences of an act (such as suicide) are far-reaching and irrevocable (Abramson, 1985). Thus, there is a realm of justifiable paternalism, within which clients' wishes must be overridden. As a counselor, whether you think assisted suicide falls within this realm of acceptable paternalism is a question you will need to answer as you deliberate your potential involvement in clients' end-of-life decision making.

In assisted suicide decisions, the value of autonomy seems to be in direct conflict with another moral principle, that of nonmaleficence, or "do no harm" (Albright & Hazler, 1995). Whether you would be willing to counsel a client who is considering PAS depends in large measure on how you interpret "doing harm." Do you believe that it is more harmful to allow or assist people to end their lives or to refuse to honor requests to die when people have made their wishes known?

The principle of beneficence also can conflict with autonomy when PAS is at issue. When terminal illness or intolerable pain is not present, the principle of beneficence is assumed to take precedence over autonomy in responding to suicide attempts (Albright & Hazler, 1995). However, when a person's life is full of pain and suffering and there is no hope for improvement in his or her condition, should the priorities given to these principles be reversed? Beneficence also imposes on helping professionals a duty to provide services that benefit the general public (Welfel, 2002). When applied to PAS, this duty raises another question: When a client requests aid-in-dying, is a counselor's foremost ethical obligation to act as an advocate for the client or as an agent of society in preventing the intentional ending of a life?

Consider how you would apply the moral principles to the case of John:

> John, age 67, is a widower with a grown daughter. He has been diagnosed with terminal cancer. His oncologist has told him that, with further surgeries and chemotherapy, he might expect to be able to live for several more years. John has requested PAS, stating that he doesn't want to die a lingering death nor is he willing to consider hospice care. He says he is a very private person and would find it unendurably humiliating to be cared for by strangers. He adds that his daughter, Serena, has offered to care for him in her home, but she is a single parent struggling to raise four children on her own and cannot afford to take time off from work. Besides, he doesn't think he could tolerate "being around those ram-

bunctious children all the time," and he wants Serena's memories of him to be good ones. He does not want to involve Serena in his decision-making process regarding aid in dying, because "she's in complete denial" of the seriousness of his illness and he knows she'll try to prevent him from hastening his death.

How would you apply the moral principles if you were to counsel John? Does he have the right as an autonomous individual to end his life now, even though he could live longer? If you were to try to persuade him to involve his daughter in the counseling process, would you be imposing limits on his right to make his own choices? How would you balance considerations of harm to John if he has to live longer in pain, and to Serena if he ends his life before she has had a chance to work through her denial?

Duty to Warn

The ACA Code of Ethics (American Counseling Association, 1995) makes an exception to the general duty of confidentiality when clients present a clear and imminent danger to themselves (Standard B.1.c). This ethical standard has its roots in the noted *Tarasoff* case, which established that mental health professionals have a duty to warn potential victims of dangerous clients (*Tarasoff v. Regents of the University of California*, 1976). What began as a legal requirement has evolved into an ethical duty and has been extended to include clients who are a danger to self as well as to others (Remley & Herlihy, 2001). Counselors must take action to protect clients who pose a danger to themselves; in other words, counselors are ethically obligated to intervene to prevent clients from attempting suicide.

Werth (1999a) examined the apparent conflict between the code of ethics and the ACA leadership's position as expressed in its *amicus* brief to the Supreme Court. The brief supported the ability of terminally ill people to choose the manner and timing of their death and, as Werth noted, it highlighted counselors' focus on self-determination and our primary responsibility to respect the dignity and promote the welfare of clients. Nowhere in the brief did the ACA indicate that counseling a person with respect to aid in dying is incompatible with its code of ethics. These conflicting messages leave counselors in a quandary.

Werth (1999a) suggested that the ACA add a statement in its next revision of the code of ethics clarifying that counselors who provide services to individuals who are considering hastening their deaths "due to the effects of a physical condition that is causing irremediable suffering have the option of breaking or not breaking confidentiality" (p. 175), depending on the specific circumstances involved. At the time of writing this chapter, the ACA is in the process of addressing this issue. The Task Force on Revision of the ACA Code of Ethics, formed in 2002, has been asked to deliberate on the assisted suicide issue and make a recommendation as to how the ethics code might be revised (M. Kocet, personal communication, February 13, 2003).

Consider the possible conflict between a duty to warn and the client's right to autonomous decision making in the following scenario:

> Tawana, age 20, was admitted to Charity Hospital after a police officer found her unconscious in an alley. She was born to a drug-addicted mother who was sent to prison when Tawana was age 5. Tawana lived in a series of foster homes until she turned 15, when she ran away from the last of her foster placements. She has lived on the streets since then, supporting herself through prostitution and drug dealing. She has lived with AIDS for several months and has requested aid in dying. She says that she has nowhere to go but the streets, is too sick to work most of the time, and is unwilling to consider hospice or other end-of-life care because she would not have access to the street drugs on which she is dependent.

Do you think that health professionals would be justified in imposing limits to Tawana's autonomy? If she were to tell you that she plans to just walk out of the hospital if her request for PAS is not granted, do you think you have a duty to warn? Could you work effectively with Tawana without prejudging which of her options would cause the least harm? For whom do you think it is most important to advocate in this situation, the client or others in society who might be harmed if she returns to the streets? What possible choices would you want to explore with her?

Counselor Values

Throughout the debate over the role of mental health professionals in PAS, it has been recognized that not every practitioner will choose to work with clients who request aid in dying. As a counselor, if you are firmly opposed to the practice, on principle, you have an obligation to refer these clients to other mental health providers. If you would consider counseling clients who are considering a request for PAS, it is vital that you do not impose your own values, even inadvertently, on these clients.

To avoid the imposition of your values is a general ethical obligation (American Counseling Association Code of Ethics, Standard A.5.b.) as well as a critically important consideration in working with PAS. The American Psychological Association (1997) advised that mental health professionals "who work in this area must approach their work in a neutral manner. Their personal beliefs on the issue should not influence the process" (p. 2). Responding to a letter to the editor that appeared in *Counseling Today,* the ACA leadership echoed this sentiment, advising that "you must be objective and not project your beliefs onto your clients" (Letters to the Editor, 1997, p. 4). In addition, several researchers (Battin, 1994; Peruzzi, Canapary, & Bongar, 1996; Werth, 1996) have pointed out the importance of being aware of one's own biases and values as a first step toward achieving the necessary neutrality. Thus, it is important that you are aware of your beliefs and values about living and dying, quality of life, and the hastening of death (Jamison, 1997).

We return to an examination of the role of counselor beliefs and values in a later section. At this point, we move on to a topic that is intertwined with issues of counselor values: the "slippery slope" phenomenon.

Slippery Slope

Opponents of the right to PAS, and even some of its strong proponents, have expressed a concern that if PAS were to become an accepted practice in certain limited situations, it could create an ethical slippery slope that could lead eventually to involuntary deaths (Gostin, 1997). The crux of the concern is that, if PAS becomes legal, the "bright line" between acceptable and unacceptable circumstances may slide from limiting it, initially, to people who are terminally ill with 6 months or less to live, to the terminally ill who may be able to survive much longer, to people who are chronically but not terminally ill, to those who are not competent to decide for them-selves (Werth, 1999b). This would have the greatest effect on the most vulnerable members of society. "The risk of harm is greatest for the many individuals in our society whose autonomy and well-being are already com-promised by poverty, lack of access to good medical care, advanced age, or membership in a stigmatized social group" (New York State Task Force on Life and the Law, 1994, p. 120).

According to some moral philosophers, a descent into this "moral quick-sand" (Battin, 1980) is inevitable because rules against assisting suicide are part of a tapestry of rules that form our larger moral code. The more threads one removes from this tapestry, the weaker the fabric becomes (Beauchamp & Childress, 1989).

Proponents of PAS counterargue that such fears are unwarranted and that, in fact, disempowered members of society would be less likely to be coerced into an assisted death if PAS were legalized. Laws regulating as-sisted suicide would protect all persons equally by providing consistent guidelines and safeguards (Dority, 1998). Assisted suicide actually would return authority and control to the individual (Jamison, 1998).

Proponents of assisted suicide also advocate for the involvement of men-tal health professionals in end-of-life decision making as another way to safe-guard against coercion of vulnerable groups. Mental health professionals can assess the degree of influence or pressure that may affect the reasoning of people who are considering PAS, thus helping to ensure that client welfare is safeguarded throughout the process (Werth, 1999b). Counselors, working from a systemic approach, can help their clients to consider environmental forces as well as intrapersonal dynamics that are pertinent to their decisions regarding assisted death.

Adaptations for Diversity

Culture is a such potent influence in shaping people's beliefs about life and death that it would be impossible to counsel clients effectively regarding hastened death decisions without considering cultural variables. American society, like most modern societies, is composed of many cultures and contains multiple ethnic groups, creating both commonalities and differences between and within groups of people (Harper, 2003). Many issues, including religious and spiritual beliefs, race, age, ageism, disabilities, gender, and socioeconomic status, play into end-of-life decisions (Farberman, 1997). The culture of the client, the culture of the counselor, and the interactions between the two inevitably affect the counseling process, and this often occurs at the unconscious level. The following sections address some aspects of culture that are particularly salient in the context of assisted suicide decision making.

Religious and Spiritual Beliefs

The case of Mary illustrates the importance of exploring the spiritual or religious beliefs of clients who are considering a request for aid in dying:

> Mary's physical condition has deteriorated rapidly since she was diagnosed with a terminal illness 8 months ago, soon after her 66th birthday. She says that she has lost her will to live and has no energy to continue to fight for her survival. She would like to request PAS rather than die a lingering death. She was raised in the Catholic faith, and although she does not attend Mass regularly or participate in church rites, she considers herself to be a practicing Catholic. Since she became ill, her parish priest has been visiting with her and has reminded her of the Church's teaching that suffering has a special place in God's plan for salvation. She has requested counseling to help her with her end-of-life issues, including how to reconcile the conflict between her desire for assisted suicide and the Church's stance against any form of euthanasia.

Religious institutions are often present in an individual's life from birth, and for many clients, their religious belief systems have a profound influence on the meaning they attribute to living and to dying, and on whether they believe that PAS is an acceptable means of dying. Counselors will be better prepared to explore these issues with clients if they are aware of the views on assisted suicide of the major religions practiced in the United States.

Most of the religions commonly practiced in the Western world are opposed to assisted suicide. In Catholic doctrine, ending one's life through assisted suicide is condemned as a crime against life. The Catholic Church's "Declaration on Euthanasia" states that the killing of a human being cannot in any way be permitted, even when the person is suffering from an incurable disease or is dying, nor is it permitted to ask for or consent to the act ("Sacred Congregation," 1980).

Euthanasia is also forbidden in conservative and Orthodox Judaism. In 1996, when the U.S. Supreme Court was preparing to deliberate on the legality of assisted suicide, the Orthodox Jewish congregation in the United States filed an *amicus curiae* brief in support of laws that ban PAS.

The church of Mormon, likewise, condemns any form of suicide, including PAS. Mormon doctrine views any form of euthanasia as a violation of the commandments of God.

Within the Islamic tradition, a person does not have a right to suicide, regardless of the situation. Islam holds that individuals do not create their own bodies; rather, they are entrusted with the care, nurturance, and safekeeping of the physical body which is owned by God. In the Islam faith, attempting to end one's life is regarded as both a crime and a sin.

The Church of England, the Lutheran church, and the Evangelical Christian church also condemn the practice of euthanasia. According to their teachings, to actively contribute to the cause of an individual's death is to directly violate the Christian duty to care for others, never to kill.

Not all philosophies or religions are opposed to the practice of assisted suicide. Albright and Hazler (1995) described how some Eastern traditions differ from typical Western beliefs. Hinduism professes the belief that in the endless cycle of birth, death, and rebirth, the goal of religion is to cease living. Indeed, self-destruction is commended when it demonstrates devotion to a deity.

Religious teachings about euthanasia will have a profound influence on the belief systems of some clients. It is important for counselors to keep in mind that individuals can profess the same faith but have varying interpretations of its teachings. Also, religious dogma may have little or no relevance for some clients. What is important is that counselors try to understand the meanings that clients ascribe to religious and spiritual issues as they relate to end-of-life decision making.

Socioeconomic Status and Social Class

Fanon described class differences in American society that result in a system of social "haves and have-nots" in which the weak are exploited by the more powerful (Bulhan, 1985). The negative effects of class dominance can be seen in poor health care, education, and social services for oppressed, disenfranchised, or less powerful populations. Kemp (1998) suggested that, in a social climate in which cutting the costs of health care is central, those in power, including insurance companies and hospitals, might view assisted suicide as a cost-saving option, especially among groups of patients who have no health insurance. This concern that assisted suicide, rather than being a program of choice for people who want it, would instead victimize ethnic minorities and the poor, was also expressed in a report made by the International Task Force on Euthanasia and Assisted Suicide. The report noted that those who support the assisted suicide movement tend to be overwhelmingly White, well off, worried, and well. Others who have similar reservations about assisted suicide fear that inequities within U.S. society will result in a disproportionately high rate of euthanasia among such peripheralized groups as ethnic minorities, the poor, and the aged (Kemp, 1998).

Economic considerations play a large role in the deliberations about assisted suicide of Arthur, the client depicted in the scenario below. If you were Arthur's counselor, how do you think you could help him deal with his financial concerns? Do you believe that he is at greater risk for assisted suicide because of his lower socioeconomic status and lack of financial resources?

> Arthur's health has slowly declined over the past 3 years because of the effects of a degenerative, incurable disease. Arthur is 56 years old. He and his wife have four children, ranging in age from 22 to 34. Since he dropped out of high school at age 15 until he became too ill to work 2 years ago, Arthur has worked at unskilled jobs mostly as a janitor and as a contract laborer. His wife has worked sporadically over the years. They have no health insurance and minimal savings. Arthur wants to explore the possibility of assisted suicide. He does not want his extended illness to drain their meager financial resources, nor does he want to become a burden to his wife and children who are, as he puts it, "barely making ends meet."

Age and Ageism

Although it is true that older adults have the highest suicide rate in the United States, Leenars (1992) suggested that the paucity of research on suicide among the elderly has led to the misconception that older people commit suicide because of old age or terminal illness. Richman (1992) stressed that illness is a biopsychosocial phenomenon and that a desire for a hastened death may be a reaction to internal and external stressors as well as the impact of life events. Although many elderly people experience illness, the deaths of family and friends, a decline in physical abilities, loss of independence, and increased social isolation, the majority of older adults choose to continue living rather than to end their lives. According to Richman, many supporters of rational suicide are guilty of ageism. Because a desire for assisted suicide is a multidetermined, systems phenomenon, counselors are uniquely suited to help the elderly explore psychological, social, and family stressors and consider assisted suicide as only one end-of-life option.

> Charles, age 87, is in great pain as a result of lung cancer that has invaded his chest wall. For the past 2 months, his physician has helped him manage the pain with morphine, but he now requires a dosage that leaves him feeling groggy and "stupid." He is considering PAS because he finds neither of his alternatives acceptable: to be alert but in agonizing pain or to

be oversedated with tolerable pain. Charles' wife died 5 years ago, and although he has two children, they live thousands of miles away and are busy raising their own children. He does not want to move away from his lifetime home to be near them, although he wishes they could visit more often. He feels lonely and isolated and thinks that a hastened death through PAS might be the kindest thing he could do for himself and for his children.

What issues do you think it is most important for a counselor to explore with Charles? Do you think that rational suicide might be an acceptable choice for him? If he were 47 rather than 87 years old, would that make a difference?

Sociorace

The sociohistorical legacy of ethnic minorities in the United States has been largely one of systematized oppression (Helms & Carter, 1990; Jones, 1993). As a result, a number of ethnic minority groups in America continue to suffer from disproportionately high rates of social ills, including domestic and community-based violence, family fragmentation, substance abuse, unemployment, poor physical and mental health, and low levels of educational attainment (Neighbors & Jackson, 1996). The slippery slope concern that was discussed earlier in the chapter is especially salient in any consideration of PAS and members of racial and ethnic minority groups. Members of these groups, like the elderly and the poor, may be more at risk for abuse of PAS.

Although scholars have called for more research on how issues of race and ethnicity relate to individual risk factors for hastened death (e.g., Farberman, 1997), these considerations rarely appear in the literature on assisted suicide. The tendency of the majority culture to minimize or ignore such minority group issues needs to be addressed. Until this occurs, members of racial and ethnic minority groups may continue to have less favorable views about PAS than their majority counterparts. A public opinion poll taken in 1994 showed that, whereas a slight majority of Whites favored PAS, African Americans opposed it by more than a 2-to-1 ratio (Tarrance Group, 1994).

In the following scenario, the individuals are members of at least two minority groups—they are Hispanic and they are gay. Do you think these cultural variables will influence how the helping professionals with whom they interact (such as physicians, hospice workers, and counselors) respond to Juan's request for PAS?

Juan, age 32, is confined to a wheelchair with advanced symptoms of AIDS that include severe pain due to the inflammation of the nerves in his limbs, nausea and vomiting on a daily basis, cystic lung infection, and diabetes. He lost his sight a month ago. He has requested PAS, stating that he wants to die while there can still be some dignity left in his manner of dying. He also wants to end the suffering of Raphael, his partner of 9 years, who has been providing care for Juan in their home.

Guidelines for Ethical and Effective Practice

To conclude this chapter, we offer some guidelines for counselors to use in their work with clients who are considering a request for aid in dying. As we have emphasized throughout the chapter, a starting place for you, as a counselor, in determining whether you are able and willing to do this work is to examine your own values and beliefs. It is important that you have confronted your own fears about death and dying so that you do not project these onto your clients. It is also crucial that you have examined your own biases and are aware of any ageist, racist, classist, or other assumptions that you might bring to your work with these clients.

We hope that the issues presented in the chapter have helped you to determine whether you believe that assisted suicide can be a rational choice under certain circumstances. Possible criteria for rational suicide have been suggested by several scholars (Callahan, 1994; Hadjistavropoulos, 1996; Werth, 1999a, 1999b; Werth & Cobia, 1995) as well as some of the professional associations (American Psychological Association, 1997; National Association of Social Workers, 1993). These include the following:

- The client's condition is unremittingly hopeless.
- The choice has been made freely, without coercion.
- The decision is not impulsive.
- All alternatives have been considered.
- The client has consulted with others, including mental health professionals.
- The choice is congruent with the client's personal values.
- The client has considered the impact of the choice on significant others, and if possible, has included them in the decision-making process.
- The choice is not a result of clinical depression or other mental illness.

As a counselor, you are uniquely qualified to help clients explore whether these criteria are true for them. Once you have established the counseling relationship and a strong therapeutic alliance, you will want to explore the client's motivations for considering PAS. Some clients may be driven to consider PAS by a desire to end physical pain and suffering. As Jamison (1998) pointed out, it may not be just the physical pain (which could possibly be managed with analgesics) but the overall experience of the illness that makes living intolerable. A combination of the side effects of medications and treatment—which could include recovery from surgery, nausea, vomiting, diarrhea, crushing fatigue, and hair loss—can come to be more than people can sustain. Cancer and AIDS, in particular, can affect multiple bodily systems and organs. Thus, it is important for counselors to explore the experience of the illness in its entirety as it is affecting the client's decision-making process.

Loss of quality of life is a strong factor in motivating some clients to seek PAS. It can be extremely frustrating to try to keep a balance between pain and the side effects of medication administered to manage the pain. For some clients, the quality of life begins to erode with the loss of physical mobility and continues with other losses such as the ability to maintain sexual relations, until they cannot perform the most basic tasks of eating, bathing, and toileting without help. For these clients, it may not be the pain that is unacceptable; rather, it is the loss of the ability to enjoy life (Jamison, 1998).

Loss of autonomy and control is a crucial motivator for some people in their decision to request an assisted death. Clients may talk about the importance of maintaining their independence, living in their own homes, engaging in their usual daily routines, and being able to take care of themselves. For these clients, exercising control over their manner and timing of death may be an extension of maintaining control in life (Jamison, 1998).

Sheer exhaustion is sometimes at the core of a person's request for PAS. For those who have been ill for a long period of time, the illness has become a lifestyle that takes its toll. The constant battle against illness may have included diagnostic procedures, surgeries, therapies, office visits, hospital stays, anxious waiting for test results, discussions and decisions about courses of treatment, and ministrations of family and friends (Jamison, 1998). It is important that you, as the counselor, are sensitive to the cumulative psychological and emotional impact of this battle.

Concerns about being a burden to family and loved ones are commonly expressed by clients who are considering a request for a hastened death. This theme has appeared in a number of the case examples we have considered. For these clients, the fear that their illness will physically, emotionally, and financially exhaust the resources of their loved ones is a crucial issue to be addressed in therapy.

In addition to discussing motivations with your client, you might listen for any contradictory values that may be present and for indications of depression. If you think that clinical depression may be a factor in the client's desire for a hastened death, there are a number of screening instruments such as the Beck Depression Inventory that you can use.

Jamison (1998) has suggested several questions you might ask the client that will help you understand what is providing the impetus for a request for PAS, including the following:

To assess impulsivity: "How long have you been thinking about making a request for aid in dying?"

To assess certainty: "Are you absolutely certain about your decision? Do you have any doubts?"

To assess immediacy: "Are you planning to do this soon? Is your mind completely made up?"

To assess availability of care: "Are you satisfied with the care you are receiving at home/nursing care facility/hospice?

To assess congruence with values: "Is this something you believe in strongly? What are your beliefs about living and dying? How long have you held these beliefs?"

To assess family involvement: "Does your family know what you are considering? Do they support you in your decision? If your family doesn't know, why haven't you told them?"

To assess awareness of alternatives: "What alternatives have you considered? What do you see as the positive and negative points in these alternatives?"

To assess for coercion: "Is anyone suggesting to you that PAS might be your best alternative? In what ways do you think your hastened death might be a blessing to others?"

An ethical obligation to keep in mind as a counselor is that you must practice only within the boundaries of your competence (ACA Code of Ethics, Standard C.2a; American Counseling Association, 1997). Clients considering a request for PAS are a specialized population, and you may wish to seek specialized training. Werth (1999b) noted that certification programs are offered by the Association for Death Education and Counseling and by the American Association of Suicidology.

PAS is likely to continue to be an emotionally charged issue. Although the practice is legal only in Oregon at the present time, more states may enact "death with dignity" laws. Certainly, the trends toward living to a more advanced age and improving medical technology will continue. Therefore, there will be a growing need for specially trained, culturally competent, and ethical counselors to assist clients with end-of-life decision making.

Summary

This chapter explored physician-assisted suicide, or PAS, an issue that challenges the core assumptions that counselors bring to their work and raises a host of complex ethical questions. A subject that is hotly debated is whether there is such a thing as rational suicide, or whether people who are terminally ill or in intolerable pain due to an incurable condition have the right to request aid in dying. Increasingly, counselors and other mental health professionals will be called on to provide services to clients who are thinking about hastening their own deaths. These counselors must struggle with balancing the need to protect client autonomy and self-determination with the need to obey the law and fulfill their responsibilities to society while remaining true to their own moral values. Courts of law and various mental health providers' professional associations have taken differing stands on PAS. Ethical issues that were discussed in this chapter include resolving conflicts among moral principles, the duty to warn, maintaining objectivity, and the potential for discrimination against vulnerable groups of people. Cultural issues such as religious and spiritual beliefs, social class and economic status, age and ageism, and race or ethnicity were considered. Guidelines for ethical practice were offered.

References

Abramson, M. (1985). The autonomy–paternalism dilemma in social work practice. *Social Casework, 66,* 387–393.

Albright, D. E., & Hazler, R. J. (1995). A right to die?: Ethical dilemmas of euthanasia. *Counseling and Values, 39,* 177–189.

American Counseling Association. (1995). *Code of ethics and standards of practice.* Alexandria, VA: Author.

American Psychiatric Association Ethics Committee. (1995). Physician-assisted suicide. *Ethics Newsletter, 11,* 1–5.

American Psychological Association. (1997). Terminal illness and hastened death requests: The important role of the mental health professional. *Professional Psychology: Research and Practice, 28,* 544–547.

Battin, M. P. (1980). Manipulated suicide. In M. P. Battin & D. Mayo (Eds.), *Suicide: The philosophical issues* (pp. 171–181). New York: St. Martin's Press.

Battin, M. P. (1994). *The least worst death: Essays in bioethics on end-of-life.* New York: Oxford University Press.

Beauchamp, T. L., & Childress, J. F. (1989). *Principles of biomedical ethics.* New York: Oxford University Press.

Bulhan, H. A. (1985). *Franz Fanon and the psychology of oppression.* New York: Plenum Press.

Callahan, J. (1994). The ethics of assisted suicide. *Health & Social Work, 19,* 237–244.

Dority, B. (1998). Arguments against legalizing physician-assisted suicide are unconvincing. In *Assisted suicide: Current controversies* (pp. 131–139). San Diego, CA: Greenhaven Press.

Emmanuel, E. J. (1994). Euthanasia: Historical, ethical, and empiric perspectives. *Archives of Internal Medicine, 154,* 1890–1901.

Farberman, R. K. (1997). Terminal illness and hastened death requests: The important role of the mental health professional. *Professional Psychology: Research and Practice, 28,* 544–547.

Gostin, L. O. (1997). Deciding life and death in the courtroom: From Quinlan to Cruzan, Glucksberg, and Vacco—A brief history and analysis of constitutional protection of the right to die. *Journal of the American Medical Association, 278,* 1523–1529.

Hadjistavropoulos, T. (1996). The systematic application of ethical codes in the counseling of persons who are considering euthanasia. *Journal of Social Issues, 52,* 169–188.

Harper, F. D. (2003). Background: Concepts and history. In F. D. Harper & J. McFadden (Eds.), *Culture and counseling: New approaches* (pp. 1–19). Boston: Pearson.

Helms, J. E., & Carter, J. (1990). *Black and White racial identity: Theory, research, and practice.* Westport, CT: Greenwood Press.

Hendin, H. (1998). *Seduced by death: Doctors, patients, and assisted suicide.* New York: Norton.

Humphry, D. (1993). *Final exit.* New York: Dell.

Jamison, S. (1997). *Assisted suicide: A decision-making guide for health professionals.* San Francisco: Jossey-Bass.

Jamison, S. (1998). Legalized physician-assisted suicide would improve treatment of the terminally ill. In *Assisted suicide: Current controversies* (pp. 115–121). San Francisco: Jossey Bass.

Jones, R. S. (1993). Double burdens, double responsibilities: Eighteenth century Black males and the African American struggle. *Journal of African American Male Studies, 1,* 1–14.

Kemp, E. J., Jr. (1998). Assisted suicide would threaten the rights of the disabled. In *Assisted suicide: Current controversies* (pp. 173–176). San Francisco: Jossey Bass.

Kiser, J. D. (1996). Counselors and the legalization of physician-assisted suicide. *Counseling and Values, 40,* 127–131.

Leenaars, A. (1992). Suicide notes of the older adult. In A. A. Leenaars, R. Maris, J. L. McIntosh, & J. Richman (Eds.), *Suicide and the older adult* (pp. 62–79). New York: Guilford Press.

Lester, D., & Leenaars, A. A. (1996). The ethics of suicide and suicide prevention. *Death Studies, 20,* 163–184.

Letters to the Editor. (1997, March). *Counseling Today,* p. 4.

Manetta, A. A., & Wells, J. G. (2001). Ethical issues in the social worker's role in physician-assisted suicide. *Health & Social Work, 26,* 160–166.

National Association of Social Workers. (1993). Client self-determination in end-of-life decisions. In *Social work speaks* (3rd ed., pp. 58–61). Washington, DC: NASW Press.

Neighbors, H. W., & Jackson, J. S. (1996). *Mental health in Black America.* Thousand Oaks, CA: Sage.

New York State Task Force on Life and the Law. (1994). *When death is sought: Assisted suicide and euthanasia in the medical context.* Albany: New York State Department of Health.

Oregon Death With Dignity Act, Or. Rev. Stat. 127. 800–127. 995 (1995).

Peruzzi, N., Canapary, A., & Bongar, B. (1996). Physician-assisted suicide: The role of mental health professionals. *Ethics & Behavior, 6,* 353–366.

Remley, T. P., & Herlihy, B. (2001). *Ethical, legal, and professional issues in counseling.* Upper Saddle River, NJ: Merrill Prentice-Hall.

Richman, J. (1992). A rational approach to rational suicide. In A. A. Leenaars, R. Maris, J. L. McIntosh, & J. Richman (Eds.), *Suicide and the older adult* (pp. 130–141). New York: Guilford Press.

Rogers, J., & Britton, P. (1994). AIDS and rational suicide: A counseling psychology perspective or a slide on the slippery slope. *Counseling Psychologist, 22,* 171–178.

Sacred Congregation for the Doctrine of the Faith Declaration on Euthanasia. (1980). Retrieved March 15, 2003 from http://www.euthanasia.com/vatican.html.

Tarasoff v. Regents of the University of California, 17 Cal. 3d 425, 551 P.2d 334, 131 Cal. Rptr. 14 (1976).

Tarrance Group. (1994, September 25–28). *A survey of voter attitudes in the United States.* Houston, TX: Author.

Vacco v. Quill, 521 U.S. 793 (1997).

Washington v. Glucksberg, 521 U.S. 702 (1997).

Welfel, E. R. (2002). *Ethics in counseling and psychotherapy.* Pacific Grove, CA: Brooks/Cole.

Werth, J. L. (1992). Rational suicide and AIDS: Considerations for the psychotherapist. *Counseling Psychologist, 20,* 645–659.

Werth, J. L. (1996). *Rational suicide? Implications for mental health professionals.* Washington, DC: Taylor & Francis.

Werth, J. L. (1999a). Mental health professionals and assisted death: Perceived ethical obligations and proposed guidelines for practice. *Ethics & Behavior, 9,* 159–183.

Werth, J. L. (1999b). When is a mental health professional competent to assess a person's decision to hasten death? *Ethics & Behavior, 9,* 141–157.

Werth, J. L., & Cobia, D. C. (1995). Empirically based criteria for rational suicide: A survey of psychotherapists. *Suicide and Life Threatening Behavior, 25,* 231–240.

Werth, J. L., & Gordon, J. R. (2002). Amicus curiae brief for the United States Supreme Court on mental health issues associated with "physician-assisted suicide." *Journal of Counseling & Development, 80,* 160–163.

Chapter 7

Suicide and the Law

Theodore P. Remley, Jr.

A ll professionals who counsel clients may at some point have to manage a suicidal client (James & Gilliland, 2001). Some counselors
deal with suicidal clients more often than others. For example, Hermann
(2002) found that school counselors have reported having to manage
suicidal clients at a very high rate, and counselors in hospital settings
often counsel suicidal patients (Bongar, Maris, Berman, & Litman, 1998;
Kiesler & Sibulkin, 1987; Silverman, Berman, Bongar, Litman, & Maris,
1998). To manage the legal risks associated with the jobs effectively, all
counselors must be prepared to determine whether a counseling client may be at risk for suicide (Packman & Harris, 1998). And counselors who provide services in their practices for suicidal clients more
often than other counselors must become very skilled in identifying
and managing clients who may be at risk for suicide.

In this chapter, the most important legal issue is discussed at length: malpractice claims against counselors whose clients have attempted or completed suicide. The incidence of lawsuits against mental health professionals is very low (Robertson, 1988); however, lawsuits against counselors based
on the suicide of a client do occur and appear to be increasing (Conner,
1994). In 1990, the American Psychologist Association's Insurance Trust
provided data indicating that the suicide of a client was the sixth most
common malpractice claim against psychologists and was the second most
costly claim to settle or litigate. Of a total of 1,892 claims, 102 were specifically related to a client's suicide (Bongar et al., 1998). This chapter summa-
rizes the general law of professional malpractice and those legal principles
applied to situations in which counselors have been sued after a client has
attempted or committed suicide. Court cases that provide important guide-

lines for practice are cited. In addition, other legal issues associated with counseling are reviewed, including the following: the requirement that counselors in some states must be licensed to practice; privacy rights of clients based on ethical and legal principles; the requirement that counselors develop and maintain competency in identifying and assisting clients who may be at risk for suicide; the responsibility counselors have to not abandon their clients; and record-keeping requirements within counseling relationships.

This chapter also offers specific recommendations for managing clients who may be at risk for suicide once they have been identified. A form for family members or friends to sign that acknowledges they have been informed of the client's potential risk is provided. Recommendations for assisting family members and friends who need to have persons evaluated to determine whether they are indeed at risk for suicide are also offered.

Finally, some diversity issues associated with counseling clients who may be at risk for suicide are offered. Counselors are cautioned to avoid imposing their own values, to be prepared for individuals from some cultures to react different from others, and to understand that in some cultures extended family members or even nonfamily members may be involved in resolving a crisis.

Counselors who read this chapter are urged to avoid overreacting with excessive anxiety about the possibility of being sued. Bongar et al. (1998) have concluded that mental health professionals are more damaged by the fear of being sued than they are by lawsuits themselves. Packman and Harris (1998) have cautioned mental health professionals to focus on providing good clinical care to clients rather than taking actions to prevent lawsuits.

Legal Issues Associated With Suicide

Although there are a number of legal issues associated with counseling and managing suicidal clients, the primary legal concern for counselors is to avoid counselor malpractice. All counselors, even when they are not dealing with suicidal clients, must adhere to federal and state statutes that affect their counseling practices. Some of the general legal duties counselors owe to clients, such as maintaining the client's privacy, are heightened or emphasized if the client becomes suicidal.

Counselor Malpractice

The most pressing concern for counselors who provide mental health services to suicidal clients is to ensure their services meet the minimum standards of care demanded by society. The word *malpractice* is derived from the Latin term *mal*, which means *bad*, and when coupled with the word *practice* means *bad practice*. Professionals who commit malpractice will be held accountable by courts to individuals who are harmed as a result of their malpractice. The five legal elements of malpractice are defined and described below in detail. In addition, the five legal elements are discussed in relation to counselors and their suicidal clients.

Licensure Requirement

Many states require that counselors be licensed to provide counseling services, unless they are exempt from licensure for some reason (Remley & Herlihy, 2001). In all states that have counselor licensure requirements, school counselors are exempt. In many states, counselors who work in nonprofit or government agencies are exempt from licensure requirements as well. It is a counselor's responsibility to determine whether a license is required for practice in his or her state. In the event a counselor was accused of wrongdoing related to a client's suicide or suicide attempt, the counselor's problems would be multiplied significantly if it was determined he or she was practicing without a license in violation of state law.

Privacy and Privileged Communication

All counselors have a general ethical obligation to their clients to keep information confidential that clients disclose within a professional counseling relationship. In addition, some counseling relationships are privileged by state or federal statutes. When a counseling relationship is privileged by statute, counselors may not disclose confidential information, even in a court of law.

However, both the ethical privacy requirement and the legal privilege requirement have exceptions. When counselors determine that clients are in danger of harming themselves through a suicide attempt, counselors are ethically and legally required to take action to prevent harm (Gladding, Remley, & Huber, 2001). If the privacy or privilege belonging to clients must be compromised or breached in the process of protecting clients from harming themselves, such actions are exceptions to the general rule that counselors must keep information confidential. Counselors must keep in mind, though, when they do have to disclose confidential information in the process of protecting clients from harming themselves that only the information that is necessary be disclosed, thereby maintaining the privacy of clients to the extent possible.

Counselor Competency

Although counselors may be hired in counseling jobs or may be licensed by a state to practice counseling, it is the ethical and legal duty of counselors to practice only within areas in which they have the knowledge and expertise to counsel. The American Counseling Association (ACA) Code of Ethics (1995) § C.2. requires that counselors limit their practices to areas in which they are competent based on their education, training, supervised experience, and professional experience. That section of the code also provides guidelines for developing new areas of practice and for dealing with difficult issues.

Counselors who have recently earned their master's degrees probably are not equipped to deal with suicidal clients on their own. Counselors without expertise in identifying and managing suicidal clients need supervision, consultation, and direction from counselors who do have that expertise. Counselors who wish to develop expertise in any new area, including providing services to suicidal clients, may develop such expertise through independent reading, workshops, university courses, or clinical supervision. There is no formula that determines when an individual counselor has developed expertise in a new area. That determination is left up to the professional judgment of each counselor. However, if a counselor is ever accused of practicing outside his or her area of competence, the burden will be on the counselor to demonstrate how he or she came to the conclusion that he or she was qualified to counsel in that area.

Abandonment

The ACA Code of Ethics (1995) § A.11.a. prohibits counselors from abandoning clients. If a counselor abandoned a client who was suicidal, and the client later harmed him- or herself, the counselor could be held legally accountable. However, a proper referral to another mental health professional who assumes responsibility for the care of a suicidal client is appropriate in many circumstances and does not constitute abandonment.

Keeping Records

In some states, the types of records kept and the length of time they are kept may be dictated by general statutes or by statutes or regulations related to counselor licensure. Agencies in which counselors are employed often dictate the contents of records that are kept on behalf of clients. Absent statutes, regulations, or agency policies, there are no general legal requirement that counselors keep records. Because counseling records are kept by most counselors, however, a counselor probably would be considered unprofessional who kept no records at all.

Clients have a legal right to see their records kept by counselors and have a legal right to have copies of those records or to have copies of the records transferred to third parties they have identified. If the counseling client is a minor or has been declared incompetent by a court, then the legal rights belong to a parent or guardian. Because clients have a legal right to their records, and because records counselors keep may at some point be disclosed to others, counselors should create records with the idea in mind that the client may eventually see them and that the records being created may some day be open to the public.

Records must be properly stored. Counselors must take reasonable precautions to ensure that counseling records are not seen by anyone who does not have a right to see them. Staff members who handle confidential records must be trained and monitored. Records must be kept in locked file drawers in locked offices. Records kept on computers must be kept in files that have passwords. Any secure system of keeping records could be breached, but counselors have a duty to take reasonable precautions to keep records confidential.

It is important for counselors to reduce to writing their thinking process in the case notes for clients who may be at risk for suicide (Packman & Harris, 1998). Consultations with colleagues and experts especially should be noted in records (Bernstein & Hartsell, 1998). If a counselor makes a decision that a client is not currently at risk after having considered that possibility, the basis for making the decision should be recorded. Counselors are not required to predict all suicide gestures, attempts, or completions, but they are expected to use sound procedures and judgment in making clinical decisions, and their reasoning should be recorded in their notes.

When providing services to suicidal clients, it is essential that counselors keep detailed records to prove they took proper steps to ensure the safety of their clients. According to Packman and Harris (1998), if actions taken by a counselor when providing service to a client who may be at risk for suicide are not written down, a judge or jury reviewing the situation later probably will assume the actions were not actually taken. It probably is impossible for counselors to create detailed records for each client they see. Routine record keeping for routine clients usually would involve less detail than records kept on a client who might be suicidal. Guidelines for keeping records that document the actions counselors have taken are included in Appendix A.

The Law of Malpractice

Prosser (1971) identified five elements that must be proven in a professional malpractice case. Those elements are duty, breach, harm, proximate cause, and damages.

A plaintiff who is suing a professional for malpractice must first prove that the professional owed a duty to the client. Professionals owe a duty only to those to whom they have agreed to provide professional services. A professional can accept an individual as a client without payment agreements and without written contracts. All that is needed is for the professional and the client to understand that a professional relationship exists.

After plaintiffs have proved that a professional owed them a duty, they then have to prove that the duty was breached. Breach of duty is usually proven by providing evidence of the care that a client can expect from a professional. The standard of care is the degree of care a reasonably prudent professional should exercise in similar circumstances (Black, 1979). Experts from the professional field usually testify as what the standard of care is in that particular field. It used to be in law that the professional standard varied from locality to locality. For example, professionals in an urban area might be expected to have more up-to-date information in the field, whereas professionals in a rural area may not have had access to new information. However, that locality standard usually is no longer applied because all professionals in the United States are expected today to stay up to date. Once the standard of care has been established in a malpractice case, it is up to the plaintiff to prove that the professional breached that standard.

After plaintiffs in a professional malpractice case have proved duty and breach of duty, the plaintiffs must then prove that actual harm occurred. Harm does not have to be physical. Harm can be monetary or emotional.

Once harm has been proven, plaintiffs must then prove that the breach of the duty by the professional was the proximate cause of the harm. Proximate cause of harm is a legal concept that is quite difficult to explain. Basically, it must be proved that had it not been for what the professional did or failed to do, the individual would not have suffered the harm.

Once the four elements listed above have been proven in a professional malpractice case, plaintiffs must prove damages. They have to place a monetary amount on the harm they suffered and convince a judge or jury to rule that the professional must compensate them for the harm they suffered.

Malpractice With Suicidal Clients

A client who has been injured in a suicide attempt might sue his or her counselor, claiming that the counselor failed to prevent the harm. In the event of a completed suicide, family members of the deceased client might sue the client's counselor, claiming that the counselor was negligent in allowing the suicide to occur.

Duty

The client or family member would have to prove the first element of the malpractice case—that the counselor owed a duty to the client. The element could be proven easily by showing that the client was being seen by the counselor for professional counseling services. Counselors should be careful to avoid counseling individuals on a casual basis. For example, if a person at a party asked a counselor for his or her advice regarding a problem and the counselor gave the person advice, a professional relationship would have been established and the counselor would then owe that person a duty.

Breach of Duty

The second element in a professional malpractice case, that the counselor breached his or her duty to the client, is usually difficult to prove in a suicide situation. The plaintiff must prove that the counselor took action or failed to take action in a manner that was materially different from what could be expected from a competent counselor. Research and clinical experience have shown that it is impossible to predict precisely whether or not an individual will attempt to take his or her own life (Goldstein, Black, Nasrallah, & Winokur, 1991; Jacobs, Brewer, & Klein-Benheim, 1999; Slaby, 1998; Stromberg et al., 1988). Therefore an error in judgment does not necessarily establish negligence (Hermann & Finn, 2002). Even though a mental health professional cannot predict whether a client will make a suicide attempt, there are agreed-upon steps knowledgeable counselors take when they are assessing whether a particular client is at risk for a suicide attempt (see chap. 5, this volume). The plaintiff in a suicide malpractice case against a counselor cannot say that the counselor was negligent simply because the client attempted or completed suicide. Instead, the plaintiff must demonstrate that the counselor did not do what a reasonable counselor would have done in a similar set of circumstances. Usually, the plaintiff will provide expert witnesses who will testify that the counselor failed to meet the standard of care in this particular situation. The counselor being sued usually will counter that type of testimony by providing experts who will testify that what the counselor did or did not do was reasonable under the circumstances, and even though the client did attempt or complete a suicide, the counselor should not be held accountable. When experts contradict each other's testimony, a judge or jury will decide which expert to believe.

Harm

If a client completes a suicide, harm to the client is simple to prove. A client who attempts suicide, though, would have to prove the third element of a professional malpractice case—that he or she suffered some harm as a result of the suicide attempt. The harm might be physical, monetary, or emotional. The more serious the harm, the more damages the client can expect to receive from the judge or jury if the client wins the lawsuit.

Proximate Cause

The most difficult element to prove for the client or the client's family member in a counselor malpractice lawsuit related to an attempted or completed suicide is proximate cause. The plaintiff must prove that the death or injuries to the client that occurred as a result of the attempted or completed suicide would not have happened if the counselor had not been negligent. Obviously, it is difficult to prove that another person (the counselor) is directly responsible for an action taken by an injured person (the client). If the counselor's negligence was outrageous, then attributing a client's attempted or completed suicide to the counselor might be possible.

An example of outrageous negligence on the part of a counselor who is providing services to a suicidal client would be if the client explicitly told the counselor that he was contemplating suicide, the client had made attempts in the past that the counselor knew about, the counselor did not ask additional questions, the counselor informed the client that suicide was always an option for everyone (thinking that by minimizing the threat, the counselor was helping the client), and the client committed suicide soon thereafter. Almost all professionals or nonprofessionals reviewing a situation like the one described here would agree that the counselor was negligent and that the client might have been prevented from committing suicide if the counselor had behaved in a more professional manner. On the other hand, when a counselor takes appropriate steps and, using sound best judgment, then determines that a client is not at risk, but the client later completes suicide, it is much harder to demonstrate that the counselor was negligent.

Damages

If a plaintiff is able to prove all of the four elements above in a counselor malpractice case related to a suicide attempt or completion, the plaintiff must then put a dollar amount on the injury that occurred and prove that the amount represents actual costs of treating the injury or dealing with the client who died, costs that represent loss of potential income, and even amounts to compensate individuals for their pain and suffering. Usually, this last element is proven through actuarial tables related to longevity and expert testimony associated with the other costs.

Lessons From Proving a Counselor Malpractice Case

By reviewing the five elements listed above that plaintiffs must prove to win a lawsuit that has been filed against a counselor related to a client's attempted or completed suicide, there are some lessons that can be learned that will help counselors effectively manage the legal risks associated with counseling suicidal clients. If counselors follow the guidelines in Appendix B, they will have a better chance of prevailing in the event they are ever sued after a client attempts or completes suicide.

Suicide Appellate Court Cases

There is no way to know how many counselors or other mental health professionals have been sued for malpractice related to suicide issues or the outcomes of all of those cases. If a lawsuit is filed in a local state or federal court and the suit is dismissed by the judge, the case is settled by the parties, or a judgment is rendered by a judge or jury, generally we know nothing about the suit unless the final disposition is appealed by one of the parties to the lawsuit. When a case from the trial level is appealed to a state or federal appellate court, then the case is summarized and is published in legal reporters. Only cases that are appealed and decisions that are rendered at the appellate level set precedent for cases that follow. And precedent is set by an appellate decision only for cases that follow in that particular state or federal jurisdiction.

While all appellate decisions are interesting and provide guidance for lawyers and mental health professionals regarding what may happen in similar cases in the future, it is important to understand that a similar case in a different jurisdiction would not be bound by a precedent set in another jurisdiction. For example, the landmark *Tarasoff* (1976) decision came from a California case that set the precedent that intended victims had to be warned by mental health professionals in some circumstances. That case created a precedent only in California. The Tarasoff principle of having to warn intended victims did not become precedent in states other than California until appellate state courts ruled similarly or state legislatures passed statutes making the principle state law. In fact, the state of Texas, in *Thapar v. Zezulka* (1999), specifically rejected the Tarasoff principle.

Most suicide malpractice lawsuits that have been reported were related to inpatient treatment of suicidal patient situations (Packman & Harris, 1998). Some inpatient and outpatient suicide cases are briefly summarized below:

- In *Meier v. Ross General Hospital* (1968), the court upheld a judgment against a physician and a hospital when a patient, following an attempted suicide, was placed in a second-floor room with a fully operable window, and the patient jumped out and killed himself.
- In *Texarkana Memorial Hospital v. Firth* (1988), a woman had been admitted to a hospital because of suicidal risk and psychosis. The locked ward to which she was admitted had no empty beds. She was sedated and was placed in an open ward with no special suicide precautions. When she woke up, she jumped from a window to her death. The hospital was held to be responsible.
- In *Bellah v. Greenson* (1978), the parents of a woman who died after taking an overdose of pills sued the woman's psychiatrist who was treating her on an outpatient basis. The court held that the psychiatrist did not owe a Tarasoff-type duty to the parents to warn them of their daughter's risk for suicide. The court held that it was a decision for a judge or jury to make as to whether the psychiatrist exercised a reasonable standard of care in this particular situation.
- In *Speer v. United States* (1981), a psychiatrist was treating a patient in an outpatient setting. The patient hoarded pills and took a lethal overdose. The psychiatrist was exonerated because he was found to have followed accepted medical standards in prescribing for the patient.

- In *Eisel v. Board of Education* (1991), a court held that school officials (including a school counselor) had a duty to investigate information from other students regarding another student's threat of suicide.
- In *Brooks v. Logan* (1995), a court held that a student's writing assignment, such as disturbing entries in a journal, could possibly make a student's suicide foreseeable.

Guidelines for Counseling and Managing Suicidal Clients

Counseling agencies and counselors in private practice need to establish procedures to be followed when a professional determines that a particular client may be at risk for suicide. Making this determination is difficult and requires that counselors exercise professional judgment. Having the knowledge to assess a client's risk for suicide is important for counselors in all settings. In addition, to protect themselves, counselors are advised to consult with their administrative supervisors, clinical supervisors, and colleagues when making difficult decisions about whether a particular client may be at risk for suicide.

Only mental health professionals whose job it is to make a decision of whether or not an individual is suicidal, and therefore must be hospitalized or watched very closely to prevent harm, should say that a particular person *is suicidal.* Counselors who may have to refer a client for an evaluation by such a mental health professional should say only that a particular client *may be suicidal.* This caution in using language could be very important if a client later does attempt or commit suicide. The term *may be suicidal,* instead of *is suicidal,* should be used in discussing the client with others and in any notes taken.

Steps to Take

Appendix C lists recommended steps to be taken when a counselor has made a determination that a minor client may be at risk for suicide. Parents or guardians must always be notified if a child is determined possibly to be at risk for suicide (Hermann & Remley, 2000). Appendix D lists similar steps when the client is an adult.

Appendix E includes a form that individuals might be asked to sign who agree to care for a client who may be at risk for suicide. Although having an individual sign such a form is not legally necessary and does not ensure a counselor will not be held accountable in the event a client harms himself or herself, having a signed form of this nature can be very helpful to demonstrate that a counselor informed a client's family member or significant person in his or her life of the situation and had a promise from the individual to seek help for the client.

Although it is not legally or even ethically required, it is best practice to assist individuals in securing evaluations for family members or friends who have been identified as perhaps being at risk for suicide. Appendix F provides a process for helping family members have evaluations completed.

The recommended steps listed in the Appendixes C through F are conservative in nature and have been developed to protect counselors if their judgment regarding a client turns out to be wrong, or if a client does attempt or complete suicide. These recommendations constitute best practice and do not reflect what most counselors do, and therefore should not be considered the standard of care clients should expect from counselors.

Professional Liability Insurance

One of the reasons counselors must have their own professional liability insurance is that they are legally required to do something that is scientifically impossible—determine the degree to which an individual may be at risk for suicide. Actually, counselors must just follow accepted procedures and use sound judgment in making such predictions. But, errors are possible. As a result, it is essential that counselors maintain their own personal professional liability insurance policies at all times. Usually, the best policies are offered by professional association insurance programs.

Adaptations for Diversity

When counselors are in the process of identifying and managing clients who may be at risk for suicide, counselors must avoid imposing their own values, which may be based on their own cultural or sociological background. Counselors must understand that some groups they may counsel may be more or less willing to take responsibility for a client who may be at risk for suicide, depending on the groups' values system (Kanel, 1999). If counselors cannot locate family members or friends who are willing to become involved in their client's potential crisis, counselors may be forced to seek assistance from emergency health care service providers.

In many cultures, extended family members or friends are as involved in a client's life as are close family members. When counseling minors who may be at risk for suicide, those to whom the counselor is legally obligated are the parents or guardians only. Information regarding the situation may be given only to the parents or guardians. When parents or guardians wish for other family members or nonfamily members to be given confidential information, counselors should obtain a written document from a parent or guardian giving permission to disclose information to others.

Summary

This chapter highlights a number of legal issues related to client suicides, including counselor malpractice, licensure requirements, privacy, privileged communication, counselor competency, abandonment, and record keeping. An overview of the elements from the law of professional malpractice is summarized, and the elements are then applied to counselor malpractice, particularly in relation to suicidal clients.

Some appellate cases related to clients who committed suicide are summarized. Guidelines for counselors for managing suicidal clients to minimize legal risks for counselors are provided. In addition, forms are provided for family members to sign when they have been notified that a family member may be at risk for suicide and for referring family members to agencies that provide evaluations to determine whether a family member may indeed be at risk for suicide.

References

American Counseling Association. (1995). *Code of ethics.* Alexandria, VA: Author.

Bellah v. Greenson, 146 Cal.Rptr. 535 (1978).

Bernstein, B. E., & Hartsell, T. L. (1998). *The portable lawyer for mental health professionals.* New York: Wiley.

Black, H. C. (1979). *Black's law dictionary.* St. Paul, MN: West.

Bongar, B., Maris, R. W., Berman, A. L., & Litman, R. E. (1998). Outpatient standards of care and the suicidal patient. In B. Bongar, A. L. Berman, R. W. Maris, M. M. Silverman, E. A. Harris, & W. L. Packman (Eds.), *Risk management with suicidal patients* (pp. 4–33). New York: Guilford Press.

Brooks v. Logan, 903 P.2d 73 (Idaho, 1995).

Conner, M. A. (Ed.). (1994). *Clinicians and the law: A legal handbook for therapists and counselors.* Providence, RI: Manisses Communications Group.

Eisel v. Board of Education, 597 A.2d 447 (Md. 1991).

Gladding, S. T., Remley, T. P., Jr., & Huber, C. H. (2001). *Ethical, legal, and professional issues in the practice of marriage and family therapy* (3rd ed.). Upper Saddle River, NJ: Prentice-Hall.

Goldstein, R. B., Black, D. W., Nasrallah, A., & Winokur, G. (1991). The prediction of suicide: Sensitivity, specificity, and predictive value of a multivariate model applied to suicide among 1,906 patients with affective disorders. *Archives of General Psychiatry, 48,* 418–422.

Hermann, M. A. (2002). A study of legal issues encountered by school counselors and perceptions of their preparedness to respond to legal challenges. *Professional School Counseling, 6,* 12–19.

Hermann, M. A., & Finn, A. (2002). An ethical and legal perspective on the role of school counselors in preventing violence in schools. *Professional School Counseling, 6,* 46–54.

Hermann, M. A., & Remley, T. P., Jr. (2000). Guns, violence, and schools: The results of school violence—Litigation against educators and students shedding more constitutional rights at the school house gate. *Loyola Law Review, 46,* 389-439.

Jacobs, D. G., Brewer, M., & Klein-Benheim, M. (1999). Suicide assessment: An overview and recommended protocol. In D. G. Jacobs (Ed.), *Guide to suicide assessment and intervention* (pp. 3–39). San Francisco: Jossey-Bass.

James, R. K., & Gilliland, B. E. (2001). *Crisis intervention strategies* (4th ed.). Belmont, CA: Wadswoth/Thomson Learning.

Kanel, K. (1999). *A guide to crisis intervention.* Pacific Grove, CA: Brooks/Cole.

Kiesler, C. A., & Sibulkin, A. E. (1987). *Mental hospitalization: Myths and facts about a national crisis.* Newbury Park, CA: Sage.

Meier v. Ross General Hospital, 69 Cal 2d 420, 71 Cal. Rptr 903, 445 P.2d 519 (1968).

Packman, W. L., & Harris, E. A. (1998). Legal issues and risk management in suicidal patients. In B. Bongar, A. L. Berman, R. W. Maris, M. M. Silverman, E. A. Harris, & W. L. Packman (Eds.), *Risk management with suicidal patients* (pp. 150–186). New York: Guilford Press.

Prosser, W. L. (1971). *Handbook of the law of torts* (4th ed.). St. Paul, MN: West.

Remley, T. P., Jr., & Herlihy, B. (2001). *Ethical, legal, and professional issues in counseling.* Upper Saddle River, NJ: Prentice-Hall.

Robertson, J. D. (1988). *Psychiatric malpractice: Liability of mental health professionals.* New York: Wiley.

Silverman, M. M., Berman, A. L., Bongar, B., Litman, R. E., & Maris, R. W. (1998). In B. Bongar, A. L. Berman, R. W. Maris, M. M. Silverman, E. A. Harris, & W. L. Packman (Eds.), *Risk management with suicidal patients* (pp. 83–109). New York: Guilford Press.

Slaby, A. E. (1998). Outpatient management of suicidal patients. In B. Bongar, A. L. Berman, R. W. Maris, M. M. Silverman, E. A. Harris, & W. L. Packman (Eds.), *Risk management with suicidal patients* (pp. 34–64). New York: Guilford Press.

Speer v. United States, 512 F. Supp. 670 (1981).

Stromberg, C. D., Haggarty, D. J., Leibenluft, R. F., McMillan, M. H., Mishkin, B., Rubin, B. L., & Trilling, H. R. (1988). *The psychologist's legal handbook.* Washington, DC: Council for the National Register of Health Service Providers in Psychology.

Tarasoff v. Regents of the University of California et al., 17 Cal. 3d 425, 118 Cal. Rptr. 129 (1974), vacated, 17 Cal. 3d 425, 551 P.2d 334, 131 Cal. Rptr. 14, Cal. Sup. Ct. (1976).

Texarkana Memorial Hospital, Inc. v. Firth, 746 S.W.2d. 494 (1988).

Thapar v. Zezulka, 994 S.W.2d 635 (Tex. 1999).

Appendix A

Documentation Through Records for Self-Protection

1. It would be impossible to write a summary of every action taken by a counselor or make an audiotape or videotape of every counseling session. Excessive documentation can take away valuable time that might be spent providing counseling services to clients.

2. On the other hand, there are circumstances in which counselors should document their actions to create a record showing that they have done what they should have done.

3. Documentation should be undertaken in circumstances in which a counselor's actions or inaction may later be reviewed by an ethics panel, a licensure board, an administrator, or within the context of a legal proceeding.

4. One of the situations in which a high level of documentation is called for occurs when a counselor determines that a client may be in danger of attempting suicide.

5. Documentation efforts should begin as soon as counselors determine they are in a situation in which documentation is important.

6. When documenting for self-protection, as much detail as possible should be included. Dates, exact times events occurred, and exact words spoken should be included to the degree details are remembered. Only factual information should be included. Thoughts, diagnoses, and conclusions of counselors should be avoided when documenting. If these kinds of things need to be written down, they should be included in clinical case notes rather than records kept for documentation.

7. The best documentation is created very soon after a conversation or event has occurred. Indicate the date and time anything is written. Never back date anything that is written. In other words, do not infer or state that something was written on an earlier date than it was actually written.

8. In the event counselors realize that documentation should have been occurring sooner, they should write a summary of what has happened up to that point in time. Include as much detail as can be remembered. The date and time the summary was written should be included on the summary.

9. Maintain a documentation file that includes the originals of notes written to counselors, copies of notes written by counselors to others, copies of relevant papers counselors cannot keep for themselves, and other papers that might be relevant to the situation.

10. Records kept for documentation should be kept secure in a locked file drawer or cabinet. If counselors agree to provide copies of their files, they should never release originals of their records, only copies.

Appendix B

Risk-Management Guidelines for Counselors That Will Assist in Prevailing If Sued in a Counselor Malpractice Case Related to a Client's Attempted or Completed Suicide

✓ If asked for casual advice regarding a person who may be suicidal, refrain from giving advice and instead refer the person asking to a mental health professional for counseling services.

✓ Make it clear in a written client agreement that counseling services are limited to the scheduled sessions and that any emergencies that occur between sessions are to addressed in an emergency environment (such as a hospital).

✓ Know how to determine whether a client may be at risk for attempting suicide. Read professional materials, attend workshops, or seek supervision from a qualified professional if skills in this area have not been developed.

✓ Consult with others in making decisions regarding client care. Consult with as many professionals as possible when making difficult decisions and document the consultations in writing.

✓ Document all steps taken in dealing with a client who may be at risk for suicide.

Appendix C

Managing a Minor Who May Be At Risk for Suicide

If you determine that a minor for whom you are responsible has exhibited some behaviors that are related to suicide but currently does not appear to be at risk for committing suicide . . .

1. If you believe that a child may be thinking about suicide or if you have observed or have information that a child has exhibited some minor behaviors that might be interpreted as suicidal, but you do not consider the situation to be an emergency, summarize in your case notes the child's behavior that supports your concern. Do not write that you believe the child may be at risk for suicide. Instead, write that although you do not believe the child may be at risk for suicide, you believe his or her parents need to be informed of the child's behaviors that concern you.

2. If you have consulted with colleagues, experts, or supervisors in reaching your position, document the consultations in your case notes.

3. Tell the child your concerns and, if appropriate, obtain an agreement from the child to inform his or her parent or guardian of your concerns. Tell the child to have his or her parent or guardian contact you after being told.

4. If the child is not capable of telling the parent or guardian himself or herself, or for some other reason asking the child to inform his or her parent or guardian does not seem like an appropriate course of action, explain to the child that you will be contacting his or her parent or guardian to inform him or her of your concern. If you are not in independent private practice, inform your supervisor of the actions you will be taking and follow any directives that he or she gives you.

5. Document in your case notes all conversations with the child, his or her guardian, and your supervisors.

If you determine that a minor for whom you are responsible MAY BE seriously at risk for committing suicide . . .

1. You are dealing with a very serious matter that requires immediate and decisive action. Make the determination that a minor may be at risk for committing suicide only if the minor has made a suicide gesture or attempt, has told you or someone else in a believable fashion that he or she plans to commit suicide, or has engaged in a pattern of behavior that the professional literature suggests is the behavior of a suicidal minor. Follow any agency or school policies that exist regarding managing suicidal children. If you are not in an independent private practice, notify your supervisor of the situ-

ation and follow any directives that he or she may give. If policies dictate or if your supervisor directs you to proceed differently from the steps below, follow the policies or the orders of your supervisor.

2. If you have consulted with colleagues, experts, or supervisors in reaching your position, document the consultations in your case notes.

3. Explain to the child that you will have to notify his or her parents or legal guardians so that they can help.

4. Assure the child that you will continue to help him or her and that you will disclose only the minimum information necessary for him or her to get assistance. Try to calm the child, but do not minimize the seriousness of the situation. Explain to the child what may happen in the next few hours, next few days, and long term.

5. Ensure that the child is not left alone and does not have any opportunity to harm himself or herself prior to turning the child over to his or her parent or guardian.

6. Contact a parent or guardian and explain that you believe his or her child may be at risk for suicide and give specific details that led to your concern. Insist that the parent or guardian come to pick up the child immediately.

7. If a parent or guardian cannot be found, make sure the child is under the supervision of a responsible person until a parent or guardian is located.

8. If you cannot contact a parent or guardian and if it is impossible to keep the child safe for an extended period of time, call an ambulance and have the child transported to a hospital that has psychiatric services. If you are not in an independent private practice, be sure to inform your supervisor and obtain his or her permission and support for taking this action. If your supervisor directs you take a different course of action, do so and document in your case notes what you were told and did. Make arrangements for someone (perhaps you) to ride in the ambulance with the child to the hospital. If you do not accompany the child to the hospital in the ambulance, give the ambulance attendant your contact information and offer to speak with the person at the hospital who will be conducting the evaluation, if requested to do so. Continue to attempt to contact the child's parent or guardian.

9. When you talk to the parent or guardian, ask him or her to take possession and responsibility immediately for the child.

10. When the parent or guardian arrives, explain to him or her that you believe that the child may be at risk for suicide, give specific details that led to your concern, instruct the parent or guardian of what he or she should do next, and ask that a document be signed that acknowledges that the parent or guardian has been informed of your concerns, has been given directions of steps to take next, and has agreed to take responsibility for his or her child. Also, have the

parent or guardian sign a form giving you permission to disclose any information you have to mental health professionals who may evaluate or treat their child in the future.

11. Explain to the parent or guardian that he or she must ensure that the child is not left alone, does not have any opportunities to harm himself or herself, and is taken for an evaluation as soon as possible to determine whether the child is at risk for suicide.

12. If a parent or guardian refuses to sign the document or communicates to you in some way that he or she will not take the situation seriously, notify your supervisor and make a report of suspected child neglect.

13. As events occur, document in your case notes in detail all of the events that transpired in relation to this situation. Be sure to date each entry and indicate the time you wrote it. Make several entries if necessary, and do not delay in writing details in your case notes.

14. When the child returns to you or your agency or school for services, obtain written permission from a parent or guardian to contact the professional who determined that the child was not at risk for suicide, or was no longer at risk for suicide.

15. Contact the child's treating physician, psychologist, or mental health provider and explain that his or her patient or client has returned to you or your agency or school for services. Ask the treating provider to summarize his or her evaluation and treatment of the child. Inquire as to whether the provider will continue to treat the child, and if so, the details of the planned treatment.

16. Also ask the treating provider the types of counseling services he or she would like for you to provide to the child. Do not agree to provide any counseling services that your position does not allow you provide (especially in a school setting). Ask the provider to tell you the circumstances under which you should return the child to him or her for further evaluation or treatment.

17. As soon as possible after you have talked to the provider, document in your case notes details of your conversation. Be sure to date the entry and indicate the time you wrote it.

Appendix D

Managing an Adult Client Who May Be At Risk for Suicide

If you determine that an adult client has exhibited some behaviors that are related to suicide but currently does not appear to be at risk for committing suicide . . .

1. If you believe that an adult client may be thinking about suicide or if you have observed or have information that an adult client has exhibited some behaviors that might be interpreted as suicidal, but you do not consider the situation to be an emergency, summarize in your case notes the client's behavior that supports your concern. Do not write that you believe the client may be at risk for suicide. Instead, write that although you do not believe the client may be at risk for suicide, you believe a significant person in his or her life needs to be informed of the client's behaviors that concern you.

2. A significant person might be your adult client's spouse, parent, adult child, other relative, domestic partner, dating partner, or close friend. Choose a person who lives with the client or who is in frequent contact with the client.

3. If you have consulted with colleagues, experts, or supervisors in reaching your position, document the consultations in your case notes.

4. Tell your adult client your concerns and, if appropriate, obtain an agreement from the client to inform a significant person in his or her life of your concerns. Tell the client to have the person he or she informs to contact you after being told.

5. If your adult client is not capable of telling the significant person him- or herself, or for some other reason asking the client to inform his significant person does not seem like an appropriate course of action, explain to the client that you will be contacting a significant person to inform him or her of your concern. If you are not in independent private practice, inform your supervisor of the actions you will be taking and follow any directives that he or she gives you.

6. Document in your case notes all conversations with your adult client, his or her significant person, and your supervisors.

If you determine that an adult client MAY BE seriously at risk for committing suicide . . .

1. You are dealing with a very serious matter that requires immediate and decisive action. Make the determination that an adult client may be at risk for committing suicide only if the client has made a suicide gesture or attempt, has told you or someone else in a believ-

able fashion that he or she plans to commit suicide, or has engaged in a pattern of behavior that the professional literature suggests is the behavior of a suicidal adult. Follow any agency policies that exist regarding managing suicidal adults. If you are not in an independent private practice, notify your supervisor of the situation and follow any directives that he or she may give. If policies dictate or if your supervisor directs you to proceed differently from the steps below, follow the policies or the orders of your supervisor.

2. If you have consulted with colleagues, experts, or supervisors in reaching your position, document the consultations in your case notes.

3. Explain to your adult client that you will have to notify a significant person in his or her life so that the individual can help.

4. Assure your adult client that you will continue to help him or her and that you will disclose only the minimum information necessary for him or her to get assistance. Try to calm the client, but do not minimize the seriousness of the situation. Explain to the client what may happen in the next few hours, next few days, and long term.

5. Ensure that your adult client is not left alone and does not have any opportunity to harm himself or herself prior to turning the client over to his or her significant person.

6. Contact a significant person in your adult client's life and explain that you believe his or her relative, partner, or friend may be at risk for suicide and give specific details that led to your concern. Insist that the significant person come to pick up the client immediately.

7. If a significant person cannot be found, make sure your adult client is under the supervision of a responsible person until a significant person is located.

8. If you cannot contact a significant person and if it is impossible to keep your adult client safe for an extended period of time, call an ambulance and have the client transported to a hospital that has psychiatric services. If you are not in an independent private practice, be sure to inform your supervisor and obtain his or her permission and support for taking this action. If your supervisor directs you take a different course of action, do so and document in your case notes what you were told and did. Give the ambulance attendant your contact information and offer to speak with the person at the hospital who will be conducting the evaluation, if requested to do so. Continue to attempt to contact the client's significant person.

9. When you talk to the significant person, ask him or her to take possession and responsibility immediately for your adult client.

10. When the significant person arrives, explain to him or her that you believe that your adult client may be at risk for suicide, give specific details that led to your concern, instruct the significant person of

what he or she should do next, and ask that a document be signed that acknowledges that the significant person has been informed of your concerns, has been given directions of steps to take next, and has agreed to take responsibility for your client.

11. Also, have the adult client sign a form giving you permission to disclose any information you have to mental health professionals who may evaluate or treat him or her in the future. If the client refuses or is not capable of signing the form, ask the family member or significant person to sign on your client's behalf.

12. Explain to the significant person that he or she must ensure that your adult client is not left alone, does not have any opportunities to harm himself or herself, and is taken for an evaluation as soon as possible to determine whether the client is at risk for suicide.

13. If a significant person refuses to sign the document or communicates to you in some way that he or she will not take the situation seriously, call an ambulance and follow the steps in Item 8 above.

14. As events occur, document in your case notes in detail all of the events that transpired in relation to this situation. Be sure to date each entry and indicate the time you wrote it. Make several entries if necessary, and do not delay in writing details in your case notes.

15. When your adult client returns to you or your agency for services, obtain written permission from your client to contact the professional who determined that your client was not at risk for suicide, or was no longer at risk for suicide.

16. Contact your adult client's treating physician, psychologist, or mental health provider and explain that his or her patient or client has returned to you or your agency for services. Ask the treating provider to summarize his or her evaluation and treatment of the client. Inquire as to whether the provider will continue to treat the client, and if so, the details of the planned treatment. Also ask the treating provider the types of counseling services he or she would like for you to provide to the client. Do not agree to provide any counseling services that your position does not allow you provide. Ask the provider to tell you the circumstances under which you should return the client to him or her for further evaluation or treatment.

17. As soon as possible after you have talked to the provider, document in your case notes details of your conversation. Be sure to date the entry and indicate the time you wrote it.

Appendix E

Notification and Agreement Form to Be Signed by Relative or Significant Person in the Life of an Individual Who May Be At Risk for Suicide

_____

Name of Person Who May Be At Risk for Suicide

I acknowledge that the mental health professional who has signed this form has told me that he or she believes that the individual listed above may be at risk for suicide. I understand that this belief is based on specific information regarding this individual. I further understand that this mental health professional is not in a position to make a determination as to whether the individual listed above is at risk for suicide.

 I agree to care for the individual listed above until he or she can be evaluated by a qualified professional to determine whether the individual is at risk. I further agree to ensure that the individual listed above is provided the mental health care he or she needs after the evaluation is completed.

 I understand that if an emergency arises, I should take the individual listed above to a hospital for emergency mental health treatment.

_____

Signature of Family Member or Significant Person
in the Individual's Life

_____

Date

_____

Signature of Mental Health Professional

_____

Date

Appendix F

Assisting Family Members or Significant Persons in the Individual's Life Arrange for an Evaluation to Determine Whether an Individual Is a Danger to Self or Others

1. These recommendations represent "best practice." Although most mental health professionals do not provide all of the information suggested in these guidelines, it would be very helpful to clients and their loved ones if it were provided.

2. A close family member or a significant person who is very close to the individual must be enlisted to assist someone who may be at risk for suicide or for harming others. It would be best if the relative or significant person lived with the individual. If the individual lives alone or lives with people who cannot help, then choose a responsible family member or significant person to help. Family members might include a spouse, adult child, parent, sibling, or other close relative. Significant persons might include a domestic partner, roommate who is close friends with the individual, or someone else who is a very close friend.

3. Explain that the individual must be cared for constantly before the evaluation takes place. Explain that constant care includes monitoring the individual's activities, ensuring someone is with the individual at all times, and making sure the individual does not have access to means of harming self or others.

4. Explain that, if necessary, the person who may be at risk should be taken to the emergency room of a hospital that offers psychiatric emergency services before an appointment with a physician occurs. Explain that it would be necessary to seek an emergency evaluation if the person who may be at risk becomes violent, refuses to cooperate with his or her care giver, or engages in behavior that alarms the caregiver in any way. Give the relative of significant person the names, addresses, and telephone numbers of local hospitals that offer psychiatric emergency services.

5. If the individual who may be at risk is covered by health care insurance or is a participant in some type of health care plan, follow the procedures for obtaining health care services required by the insurance or health care plan. If the procedures are not known, the family member or significant person should call the health care plan's information number and ask what procedures they should follow to have the individual's mental status evaluated to determine whether he or she is a danger to self or others.

6. If the process for scheduling an appointment takes too long, then the emergency treatment option of the health care insurance or health care plan should be utilized.

7. The major types of health care plans include the following:
   A. Health Maintenance Organization (HMO). If the individual is an HMO member, then he or she should be scheduled to see his or her primary care physician. Use the expedited appointment option for HMO services if it would take too long to schedule an appointment with the individual's primary care physician.
   B. Preferred Provider Organization (PPO) or Exclusive Provider Organization (EPO). If the individual is a PPO or an EPO member, then he or she should make an appointment according to that organization's procedures. The PPO or EPO may require that the appointment be made with the individual's primary care physician. Use the expedited option for PPO or EPO services if it would take too long to schedule an appointment with the individual's primary care physician. If seeing the primary care physician is not required, an appointment should be made directly with a psychiatrist who is on the PPO or EPO list of providers.
   C. Traditional health insurance. If the individual has traditional health insurance, then he or she should make an appointment to see a psychiatrist.
8. If the individual who may be at risk does not have any type of health insurance or is not a member of any type of health care plan, then the public mental health system should be utilized. Follow the steps below:
   A. Provide the family member or significant person with the name, address, and telephone number of the community mental health facility in the political jurisdiction in which the person who may be at risk lives that performs mental health evaluations for indigent persons.
   B. Explain how the mental health facility accepts referrals and its policies for performing mental health evaluations for indigent persons.
9. Give the family member or significant person your contact information and offer to speak with the professional who performs the evaluation if the individual is interested in speaking to you.
10. Ask the family member or significant person to contact you after the evaluation has taken place to summarize the results of the evaluation and to give you the name and telephone number of the person who completed the evaluation.

3.
Counseling Suicidal Clients and Survivors

Part Three of this book contains myriad applied information and applications for counselors to use when counseling suicidal clients along the life span continuum. Chapter 8, Counseling Suicidal Children, by Tamara Davis, explores the realities of suicide among children. The chapter begins with a literature review of what we know about children and suicide. Discussion of the signs and symptoms in children, both in terms of behavior and developmental milestones, sheds light on ways that counselors, educators, and family members can recognize when a child is at risk for self-harm. Multimodal treatment approaches and counseling strategies are described, followed by the presentation of two case studies.

Chapter 9, Counseling Suicidal Adolescents, coauthored by Douglas R. Gross and myself, discusses risk factors, myths, and a four-part profile for recognizing signs and symptoms in suicidal adolescent clients. This is followed by an explanation of approaches to prevention from individual, family, school, and community perspectives. The subsequent subsection on approaches to intervention uses the same four perspectives to provide the reader with guidelines for practice. Risk assessment, crisis counseling, guidelines for postvention, adaptations for diversity, and case study material are also provided to give counselors as many concrete suggestions as possible in a single chapter.

Chapter 10, Counseling Suicidal Adults: Rebuilding Connections, by Suzanne R. S. Simon, a doctoral student in special and counselor education at Portland State University, explores the topic of counseling suicidal adults through the periods of early (age 25–34), middle (age 35–65), and late (over 65) adulthood. The stage theories of Erik Erickson and Daniel Levinson provide the underpinning for ensuing discussion of risk assessment, crisis management, and interventions in the lives of early, middle, and late-stage suicidal adults. The stories of Beth, John, and Gloria provide the reader with concrete case study material as perspectives of the individual client, the counselor, the family, and the community are explored.

The final chapter of the book, Counseling Suicide Survivors (chap. 11), by Dale Elizabeth Pehrsson and Mary Boylan of Oregon State University, begins with the case of Delilah. Through the lens of this case study, the consequences of suicide for suicide survivors, suicide survivors and development, implications for counseling suicide survivors, and adaptations for diversity are addressed. I am sure the readers will find this chapter helpful because counseling suicide survivors may be a necessary part of the role of the counselor in a variety of settings.

Chapter 8
Counseling Suicidal Children

Tamara Davis

Childhood is a time when life is supposedly carefree, full of fun, excitement, and opportunity. Although adversity may arise, most children seem remarkably resilient and able to put their world back in order again. Despite the hurdles and obstacles that sometimes present themselves in childhood, most children learn coping mechanisms and strategies to help them through even the most horrific events. However, some children do not cope so readily and may internalize the difficulties they are facing. It seems hard to imagine that children entertain the thought of self-harm and, even more serious, suicide. To consider childhood and suicide simultaneously seems unrealistic and truly disturbing. However, the topic of suicidal children should be explored because, despite our general desire not to acknowledge it, the reality is that children do think about suicide, and some even complete the act.

This chapter explores the realities of suicide among children. For the purposes of this discussion, childhood is defined as the chronological ages of 5–12. A review of the literature provides what is known about children and suicide, including statistics and research that specifically addresses the suicidal child. Discussions of the signs and symptoms, both in terms of behavior and in terms of developmental milestones, shed light on ways that counselors, educators, and family members can recognize when a child is at risk for self-harm. Finally, multimodal treatment approaches and counseling strategies are provided. Two case studies are offered as examples of counseling interventions, one in which the outcome was successful and the other in which obstacles interfere with effective treatment.

Do Children Commit Suicide?

Statistics indicate that the rate of suicide among children, even those under the age of 10, may be grossly underestimated. In fact, it is difficult to find statistics for children younger than 10, although there is evidence that young children have committed suicide. The National Center for Health Statistics (2001) ranked suicide as the third leading cause of death among children ages 10–14. This ranking remains consistent throughout adolescence and early adulthood. The rate of suicide among children ages 10–14 increased 109% between 1980 and 1997 (National Center for Injury Prevention and Control, 1999). According to the National Institute of Mental Health (2000), the suicide rate among children ages 10–14 was 1.5 per 100,000 children, with the gender ratio being 4:1 (males:females). The completed suicide gender ratio remains consistent and becomes even slightly higher for males into early adulthood, although more females than males attempted suicide (National Institute of Mental Health, 1999).

But what about younger children? The research is lacking in terms of providing statistics or information about the likelihood of suicide in very young children. The National Center for Health Statistics (2001) reported that the leading cause of death for children 5–9 years old was unintentional injury, with more than half occurring in motor vehicle accidents. The second leading cause of death was cancer. This remained consistent in children 10–14 years olds. These statistics imply that children are not committing suicide; if young children die, it is usually due to some other cause, particularly an accident. However, these statistics should be interpreted rather cautiously. According to the *Merck Manual of Diagnosis and Therapy* (Beers & Berkow, 1999), it is difficult for the cause of death in children to be designated as suicide because such a designation typically requires proof of intent. Therefore, if a gun is fired or a child takes too many pills, society does not want to believe that the act was intentional, and it is easier to accept that a child dies accidentally than to consider the circumstances that might result in the suicide of a child. According to Mishara (1999):

> My discussions with various coroners and medical examiners revealed that coroners are often reluctant to classify self-inflicted deaths in children as suicides because there is a general belief that children do not fully understand the implications of their actions and thus may be incapable of committing suicide, even when their self-inflicted injury or lethal behavior resulted in death. (p. 106)

A report by Miller (2000, as cited by Hirshberg & Sinha, 2002) investigated the relationship between accessibility to guns and the number of child suicides. Miller reported that "in the five states where people own the highest number of firearms, far more suicides are committed by kids between the ages of 5 and 15 than in the five states with lowest gun ownership" (p. 36). Miller suggested that the availability of guns makes suicidality among children more likely.

While there is significant and extensive research on adolescent suicide, it seems difficult for society to handle the reality that children may become so distraught that they commit suicide. As professional counselors, it is beneficial and worthwhile to consider the likelihood that an accidental death of a child might somehow be intentional and, therefore, preventable.

What We Know About Children and Suicide: Contributing Factors

Although the research on young children and suicide is sparse, it does seem that there are conditions or circumstances that are related to childhood suicide. These include family, social, and academic factors.

Family Factors

An article in *Mental Health Weekly* ("Children Whose Parents Attempt Suicide," 2002) reported that the children of parents who have attempted suicide have an increased risk of attempting suicide in their lifetime. Wise and Spengler (1997) concurred with this report and stated that parental suicidal behavior and depression are key factors influencing the suicidal behavior of children. Yang and Clum (2000) cited other family characteristics that have comorbidity with childhood suicide, such as family violence, including child abuse and neglect, marital discord, a general poor family environment, and child maltreatment. They found that early negative life events contributed to feelings such as low self-esteem and hopelessness and created cognition that established a relationship between early negative life events and suicidal ideation. The long-term effects of unstable home environments and dysfunctional families also put children at risk for suicidal behavior later in their lives. Whether it is an attempt to model parent behavior or an attempt to escape from unhappiness, children may choose to end their lives much earlier if it seems to be the only way out of their present circumstances.

Social Factors

Koki (1999) gathered reports from Norway, England, and Japan and found that children who have experienced severe episodes of bullying have later committed suicide. This research is supported by claims that the majority of school violence prevention efforts (including antibullying programs) are not targeted toward young children (Speaker & Petersen, 2000). Therefore, much of the social and emotional damage of bullying and harassment has been done prior to the onset of antiviolence programs. The longevity of childhood bullying may extend into adolescence, which is a more likely time for suicide to occur. Fried and Fried (1996) reviewed research that indicated that prolonged exposure to bullying may lead to either withdrawn or aggressive behavior and may also lead to suicide. Thus, it is important that significant adults in a child's life pay attention to the relationships and social situations that children are a part of and intervene when bullying and teasing begin.

Academic Factors

Research in the 1980s connected childhood suicide to poor school performance (Stillion, McDowell, & May, 1989) and having a diagnosed learning disability (Peck, 1985, as cited in Wise & Spengler, 1997). Other research indicated that children who have above-average intelligence are more likely to become suicidal (Kosky, 1983). A significant finding by Orbach (1988) was that a more significant contributing factor to a child's suicidal behavior is the belief that he or she is a failure in more than one area (e.g., at school and at home). This would suggest that children who feel unsuccessful academically and in their family environment might be twice as likely to consider suicide as a viable alternative. The lack of recent research in this area is a problem that counselors should note.

Myths About Children and Suicide

There are several myths about children and suicide that should be addressed. Because society does not like to consider the possibility that a child is suicidal, one tends to develop misconceptions about a child's perception of suicide.

Wise and Spengler (1997) identified the following as myths about children and suicide:

1. *Children do not commit suicide.* As mentioned earlier, the reality is blurred because of underreporting, misreporting, and incomplete data.
2. *Children do not understand the concept and finality of death.* Speece and Brent (1992, as cited in Wise & Spengler, 1997) suggested that children understand the finality of death between the ages of 5 and 12. Younger children perceive death like sleep, so there is the belief they will wake up from death. By ages 9–10, children understand that death is irreversible and is the end of life. Mishara (1999) surveyed 65 students in Grades 1–5 and found that 71% understood that death is final and 88% understood that death is universal.
3. *Children are incapable of planning suicide.* Wise and Spengler (1997) cited research that supports that documented suicides of children between the ages of 6–12 show intentional actions that lead to death. These included jumping from heights, intentional drowning, stabbing, running in front of moving vehicles, and hanging. Mishara (1999) found that when identifying how someone commits suicide, 58% of the children mentioned a knife, 34% jumping, 31% using a gun, 25% poison, and 12% intentionally being hit by a car. Other responses included drowning, hanging, setting oneself on fire, and banging one's head against a wall.

But do children think about killing themselves? Mishara's (1999) survey revealed the shocking answer: yes. Nine of the children in his study (13.8%)

said they had thought about killing themselves at one time but were not currently suicidal. Not surprisingly, the older the student, the greater likelihood of talking about suicide with others. These truths have important implications for counselors in all settings. It is imperative that practitioners assess childhood suicidality in the counseling setting to understand and respond to the potential for a child to commit suicide.

Signs and Symptoms of a Suicidal Child

It is difficult to describe how a suicidal child looks or the signs and symptoms that might be present in a child with suicidal ideation. Bailey (2001) presented the spectrum of suicide that might occur from the cognitive beginning to its tragic end:

- preoccupation with death or death themes
- suicidal thoughts (ideation)
- conscious and unconscious suicidal behavior
- suicide gestures and attempts
- suicidal plans
- suicide completion

Counselors and significant adults in a young person's life should intervene at the first indication of self-harming behavior. While this list serves as a possible progression of suicidal behavior, it should not be considered an absolute. Many children are able to mask their internal thoughts of suicide, which perpetuates society's hesitancy in acknowledging childhood suicide.

Many researchers have attempted to identify the symptomatology and "tell-tale" signs of suicide. A compilation of these symptoms are listed in Exhibit 8.1. The list in Exhibit 8.1 evokes some interesting questions about how suicidality presents itself in young children. How does one discriminate between developmental changes and suicidal symptoms? Should we jump to the conclusion that every major mood swing or behavior change is a sign of suicidal tendencies? Do we assume that any bizarre behavior or sudden shift in relationships is an indication that suicide is eminent? These answers can be addressed through professional assessment and a thorough exploration and evaluation of the child's mental, physical, and social environment.

The symptoms listed in Exhibit 8.1 are probably not surprising. These are the signs and symptoms associated with suicidal behavior in adolescents as well. However, recent studies have explored other behaviors and symptoms that may also be indicative of suicidal children.

Anxiety

A term that has been explored with reference to its relationship to childhood suicidal ideation is "anxious suicidality" (Allan, Kashani, Dahlmeier,

Exhibit 8.1

Signs and Symptoms of a Suicidal Child

- Preoccupation with death themes in conversation, writing, music, drawing
- Unexpected social isolation
- Peer or friend with recent suicidal behavior
- Writing and leaving suicide notes to be found
- Accident-prone or high-risk behavior
- Obtaining a weapon or means of suicide
- Belligerent or acting-out behavior
- Running away from home
- Giving away possessions
- Persistent thoughts about suicide
- Previous near-fatal attempts
- Episodes of acute depression
- Reported changes in eating or sleeping patterns
- Defiance, rebelliousness, or violence
- Neglect of appearance or personal hygiene
- Mood or personality changes
- Boredom, lack of concentration
- Drastic declines in quality of school work

Note. From Bailey (2001) and Helsel (2001).

Beck, & Reid, 1998, p. 251). Research has not typically examined the connection between anxiety disorders, such as phobias and panic disorders, and suicide ideation. In a study of 27 children (ages 8–11 years) with suicide ideation (as measured by the Scale for Suicide Ideation), Allan et al. found that children who scored high on measures of suicide ideation and anxiety were more active and more likely to have intense emotional reactions to events than those with low anxiety. It is interesting to note that groups with low anxiety and suicide ideation and groups with high anxiety and suicide ideation did not differ on measures of depression and hopelessness. Another result of the study was that the children with comorbid suicidality and high anxiety also exhibited other problems such as overall unhappiness and parental history of psychopathology (Allan et al., 1998). This implies that when students have anxiety coupled with one or more comorbid contributing factors, such as negative life events, the tendency toward suicidal ideation may be more likely than for those children with suicide ideation only.

Suicide Gestures

Parasuicide

Parasuicidal gestures may be overt or covert. Overt examples would be the child who repeatedly indicates that "I'm going to kill myself" or "I wish I could die." More covert measures might be giving away personal belongings or wearing clothing to cover failed attempts at suicide. Helsel (2001) reviewed the literature and cited signs of parasuicide, such as leaving suicide notes, telling others about pending suicide plans, or showing signs of self-mutilation.

These types of gestures are atypical of normal developmental childhood behavior. However, it is not unusual for a child to state, "I just want to die" or "I could just kill myself." Children often speak in extremes as a way of getting the attention of others. However, it is very important to assess the impetus behind such statements and to inform children of the seriousness of the threat. Poppenhagen and Qualley (1998) indicated that more covert statements, such as "I just can't take it anymore," should be evaluated just as intensely as more obvious statements. Above all else, it is professionally and ethically responsible to err on the side of caution and to follow protocol when a child threatens suicide.

Self-Mutilation

One of the most disturbing trends among youth today is the rise in the incidence of self-mutilating behavior. The behavior of cutting and self-harm has gained popularity in recent years. When defining self-injurious behavior, it is important to recognize there is a wide range of behaviors. Martinson (2001) listed the following as examples:

- carving
- scratching
- branding
- marking
- burning/abrasions
- biting
- bruising
- hitting
- picking and pulling skin and hair

The intent of the injury also affects the labeling of the behavior as self-injurious. If the purpose is for sexual gratification, body decoration, spiritual enlightenment via ritual, or fitting in with peers, the behavior should not be considered self-injury.

In the research, self-mutilation is defined as "deliberate self-harm without the intent to die" (Stanley, Gameroff, Michalsen, & Mann, 2001, p. 427). However, this does not mean that children who self-harm may not be suicidal. Stanley et al. noted that there may be a subtype of suicidal behavior in which the intention is death but the behavior manifests itself as self-mutilation. Their study, though conducted with adults with a history of self-mutilation, has some important implications for those who might work with suicidal children. They found that adult self-mutilators may be at a greater risk for suicide than nonmutilators because of the feelings of hopelessness and

217

depression that are characteristic of suicide attempts, the instability that characterizes suicidal ideation, and the belief that they will be rescued after a suicide attempt based on the history of being rescued when self-mutilating.

The implications for children are not clearly evident, but some general parallels may be drawn. Because self-injury is perceived as a release from psychological pain, there is a boundary in which the self-injurious behavior is not enough to reduce the pain; therefore, suicidal behavior or extreme self-injury may be the only escape from pain. Although there is no concrete evidence to support that self-mutilating children are more likely to be suicidal, it seems reasonable that children who self-injure are seeking attention or asking for help, and if their call goes unanswered, they might progress to suicidal behavior. Martinson (2001) stated:

> People who inflict physical harm on themselves are often doing it in an attempt to maintain psychological integrity—it's a way to keep from killing themselves. . . . And, although some people who self-injure *do* later attempt suicide, they almost always use a method different from their preferred method of self harm. (p. 3)

While self-mutilation may not be a direct sign or symptom of suicide, it is a behavior that should be addressed through intensive counseling.

Assessing Child Suicide

Formal Assessment

Just as the research regarding childhood suicide is lacking, there are few formal assessment instruments that are appropriate for use with children. First, the Child Suicide Potential Scales (Pfeffer et al., 1979, as cited by Wise & Spengler, 1997) consists of eight scales based on suicidal risk factors for children ages 6–12. Another instrument is the Suicidal Ideation Questionnaire–JR (Reynolds, 1987). The weakness of this inventory is that it only goes as low as Grades 7–9, which makes its applicability and usefulness with young children questionable. Although there are other inventories related to childhood depression, inventories used to assess childhood suicide are seemingly nonexistent. This seems to parallel the general attitude toward childhood suicide.

Informal Assessment

If a child nonchalantly mentions suicide or threatens self-harm, adults need to respond. Does the child truly feel this way? What do they mean by the statement? Have they felt this way before? Do they have a plan for doing this to themselves? In some situations, children may say, "No, I was just kidding" or "I don't really want to hurt myself, I'm just mad." While these statements may be true, adults should seek services from trained personnel such as school counselors, psychologists, or other mental health professionals to discuss the threat with the child. A child may honestly have no intention of harming him- or herself. Sometimes, children make a statement to get others to pay more attention to them. Everyone pays attention when children threaten to harm themselves. If it is discovered that a child is using the threat of suicide to get the time and attention of others, it should be addressed by significant adults in the child's life. For this reason, even the most minimal threat should be brought to the attention of the child's parent or guardian. Exploring the intent as well as the feelings behind such statements is necessary, and counselors in all areas have an ethical responsibility to explore and report a child's intent to harm him- or herself.

Addressing a child's overt suicidal threat is not easy, but it is much more difficult to determine if a child's covert behavior is suicidal. When a child is shy or withdrawn, it is difficult to assess if the mood or attitude is part of the child's personality or if it is indicative of depression or psychological issues. The best way to assess a child's frame of mind and feelings about life circumstances is to evaluate the situation. Possible questions might include the following:

- I noticed you were playing by yourself when you were at recess. Do you like to spend time alone?
- When you are spending time alone, what do you think about?
- What things make you happy? What things make you sad?
- What do you like about school/home/day care? Are there things that you don't like?

If at any time during the questioning the child indicates deep depression or suicidal thinking, the line of questioning will become more specific to suicide. This questioning is discussed in the next section ("Treating the Suicidal Child").

Another verbal strategy for assessing a child's level of suicidality is a technique from solution-focused brief counseling called *scaling*. The technique involves asking the client (in this case, the child): "On a scale of 1 to 5, with 1 being *not at all* and 5 being *all the time*, how much do you think about hurting yourself?" A counselor is going to respond somewhat differently to the child who says "1" and the child who says "5." The scaling question is a good way to assess the level of seriousness of the suicidal child, and the response may have specific implications for treatment.

Developmentally, young children may not be able to verbalize their thoughts and feelings, or children may not be ready to verbally express the feelings they are having. One way to assess a child's thinking and feeling is through play observation. Pfeffer (1986) suggested that direct observation of a child's play can provide important information into the child's thoughts and emotions. Three common characteristics of a suicidal child's play are (a) developmentally inappropriate play, particularly that of younger children,

(b) repeated dangerous and reckless behaviors using self as the object of attack, and (c) acting out scenes or fantasies of death or violence (Pfeffer, 1986). Again, it is not atypical for children to play "war" or to have objects battle each other or even destroy each other. However, if the destruction or harm seems to be turned inward toward the child, there may be reason for concern.

Another important assessment feature is the *continuity* of suicidal feelings over time. A history of suicidal thoughts and feelings is a key indicator that the issues that originally prompted the suicidal ideation have either not changed or not dissipated. Once the assessment of suicidality is made, a treatment plan must be developed. The next section focuses on treatment plans and provides strategies for school counselors, mental health counselors, and parents in a collaborative approach to treatment for the suicidal child.

Treating the Suicidal Child

Because suicidal tendencies are comorbid with several *Diagnostic and Statistical Manual of Mental Disorders—Text Revision* (*DSM–IV–TR*; American Psychiatric Association, 2000) categories, it is critical that a suicidal child is examined by a physician and a mental health professional with medical training (e.g., psychiatrist, psychologist) in the event that medication seems to be a treatment choice. Depending on the diagnosis, antidepressants, such as Zoloft or Paxil, might be prescribed in small doses to address the depressive symptoms. Other mood stabilizers that might be used with children include mood stabilizers such as Depakote or Tegretol. Bailey (2001) indicated that it is not unusual for doctors to prescribe a selective serotonin reuptake inhibitor (SSRI) with an atypical antidepressant, such as Wellbutrin or Effexor, to boost the effect of the SSRI alone. Although psychiatric medications can be an effective treatment alternative, it is critical that the side effects of medication on young children be considered. Because there are relatively few clinical trials with these types of medication with young children, medical personnel must use caution when prescribing medication as a means of treatment. A thorough exploration of potential side effects as well as the physical and emotional effects of taking such medications will need to be conducted and explained to parents or guardians of suicidal children. While medication may be a viable choice of treatment, it should not be viewed as the "fix" for suicidal thoughts and feelings in children.

Research on treatment with depression and suicidal children consistently promotes multimodal assessment and multimethod treatment. Medication alone is probably not going to solve the problem, just as one formal inventory is not going to give the complete picture of the suicidal child. Medication in combination with counseling or psychotherapy for the child as well as collaboration with the family attacks the issue from all angles and provides a more comprehensive approach to treatment. Addressing the suicidal child from varying perspectives increases the likelihood that one of the treatments, if not all, will be successful.

Counseling Suicidal Children

When preparing to work with a suicidal child, counselors should use a holistic approach. Counseling interventions should occur with the individual child, the school, community mental health professionals, and the family. I discuss each of these separately but emphasize the need for collaborative efforts to comprehensively address the issues of the suicidal child.

Individual

Although the setting will influence counseling suicidal children, there are some general techniques that can be used when working with the child individually. Regardless whether the professional is a school counselor, a licensed professional counselor, or a member of a mental health facility, the one constant is that as soon as a suicidal child is brought to the attention of the professional, intervention must occur. The ethical and legal responsibilities of *due care* require that counselors respond when they are aware of clients in danger of harming themselves or others.

When meeting with a young child, it is important that the counselor not overwhelm him or her right away by bombarding the child with questions about his or her suicidal thoughts and feelings. In fact, the child may be hesitant to open up right away, especially if the child is not familiar with the counselor. Allowing time for the child to get comfortable and beginning to establish rapport is going to be a key component in helping the child feel safe enough to disclose personal information. With young children, it is often good to have books, art supplies, clay, puppets, or other materials that might foster play. As mentioned earlier, there may be some indication during the observation of play that the child is suicidal. Drawing or coloring is another avenue to help the child become more comfortable in the counseling setting. The child should be given time to adjust to the unfamiliar surrounding.

Although the tasks of building trust and rapport often take more than one session, the immediacy of the suicidal threat and the concern that the child may be suicidal prevent the counselor from allowing the child to leave the counseling setting without a plan of action. Ideally, the parent has already been contacted or has been working collaboratively with the counselor and is aware of the child's suicidal thoughts or behaviors. If the parent is not aware of the child's threats or behaviors about suicide, the counselor must make contact with the parent/guardian to inform them. The ethical and legal obligations and "duty to warn" are very clear about this professional responsibility.

Assessing Intent and the Plan. Once the child seems to feel comfortable in the counseling setting, it is appropriate to begin gently confronting the issue. Sometimes, if the counselor is privy to information about the child making specific suicidal threats, it is suitable for the counselor to refer to that information. For example: "I understand that you wrote something in your journal about hurting yourself. Would you like to tell me about that?" If the child is amenable to talking about the behavior, other probing questions might follow:

- Is this the first time you have thought about this? If not, when else has this been something you have thought about?
- Tell me what you mean when you say you want to _____ (hurt yourself, kill yourself, die).
- Do you know someone else who has done this? If so, who and how did you know them?
- Have you thought about a plan for killing yourself? What types of ways have you thought about?
- What would others who are left behind do without you? How would your _____ (mother, father, sibling, friend, etc) feel?
- How do you think that things would be better if you weren't here?
- Ask the Miracle Question: If you woke up tomorrow and the problem was gone, what would that look like? Would the problem be gone and would you still be here?
- What would you like to say to the people in your life about how you are feeling right now?
- Tell me about the important people in your life. How would they miss you if you weren't here?
- What are some ways that we can work together to help you feel better about things? Tell me what would make this situation seem better and if there is anything that would make you want to continue to live.

In the first few question, the counselor is questioning the intent and threat of suicide. If the child immediately retreats from suicidal talk (e.g., "I was only kidding"), the counselor should be cautious about accepting this as the truth. It could be that the child is trying to divert away from the topic because the child feels that if he or she is honest, he or she might get into trouble. This fear might exacerbate suicidal thoughts, feelings, and behaviors.

When assessing the seriousness of the suicidal threat, it is crucial to see if the child has a plan. One way to ascertain that a person has seriously contemplated committing suicide is if the person has a well-thought plan for carrying out the suicide. This is not to say that the lack of a plan means that suicide is not being considered, so proceeding with counseling and explorative questions is still needed.

Counseling Suicidal Children in School

If the child's suicidal threat has occurred at school, the school counselor and/or school psychologist should take the lead in exploring and assessing intent. In addition, school administration and other involved school personnel should be alerted to the fact that the child has implied that he or she is suicidal, in the event that the child runs or tries to leave the building. All involved parties must collaborate to make sure that the child is in a safe environment or space in which there are no opportunities for self-harm or escape.

While the school counselor or school psychologist is talking with the child, someone, preferably a school administrator or another school-based mental health professional, should try to contact the parents or guardians of the child to inform them of the situation. Ideally, the parent/guardian would be asked to come to the school to collaborate with school personnel in terms of the next steps in the plan. If a parent cannot be reached, the child should remain in a secure location and not be allowed to leave without constant supervision. When the parent is contacted, it should be made perfectly clear that the child has indicated a desire to seriously harm him- or herself and that the school will keep the child until the parent can come address the situation.

When the parent arrives, a private discussion with the school counselor or school psychologist should reveal to the parent what the child has said. Any other observations or signs that the child is a threat to himself or herself should be shared. At this time, it is appropriate to ask if the child is being seen by an external mental health professional. If there is an established relationship with a therapist outside of school, the parent is encouraged to call the professional immediately and make an appointment as soon as possible. If no prior relationship has been established, the school counselor and/or school psychologist might suggest taking the child to the closest hospital that specializes in suicidal treatment. Resistance to this might be addressed by suggesting that the parent take the child to their family physician first and have the doctor conduct an assessment.

Finally, the child should only be allowed to leave the school building after being released to the parent/guardian. In addition, it is helpful for school personnel to know what steps the parent/guardian is going to take to address the suicidal behavior. This knowledge will help school personnel plan for follow-up when the student returns to the school building. It is also a good idea for the school counselor and/or school psychologist to indicate that they will contact the family later that day or the next day to see how the child is doing and what the plan of action entailed. Finally, documentation of the events and the actions taken will provide legal support should there be any question about the actions of school personnel.

When the suicidal child returns to the building, whether it is the next day or several days or weeks later, it is imperative that the school counselor connect with the student right away for several reasons. First, the student may feel awkward for missing school and may be overwhelmed by missed school work, so providing support for a smooth transition will be critical. This may entail talking with the child's teachers and asking for reduced work or limited makeup assignments so the child does not feel burdened. Second, the student may wonder how much the other students know. If the child has been hospitalized, the child might feel like other children perceive him or her as "sick" or "crazy" and may be overly sensitive to the comments and actions of students. Third, if the child is taking medication related to the suicidal behavior, it may require a change in the child's school schedule so that he or she can go to the school nurse or office to take medication during the day. This can be a difficult time for students who are not used to the routine. The school counselor or school psychologist might work with the school nurse for the child to take the medication in private or in an area that is not visible to others until the child feels more comfortable. Finally, the school counselor should consult with outside mental health professionals who are involved with the child's case. Acquiring parent permission for release of information will be an important task so that dialogue and collaboration between all members of the child's treatment team can take place. If a student is in outside individual or group counseling, the school counselor may seek to serve as a support that is available to the student but may not want to provide intensive counseling services in school since the underlying issues are being addressed through outside counseling. Most importantly, the school counselor needs to be aware and available in the event that the child lapses back into suicidal ideation or suicidal behavior.

Counseling Suicidal Children: Mental Health Counselors

Counseling suicidal children in private practice differs slightly from the school experience. Chances are that the signs and symptoms of suicidal behavior may be the issues that brought the child to counseling in the first place. If a child is in a counseling session and says or does something that seems indicative of suicide, the counselor should begin the assessment process. Once the level of intent has been explored, the counselor should involve the parent/guardian as soon as possible. As was the case in the school setting, the counselor does not want the child to leave the premises until the parent is present and a plan of action is in place. Further, if the counselor is a child psychologist or psychiatrist, plans for a more thorough assessment should be made to determine if medication or hospitalization is needed. Follow-up is needed, and considerations of family counseling may be a reasonable course of counseling. If the counselor does not have the psychological training or expertise to assess the level of threat to the child, it is important that the counselor seek help and support from colleagues or professionals with more specialized training. Again, referral to a hospital or mental health facility that can do a more intensive psychological assessment and intervention plan is appropriate.

Counseling the Suicidal Child: Family Interventions

As mentioned earlier, childhood suicidal ideation and behavior is often linked to issues that are occurring within the family. Parental divorce, death of a loved one, and family discord may all result in stress on a child, and the potential for relief from the uncomfortable situation may be appealing for the child. Therefore, professional counselors cannot discount family counseling as an approach with suicidal children. In fact, addressing the family's involvement in and perpetuation of suicidal behavior in children is a critical component of multimodal intervention.

When working with the family of a suicidal child, the first priority should be a comprehensive intake, including family history. It is critical to know if there has been a history of suicide, depression, or other mental heath issues in the family. Birth order and sibling relationships are also important pieces of information as the counselor gathers data about the family. Family history provides insight that will help gauge how the counseling process should occur and whether the interventions should be individual or with the entire family.

Orbach (1988) identified several goals of counseling the families of suicidal children, including (a) identifying the unresolvable problem, (b) dealing with the family's coping and problem-solving strategies, (c) helping the family deal with other crises, and (d) promoting positive family interchanges. I discuss each of these in turn.

Identifying the Unresolvable Problem. When it becomes obvious that one of the issues of the suicidal child is related to family problems, it is important to interview the family members, either individually or in different combinations, to determine what the problem is. This may take several sessions as families often bury and deny family problems rather than confront the emotions that will result from bringing them to the surface. Orbach (1988) acknowledged that families may demonstrate defense mechanisms such as opposition, aggression, and denial. When a counselor meets with family members for the first time, it should be made perfectly clear that the suicidal child's thoughts, feelings, and behaviors are, at least in part, related to whatever the problem is with the family and that in order for the child to work through his or her problems, the family must address the "unresolvable" problem. Emphasizing the suicidal child's cry for help may motivate family members to commit to the counseling process and be more open to identifying the key problems and issues.

It may be that the "family secret" has never been addressed openly or even been acknowledged. For this reason, it is a good idea for counselors who specialize in individual counseling to partner with an experienced family therapist to help address family dynamics and systems. The intensity of this process may be better addressed by more than a single counselor or therapist.

Dealing With the Family's Coping and Problem-Solving Strategies. A major focus of working with the families of a suicidal child is to help family members realize that the coping and problem-solving strategies they are using are not working, particularly for the child who no longer wants to live in this world, much less in the family. Counseling strategies must emphasize finding new ways of dealing with old problems. Again, the input and expertise of a trained family counselor is valuable during this process.

It is not unusual for the suicidal child to be the focus of a family's, particularly parental, frustration, which results in high, and often unrealistic, expectations for the children. Suicidal thoughts and behaviors often occur because a child feels he or she cannot measure up to the expectations of parents or other family members. Family patterns of coping mechanisms might involve rigid expectations and pressure on the child. Counseling strategies must address these rigid expectations and reveal how they affect the children's feelings about themselves and their life. As Orbach (1988) stated: "Once they are willing to relinquish unrealistic expectations and to consider realistic compromises, they can begin to find new and more efficient means of dealing with life's problems" (p. 233).

Helping the Family Deal With Other Crises. Typically, family chaos may result from other family crises or events that may have affected the family balance. Death of a family member, especially by suicide, may be the trigger that disrupts the family dynamic and creates emotional discord among family members. The suicidal child might view death as the escape from the chaos as well as an opportunity to "join" the deceased family member. Counseling interventions must immediately address the emotions that are part of the grieving process: anger, guilt, sadness, and loss.

Other types of family crisis also result in strained family relationships. Loss of a job, loss of home, marital discord, and sibling issues are just a few examples of the types of problems that can unravel the most functional family. In a child's eyes, the family unit represents stability, safety, and security. When that image is shattered, the child may feel isolated, unstable, unsafe, and insecure. This threat to the most basic of human needs may result in a child believing that the world is not a good or safe place to live; therefore, alternatives to living may be a logical thought to a young child.

When working with the family of the suicidal child, the counselor may need to meet with members individually to get the spectrum of perspectives on family relationships, situations, and circumstances. Understanding how other family members perceive certain situations may provide valuable insight into family issues. In particular, assessing how the family perceives the suicidal child's role in the family is an important exploration that may provide information that will help guide further counseling interventions and goals.

Promoting Positive Family Interchanges. If counseling reveals that the family is a factor in the child's suicidal plans or statements, the counselor must focus on the family dynamic or circumstance that triggers the suicidal thoughts or plans. Counseling interventions may be behavioral and involve specific changes in behavioral responses to family events to provide stability for the child. Other interventions might be more cognitive and challenge the family's basic thinking about how things should be and emphasize, more appropriately, how they are and how to make them better.

Other counseling interventions based on family systems, Adlerian, and choice theory, for example, may have appropriate applications to a family situation. Deciding on the counseling methods and techniques to use should be an ongoing process for the counselor with the primary focus always being the suicidal child's role in the family drama.

Whether the family is or is not a catalyst for the suicidal child's ideation and behaviors, it is imperative to get the family involved and committed to the treatment of the suicidal child. For siblings who are not suicidal, it will be difficult for them to understand why someone would want to kill themselves. Providing an explanation of why some people are suicidal and the emotions and circumstances that trigger suicidal thoughts may help siblings become more supportive of the suicidal child. It is also difficult for families to admit that a family member may have a mental disorder or may need intensive mental health intervention. Counselors must help families understand the dynamics of mental health as well as the many life events and situations that can easily alter and affect healthy mental development. Family support and encouragement as well as an increased family awareness of suicidal threat should be emphasized from the onset of counseling services.

Multimodal Intervention

It is obvious that treating a suicidal child does not involve an isolated intervention effort. Effective treatment must occur as a result of collaborative efforts of mental health and school personnel as well as the involvement and support of the family of the suicidal child. Approaching the suicidal child from a holistic perspective addresses the factors that could trigger a suicidal event. School counselors must always be aware of the emotional and social development of young children because the balance is so fragile when children are young. If a suicidal child presents him- or herself at school, school personnel must involve the family as well as encourage the involvement of mental health counselors and, perhaps, even medical intervention depending on the severity of the child's condition. Professional counselors and therapists must also collaborate with child psychologists and psychiatrists to determine if medical intervention or hospitalization is warranted. Further, dialogue with school counselors and school psychologists is crucial to the progress of the suicidal child in school to provide the most comprehensive, yet not redundant, services for children. Finally, involvement of the family, whether through family counseling or providing strategies that the family can implement to support and monitor their loved one, is crucial to the successful treatment of the suicidal child.

Probably the most important function of multimodal intervention is the gathering of all involved parties to assess, monitor, and evaluate the progress of the suicidal child. If each person works independently of the others, it will be difficult to provide effective intervention for the suicidal child. Collaboration and cooperation is key in the holistic treatment of the suicidal child, and there is much greater likelihood of successful intervention if all parties are working together toward a common goal—a happy, healthy, living child.

Adaptations for Diversity

The research on suicidal children is alarmingly sparse. Sadly, research on diversity as it relates to suicide among children is all but nonexistent. The statistics that are available reveal information mainly about adolescent suicide. A report by the Surgeon General (1999) indicated that from 1980 to 1996, the suicide rate for African American males age 15–19 increased 105%, which was the most rapid increase among all groups. Another report by the 1997 Youth Risk Behavior Surveillance System (as cited by the Surgeon General) indicated that Hispanic high school students were significantly more likely than White students to have reported a suicide attempt. A report by the Centers for Disease Control and Prevention (1996) revealed that 64% of the suicides among Native Americans between the years of 1979 and 1992 were among males ages 15–24. Obviously, information regarding children, diversity, and suicide is remarkably lacking.

There are, however, some obvious considerations when working with diverse children and families in the area of suicide.

1. Consider the diversity factors that might contribute to the child's suicidality (e.g., cultural customs/traditions, socioeconomic status, language barriers, social factors).
2. Explore the family's thoughts about suicide. Is it taboo? Could the child be "disowned" for having suicidal thoughts? Is it perceived as noble to kill oneself for a cause or to prevent shame?
3. Consider the cultural expectations and factors that could contribute to a child's suicidal intent. For example, if a culture places a tremendous amount of importance on educational success and the child is struggling academically, could family pressure or the shame associated with failure be the impetus of the suicidal thoughts?
4. When counseling the suicidal child and family, be cognizant of one's own worldview and the biases that might be evident. Explore the cultural understanding of and beliefs about suicide in the culture and proceed respectfully.

One area that is not addressed here is the suicidality of sexual minority youth. The Surgeon General (1999) reported that "gay and lesbian youth are 2–3 times more likely to commit suicide than other youth and that 30% of all attempted suicides or completed youth suicides are often related to issues of sexual identity" (p. 1). Although sexual identity may begin to develop in late elementary school, it is developmentally improbable that a young child's sexual orientation might result in suicidal behavior. However, teasing about being gay or accusing a young child of liking a child of the same sex might result in a child feeling isolated or withdrawn and could potentially lead to thoughts of suicide. Any sort of sexual harassment or indication that a child is being teased or bullied about sexual orientation should be addressed through school intervention as well as family involvement.

Issues of diversity—ethnicity, culture, socioeconomic status, and gender—are certainly going to influence the development of children at a very young age. When a child is potentially suicidal, it is important to consider and explore these factors as they relate to the child's self-concept, social relationships, and emotional development.

Case Example: Joey

The following is a case study of an 8-year-old biracial boy who has had a history of self-harming and suicidal behavior since the age of 6.

Presenting Problem. Joey's propensity to suicidal behavior manifested itself in the school setting early in his school career. He demonstrated symptoms of manic depression, with extreme highs and lows in his mood patterns. In addition to self-injury, such as banging his head on a wall or table until there was a bump on his head, he would constantly say to the school counselor and other school personnel that he "wanted to lay in the street and let cars run over him."

Family Background. Joey's mother is Native American and has lived in the community for 4 years. She graduated from high school and is currently a receptionist for a local car dealer. She lives with her boyfriend, who has been in the house for approximately 2 years. While there has been some indication of abuse to the mother, Joey denies any abuse himself.

Joey's biological father is African American. He is incarcerated for multiple misdemeanors and one assault and battery that ended up paralyzing the victim. He is not eligible for parole for 3 years. The mother reported that the father had a history of educational problems and also experienced severe mood swings for which he refused medication. Joey has recently had a visit with the biological father, and the mother believes this has triggered these extreme behaviors.

Joey has two younger siblings, both male, but it is unsure who their biological father is. Neither child exhibits the same behavior as Joey.

Joey's mother and the boyfriend insist that Joey does not behave like this at home and that they do not see any indication of depression or mania in his interaction with family members. They are resistant to intervention.

Symptomatology. In kindergarten and first grade, Joey developed no peer relationships because he would tell his teachers that students were picking on him and making fun of him, but no children had interacted with him. Students did avoid him because if they would try to talk to him, he would start crying and hitting himself. As the paranoia became more extreme, school personnel decided there was a need for deeper exploration, and Child Study referral was made at the end of the second grade.

Suicidal gestures included head banging, scratching until bleeding, throwing himself against walls and chairs, and constantly telling others that he wants to "kill himself and die."

Also, in a conversation with a school psychologist, Joey claimed to hear voices and exhibited signs of hallucinations. He has not lashed out at other students or school personnel.

Interventions. Behavior contracts and constant interaction with the school counselor and school psychologist have not been effective with Joey. One day in school, the suicidal behaviors and suicide ideation reached extreme levels in the classroom and Joey had a large bump on his head from banging it on the table. The school counselor came and took Joey away from the class and into a quiet office. The mother was called and when she came to pick him up, school officials informed her that Joey needed to be seen in a mental health facility or hospital. The mother left and attempted to take Joey for treatment, but later claimed that no hospitals would take her insurance. Joey returned to school the next day.

Joey's behaviors were even more extreme in the days to follow. Again, school personnel instructed the mother that Joey was in grave danger and needed to be treated. The mother refused to take him for treatment, at which point the school counselor and school psychologist involved Child Protective Services (CPS). The CPS worker coerced the mother into taking Joey to the hospital with the promise of financial help to pay for the treatment. He was in the hospital for 7 days. The *DSM–IV–TR* (American Psychiatric Association, 2000) diagnosis was attention deficit hyperactivity disorder and depression. He was placed on low dosages of Zoloft and an SSRI, although they wanted to do more screening to assess the best psychopharmacological treatment. The mental health facility wanted to keep Joey for further evaluation, but his mother refused.

Joey returned to school where he was placed in a classroom with a 2:1 student-to-teacher ratio. The Child Study Team is evaluating Joey to determine the best educational placement for him. The medication seems to have helped minimally, but Joey still has self-harming thoughts and talks about killing himself. He talks of walking in front of cars and having them run over him.

Multimodal Intervention. A team of professionals from school and the mental health community have been a part of Joey's case. These include the school counselor, the school social worker, members of the Child Study Team, the school psychologist, a neurologist, Child Protective Services, and hospital professionals such as a medical pediatrician, child psychiatrists, and the hospital social worker. The mother and boyfriend have cooperated with appointments and meetings, but as soon as the intervention becomes more intensive, such as hospitalization or residential placement, their cooperation waivers. Joey continues to take the medication, sees an outside child psychiatrist, and has constant support at school. He is unable to develop friendships and finds little joy in school or home activities. He still hears voices and desires to kill himself and "be gone from the world."

This case study illustrates how children suffer and may develop suicidal ideation and behavior. Despite several interventions, Joey's progress has been minimal. The crucial piece of the problem is the lack of cooperation from his biological mother. Each member of the team of professionals who are involved in Joey's case needs to persuade her to seek more intensive treatment for her child. It is difficult for parents to admit that their child has a mental disorder or illness. Professional counselors and mental health professionals must collaborate to try to convince the parent that intervention may be the only way to ensure that Joey has the best chance of salvaging a happy childhood.

The next case study is a more acute incident where the child does not have a history of suicidal behavior, but an event triggers the self-harming cognition and threat of suicide.

Case Example: Alex

Alex was a fifth-grade student in a special needs program for emotionally disturbed children. One day, upon receiving a bad grade on a paper, he became very agitated with the teacher, threatening to harm her and the other students. The teacher informed the administration and everyone decided that because of his threats, Alex was going to be suspended for the rest of the day. As the teacher escorted Alex up the hall, Alex said: "I'm glad I'm going home. My dad will be at work and I can go into the bathroom and get his razor blades and kill myself."

The teacher continued walking Alex to the office and informed the principal of Alex's comments. The administrator immediately called the school counselor and school psychologist into the office, and Alex was put into a room that had been cleared of all potentially harmful objects. He was not belligerent or out of control but continued to discuss his plans to kill himself as soon as he got home.

The administration made attempts to get in touch with Alex's father but was unable to reach him at his job. A phone call was made to the noncustodial parent who refused to be bothered with anything regarding Alex. Because of the suicidal threats, the counselor and psychologist explored the option of transporting Alex to the hospital to have him admitted for psychiatric evaluation. However, the school would not accept liability for transporting him to the hospital. A phone call to the police indicated that they would not transport the child without consent from the parent because the student was no longer belligerent and not a present threat to himself or others.

Attempts to contact the father continued through the afternoon. The counselor and teacher rotated shifts in being in the room with Alex, never leaving him alone. Alex had calmed down and asked for class work because he was getting bored. The teacher also recalled that Alex was being seen by a therapist outside of the school, and attempts were made to contact the counselor.

Approximately 5 hours after Alex's comment about killing himself, his father was finally located and came to pick Alex up. The therapist had also called and said the father had made an emergency appointment for Alex and would be bringing him directly to his office. The school released Alex to his father and requested that the therapist be given a release of information to discuss the case with the school counselor. The collaborative efforts of the school and community agencies worked successfully in this case.

This case does not have the history or intensity of the first case but is nonetheless an example of how multimodal intervention can be successful with a suicidal child. While the stories are as different as the children themselves, it is evident that suicide among children should not be taken lightly, nor is it a phenomenon that should be ignored. Counseling efforts should focus on prevention by recognizing the signs and symptoms that are indicative of suicidal thoughts, feelings, and behaviors so that intervention is proactive rather than reactive. Immediate intervention to secure the safety of the child is the top priority of counseling, followed by intensive counseling and a clear plan of action in which all members of the treatment team understand their intervention roles and fulfill them successfully.

Summary

This chapter has explored a topic that, in general, is not comfortable for society. No one wants to think that children are suffering to the point that they would harm or kill themselves. However, it is a disservice to children if counselors and other mental health professionals do not respond to the signs and symptoms of suicidal behavior. Intervention must be multimodal and involve a team effort from schools, community agents, mental health facilities, and family. By addressing the issues from a holistic approach, there is greater likelihood that a comprehensive plan will successfully treat the suicidal child. Further research is needed in all facets of the areas related to child suicide to help counseling professionals deal more effectively with issues related to the suicidal child. It is the most and the best that we as counselors can do for children who desperately need our professional help.

References

Allan, W. D., Kashani, J. H., Dahlmeir, J. M., Beck, N., & Reid, J. C. (1998). "Anxious suicidality": A new type of childhood ideation? *Suicide & Life-Threatening Behavior, 28,* 251–260.

American Psychiatric Association. (2000). *Diagnostic and statistical manual of mental disorders* (4th ed., Text Revision). Washington, DC: Author.

Bailey, G. W. (2001, March). *The many faces of depression: Assessing depression and suicide in children and adolescents.* Paper presented at the INOVA Kellar Center, Fairfax, VA.

Beers, M. H., & Berkow, M. D. (Eds.) (1999). Suicide in children and adolescents. In *The Merck manual of diagnosis and therapy* (Chap. 274, Sec. 19). Whitehouse Station, NJ: Merck & Co., Inc.

Centers for Disease Control and Prevention. (1996). *Violence surveillance summary series, No. 2.* Atlanta, GA: Author.

Children whose parents attempt suicide are at high risk for attempting suicide. (2002, September 16). *Mental Health Weekly, 12,* p. 5.

Fried, S., & Fried, P. (1996). *Bullies and victims: Helping your child through the schoolyard battlefield.* New York: Evans.

Helsel, D. C. (2001). Does your school track the suicidal student? *The Clearing House, 75,* 92–95.

Hirshberg, C., & Sinha, G. (2002). Child suicide by the numbers. *Popular Science, 261,* 36.

Koki, S. (1999). *Bullying in schools should not be par for the course.* Honolulu, HI: Pacific Resources for Education and Learning. (ERIC Document Reproduction Service No. ED465200)

Kosky, R. (1983). Childhood suicidal behavior. *Journal of Child Psychology and Psychiatry and Allied Disciplines, 24,* 457–468.

Martinson, D. (2001). Self injury. Retrieved March 9, 2003 from http://www.focusas.com/SelfInjury.html.

Mishara, B. L. (1999). Conceptions of death and suicide in children ages 6–12 and their implications for suicide prevention. *Suicide and Life-Threatening Behavior, 29,* 105–118.

National Center for Health Statistics. (2001). Vital statistics of children, Year 2000, *Health and Health Care in Schools, 2*(10). Retrieved January 13, 2003 from http://www.healthinschools.org/ejournal/dec01_02.htm

National Center for Injury Prevention and Control. (1999). *Suicide in the United States: Suicide prevention fact sheet.* Retrieved January 13, 2003 from http://www.cdc.gov.ncipc/factsheets/suifacts.htm

National Institute of Mental Health. (2000). *Suicide facts.* Retrieved January 13, 2003 from http://www.nimh.nih.gov/research/suifact.htm

Orbach, I. (1988). *Children who don't want to live.* San Francisco: Jossey-Bass.

Pfeffer, C. R. (1986). *The suicidal child.* New York: Guilford Press.

Poppenhagen, M. P., & Qualley, R. M. (1998). Adolescent suicide: Detection, intervention and prevention. *Professional School Counseling, 1*, 30–35.

Reynolds, W. M. (1987). Suicidal Ideation Questionnaire. *Research Psychologists Press.* Retrieved March 9, 2003 from http://www.rpp.on.ca/siq.htm

Speaker, K. M., & Petersen, G. J. (2000). School violence and adolescent suicide: Strategies for effective intervention. *Educational Review, 52*, 65–73.

Stanley, B., Gameroff, M. J., Michalsen, V., & Mann, J. J. (2001). Are suicide attempters who self-mutilate a unique population? *The American Journal of Psychiatry, 158*, 427–432.

Stillion, J. M., McDowell, E. E., & May, J. H. (1989). *Suicide across the life span: Premature exits.* New York: Hemisphere.

Surgeon General. (1999). *The Surgeon General's call to action to prevent suicide, 1999. At a glance: Suicide among the young.* Retrieved January 13, 2003 from http://www.surgeongeneral.gov/library/calltoaction/fact3.htm

Wise, A. J., & Spengler, P. M. (1997). Suicide in children younger than age fourteen: Clinical judgment and assessment issues. *Journal of Mental Health Counseling, 19*, 318–335.

Yang, B., & Clum, G. A. (2000). Childhood stress leads to later suicidality via its effects on cognitive functioning. *Suicide & Life-Threatening Behavior, 30*, 183–198.

Chapter 9

Counseling Suicidal Adolescents

David Capuzzi and Douglas R. Gross

The adolescent at risk for suicidal preoccupation and behavior has become an increasing concern for schools and communities throughout the United States (King, 2001b). Between 1960 and 1988, the suicide rate among adolescents increased much more dramatically than it did in the general population. The adolescent suicide rate rose by 200% compared with an increase in the general population of approximately 17% (Garland & Zigler, 1993). Current literature (National Institute of Mental Health, 2002) ranks suicide as the third leading cause of death for our nation's youth.

The topic of adolescent suicide has been a major focus for newspaper features, television specials, and legislative initiatives as the problem of adolescent suicide has reached epidemic proportions (Hafen & Frandsen, 1986). In 1999, U.S. Surgeon General David Satcher made urgent recommendations to the public regarding suicide, stating that "the country is facing an average of 85 suicides and 2,000 attempts per day" (p. 1). In 2000, there were nearly 4,000 adolescent suicides recorded, accounting for 15% of deaths between the ages of 15 and 24 (National Center for Health Statistics, 2002). Such data provide the basis for ranking suicide as the third leading cause of death among the 11–24 age group (National Institute of Mental Health, 2002). Centers for Disease Control and Prevention (2000) surveillance data from 1999 reported that 19.3% of high school students had

This chapter originally appeared in the fourth edition of *Youth at Risk: A Prevention Resource for Counselors, Teachers, and Parents* by David Capuzzi and Douglas R. Gross published by the American Counseling Association (ACA) in 2004. It has been reprinted with this title with the permission of ACA.

seriously considered attempting suicide, 14.5% had made plans to attempt suicide, and 8.3% had made more than one suicide attempt during the 12-month period prior to the survey. Because teachers in typical U.S. high school classrooms can expect to have at least one young man and two young women who attempted suicide in the previous year (King, 2000), counselors, teachers, and parents are becoming more and more concerned about their responsibilities. Many states are requiring that schools include guidelines for suicide prevention, crisis management, and postvention in their written tragedy response plans.

Problem Definition

Ethnic and Gender Differences

The suicide rate is higher among adolescent males than among adolescent females (although adolescent females attempt three to four times as often as adolescent males). Caucasian adolescent males complete suicide more often than any other ethnic group (Canetto & Sakinofsky, 1998; Metha, Weber, & Webb, 1998; Price, Dake, & Kucharewski, 2001). A number of explanations to account for the differences in rates between genders and races have been proposed, but no clear answers have been found. As early as 1954, Henry and Short provided an explanation based on a reciprocal model of suicide and homicide that suggested that some groups were seen as more likely to express frustration and aggression inwardly and others were more likely to express them outwardly. Empirical data, however, do not support this reciprocal relationship. Some models used to explain racial differences in suicide have suggested that the extreme stress and discrimination that African Americans in the United States confront help to create protective factors, such as extended networks of social support that lower the risk and keep the suicide rates for African American adolescents lower than those of Caucasian adolescents (Borowsky, Ireland, & Resnick, 2001; Bush, 1976; Gibbs, 1988). It is important to note, however, that despite the overall pattern suggested by the data, during the period between 1980 and 1994, the suicide, rates for African American adolescent males showed a 320% increase in the 10–14 age group and a 196% increase in the 15–19 age group (Lyon et al., 2000; Metha et al., 1998).

Native Americans have the highest adolescent suicide rates of any ethnic group in the United States (Committee on Adolescence, 2000). There is considerable variability across tribes; the Navajos, for example, have suicide rates close to the national average of 11 to 13 per 100,000 of the population, whereas some Apache groups have rates as high as 43 per 100,000 (Berlin, 1987). The high suicide rates in the Native American population have been associated with factors such as alcoholism and substance abuse, unemployment, availability of firearms, and child abuse and neglect (Berman & Jobes, 1991). In general, less traditional tribes have higher rates of suicide than do more traditional tribes (Wyche, Obolensky, & Glood, 1990). Suicide rates for both Asian American and Hispanic American adolescents continue to be lower than those for African American and Native American youth, even though the 1980–1994 time period bore witness to much higher rates than previously recorded (Metha et al., 1998).

Methods

The use of firearms outranks all other methods of completed suicides; firearms are now being used by both genders. Studies in the United States show that availability of guns increases the risk of adolescent suicide (Brent et al., 1993; Committee on Adolescence, 2000). The second most common method is hanging, and the third most common is gassing. Males use firearms and hanging more often than do females, but females use gassing and ingestion more often than do males for completed suicides (Berman & Jobes, 1991). The most common method used by suicide attempters is ingestion or overdose.

Risk Factors

As noted by Garland and Zigler (1993) and Shaffer and Craft (1999), the search for the etiology of suicide spans many areas of study (Orbach, 2001). Risk factors that have been studied include neurotransmitter imbalances and genetic predictors, psychiatric disorders, poor self-efficacy and problem-solving skills, sexual or physical abuse, concerns over sexual identity or orientation, availability of firearms, substance abuse, violent rock music, divorce in families, unemployment and labor strikes, loss, disability, giftedness, and phases of the moon. It is important to note that almost all adolescent suicide victims have experienced some form of psychiatric illness. The most prevalent psychiatric disorders among completed adolescent suicides appear to be affective disorders, conduct disorder or antisocial personality disorder, and substance abuse (Shaffer, 1988; Shaffer & Craft, 1999). Among affective disorders, particular attention should be paid to bipolar illness and depressive disorder with comorbidity such as attention deficit disorder, conduct disorder, or substance abuse (Rohde, Lewinsohn, & Seeley, 1991).

The suicide of a family member or a close friend of the family can also be a risk factor for adolescent suicide; prior attempts also escalate risk. An adolescent experiencing a physical illness that is chronic or terminal can also be at higher risk (Capuzzi, 1994). Many researchers have studied cognitive and coping style factors, such as generalized feelings of hopelessness and poor interpersonal problem-solving skills, as risk factors for adolescent suicide (Garland & Zigler, 1993). High neuroticism and low extraversion, high impulsiveness, low self-esteem, and an external locus of control have also been studied and can be used to predict risk (Beautrais, Joyce, & Mulder,

1999). Alcohol and drug abuse, the breakup of a relationship, school difficulties or failure, social isolation, a friend who committed suicide, chronic
levels of community violence, and availability of lethal methods have also
been studied and identified as risk factors (Price et al., 2001).

The best single predictor of death by suicide seems to be a previous
suicide attempt (King, 2000; Shaffer, Garland, Gould, Fisher, & Trautman,
1988). Some studies indicate that as many as 40% of attempters will make
additional suicide attempts, and as many as 10%–14% of these individuals
will complete suicide (Diekstra, 1989).

Precipitants

Often, completed suicide is precipitated by what, to the adolescent, is interpreted as a shameful or humiliating experience (e.g., failure at school or
work, interpersonal conflict with a romantic partner or parent). There is
mounting evidence indicating that adolescents who do not cope well with
major and minor life events and who do not have family and peer support
are more likely to have suicidal ideation (Mazza & Reynolds, 1998; Stanard,
2000). The humiliation and frustration experienced by some adolescents
struggling with conflicts connected with their sexual orientation may precipitate suicidal behavior (Harry, 1989), although being gay or lesbian, in
and of itself, may not be a risk factor for suicide (Blumenthal, 1991; Russell
& Joyner, 2001). Hoberman and Garfinkel (1988) found that the most common precipitant of suicide in a sample of 229 youth suicides was an argument with a boyfriend, a girlfriend, or a parent (19%) followed by school
problems (14%). Other humiliating experiences such as corporal punishment and abuse also serve as precipitants; the experience of sexual or physical
assault seems to be a particularly significant risk factor for adolescent women
(Hoberman & Garfinkel, 1988).

Understanding the Myths

The biggest problem connected with the topic of adolescents at risk for
suicide is the fact that parents, teachers, mental health professionals, and
the adolescent population itself are not made aware of a variety of myths and
misconceptions as well as the signs and symptoms associated with adolescent suicide. Because subsequent case study prevention and intervention
information in this chapter is based on prior awareness of these areas, the
following information about myths and the suicidal profile is pertinent.

It is important to disqualify myths and misconceptions surrounding the
topic of adolescent suicide at the beginning of any initiative to provide
prevention, crisis management, and postvention services. Some of the most
commonly cited misconceptions include the following (Capuzzi, 1988, 1994;
Capuzzi & Gross, 2000; King, 1999):

Adolescents Who Talk About Suicide Never Attempt Suicide. This is probably one of the most widely believed myths. All suicidal adolescents make attempts (either verbally or nonverbally) to let a friend, parent, or teacher know that life seems to be too difficult to bear. Because a suicide attempt is a cry for help to identify options, other than death, to decrease the pain of living, always take verbal or nonverbal threats seriously. Never assume such threats are only for the purpose of attracting attention or manipulating others. It is better to respond and enlist the aid of a professional than it is to risk the loss of a life.

Suicide Happens With No Warning. Suicidal adolescents leave numerous hints and warnings about their suicidal ideations and intentions. Clues can be verbal or in the form of suicidal gestures, such as taking a few sleeping pills, becoming accident prone, reading stories focused on death and violence, and so on. Quite often, the social support network of the suicidal adolescent is small. As stress escalates and options, other than suicide, seem few, suicidal adolescents may withdraw from an already small circle of friends, thus making it more difficult for others to notice warning signs.

Most Adolescents Who Attempt Suicide Fully Intend to Die. Most suicidal adolescents do not want to end their lives. They feel desperate and ambivalent about whether it would be better to end their lives and, thus, their emotional pain or try to continue living. This confusion is usually communicated though behavior and verbal communication (both of which are discussed in a subsequent subsection of this chapter).

Adolescents From Affluent Families Attempt or Complete Suicide More Often Than Adolescents From Poor Families. This, too, is a myth. Suicide is evenly divided among socioeconomic groups.

Once an Adolescent is Suicidal, He or She is Suicidal Forever. Most adolescents are suicidal for a limited period of time. In our experience, the 24–72-hour period around the peak of the crisis is the most dangerous. If counselors and other mental health professionals can monitor such a crisis period and transition the adolescent into long-term counseling/therapy, there is a strong possibility there will never be another suicidal crisis. The more effort that is made to help an adolescent identify stressors and develop problem-solving skills during this postsuicidal crisis period and the more time that passes, the better the prognosis.

If an Adolescent Attempts Suicide and Survives, He or She Will Never Make an Additional Attempt. There is a difference between an adolescent who experiences a suicidal crisis but does not attempt suicide and an adolescent who actually makes an attempt. An adolescent who carries through with an attempt has identified a plan, had access to the means, and maintained a high enough energy level to follow through. He or she may believe that a second or third attempt may be possible. If counseling/therapy has not taken place or has not been successful during the period following an attempt, additional attempts may be made. Most likely, each follow-up attempt will become more lethal.

239

Adolescents Who Attempt or Complete Suicide Always Leave Notes. Only a small percentage of suicidal adolescents leave notes. This is a common myth and one of the reasons why many deaths are classified and reported as accidents by friends, family members, physicians, and investigating officers when suicide has actually taken place.

Most Adolescent Suicides Happen Late at Night or During the Predawn Hours. This myth is not true for the simple reason that most suicidal adolescents actually want help. Mid to late morning and mid to late afternoon are the time periods when most attempts are made because a family member or friend is more likely to be around to intervene than would be the case late at night or very early in the morning.

Never Use the Word Suicide When Talking to Adolescents Because Using the Word Gives Some Adolescents the Idea. This is simply not true; you cannot put the idea of suicide into the mind of an adolescent who is not suicidal. If an adolescent is suicidal and you use the word, it can help an adolescent verbalize feelings of despair and assist with establishing rapport and trust. If a suicidal adolescent thinks you know he or she is suicidal and realizes you are afraid to approach the subject, it can bring the adolescent closer to the point of making an attempt by contributing to feelings of despair and helplessness.

The Most Common Method for Adolescent Suicide Completion Involves Drug Overdose. Guns are the most frequently used method for completing suicide among adolescents, followed by hanging. The presence of a gun or guns in the home escalates the risk of adolescent suicide by approximately five times even if such firearms are kept locked in a cabinet or drawer. Restricting the presence of and access to guns significantly decreases the suicide rates among adolescents.

All Adolescents Who Engage in Suicidal Behavior are Mentally Ill. Many adolescents have entertained the thought of suicide, but this does not indicate mental illness. Adolescents who attempt or complete suicide are usually not suffering from a mental disorder but are having a great deal of difficulty coping with life circumstances.

Every Adolescent Who Attempts Suicide is Depressed. Depression is a common component of the profile of a suicidal adolescent, but depression is not always a component. Many adolescents simply want to escape their present set of circumstances and do not have the problem-solving skills to cope more effectively, lower stress, and work toward a more promising future.

Suicide is Hereditary. Although suicide tends to run in families, just as physical and sexual abuse does, and has led to the development of this myth, suicide is not genetically inherited. Members of families do, however, share the same emotional climate because parents model coping and stress management skills as well as high or low levels of self-esteem. The suicide of one family member tends to increase the risk among other family members that suicide will be viewed as an appropriate way to solve a problem or set of problems.

In conjunction with this myth, it should be noted that some adolescents are predisposed, because of genetic factors, to depression as a response to life circumstances. Because of the connection between depression and suicide, many have mistakenly come to the belief that suicide can be genetically inherited.

If an Adolescent is Intent on Attempting Suicide, There is Nothing Anyone Can Do to Prevent Its Occurrence. Two of the most important things a counselor, teacher, or parent can do are to know the risk factors and warning signs connected with adolescent suicide and to know how to respond. It is important for counselors to be prepared to provide preventive and crisis management services and for teachers and parents to know how to facilitate a referral to a qualified professional. Suicide can be prevented in most cases.

Recognizing the Profile

A number of experts (Beautrais et al., 1999; Capuzzi, 1994; Capuzzi & Golden, 1988; Cavaiola & Lavender, 1999; Cohen, 2000; Curran, 1987; Davis, 1983; Fernquist, 2000; Hafen & Frandsen, 1986; Hussain & Vandiver, 1984; Johnson & Maile, 1987; Mazza & Reynolds, 1998) believe that about 90% of the adolescents who complete suicide (and lethal first attempts can result in completions) give cues to those around them in advance. Whether these cues or hints are limited or numerous will depend on the adolescent because each adolescent has a unique familial and social history. It is important for adults (and young people as well) to recognize the signs and symptoms to facilitate intervention. A comment such as "I talked with her a few days ago and she was fine—I am so shocked to learn of her death" may mean that no one was aware of the warning signs. One of the essential components of any staff development effort is teaching the profile of the suicidal or potentially suicidal adolescent so that referral and intervention can take place. Behavioral cues, verbal cues, thinking patterns and motivations, and personality traits are the four areas that are described below.

Behavioral Cues

The following are some behavioral cues that can be possible warning signs of adolescents who are suicidal:

Lack of Concern About Personal Welfare. Some adolescents who are suicidal may not be able to talk about their problems or give verbal hints that they are at risk for attempting suicide. Sometimes such adolescents become unconcerned with their personal safety in the hopes that someone will take notice. Experimenting with medication, accepting dares from friends, reckless driving, carving initials into the skin of forearms, and so on may all be ways of gesturing or letting others know "I am in pain and don't know how to continue through life if nothing changes."

Changes in Social Patterns. Relatively unusual or sudden changes in an adolescent's social behavior can provide strong cues that such a young person is feeling desperate. A cooperative teenager may suddenly start breaking the house rules that parents have never had to worry about enforcing. An involved adolescent may begin to withdraw from activities at school or end long-term friendships with school and community-related peers. A stable, easygoing teenager may start arguing with teachers, employers, or other significant adults with whom prior conflict was never experienced. Such pattern changes should be noted and talked about with an adolescent who does not seem to be behaving as he or she usually has in the past.

A Decline in School Achievement. Many times, adolescents who are becoming more and more depressed and preoccupied with suicidal thoughts are unable to devote the time required to complete homework assignments and maintain grades. If such an adolescent has a history of interest in the school experience and has maintained a certain grade point average, loss of interest in academic pursuits can be a strong indication that something is wrong. The key to assessing such a situation is the length of time the decline lasts.

Concentration and Clear Thinking Difficulties. Suicidal adolescents usually experience marked changes in thinking and logic. As stress and discomfort escalate, logical problem solving and option generation become more difficult. It becomes easier and easier to stay focused on suicide as the only solution as reasoning and thinking become more confused and convoluted. "It may become more and more obvious that the adolescent's attention span is shorter and that verbal comments bear little relationship to the topic of a conversation" (Capuzzi, 1988, p. 6).

Altered Patterns of Eating and Sleeping. Sudden increases or decreases in appetite and weight, difficulty with sleeping, or wanting to sleep all the time or all day can all be indicative of increasing preoccupation with suicidal thoughts. These altered patterns can offer strong evidence that something is wrong and that assistance is required.

Attempts to Put Personal Affairs in Order or to Make Amends. Often, once a suicide plan and decision have been reached, adolescents will make last-minute efforts to put their personal affairs in order. These efforts may take a variety of directions: attempts to make amends in a troubled relationship, final touches on a project, reinstatement of an old or neglected friendship, or the giving away of prized possessions (skis, jewelry, compact discs, collections, etc.).

Use or Abuse of Alcohol or Drugs. Sometimes troubled adolescents use or abuse alcohol or other drugs to lessen their feelings of despair or discontent. Initially, they may feel that the drug enhances their ability to cope and to increase feelings of self-esteem. Unfortunately, the abuse of drugs decreases ability to communicate accurately and problem solve rationally. Thinking patterns become more skewed, impulse control lessens, and option identification decreases. Rapid onset of involvement with illicit or over-the-counter drugs is indicative of difficulty with relationships, problem solving, and ability to share feelings and communicate them to others.

Unusual Interest in How Others are Feeling. Suicidal adolescents often express considerable interest in how others are feeling. Because they are in pain but may be unable to express their feelings and ask for help, they may reach out to peers (or adults) who seem to need help with the stresses of daily living. Such responsiveness may become a full-time pastime and serve to lessen preoccupation with self and serve as a vehicle for communicating, "I wish you would ask me about my pain" or "Can't you see that I need help too?"

Preoccupation With Death and Violence Themes. Reading books or poetry in which death, violence, or suicide is the predominating theme can become the major interest of an adolescent who is becoming increasingly preoccupied with the possibility of suicide. Such adolescents may be undecided about the possibility of choosing death over life and may be working through aspects of such a decision with such reading. Other examples of such preoccupation can include listening to music that is violent; playing violent video games; writing short stories focused on death, dying, and loss; drawing or sketching that emphasizes destruction; or watching movies or videos that emphasize destruction to self and others.

Sudden Improvement After a Period of Depression. Suicidal adolescents often fool parents, teachers, and friends by appearing to be dramatically improved, after a period of prolonged depression, in a very short period of time. This improvement can sometimes take place overnight or during a 24-hour period and encourages friends and family to interpret such a change as a positive sign. It is not unusual for this type of change to be the result of a suicide decision and the formulation of a concrete suicide plan on the part of the adolescent at risk. It may mean that the suicide attempt (and the potential of completion) is imminent and that the danger and crisis are peaking. The important point for family and friends to remember is that it is not really logical for a depression to lessen that rapidly. It takes time, effort, and, at times, medical assistance to improve coping skills and lessen feelings of depression, just as it took time (months or years) to develop nonadaptive responses to people and circumstances and feelings of hopelessness.

Sudden or Increased Promiscuity. It is not unusual for an adolescent to experiment with sex during periods of suicidal preoccupation in an attempt to refocus attention or lessen feelings of isolation. Unfortunately, doing so sometimes complicates circumstances because of an unplanned pregnancy or an escalation of feelings of guilt.

Verbal Cues

As noted by Schneidman, Farberow, and Litman (1976), verbal statements can provide cues to self-destructive intentions. Such statements should be assessed and considered in relation to behavioral signs, changes in thinking patterns, motivations, personality traits, and so on. There is no universal language or style for communicating suicidal intention. Some adolescents will openly and directly say something like "I am going to commit suicide" or "I am thinking of taking my life." Others will be far less direct and make statements such as "I'm going home," "I wonder what death is like," "I'm tired," "She'll be sorry for how she has treated me," or "Someday I'll show everyone just how serious I am about some of the things I've said!"

The important thing for counselors, parents, teachers, and friends to remember is that when someone says something that could be interpreted in a number of ways, it is always best to ask for clarification. It is not a good idea to make assumptions about what a statement means or to minimize the importance of what is being communicated. Suicidal adolescents often have a long-term history of difficulty with communicating feelings and asking for support. Indirect statements may be made in the hopes that someone will respond with support and interest and provide or facilitate a referral for professional assistance (Capuzzi & Gross, 2000).

Thinking Patterns and Motivations

In addition to the areas previously described, thinking patterns (Gust-Brey & Cross, 1999) and motivations of suicidal adolescents can also be assessed and evaluated. For such an assessment to occur, it is necessary to encourage self-disclosure to learn about changes in an adolescent's cognitive set and distortions of logic and problem-solving ability. As noted by Velkoff and Huberty (1988), the motivations of suicidal adolescents can be understood more readily when suicide is viewed as fulfilling one of three primary functions: (a) an avoidance function that protects the individual from the pain perceived to be associated with a relationship or set of circumstances; (b) a control function that enables an adolescent to believe he or she has gained control of someone or something thought to be out of control, hopeless, or disastrous; or (c) a communication function that lets others know that something is wrong or that too much pain or too many injuries have been accumulated.

Often suicidal adolescents distort their thinking patterns in conjunction with the three functions of avoidance, control, and communication so that suicide becomes the best or only problem-solving option. Such distortions can take a number of directions. All-or-nothing thinking, for example, can enable an adolescent to view a situation in such a polarized way that the only two options seem to be continuing to be miserable and depressed or carrying out a suicide plan; no problem-solving options to cope with or overcome problems may seem possible (Capuzzi, 1988; Capuzzi & Gross, 2000). Identification of a single event that is then applied to all events is another cognitive distortion, that of overgeneralization. Being left out of a party or trip to the mountains with friends may be used as "evidence" for being someone no one likes, a "loser," or someone who will always be forgotten or left out. "I can't seem to learn the material for this class very easily" becomes "I'm never going to make it through school" or "I'll probably have the same difficulties when I start working full time." Adolescents who are experiencing stress and pain and who are becoming preoccupied with suicidal thoughts often experience more and more cognitive distortions. Such distortions result in self-talk that becomes more and more negative and more and more supportive of one of the following motivations for carrying through with a suicide plan:

- wanting to escape from a situation that seems (or is) intolerable (e.g., sexual abuse, conflict with peers or teachers, pregnancy, etc.)
- wanting to join someone who has died
- wanting to attract the attention of family or friends
- wanting to manipulate someone else
- wanting to avoid punishment
- wanting to be punished
- wanting to control when or how death will occur (an adolescent with a chronic or terminal illness may be motivated in this way)
- wanting to end a conflict that seems unresolvable
- wanting to punish the survivors
- wanting revenge

Personality Traits

As noted by Capuzzi (1988), it would be ideal if the research on the profile of the suicidal adolescent provided practitioners with such a succinct profile of personality traits that teenagers at risk for suicide could be identified far in advance of any suicidal risk. Adolescents who fit the profile could then be assisted through individual and group counseling and other means. Although no consensus has yet been reached on the usual, typical, or average constellation of personality traits of the suicidal adolescent, researchers have agreed on a number of characteristics that seem to be common to many suicidal adolescents (Orbach, 2001).

Low Self-Esteem. A number of studies (Beautrais et al., 1999; Cull & Gill, 1982; Faigel, 1966; Freese, 1979; King, 1999; Price et al., 2001; Stein & Davis, 1982; Stillion, McDowell, & Shamblin, 1984) have connected low self-esteem with suicide probability. Our counseling experience as well as the experience of other practitioners seems to substantiate the relationship between low self-esteem and suicide probability. Almost all such clients have issues focused on feelings of low self-worth, and almost all such adolescents have experienced these self-doubts for an extended time period.

Hopelessness/Helplessness. Most suicidal adolescents report feeling hopeless and helpless in relation to their circumstances as well as their ability to cope with these circumstances. The research support (Beautrais et at, 1999;

Cull & Gill, 1982; Jacobs, 1971; Kovacs, Beck, & Weissman, 1975; Peck, 1983; Stanard, 2000) for verification of what clinicians report is growing. Most practitioners can expect to address this issue with suicidal clients and to identify a long-term history of feeling hopeless and helpless on the part of most clients.

Isolation. Many, if not most, suicidal adolescents tend to develop a small network of social support. They may find it uncomfortable to make new friends and rely on a small number of friends for support and companionship. (This may be the reason why so often those around a suicide victim state they did not notice anything unusual. The suicidal adolescent may not be in the habit of getting close enough to others so that changes in behavior, outlook, and so on can be noted.) A number of authorities (Gust-Brey & Cross, 1999; Hafen, 1972; Kiev, 1977; Peck, 1983; Sommes, 1984; Stein & Davis, 1982) support this observation.

High Stress. High stress coupled with poor stress management skills seems to be characteristic of the suicidal adolescent. A number of studies have addressed this trait in terms of low frustration tolerance (Cantor, 1976; Kiev, 1977; Stanard, 2000).

Need to Act Out. Behaviors such as truancy, running away, refusal to cooperate at home or at school, use or abuse of alcohol or other drugs, and experimentation with sex are frequently part of the pattern present in the life of a suicidal adolescent. Such behaviors may be manifestations of depression. Often, adults remain so focused on the troublesome behavior connected with an adolescent's need to act out that they may overlook underlying depressive episodes.

Need to Achieve. Sometimes, adolescents who are suicidal exhibit a pattern of high achievement. This achievement may be focused on getting high grades, being the class clown, accepting the most dares, wearing the best clothes, or any one of numerous other possibilities. In our counseling experience, this emphasis on achievement often is a compensation for feelings of low self-esteem. Readers should be cautioned, however, about jumping to the conclusion that every adolescent who achieves at a high level is suicidal. This trait, along with all of the other traits and characteristics connected with the profile of the suicidal adolescent, must be assessed in the context of other observations.

Poor Communication Skills. Suicidal adolescents often have a history of experiencing difficulty with expression of thoughts and feelings. Such adolescents may have trouble with identifying and labeling what they are feeling; self-expression seems awkward if not stressful. It is not unusual to discover that adolescents who have become preoccupied with suicidal thoughts have experienced a series of losses or disappointments that they have never been able to discuss and, understandably, integrate or resolve.

Other-Directedness. Most suicidal adolescents are "other-directed" rather than "inner-directed." They are what others have told them they are instead

246

of what they want to be; they value what others have said they should be instead of what they deem to be of personal value and worth. This trait may also be linked to low self-esteem and may lead to feelings of helplessness or inability to control interactions or circumstances around them.

Guilt. Usually connected with feelings of low self-esteem and a need to be other-directed, the guilt experienced by many suicidal adolescents is bothersome and sometimes linked to a "wanting to be punished" motivation for suicide. Some statements common to the guilt-ridden suicidal adolescent might include "Nothing I do seems to be good enough," "I feel so bad because I disappointed them," or "I should not have made that decision and should have known better."

Depression. Depression is a major element (Mazza & Reynolds, 1998) in the total profile of the suicidal adolescent. Hafen and Frandsen (1986) pointed out that there are sometimes differences between depression in an adult and depression in an adolescent. Adults are often despondent, tearful, sad, or incapable of functioning as usual. Although adolescents sometimes exhibit these characteristics, they may also respond with anger, rebelliousness, truancy, running away, using and abusing drugs, and so on. Those adults and peers who associate depression only with feelings of sadness and despondency may not recognize depression in adolescents who mask the depression with behavior that creates discomfort in family and school environments.

As noted by Capuzzi (1988),

> Given the complexity of being an adolescent in the late 1980's, coupled with the normal ups and downs of the developmental stage of adolescence, it is normal for every adolescent to experience short periods of depression. But when depressive periods become more and more frequent, longer and longer, and of such intensity that the adolescent has difficult functioning at school and at home, they could be a strong warning sign of suicide potential, especially if other aspects of behavior, verbalization, motivations and cognitive distortions have been observed. (p. 10)

It is extremely important for counselors and other professionals who may be working with suicidal adolescents to complete additional coursework or training experiences to learn about the different types of depression. Although familiarity with resources and guidelines such as those provided by McWhirter and Kigin (1988) and the *Diagnostic and Statistical Manual of Mental Disorders—Text Revision* (American Psychiatric Association, 2000) are readily available to mental health practitioners, case supervision and consultation may be needed to accurately determine the nature of a depressive episode. Frequently, well-meaning practitioners fail to discriminate between depression created by a constellation of factors (negative self-talk, poor problem-solving skills, high stress, etc.) and depression that is a result of the body chemistry an adolescent inherited at birth. Treatment or counseling plans are different based on the kind of depression being experienced.

Counselors, therapists, and core or crisis team members need to liaison with nurse-practitioners and psychiatrists when medical assessment and subsequent medication are appropriate for depression.

Poor Problem-Solving Skills. Most parents notice differences in the problem-solving ability of their children. Some children are more resourceful than others in identification of problem resolution options. Suicidal adolescents seem, in our experience, to have less ability to develop solutions to troublesome situations or uncomfortable relationships. This may be a reason why suicidal preoccupation can progress from a cognitive focus to an applied plan with little dissonance created by the formulation and consideration of other problem-solving options and decisions.

Case Study

Jim was a 17-year-old high school junior and the son of affluent, well-educated parents. Jim's dad was a successful attorney, and his mom was an assistant superintendent for the local school district. Jim's sister, Janell, was 15, well liked, a cheerleader, and involved in a variety of school and community-related activities. Janell had a beautiful singing voice and frequently accepted prominent roles in school, church, and community musical productions.

Although Jim had a few close friends, he preferred to spend most of his time reading and studying and was a straight A student. He accepted an opportunity to spend most of his junior year traveling and studying in Europe and thought such an experience would provide an excellent educational option as well as time away from his parents. Jim resented the high expectations his parents placed on both him and Janell and felt that his father did not approve of an earlier decision not to participate in varsity sports. Both parents, Jim felt, pressured him to be involved in school and community civic and social organizations; Jim preferred more solitary and intellectual pursuits. Jim felt somewhat self-conscious and awkward in social situations and never felt that he could present himself as well as his sister or in a way acceptable to his parents. He felt directed and criticized by both parents and resented the fact that his parents always seemed too busy to listen to him talk about things of importance to him. He really resented his father's lack of approval and felt that no one in his family seemed to really understand his point of view.

Jim had experienced periodic episodes of depression, and because he had decided that it was best not to talk with family members about his feelings, he usually tried to keep his sister and his parents from knowing that he felt really down. Jim noticed that his depression was the worst when he was under a lot of stress with respect to completing class assignments and during times that his parents pressured him into social situations. Bob, Jim's best friend, got so concerned about Jim toward the end of the exam period in the spring of their sophomore year that he told Jim's parents. Jim's parents took him to a psychiatrist, who prescribed an antidepressant and recommended weekly therapy. Jim's parents were angry with their son, resented the additional expense, and demanded that Jim get better as soon as possible. Janell hoped her friends would not find out because she was in the midst of being nominated for Queen of the Rose Festival and had already been selected as a Rose Festival Princess. Jim did not like the psychiatrist and felt as criticized by him as he did by his parents. He disliked the side effects of the medication, often skipped his weekly therapy session, and could hardly wait to leave home in late August to attend the orientation session at Cambridge prior to initiation of his travel/study itinerary.

Shortly after Thanksgiving Jim's parents received a call from Switzerland; Jim had nearly died after an overdose of his medication and was recovering in a hospital in Zurich. Jim was sent home during the first part of December.

Approaches to Prevention

Individual

Individually focused preventive counseling with Jim could have been focused in several ways. Jim could have benefited from a therapeutic relationship that included self-esteem enhancement as part of the treatment plan. If counseling/therapy had been initiated during elementary school years, Jim might not have responded with depression and, to a great extent, isolation and withdrawal from all but a few friends who provided a limited network of social support. Jim might also have been encouraged to share feelings and communicate with his parents. He also would have benefited from assertiveness training to assist him with sending needed messages to his parents at times when his parents were more preoccupied with career-related responsibilities and interests. Jim's counselor/therapist would probably have worked with him to become more aware of stressors and more adept at managing stress and removing stressors from his environment. Possibly, the combination of efforts made by his parents in couples' counseling and by Jim in the context of his individual work would have resulted in outcomes very different from those described in the previous case description.

Family

Most suicidal adolescents have developed their at-risk profiles over time beginning during early childhood. In families in which there is more than one child, it is often easy for parents to identify differences in self-esteem, communication skills, stress management, problem solving, and so on. By the time a child is in elementary school, there may be visible indicators or traits that, if no intervention takes place, will result in the child's involvement in one or several at-risk behaviors. It is our opinion that such a child, by the time the middle school or junior high transition occurs, will be vulnerable to becoming pregnant, contracting AIDS, abusing drugs, developing an eating disorder, dropping out of school, or attempting or completing suicide.

Jim's family could have noted Jim's low self-esteem, discomfort with respect to sharing feelings, depression, response to stress, poor stress-management skills, and his resentment toward them. They might have been able to detect changes in his thinking patterns or fluctuations in day-to-day behaviors had they developed a relationship with him that included more open lines of communication. Jim's parents did not realize that their son experienced even higher levels of stress in conjunction with the European study program and felt compelled to succeed at all costs. Jim also did not anticipate the amount of interchange and collaboration required by the group living situations he found himself in as he and his peers and teachers traveled from one community to another and had begun to feel less self-assured than ever. Ideally, Jim's parents should have sought counseling assistance for themselves and their son when Jim was in elementary school. A counselor might have done an assessment of possible risk factors connected with Jim's family of origin and the families of his grandparents so that counseling could have compensated for predisposing factors and included an educational component for Jim's parents.

School and Community

There are a number of steps that can be taken to involve both the school and the community in prevention efforts (King, 2001a). In general, it is easier to initiate efforts in the school setting than it is in the context of a mental health center because schools can easily access young people, reach and prepare school faculty and staff, involve parents, and collaborate with mental health professionals from the surrounding community.

A number of steps must be taken to facilitate a successful school–community prevention effort. Collaboration with administrators, faculty/staff in-service, preparation of crisis teams, providing for individual and group counseling options, parent education, and classroom presentations are described in the following subsections.

Collaboration With Administrators. There is a compelling need for prevention, crisis management, and postvention programs for the adolescent suicide problem to be put in place in elementary, middle, and high schools throughout the country (Metha et al., 1998; Speaker & Petersen, 2000; Zenere & Lazarus, 1997). Based on our experience in the process of working with school districts all over the United States, one of the biggest mistakes made by counselors, educators, and coordinators of counseling/student services is to initiate programs and services in this area without first obtaining commitment and support of administrators and others in supervisory positions. Too often efforts are initiated and then canceled because little or no negotiation with those in decision-making positions has taken place (Adelman & Taylor,

2000). Building principals and superintendents must be supportive; otherwise all efforts are destined for failure. Developing understanding of the parameters connected with suicide prevention and intervention must start with the building principal and extend to all faculty and staff in a given building (Adelman & Taylor, 2000; King, 2001a) so that advance understanding of why quick action must take place is developed. During a crisis, schedules must be rearranged, and faculty and staff may be called on to teach an extra class, assist with an initial assessment, and so on. Everyone connected with a given building must have advance preparation.

In addition to the groundwork that must be done on the building level, it is also important to effect advance communication and planning on the district level. The superintendent, assistant superintendent, curriculum director, staff development director, student services coordinator, research and program evaluation specialist, and others must all commit their support to intervention efforts. When administrators have the opportunity to listen to an overview of proposed efforts and ask questions, a higher level of commitment can be established, and efforts can be more easily expedited. The probability of extending proposed programming to all schools in a given district is also increased.

Faculty/Staff In-Service. Because teachers and other faculty and staff usually learn of a student's suicidal preoccupation prior to the situation being brought to the attention of the school counselor or another member of the core or crisis team (assuming such a team exists), all faculty and staff must be included in building- or district-level in-service on the topic of adolescent suicide. Teachers, aides, secretaries, administrators, custodians, bus drivers, food service personnel, librarians, and school social workers all come in contact with adolescents at risk for suicide. It is imperative that all such adults be educated about both adolescent suicide and building and district policies and programs for prevention, crisis management, and postvention. There are a growing number of publications that provide excellent guidelines for elements of prevention programming focused on school faculty and staff (Davidson & Range, 1999; Kirchner, Yoder, Kramer, Lindsey, & Thrush, 2000; Metha et al, 1998; Speaker & Petersen, 2000; Zenere & Lazarus, 1997). When a young person reaches out to a trusted adult, that adult must have a clear understanding and a considerable amount of self-confidence so he or she knows exactly what to say and do as well as what not to say and do.

Many schools and school districts have actually precipitated suicide attempts by not providing for faculty/staff in-service on the topic prior to introducing discussion among student groups. When middle and high school students participate in educational programs on the topic of adolescent suicide, they begin to realize that they, as well as some of their friends, are at risk and they approach admired adults for assistance. Adults in the school who have no knowledge of what to do and who have not had the opportunity to have their questions answered and their apprehension lowered may be threatened by what a student is sharing and fail to make appropriate comments and decisions. Highly stressed, depressed, suicidal adolescents do not have the perspective to realize that such responses are connected with discomfort on the part of the adult and have little to do with what could be interpreted as disapproval and lack of acceptance. Awkward and minimal responses to suicidal self-disclosure on the part of a trusted adult can be interpreted by the adolescent as the loss of the last link to society and provide additional reinforcement for finalizing a suicide plan.

It is unethical not to prepare school faculty and staff in advance of the presentation of information on suicide to the students in a school. To do so could also become the basis for legal action by parents and family members. Much of the content in this chapter can become the basis for necessary in-service efforts.

Preparation of Crisis Teams. Many schools have crisis or core teams composed of faculty, staff, and parents connected with a particular building. These teams often exist in conjunction with a program for the prevention and intervention efforts necessary to cope with the drug problem among the young people in today's schools. Such teams usually consist of some combination of teachers, counselors, parents, social workers, school psychologists, school nurses, and school administrators. Usually these teams have been educated about traits that place adolescents at risk for substance use and abuse and have had supervision and instruction on the use of appropriate communication, diagnostic, and intervention skills necessary to begin the long-term process of recovery from alcoholism and other addictions. With education beyond that which is provided during the faculty/staff in-service discussed previously, as well as additional supervision and evaluation of clinical skills, a core or crisis team can be taught how to facilitate prevention efforts in a school as well as how to respond to a student already experiencing a suicidal crisis or in need of postvention efforts. In addition, such a team can be expected to write a policy statement that covers all parameters connected with prevention, crisis management, and postvention efforts. Such a policy could be adopted in other schools; in reality, except for specifics connected with a given building, the same policy statement should be adopted and followed throughout a school district. It is important to realize that everyone who is called on to assist a suicidal adolescent must know what to do. Confusion or lack of certainty about a chain of command or notification of parents procedures can result in delays and interfere with efforts to save a young person's life.

Individual and Group Counseling Options. Prior to providing students with any information about suicide and suicide prevention efforts in a school, arrangements must be made for the individual and group counseling services that will be needed by those who seek assistance for themselves or their friends. Unless such counseling options are available, any effort at prevention, crisis management, or postvention will be doomed to failure. This may present a problem to school personnel, particularly on the secondary level, unless there is a commitment on the part of administrators to free counselors from scheduling, hall monitoring, and other duties not related to the emerging role of the counselor of the 21st century. Working with suicidal adolescents requires a long-term commitment on the part of those interested in intervening. No counselor, psychologist, or social worker can undo the life experiences and self-perceptions of a lifetime without providing consistent, intensive opportunities for counseling.

If the school district cannot make a commitment to providing counseling, then arrangements for referral to community agencies and private practitioners must be made. It is important to provide adolescents and their families with a variety of referral possibilities along with information on fee schedules. There may be some question about whether the school district will be liable for the cost of such counseling if the referral is made by the school. (This issue should be explored by whatever legal counsel is retained by the district.) The dilemma, of course, is that unless counseling takes place when a suicidal adolescent has been identified, the probability is high that an attempt or a completion will take place. If the school is aware of a teenager's suicidal preoccupation and does not act in the best interests of such a teenager, families may later bring suit against the district. Counselors in the school and members of the mental health network in the community must preplan to work in concert for the benefit and safety of adolescents at risk for suicide.

Parent Education. Parents of students in a school in which a suicide prevention program is to be initiated should be involved in the school's efforts to educate, identify, and assist young people in this respect. Parents have a right to understand why the school is taking such steps and what the components of a schoolwide effort will be. Evening or late-afternoon parent education efforts can be constructive and engender additional support for a school or school district. Parents have the same information needs as faculty and staff with respect to the topic of adolescent suicide. They will be more likely to refer themselves and their children to the school for assistance if they know of the school's interest in adolescent suicide prevention, have had an opportunity to ask questions about their adolescent sons' and daughters' behavior, and have been reassured about the quality and safety of the school's efforts.

Classroom Presentations. There is continuing debate surrounding the safety of adolescent suicide prevention programs that contain an educational component that is presented to adolescents. This debate is similar to the one that emerged years ago when schools initiated staff development and classroom presentations on the topic of physical and sexual abuse. There are a number of advocates of education and discussion efforts that are focused on students in conjunction with a schoolwide suicide prevention effort (Capuzzi, 1988, 1994; Capuzzi & Golden, 1988; Curran, 1987; Ross, 1980;

Sudak, Ford, & Rushforth, 1984; Zenere & Lazarus, 1997). Providing adolescents with an appropriate forum in which they can receive accurate information, ask questions, and learn about how to obtain help for themselves and their friends does not precipitate suicidal preoccupation or attempts (Capuzzi, 1988, 1994; Capuzzi & Gross, 2000). Because newspaper and television reports of individual and cluster suicides do not usually include adequate education on the topic, and because many films have unrealistically presented or romanticized the act of suicide, it is important for schools to address the problem in a way that provides information and encourages young people to reach out for help prior to reaching the point of despair.

A carefully prepared and well-presented classroom presentation made by a member of the school's core team (or another presenter who has expertise on the topic) is essential. Such a presentation should include information on causes, myths, and symptoms as well as information about how to obtain help through the school. *Under no circumstances should media be used in which adolescents are shown a suicide plan.* In addition, on the elementary level, school faculty should not present programs on the topic of suicide prevention; their efforts are better focused on developmental counseling and classroom presentations directed at helping children overcome traits (such as low self-esteem or poor communication skills) that may put them at risk for suicidal behavior at a later time. Although these efforts should be continued through secondary education, middle and high school students are better served through presentations that address adolescent suicide directly. (Middle and high school students almost always have direct or indirect experience with suicide and appreciate the opportunity to obtain information and ask questions.)

Legal Considerations

Prior to discussing intervention strategies in the next section of this chapter, it seems appropriate to comment about some legal aspects of suicide prevention and intervention efforts in schools. In an excellent review of the results of school violence litigation against schools, Hermann and Remley (2000) noted that, even though those who are employed by school districts are expected to exert reasonable care to prevent harm to students, the courts have been reluctant to find educators liable for injuries related to violence or self-harm. State law claims usually fail because much of today's school violence (and suicide attempts and completions are components of school violence) results from what can be termed *spontaneous acts of violence.* This fact should not, however, lull school personnel into a false sense of security or complacency. A growing number of legal opinions have indicated that an unanticipated act of violence can be predictable and, thus, actionable under state law. Therefore, counselors, teachers, administrators, and other members of school staffs can protect themselves, as well as the youth they serve, by writing and implementing suicide prevention, crisis management, and postvention policy and procedures. These policy and procedures documents should mandate staff development for all school personnel so that all adults in the school setting recognize risk factors, possible behavioral, verbal, cognitive, and personality indicators, as well as role responsibilities and limitations. What we view as best practices are more likely to be followed if schools take a proactive rather than a reactive stance to this growing epidemic in our country's youth.

Intervention Strategies

Individual and Family

There are times that adolescents at risk for suicide are not identified until a crisis state has been reached. In such circumstances, it is important for all concerned to initiate action for the purpose of assessing lethality and determining appropriate follow-up. Because many professionals who are not counselors lack experience with adolescents who are in the midst of a personal crisis, the following guidelines may prove helpful. Note that these guidelines can be read in the context of working with Jim, the student in the case study. The assumption that one would have to make, however, is that all the adults traveling with Jim and his peers would have participated in staff development efforts and would include a counselor or other professional who could assess suicidal risk. An additional assumption is that families would be supportive of the use of these guidelines, either because they realized that the situation had escalated beyond their capacity to handle the situation or because they had participated in a school-sponsored presentation to the community on the topic of adolescent suicide prevention and intervention.

1. *Remember the meaning of the term* crisis management. When thinking of crisis management, it is important to understand the meaning of the word *crisis* as well as the word *management.* The word *crisis* means that the situation is not usual, normal, or average; circumstances are such that a suicidal adolescent is highly stressed and in considerable emotional discomfort. Adolescents in crisis usually feel vulnerable, hopeless, angry, low in self-esteem, and at a loss for how to cope. The word *management* means that the professional involved must be prepared to apply skills that are different from those required for preventive or postvention counseling. An adolescent in crisis must be assessed, directed, monitored, and guided for the purpose of preventing an act of self-destruction. Because adolescents who are experiencing a suicidal crisis may be quite volatile and impulsive, the need for decisive, rapid decision making on the part of the intervener is extremely important.

2. *Be calm and supportive.* A calm, supportive manner on the part of the intervener conveys respect for the perceptions and internal pain of an adolescent preoccupied with suicidal thoughts. Remember that such an adolescent usually feels hopeless and highly stressed. The demeanor and attitude of the helping person are pivotal in the process of offering assistance.

3. *Be nonjudgmental.* Statements such as "You can't be thinking of suicide; it is against the teachings of your church" or "I had a similar problem when I was your age and I didn't consider suicide" are totally inappropriate during a crisis situation. An adolescent's perception of a situation is, at least temporarily, reality and that reality must be respected. The same caution can be applied to the necessity of respecting a suicidal adolescent's expression of feelings whether these feelings are those of depression, frustration, fear, or helplessness. Judgmental, unaccepting responses and comments only serve to further damage an already impaired sense of self-esteem and decrease willingness to communicate. Adolescents could sink further into depression or increase their resolve to carry through with a suicide plan if others are critical and unwilling to acknowledge what appear, to the adolescent, to be insurmountable obstacles.

4. *Encourage self-disclosure.* The very act of talking about painful emotions and difficult circumstances is the first step in what can become a long-term healing process. A professional helper may be the first person with whom such a suicidal adolescent has shared and trusted in months or even years, and it may be difficult to do simply because of lack of experience with communicating thoughts and feelings. It is important to support and encourage self-disclosure so that an assessment of lethality can be made early in the intervention process.

5. *Acknowledge the reality of suicide as a choice but do not normalize suicide as a choice.* It is important for practitioners to let adolescents know that they are not alone and isolated with respect to suicidal preoccupation. It is also important to communicate the idea that suicide is a choice, a problem-solving option, and that there are other choices and options. This may be difficult to do in a way that does not make such an adolescent feel judged or put down. An example of what could be said to an adolescent in crisis is, "It is not unusual for adolescents to be so upset with relationships or circumstances that thoughts of suicide occur more and more frequently; this does not mean that you are weird or a freak. I am really glad you have chosen to talk to me about how you're feeling and what you are thinking. You have made a good choice since, now, you can begin exploring other ways to solve the problems you described."

6. *Actively listen and positively reinforce.* It is important, during the initial stages of the crisis management process, to let the adolescent at risk for suicide know you are listening carefully and really understanding how difficult life has been. Not only will such careful listening and communicating, on the part of the professional, make it easier for the adolescent to share, but it will also provide the basis for a growing sense of self-respect. Being listened to, heard, and respected are powerful and empowering experiences for anyone who is feeling at a loss for how to cope.

7. *Do not attempt in-depth counseling.* Although it is very important for a suicidal adolescent to begin to overcome feelings of despair and to develop a sense of control as soon as possible, the emotional turmoil and stress experienced during a crisis usually make in-depth counseling impossible. Developing a plan to begin lessening the sense of crisis an adolescent may be experiencing is extremely important, however, and should be accomplished as soon as possible. Crisis management necessitates the development of a plan to lessen the crisis; this plan should be shared with the adolescent so that it is clear that circumstances will improve. Counseling/therapy cannot really take place during the height of a suicidal crisis.

8. *Contact another professional.* It is a good idea to enlist the assistance of another professional, trained in crisis management, when an adolescent thought to be at risk for suicide is brought to your attention. School and mental health counselors should ask a colleague to come into the office and assist with assessment. It is always a good idea to have the support of a colleague who understands the dynamics of a suicidal crisis; in addition, the observations made by two professionals are likely to be more comprehensive. Because suicidal adolescents may present a situation that, if misjudged or mismanaged, could result in a subsequent attempt or completion, it is in the best interests of both the professional and the client for professionals to work collaboratively whenever possible. It should also be noted that liability questions are less likely to become issues and professional judgment is less likely to be questioned if assessment of the severity of a suicidal crisis and associated recommendations for crisis management have been made on a collaborative basis. *No matter what the circumstances, document all that is done on behalf of the youth through keeping careful case notes.*

9. *Ask questions to assess lethality.* A number of dimensions must be explored to assess lethality. This assessment can be accomplished through an interview format (a crisis situation is not conducive to the administration of a written appraisal instrument). The following questions help determine the degree of risk in a suicidal crisis; all of them do not need to be asked if the interview results in the spontaneous disclosure of the information:

- *"What has happened to make life so difficult?"* The more an adolescent describes the circumstances that have contributed to feelings of despair and hopelessness, the better the opportunity for effective crisis management. The process of describing stress-producing interpersonal situations and circumstances may begin to lower feelings of stress and reduce risk. It is not unusual for an adolescent in the midst of a suicidal crisis to describe a multifaceted set of problems with family, peers, school, drugs, and so on. The more problems an adolescent describes as stress-producing and the more complicated the scenario, the higher the lethality or risk.

- *"Are you thinking of suicide?"* Although this may not be the second question asked during an assessment of risk (ask it when you think the timing is right), it is listed here because it is the second most important question to ask. Adolescents who have been preoccupied with suicidal thoughts may experience a sense of relief to know there is someone who is able to discuss suicide in a straightforward manner. Using the word *suicide* will convey that the helping professional is listening and is willing to be involved; using the word *suicide* will not put the idea of suicide in the mind of a nonsuicidal adolescent. This particular question need not be asked until such time the assessor has developed the rapport and trust of the adolescent; timing is important in this regard so that relief rather than resistance is experienced on the part of the adolescent.

- *"How long have you been thinking about suicide?"* Adolescents who have been preoccupied with suicide for a period of several weeks are more lethal than those who have only fleeting thoughts. One way to explore several components of this question is to remember the acronym FID: When asking about suicidal thoughts, ask about *frequency* or how often they occur, *intensity* or how dysfunctional the preoccupation is making the adolescent ("Can you go on with your daily routine as usual?"), and *duration* or how long the periods of preoccupation last. Obviously, an adolescent who reports frequent periods of preoccupation so intense that it is difficult or impossible to go to school, to work, or to see friends, and for increasingly longer periods of time so that periods of preoccupation and dysfunction are merging, is more lethal than an adolescent who describes a different set of circumstances.

- *"Do you have a suicide plan?"* When an adolescent is able to be specific about the method, the time, the place, and who will or will not be nearby, the risk is higher. (If the use of a gun, knife, medication or other means is described, ask if that item is in a pocket or purse and request that the item be left with you. Never, however, enter into a struggle with an adolescent to remove a firearm. Call the police or local suicide or crisis center.) Most adolescents will cooperate with you by telling you about the plan and allowing you to separate them from the means. Remember, most suicidal adolescents are other-directed; such a trait should be taken advantage of during a crisis management situation. Later, when the crisis has subsided and counseling is initiated, the adolescent's internal locus of control can be strengthened.

- *"Do you know someone who has committed suicide?"* If the answer to this question is yes, the adolescent may be of higher risk, especially if this incident occurred within the family or a close network of friends. Such an adolescent may have come to believe that suicide is a legitimate problem-solving option.

- *"How much do you want to live?"* An adolescent who can provide only a few reasons for wishing to continue with life is of higher risk than an adolescent who can enumerate a number of reasons for continuing to live.

- *"How much do you want to die?"* The response to this question provides the opposite view of the one above. An adolescent who gives a variety of reasons for wishing to die is more lethal than an adolescent who cannot provide justification for ending life. It may be unnecessary to ask this question if the previous question provided adequate data.

- *"What do you think death is like?"* This question can be an excellent tool for assessment purposes. Adolescents who do not seem to realize that death is permanent, that there is no reversal possible, and that they cannot physically return are at higher risk for an actual attempt. Also, adolescents who have the idea that death will be "romantic," "nurturing," or "the solution to current problems" are at high risk.

- *"Have you attempted suicide in the past?"* If the answer to this question is yes, then the adolescent is more lethal. Another attempt may occur that could be successful because a previous attempter has the memory of prior efforts and the fact that he or she conceptualized and carried through with a suicide plan. An additional attempt may correct deficits in the original plan and result in death.

- *"How long ago was this previous attempt?"* is a question that should be asked of any adolescent who answers yes to the previous question. The more recent the previous attempt, the more lethal the adolescent and the more critical the crisis management process.

- *"Have you been feeling depressed?"* Because a high percentage of adolescents who attempt or complete suicide are depressed, this is an important question. Using the acronym FID to remember to ask about frequency, intensity, and duration is also helpful in the context of exploring an adolescent's response to this question. As previously discussed, a determination needs to be made about the existence of clinical depression if such a condition is suspected. Adolescents who report frequent, intense, and lengthy periods of depression resulting in dysfunctional episodes that are becoming closer and closer together, or are continuously experienced, are at high risk.

- *"Is there anyone to stop you?"* This is an extremely important question. If an adolescent has a difficult time identifying a friend, family member, or significant adult who is worth living for, the probability of a suicide attempt is high. Whomever the adolescent can identify should be specifically named; addresses, phone numbers, and the relationship to the adolescent should also be obtained. (If the adolescent cannot remember phone numbers and addresses, look up the information, together, in a phone book.) In the event it is decided that a suicide watch should be initiated, the people in the network of the adolescent can be contacted and asked to participate.

- *"On a scale of 1 to 10, with 1 being low and 10 being high, what is the number that depicts the probability that you will attempt suicide?"* The higher the number, the higher the lethality.

- *"Do you use alcohol or other drugs?"* If the answer to this question is yes, the lethality is higher because use of a substance further distorts cognition and weakens impulse control. An affirmative response should also be followed by an exploration of the degree of drug involvement and identification of specific drugs.

- *"Have you experienced significant losses during the past year or earlier losses you've never discussed?"* Adolescents who have lost friends because of moving, vitality because of illness, their family of origin because of a divorce, and so on are vulnerable to stress and confusion and are usually at higher risk for attempting or completing suicide if they have been preoccupied with such thoughts.

- *"Have you been concerned, in any way, with your sexuality?"* This may be a difficult question to explore, even briefly, during a peaking suicidal crisis. Generally, adolescents who are, or think they may be, gay or lesbian are at higher risk for suicide. It is quite difficult for adolescents to deal with the issue of sexual orientation because of fear about being ridiculed or rejected. They may have experienced related guilt and stress for a number of years, never daring to discuss their feelings with anyone.

- *"When you think about yourself and the future, what do you visualize?"* A high-risk adolescent will probably have difficulty visualizing a future scenario and will describe feeling too hopeless and depressed to even imagine a future life.

As noted at the beginning of this discussion, it is not necessary to ask all of these questions if the answers to them are shared during the course of the discussion. Also, it is appropriate to ask additional questions after a response to any of the above when it seems constructive to do so. It should be noted that the interviewing team must make judgments about the truthfulness of a specific response by considering the response in the total context of the interview.

10. *Make crisis management decisions.* If, as a result of an assessment made by at least two professionals, the adolescent is at risk for suicide, a number of crisis management interventions can be considered. They may be used singly or in combination; the actual combination will depend on the lethality determination, resources and people available, and professional judgment. It is the responsibility of the professionals involved, however, to develop a crisis management plan to be followed until the crisis subsides and long-term counseling or therapy can be initiated.

- *Notify parent/legal guardians.* Parents of minors must be notified and asked for assistance when an adolescent is determined to be at risk for a suicide attempt. Often, adolescents may attempt to elicit a promise of confidentiality from a school or mental health counselor who learns about suicidal intent. Such confidentiality is not possible; the welfare of the adolescent is the most important consideration, and parents should be contacted as soon as possible.

Sometimes parents do not believe that their child is suicidal and refuse to leave home or work and meet with their son or daughter and members of the assessment team. At times, parents may be adamant in their demands that the school or mental health professional withdraw their involvement. Although such attitudes are not conducive to the management of a suicidal crisis, they are understandable because parents may respond to such information with denial or anger to mask true emotions and cope with apprehensions that perhaps their child's situation reflects their personal inadequacies as people and parents. Because an adolescent at risk for a suicide attempt cannot be left unmonitored, this provides a dilemma for a school or a mental health agency. Because conforming to the wishes of uncooperative parents places the adolescent at even greater risk, steps must be taken despite parental protests. Although some professionals worry about liability issues in such circumstances, liability is higher if such an adolescent is allowed to leave unmonitored and with no provision for follow-up assistance. It may be necessary to refer the youth to protective services for children and families when parents or guardians refuse to cooperate. Schools and mental health centers should confer with legal counsel to understand liability issues and to make sure that the best practices are followed in such circumstances.

- *Consider hospitalization.* Hospitalization can be the option of choice during a suicidal crisis (even if the parents are cooperating) when the risk is high. An adolescent who has not been sleeping or eating, for example, may be totally exhausted or highly agitated. The care and safety that can be offered in a psychiatric unit of a hospital are often needed until the adolescent can experience a lowered level of stress, obtain food and rest, and realize that others consider the circumstances painful and worthy of attention. In many hospital settings, multidisciplinary teams (physicians, psychiatrists, counselors, social workers, nurses, nurse-practitioners, teachers) work to individualize a treatment plan and provide for outpatient help as soon as the need for assistance on an inpatient basis subsides.
- *Write contracts.* At times, professionals may decide that developing a contract with the adolescent may be enough to support the adolescent through a period of crisis and into a more positive frame of mind after which the adolescent would be more receptive to long-term counseling or therapy. Such a contract should be written out and signed and dated by the adolescent and the counselor. The contract can also be witnessed and signed by other professionals, friends, or family members.

  Contracts should require the adolescent to:

  1. Agree to stay safe.
  2. Obtain enough food and sleep.
  3. Discard items that could be used in a suicide attempt (guns, weapons, medications, etc.).
  4. Specify the time span of the contract.
  5. Call a counselor, crisis center, and so on if there is a temptation to break the contract or attempt suicide.
  6. Write down the phone numbers of people to contact if the feeling of crisis escalates.
  7. Specify ways time will be structured (walks, talks, movies, etc.).

- *Organize suicide watches.* If hospital psychiatric services on an inpatient basis are not available in a given community and those doing the assessment believe the suicide risk is high, a suicide watch should be organized by contacting the individuals whom the adolescent has identified in response to the question, "Is there anyone to stop you?" After receiving instruction and orientation from the professional, family members and friends should take turns staying with the adolescent until the crisis has subsided and long-term counseling or therapy has begun. In our opinion, it is never a good idea to depend on a family member alone to carry out a suicide watch; it is usually too difficult for family members to retain perspective. Friends should be contacted and included in a suicide watch even though confidentiality, as discussed earlier, cannot be maintained.

• *Refuse to allow the youth to return to school without an assessment by a mental health counselor, psychologist, psychiatrist, or other qualified professional.* An increasing number of school districts are adopting this policy. Although it could be argued that preventing a suicidal youth from returning to school might exacerbate suicidal ideation and intent, this policy increases the probability that the youth will receive mental health counseling and provides the school with support in the process of preventing the youth from engaging in self-harm.

School and Community

When an adolescent has attempted or completed a suicide, it is imperative, particularly in a school setting, to be aware of the impact of such an event on the "system." Usually, within just a few hours, the fact that an adolescent has attempted or completed suicide has been chronicled through the peer group. This could present a problem to the faculty and staff in a given school building because not answering questions raised by students can engender the sharing of misinformation or rumors and encouraging open discussion could embarrass an attempter on his or her return.

The following guidelines should prove helpful. Had Jim been in the regular school program when he made his attempt, these guidelines would have been put into effect immediately.

1. The principal of the building in which a student has attempted or completed suicide (even though such an incident most likely occurred off the school campus) should organize a telephone network to notify all faculty and staff that a mandatory meeting will take place prior to school the next morning. (Prior to the meeting, the principal should confirm the death through the coroner's office or through the student's family.) The principal should share information and answer questions about what happened during such a meeting. In the case of a suicide completion, it is recommended that the principal provide all faculty and staff with an announcement that can be read, in each class rather than over a public address system, so that everyone in the school receives the same information. The announcement should confirm the loss and emphasize the services the school and community will be providing during the day and subsequent days. Details about the circumstances or the family of the deceased should not be given so that confidentiality is maintained in that regard.

263

2. Faculty and staff should be instructed to answer student questions that spontaneously arise but should be told not to initiate a discussion of suicide in general.

3. Faculty and staff should be told to excuse students from class if they are upset and need to spend time in the office of the building counselor or another member of a core or crisis team.

4. Parents who are upset by the suicidal incident should be directed to a designated individual to have questions answered. Parents should also be provided with options for counseling, whether this counseling is provided by school personnel or referred to members of the mental health community.

5. At times, newspaper and television journalists contact the school for information about both the suicide attempt or the completion and the school's response to the aftermath. Again, it is important to direct all such inquiries to a designated individual to avoid the problems created by inconsistency or sharing inaccurate information.

6. If a suicidal attempt occurs prior to the initiation of prevention and crisis management efforts in a given building, it is not a good idea to immediately initiate classroom mental health education even if faculty, staff, and core teams have been prepared and a written policy has been developed. Allow sufficient time to pass to prevent embarrassment to the returning student and his or her family.

7. Be alert to delayed or enhanced grief responses on the part of students prior to the anniversary of a suicide completion. Often students will need opportunity to participate in a support group with peers or individual counseling prior to and, perhaps, beyond the anniversary date.

8. Do not conduct a memorial service on the school campus after a suicide because doing so may provide reinforcement to other students preoccupied with suicidal ideation. This means that it is unwise to conduct an on-campus memorial service after a death for any reason—it is difficult to explain why a student who has committed suicide is not being remembered when another student, faculty, or staff has been memorialized previously. Excuse students to attend the off-campus memorial or funeral. Do the same thing after deaths for other reasons.

9. Early in the sequence of events, as listed above, one or two individuals from the school should contact the family and ask if there is any support they might need that the school can provide. It is a good idea to offer such assistance periodically, as time passes, because so many families are left alone with their grief once the memorial or funeral has taken place.

Adaptations for Diversity

It is important to note that the information contained in the introductory section of this chapter suggests a number of adaptations for diversity, particularly with respect to prevention efforts. Because data suggest that Caucasian adolescent males are the highest risk group for suicide, extra efforts should be made to involve those young men who may be vulnerable in early prevention efforts. Individual and group counseling, focused on some of the personality traits described earlier, could and should be initiated in the elementary school years. Such early prevention efforts are preferable to waiting until suicidal preoccupation develops and observations about behavior can be observed. Because Native Americans have the highest adolescent suicide rates of any ethnic group in the United States, teachers, counselors, and parents should be alerted to early signs so that efforts can be made to avert the development of at-risk behaviors.

The etiology of suicide is something that all adults should be made aware of so that young people experiencing psychiatric illness, abuse, confusion about sexual identity, chronic or terminal physical illness, and so on (see discussion earlier in the chapter) can be monitored, supported, and referred for counseling/therapy when needed. Staffing sessions should be routinely conducted in elementary, middle, and high school settings so that young people who may be at risk for suicide attempts or completions could be routinely monitored and assisted. Because we know that adolescents who experience what they interpret as shameful or humiliating experiences with peers and with family members may, at times, be at high risk, these young people should also be the focus of observation and action should the need for prevention or intervention efforts be identified. In general, the more adults can be made aware of both risk factors and the suicidal profile, the earlier and more effective the prevention or intervention efforts.

Summary

We believe that individuals who are interested in working with suicidal youth must obtain more extensive information than that provided in this chapter. In addition, such individuals should obtain supervision from professionals qualified to provide such supervision after observing actual assessment interview and counseling/therapy sessions. Generally, neither assessment nor preventive or postvention sessions should be attempted by anyone who has graduated from a graduate program with less than a 2-year coursework and practicum/internship requirement. (In the case of counselors, such a graduate program should follow the standard set by the Council for the Accreditation of Counseling and Related Educational Programs.) In addition, membership in the American Association of Suicidology, participation in workshops and conferences focused on the topic of adolescent suicide, and consistent reading of the journal *Suicide and Life-Threatening Behavior* and other related books and journals are imperative.

Readers should also be cautioned not to use the material in this chapter as the sole basis for mental health education on the topic of adolescent suicide prevention or faculty/staff development in schools. This chapter provides an overview and an excellent starting point for professionals. Those without expertise on the topic or graduate preparation as a counselor, social worker, psychologist, psychiatric nurse, or other helping professions will not be able to answer questions of clients, families, and other professionals on the basis of reading a single chapter on this topic. Finally, anyone reading this chapter should be cautioned against initiating an adolescent suicide prevention, crisis management, and postvention program without writing a description of the various components so it can be checked by other professionals (including attorneys) and followed by all those involved in such an initiative.

An adolescent who becomes suicidal is communicating the fact that he or she is experiencing difficulty with problem solving, managing stress, expressing feelings, and so on. It is important for us to respond in constructive, safe, informed ways because the future of our communities (whether local, national, or international) is dependent on individuals who are positive, functional, and able to cope with the complex demands of life. As research and clinical experience provide additional and more sophisticated information about adolescent suicide, it will be necessary to incorporate this information into prevention, crisis management, and postvention efforts. To abdicate our responsibility to do so would communicate a lack of interest in the youth of today and a lack of concern about the future of society.

References

Adelman, H. S., & Taylor, L. (2000). Moving prevention from the fringes into the fabric of school improvement. *Journal of Educational and Psychological Consultation, 11,* 7–36.

American Psychiatric Association. (2000). *Diagnostic and statistical manual of mental disorders* (4th ed., Text Revision). Washington, DC: Author.

Beautrais, A. L., Joyce, P. R., & Mulder, R. T. (1999). Personality traits and cognitive styles as risk factors for serious suicide attempts among young people. *Suicide and Life-Threatening Behavior, 29,* 37–47.

Berlin, I. N. (1987). Suicide among American Indian adolescents: An overview. *Suicide and Life-Threatening Behavior 17,* 218–232.

Berman, A. L., & Jobes, D. A. (1991). *Adolescent suicide: Assessment and intervention.* Washington, DC: American Psychological Association.

Blumenthal, S. J. (1991). Letter to the editor. *Journal of the American Medical Association, 265,* 2806–2807.

Borowsky, I. W, Ireland, M., & Resnick, M. D. (2001). Adolescent suicide attempts: Risks and protectors. *Pediatrics, 107,* 485–493.

Brent, D. A., Perper, J. A., Moritz, C., Baugher, M., Schweers, J., & Roth, C. (1993). Firearms and adolescent suicide: A community case-control study. *American Journal of Diseases in Children, 747,* 1066–1072.

Bush, J. A. (1976). Suicide and Blacks. *Suicide and Life-Threatening Behavior, 6,* 216–222.

Canetto, S. S., & Sakinofsky, I. (1998). The gender paradox in suicide. *Suicide and Life-Threatening Behavior, 28,* 1–23.

Cantor, P. (1976). Personality characteristics found among youthful female suicide attempters. *Journal of Abnormal Psychology, 85,* 324–329.

Capuzzi, D. (1988). *Counseling and intervention strategies for adolescent suicide prevention* (Contract No. 400-86-0014). Ann Arbor, MI: ERIC Counseling and Personnel Services Clearinghouse.

Capuzzi, D. (1994). *Suicide prevention in the schools: Guidelines for middle and high school settings.* Alexandria, VA: American Counseling Association.

Capuzzi, D., & Golden, L. (Eds.). (1988). *Preventing adolescent suicide.* Muncie, IN: Accelerated Development.

Capuzzi, D., & Gross, D. (2000). "I don't want to live": The adolescent at risk for suicidal behavior. In D. Capuzzi, & D. Gross (Eds.), *Youth at risk: A prevention resource for counselors, teachers, and parents* (3rd ed., pp. 319–352). Alexandria, VA: American Counseling Association.

Cavaiola, A. A., & Lavender, N. (1999). Suicidal behavior in chemically dependent adolescents. *Adolescence, 34,* 735–744.

Centers for Disease Control and Prevention. (2000). CDC Surveillance Summaries (No. 55-5). *MMWR, 49,* 10.

Cohen, E. M. (2000). Suicidal ideation among adolescents in relation to recalled exposure to violence. *Current Psychology, 19,* 46–56.

Committee on Adolescence. (2000). Suicide and suicide attempts in adolescence. *Pediatrics, 105,* 871–874.

Cull, J., & Gill, W. (1982). *Suicide probability scale manual.* Los Angeles: Western Psychological Services.

Curran, D. F. (1987). *Adolescent suicidal behavior.* Washington, DC: Hemisphere.

Davidson, M. W., & Range, L. M. (1999). Are teachers of children and young adolescents responsive to suicide prevention training modules? Yes. *Death Studies, 23,* 61–71.

Davis, P. A. (1983). *Suicidal adolescents.* Springfield, IL: Charles C Thomas.

Diekstra, R. F. (1989). Suicidal behavior in adolescents and young adults: The international picture. *Crisis, 10,* 16–35.

Faigel, H. (1966). Suicide among young persons: A review of its incidence and causes, and methods for its prevention. *Clinical Pediatrics, 5,* 187–190.

Fernquist, R. M. (2000). Problem drinking in the family and youth suicide. *Adolescent Psychology, 35,* 551–558.

Freese, A. (1979). *Adolescent suicide: Mental health challenge.* New York: Public Affairs Committee.

Garland, A. F., & Zigler, E. (1993). Adolescent suicide prevention: Current research and social policy implications. *American Psychologist, 43,* 169–182.

Gibbs, J. T. (1988). Conceptual, methodological, and sociocultural issues in Black youth suicide: Implications for assessment and early intervention. *Suicide and Life-Threatening Behavior, 18,* 73–79.

Gust-Brey, K., & Cross, T. (1999). An examination of the literature base on the suicidal behaviors of gifted students. *Roeper Review, 22,* 28–35.

Hafen, B. Q. (Ed.). (1972). *Self-destructive behavior.* Minneapolis, MN: Burgess.

Hafen, B. Q., & Frandsen, K. J. (1986). *Youth suicide: Depression and loneliness.* Provo, UT: Behavioral Health Associates.

Harry, J. (1989). *Sexual identity issues: Report of the Secretary's Task Force on Youth Suicide: Vol. 2. Risk factors for youth suicide* (DHHS Publication No. ADM 89-1622). Washington, DC: Government Printing Office.

Henry, A. F., & Short, J. F. (1954). *Suicide and homicide.* Glencoe, IL: Free Press.

Hermann, M. A., & Remley, T. P., Jr. (2000). Guns, violence, and schools. The results of school violence litigation against educators and students shedding more constitutional rights at the school house gate. *Loyola Law Review, 46,* 389–439.

Hoberman, H. M., & Garfinkel, B. 0. (1988). Completed suicide in children and adolescents. *Journal of the American Academy of Child and Adolescent Psychiatry, 27,* 688–695.

Hussain, S. A., & Vandiver, K. T. (1984). *Suicide in children and adolescents.* New York: SP Medical and Scientific Hooks.

Jacobs, J. (1971). *Adolescent suicide.* New York: Wiley.

Johnson, S. W., & Maile, L. J. (1987). *Suicide and the schools: A handbook for prevention, intervention, and rehabilitation.* Springfield, IL: Charles C Thomas.

Kiev, A. (1977). *The suicidal patient.* Chicago: Nelson-Hall.

King, K. A. (1999). Fifteen prevalent myths concerning adolescent suicide. *Journal of School Health, 69,* 159–161.

King, K. A. (2000). Preventing adolescent suicide: Do high school counselors know the risk factors? *Professional School Counseling, 3,* 255–263.

King, K. A. (2001a). Developing a comprehensive school suicide prevention program. *Journal of School Health, 71,* 132–137.

King, K. A. (2001b). Tri-level suicide prevention covers it all. *Education Digest, 67,* 55–61.

Kirchner, J. E., Yoder, M. C., Kramer, I. L., Lindsey, M. S., & Thrush, C. (2000). Development of an educational program to increase school personnel's awareness about child and adolescent depression. *Education, 121,* 235–246.

Kovacs, M., Beck, A., & Weissman, A. (1975). The use of suicidal motives in the psychotherapy of attempted suicides. *American Journal of Psychotherapy, 29,* 363–368.

Lyon, M. E., Benoit, M., O'Donnell, R. M., Getson, P. R., Silber, I., & Walsh, T. (2000). Assessing African American adolescents' risk for suicide attempts. *Adolescence, 35,* 121–134.

Mazza, J. J., & Reynolds, W. M. (1998). A longitudinal investigation of depression, hopelessness, social support, and major and minor life events and their relation to suicidal ideation in adolescents. *Suicide and Life-Threatening Behavior, 28,* 358–374.

McWhirter, J. J., & Kigin, T. J. (1988). Depression. In D. Capuzzi & L. Golden (Eds.), *Preventing adolescent suicide* (pp. 149–186). Muncie, IN: Accelerated Development.

Metha, A., Weber, B., & Webb, L. D. (1998). Youth suicide prevention: A survey and analysis of policies and efforts in the 50 states. *Suicide and Life-Threatening Behavior, 28,* 150–164.

National Center for Health Statistics. (2002). Deaths: Leading causes for 2000. *National Vital Statistics Reports, 50,* 16.

National Institute of Mental Health. (2002). *Suicide facts.* Retrieved November 21, 2002, from http://www.nimh.nih.gov/research/suifact.cfm

Orbach, I. (2001). Therapeutic empathy with the suicidal wish: Principles of therapy with suicidal individuals. *American Journal of Psychotherapy, 55,* 166–184.

Peck, D. (1983). The last moments of life: Learning to cope. *Deviant Behavior, 4,* 313–342.

Price, J. H., Dake, I. A., & Kucharewski, R. (2001). Assets as predictors of suicide attempts in African American inner-city youths. *American Journal of Health Behavior, 25,* 367–375.

Rohde, P., Lewinsohn, P., & Seeley, J. R. (1991). Comorbidity of unipolar depression: Comorbidity with other mental disorders in adolescents and adults. *Journal of Abnormal Psychology, 100,* 214–222.

Ross, C. (1980). Mobilizing schools for suicide prevention. *Suicide and Life-Threatening Behavior, 10,* 239–243.

Russell, S. I., & Joyner, K. (2001). Adolescent sexual orientation and suicide risk: Evidence from a natural study. *American Journal of Public Health, 91,* 1276–1281.

Satcher, D. (1999). *Remarks at the release of the Surgeon General's call to action to prevent suicide.* Retrieved November 21, 2002, from http://www.surgeongeneral.gov/library/calltoaction/remarks.htm

Schneidman, B., Farberow, N., & Litman, R. (1976). *The psychology of suicide.* New York: Jason Aronson.

Shaffer, D. (1988). The epidemiology of teen suicide: An examination of risk factors. *Journal of Clinical Psychiatry, 49,* 36–41.

Shaffer, D., & Craft, L. (1999). Methods of adolescent suicide prevention. *Journal of Clinical Psychiatry, 60,* 70–74.

Shaffer, D., Garland, A., Gould, M., Fisher, P., & Trautman, P. (1988). Preventing teenage suicide: A critical review. *Journal of the American Academy of Child and Adolescent Psychiatry, 27,* 675–687.

Sommes, H. (1984). The troubled teen: Suicide, drug use, and running away. *Women and Health, 9,* 117–141.

Speaker, K. M., & Petersen, G. J. (2000). School violence and adolescent suicide: Strategies for effective intervention. *Educational Review, 52,* 65–73.

Stanard, R. P. (2000). Assessment and treatment of adolescent suicidality. *Journal of Mental Health Counseling, 22,* 204–217.

Stein, M., & Davis, J. (1982). *Therapies for adolescents.* San Francisco: Jossey-Bass.

Stillion, J., McDowell, E., & Shamblin, J. (1984). The suicide attitude vignette experience: A method for measuring adolescent attitudes toward suicide. *Death Education, 8,* 65–81.

Sudak, H., Ford, A., & Rushforth, N. (1984). Adolescent suicide: An overview. *American Journal of Psychotherapy, 38,* 350–369.

Velcoff, P., & Huberty, T. J. (1988). Thinking patterns and motivation. In D. Capuzzi & L. Golden (Eds.), *Preventing adolescent suicide* (pp. 111–147). Muncie, IN: Accelerated Development.

Wyche, K., Obolensky, N., & Glood, B. (1990). American Indian, Black American, and Hispanic American youth. In M. J. Rotheram-Borus, J. Bradley, & N. Obolensky (Eds.), *Planning to live: Evaluating and treating suicidal teens in community settings* (pp. 353–389). Tulsa, OK: University of Oklahoma Press.

Zenere, F. J., III, & Lazarus, P. J. (1997). The decline of youth suicidal behavior in an urban, multicultural public school system following the introduction of a suicide prevention and intervention program. *Suicide and Life-Threatening Behavior, 27,* 387–403.

Chapter 10

Counseling Suicidal Adults
Rebuilding Connections

Suzanne R. S. Simon

Beth, age 23, recently gave birth to her second child. She and her husband just relocated far from family and friends to a new city because of his job transfer. Lately, she has been having difficulty sleeping, has been crying frequently, and feels increasingly overwhelmed. Beth feels alone and is frightened to tell her husband about her fears because of the pressure he is under with his new position.

John, age 56, does not get the promotion he is expecting for the second time in 6 months. He has become increasingly agitated and volatile both at home and at work. His wife is concerned about John's alcohol use and smoking, especially since he had a heart attack 2 years ago. John told his wife that he feels like a failure and that his parents were right about him—he wouldn't amount to anything.

Gloria, age 75, provided full-time care for her husband who died less than a year ago after living with Alzheimer's disease for almost 7 years. Gloria was devoted to her husband and became increasingly isolated at home because of his needs. Her own decline in health due to diabetes has contributed to problems with vision and increased fatigue. After her husband's death, she felt conflicted by profound feelings of loss, relief, and resulting guilt. She has no living relatives or close friends. Gloria recently told her mail carrier that she has been so "out of touch" and is too tired to "return to life" without her husband and believes that no one would miss her anyway if she were gone.

Adulthood is a time of forming relationships, starting families, and establishing careers. But aging also includes many transitions that can strengthen bonds or bring profound losses. Connectedness sustains the human experience, yet "every 17 minutes in America, someone commits suicide" (Jamison, 1999, p. 309). According to the Centers for Disease Control and Prevention (2002), suicide rates increase with age and are highest among Americans over age 65. The experiences of Beth, John, and Gloria can offer a glimpse into the complexities of assessing potential risk for suicidal behavior. Each of their stories is unique and influenced by a variety of factors, including age-related life experiences. With further exploration, however, similarities might also be found. Feelings of hopelessness, helplessness, and isolation are threaded through each of their experiences. The suicidal adult's life, though often severed from various support systems, *depends* on connections and the awareness and sensitivity of family, community, and mental health counselors. Ultimately, a counselor's skilled assessment and intervention can be the first step for the client to reconnect with self, others, and life.

This chapter explores adult suicide risk, assessment, and intervention through the periods of early (age 25–34), middle (age 35–65), and late (over 65) adulthood. The goal of using a framework contextualized within the span of adulthood is not to stratify but rather is intended as a resource for better understanding the multifacetedness of the complex interrelation of factors contributing to adult suicide. A brief chapter overview includes suicide research trends, a review of two adult stage development theories as they relate to life transitions, and research highlights noting suicidal precipitants and risk factors. Risk assessment, crisis management, and intervention are viewed through each of the three periods of adulthood and conceptualized through the stories of Beth, John, and Gloria. The perspectives of the individual client, counselor, family, and community are woven into each case study. Prevention and postvention strategies are explored across the adult life span, and adaptations for diversity are also considered.

Overview

Trends and Implications

Findings of most suicidologists are consistent that women attempt suicide more than men, men complete suicide attempts more often than women, the elderly commit suicide more than any other age group, and suicide is most common in the psychiatrically disturbed (Adam, 1990; Blumenthal & Kupfer, 1990; Hendren, 1990; Jamison, 1999; Lester, 1997). Regardless of this strong knowledge base, it is difficult to predict who will attempt or complete suicide (Jamison, 1999; Moscicki, 1999). Though a pursuit of trends and themes has contributed to a better understanding of the who, how, when, and where of suicide, the *why* is still unclear (Jamison, 1999). Researchers such as Shneidman (1999), for example, believe that attempting to get at the meanings of and motivations for suicide to offer appropriate interventions and care has been problematic because of the complexities of individual life experience. Doyle (1999) contended that suicidal behavior must be contextualized to be understood, and Jamison (1999) emphasized that the interaction of intrapersonal perceptions, social influences, mental illness, and traumatic events manifest in unique ways for each individual.

A review of some of the literature makes clear that there are, however, effective ways to explore suicidal behaviors and those at risk from a variety of perspectives, including environmental (Blumenthal & Kupfer, 1990; Lester, 1997), genetic/heredity (Lester, 1986), and psychodynamic (Jamison, 1999; Lester, 1997) frameworks. Vaillant and Blumenthal (1990) and Stillion and McDowell (1996), however, offered an enhanced perspective for this chapter's discussion by considering behaviors and risks through the "lens of adult development over the lifespan as one possible way to understand the complex and intricate interrelationships that can lead to suicide" (Vaillant & Blumenthal, 1990, p. 12). Lester (1997) added that "suicide is the result of a gradual process that unfolds within an individual" (p. 2) and across the life journey. Because effective assessment and rapport building are key components of successful crisis intervention, counselors may want to consider interviewing techniques that are age related (see Hendren, 1990). An awareness of stressors considered within the context of various life stages can facilitate a better understanding of the *meaning* and potential impact that these challenges have within a given life stage for an adult at risk for suicide.

While frameworks and models can be productive tools for assessment and interventions, researchers agree that predictions and generalizations for suicide are problematic and should be viewed as cautionary (Adam, 1990; Jamison, 1999; Lester, 1997; Osgood & Thielman, 1990). Suicidologists also emphasize that suicide manifests uniquely and is difficult to classify. In terms of seeking appropriate treatment, it is important to realize that most major studies reveal that 90%–95% of people who commit suicide have a diagnosable mental illness (Jamison, 1999). Other researchers find that personality traits such as hostility, impulsivity, and depression are most commonly linked to an increased risk of suicide (Lester, 1997; Vaillant & Blumenthal, 1990). In addition, the most evident indicators of crisis are often behaviors that reflect a withdrawal or disconnect from just those life experiences the person in crisis holds as most meaningful. Lack of interest in favorite activities, agitation, withdrawal from relationships, sleep disturbances, and the decreased sense of finding pleasure are just a few signals that someone is experiencing a life challenge. Further, some suicidologists (Blumenthal & Kupfer, 1990; Jamison, 1999) suggest that when the most common element in suicide, mental illness, interacts with social, environmental, and behavioral factors, evaluating the role of these indicators is complex. The shifting impacts of related stressors such as unemployment, substance abuse, medical illness, or loss are perceived uniquely across the life span. Yet, in an attempt to better understand suicide to more appropriately treat and prevent, viewing suicide through an additional lens of adult stage developmental theory may be productive.

Stage Development Theories and Life's Transitions

Inquiries into the human life course and aging have emerged as various stage and developmental theories that attempt to link ages and tasks through different paradigms. The works of Erik Erikson (1978) and Daniel Levinson (1986) have been influential in contributing to the knowledge base that attempts to conceptualize a sequential aging process. Theorists from a variety of disciplines offer models that enhance an understanding of the life course through such frames as humanistic (Maslow, 1968; Rogers, 1961) or psychosocial (Loevinger, 1976). Additionally, some current researchers (Eastmond, 1991; Gilligan, 1982; Hughes & Graham, 1990; Peck, 1986) are calling into question potential gaps of gender and culture that exist in many of these models. Clearly, just as aging itself is a process of understanding and awareness, so too is the development and conceptualization of frameworks seeking to better understand how human experience unfolds over the life course. Consideration of developmental theories is offered in this chapter as an additional resource tool for counseling adults in crisis.

A detailed survey of stage development and aging theory is beyond the scope of this chapter. For the purposes of this section, key elements of the theories of Erikson (1978, 1982) and Levinson (1986) are noted as relevant to the discussion of suicide in adulthood. Erikson's (1978) model of life stages captures the dynamic of struggle between either accomplishing a primary task or experiencing a negative result. Young adulthood is seen as a time of search for *intimacy* instead of *isolation*; middle age involves activity or *generativity* as opposed to *stagnation*; and old age is perceived as a period of achievement of *integrity* with a meaningful perception of a unified self instead of *despair*. Erikson offers a relevant adjunct to human development theory with lifelong growth potential that results in profound psychosocial adjustments. And although his framework could be more fully elaborated across gender and cultural perspectives, the foundation of his model captures the vital relationship between internal and external life forces.

Daniel Levinson grounds his perspective in the belief that humans are in a process of establishing a self—*individuation*—by maintaining boundaries between the inner self and the outer world (Levinson, Darrow, Klein, Levinson, & Mckee, 1978). Stillion and McDowell (1996) further elucidated this key point by noting that this process "propels one to reach for uniqueness and to realize his capabilities in doing so" (p. 37). In his life cycle model, Levinson characterized a person's life with specific periods of stability and transition that form an evolving life structure. During times of *consistency* certain patterns are strengthened but are called into question or changed during times of *transition* (Levinson & Levinson, 1996). Relevant to this chapter's discussion is Levinson's emphasis that what each person holds as most important gains the most attention and therefore most influences all other aspects of the life structure.

As previously mentioned, this attempt to conceptualize life experience through age-related perspectives does not assume that events are age specific—stressors associated with marriage, family, or career occur throughout adulthood. However, one of the goals of this discussion about suicide within different adult stages is to consider the potential impact and interrelatedness of experiences that are more common to specific age ranges. On the basis of their research, Stillion and McDowell (1996) highlighted key elements of three periods of adulthood that suggest age-related trends and characteristics. They identified young adulthood (age 25–34) as a time of peak mental and physical capabilities with an increasing need to establish commitments in "work, marriage, and parenthood as well as a rigorous reevaluation of those commitments" (p. 121). Middle adulthood (age 35–65) is conceptualized as a period for significant opportunities for accomplishments, increased responsibilities, and intensive reflection and evaluation. Finally, Stillion and McDowell noted that biological changes, including sensory loss, along with an increase in chronic illness and a shift in traditional sex roles contribute to profound transitions experienced in older adulthood.

Risk Factors and Precipitants for Suicidal Adults

In comparing suicidal behavior of adults, researchers find that older adults use more lethal weapons, suffer from more medical problems, and try to escape pain (Hendren, 1990; Lester, 1997; Vaillant & Blumenthal, 1990), whereas younger adults are more likely to self-punish, seek revenge, or respond impulsively to interpersonal problems (Lester, 1997). Steffens and Blazer (1999) highlighted the key late-life risk factors as depression, feelings of hopelessness, major medical illness, bereavement for loss of a significant loved one, and previous suicide attempts. Jamison (1999) asserted that most studies show that the elderly are "inadequately treated for depression" (p. 21). And, when left untreated, depression in older adults manifests in somatic symptoms (Hendren, 1990), which contribute to a vicious cycle of emotional and physical illness that obscures underlying symptoms of depression.

Stillion and McDowell (1996) also suggested that middle adulthood is the least "empirically developed" (p. 152) stage, although they added that the stressors of this period include loss related to youthful perspectives of self, children leaving home, changes in perspective of time, increased use of alcohol, and an increase in multiple negative life events. Kahn (1990) emphasized that long dormant conflicts with parents emerge during middle adulthood, along with feelings of defeat, disappointment, and lowered expectations. And Viorst (1986) conceptualized middle adulthood as a period of many losses, including loss of the perception of a youthful self, children growing up and leaving home, and the death of parents. In revisiting Levinson et al.'s (1978) framework for middle adulthood as a time of transition, Pascual-Leone and Irwin (1998) elucidated Levinson's concept of the "midlife crisis" as a process in which the "polarities constructed in earlier periods break down . . . [and] life is no longer simply a matter of either/or" (pp. 54–55). Their point makes clear that although stage development is conveyed as a linear process, there also exist simultaneous challenges and shifts occurring within and between these periods. This awareness can be superimposed onto suicidal risk and its complicated symptomatology and mirror the complexities of aging.

Crisis Assessment, Management, and Intervention

In an attempt to illuminate the complexities of crisis and suicidal risk within different periods of adulthood, let us revisit the case studies of Beth, John, and Gloria. A primary goal in this exploration is to capture the dynamic aspect of connectedness as it both informs and reflects the shifting experience of pain that can lead to feelings of hopelessness, helplessness, and the ultimate attempt to disconnect. The interrelations with family, friends, work, and community that define humans as social beings contribute to both the tension and sustenance for a person in crisis. The duality of *needing others* and feeling *overwhelmed by* these relations is the fragile boundary that must be traversed by client, counselor, loved ones, and the larger community to facilitate appropriate intervention and treatment for suicidal risk. A key component of initial assessment is to determine a client's supports and stressors, and it is therefore important to understand that the meanings of the stressors are often both/and instead of either/or. Enmeshed within this awareness is the assumption that the desire to withdraw or disconnect through suicide is an attempt to *cut out* or *release from* the tensions of competing needs rather than being able to balance or reconcile conflicts.

Additionally, some researchers agree that the most effective ways to prevent suicide include recognizing the signs of someone at risk (Lester, 1997); using effective interviewing techniques (Hendren, 1990); reviewing predisposing factors such as personality, history of suicide, psychiatric illness, and life stressors (Jacobs, Brewer, & Klein-Benheim, 1999; Jamison, 1999); evaluating the availability and lethality of methods (Jamison, 1999); and recognizing that people with depression are at the highest risk for suicide (Hendren, 1990; Jamison, 1999; Kahn, 1990; Lester, 1997). Threaded throughout the literature is the key emphasis on the need for counselors to fully explore their own feelings about and reactions to suicide. Researchers noted a profound relationship between ability, skill level, and treatment impact on clients in crisis and the counselor's perception of suicide personally and professionally. For example, Firestone (1997) asserted that practitioners have themselves "rarely experienced the profound sense of lone-liness, devastating shame, unworthiness, and vicious self-recriminations that suicidal individuals feel" (p. 220). He believed this lack of personal experi-ence can lead to faulty judgment. Doyle (1990) added that working with suicidal patients provokes anxiety and demands total involvement, and that many of the client's behaviors can "alienate the counselor and threaten the professional equilibrium" (pp. 381–382).

Therefore, fundamental to appropriately assessing, intervening, and building a strong counselor and client alliance is the counselor self-manag-ing (Doyle, 1990). In his review of research related to treatment strategies, Firestone (1997) outlined the key components in effective case manage-ment of a suicidal client that incorporate clinical, legal, and ethical aspects of the counseling relationship:

- achieving acceptable standards of care as measured by skill and diligence similar to practitioners in like circumstances
- accurate assessment of risk factors
- productive interviewing emerging from rapport and feelings of support
- assessing collateral behavior with permission of client to interview significant others
- careful documentation and consultation with care providers
- involvement of family and significant others
- hospitalization when appropriate secondary to level of risk, with involvement and follow-up
- application of antisuicide contracting
- knowledge of community resources
- technical and personal competence

Hendren (1990) emphasized the importance of skilled interviewing with expediency and immediacy and suggested a developmental approach to interviewing that takes into account the client's age and life experiences as effective tools to guide questions and probes. In general, researchers encourage counselors to ask direct questions about suicidal ideation and intent as appropriate and necessary. It is a myth that asking specific ques-tions will either encourage or "give someone the idea" to attempt suicide. Most suicidologists agree that such questions elicit feelings of confidence and build trust with a client in crisis who believes the counselor skilled, confident, and takes the client's intent seriously (see Jamison, 1999; Lester, 1997). Additionally, the counselor must be resourceful, flexible, and clear about the extent and limits of the assistance that is being offered. To move from assessing to implementing a treatment plan, a genuine agreement must be reached by both client and counselor (Doyle, 1990).

To make more vivid age-related assessment and intervention dynamics, I explore the stories of Beth, John, and Gloria in the following sections.

These stories include strategies that rely heavily on the research and perspectives offered by Firestone (1997), Jacobs et al. (1999), and Stillion and McDowell (1996).

Suicide and Young Adulthood: Beth

It has been 2 months since Beth, her husband, and their children have moved to a new city and apartment. They have a strong and supportive marriage. Because of her husband's new job, he has been spending long hours at work and Beth has been trying not to bother him with her problems. As a result, communication between them has declined. Beth only leaves the apartment to run necessary errands and struggles to be "a good mother" for the children. Beth's parents want to visit, but Beth is embarrassed by the cluttered apartment because she and her husband have only unpacked a few boxes. Beth has not had the energy to arrange furniture or decorate. Her two best friends have called and sent cards, but Beth has not responded back to them. She is afraid she will fall apart on the phone, though she does not even know why.

As the weeks progress, Beth's husband notices that she is often asleep when he gets home for dinner and she has trouble getting out of bed in the morning. He knows she is still recovering from her pregnancy and that she is missing both family and friends back home. He misses them too, but he believes this job opportunity will lead to future success. He feels Beth is just going through another rough time, similar to the one she went through when their first child was born. To help Beth, her husband has been doing the shopping and caring for the children before and after work so that she can rest.

Beth's husband tells her that he has to attend a week-long seminar in another state, and he suggests she call her parents and have them visit while he is gone. Beth says she will "think about" his suggestion but decides not to because having family will only make it more difficult for her. After being gone for a few days, Beth's husband calls home and discovers that she has not been out of the apartment and has stayed in bed most of the time. He asks how she and the children are doing and she responds that "they are fine" and she adds that maybe his life would be better if he did not have them to worry about. Beth begins to sob. He asks her to tell him what is wrong. She expresses that she cannot find the words to describe what she is feeling, and she believes that it will just get worse because she doesn't *know* what is wrong. She tells him that she just wants to give up. Beth's husband says that he will return home immediately and asks Beth to promise to keep the phone close and wait for him. Beth agrees to wait.

Within Erikson's (1978) theory of a dynamic struggle between isolation and intimacy, Beth may be perceived as experiencing profound feelings of detachment. The interruptions resulting from relocation and the birth of her second child have shaken Beth's sense of self, and her relation to outer influences are being called into question (Levinson & Levinson, 1996).

Her current life is a paradox of beginnings and losses that compete for past understandings and new ways of coping. The crisis Beth is experiencing has manifested in both subtle and overt ways:

Risks and Signs
- change in sleeping patterns
- decline in attention to personal appearance
- loss of energy and interest
- withdrawal and lethargy
- unexpressed feelings of depression and hopelessness
- expressed feelings of giving up

Life Circumstances Affecting Risk
- loss and disruption of support networks
- birth of child
- relocation

Beth's Counselor

Overview. In Beth's case, the counselor's role will be to assess issues of suicidality within the context of Beth's current life situation and also to evaluate predisposing factors. As a young adult, Beth's experiences capture the tension that exist as a result of her wanting to be independent and her struggle with anxiety due to increased parental responsibilities. She is grieving over losses due to the relocation. Balancing her needs with those of the family has become difficult. With Beth's permission, the counselor meets with her husband to better understand how Beth's behaviors and mood have been unfolding over the last months and in relation to her mood and actions over the last few years.

Assessment and Intervention. The counselor's primary goal is to assess Beth's current level of safety in terms of risk for harm to self or others. In addition, the counselor's goals should include relief of Beth's acute level of pain; intervention and treatment to diffuse potential lethality; establishment of an alliance; support of Beth in finding and seeing options; and, ultimately, help Beth to find hope (Doyle, 1990). After taking a detailed history, the counselor notes the following key points:

1. *Current plan and level of lethality.* Although Beth expressed feelings of "giving up," she has not thought about a suicide plan, nor does she have access to means. The counselor has a responsibility to assess Beth's risk for harm toward the children and incorporates direct questions about them throughout the intervention.
2. *History, including past attempts and family incidence.* Beth has had a previous episode of depression after the birth of her first child but does not recall any experiences of melancholy or depression prior to that. Additionally, after she gave permission to the counselor to

279

speak with family members, the counselor notes that there has been no reported family history of mental illness or suicide attempts.

3. *Support status.* Beth has consistent and loving support of her husband. Additionally, even though family and friends are separated by distance, they are caring and involved and want to provide support.

4. *Risk factors (depression, mental status, substance abuse).* Beth's isolation and grief response to moving away from loved ones are key factors in her current crisis experience. Additionally, her depression will be treated with both counseling and pharmacological interventions. Beth has no history of substance abuse.

5. *Questions and probes.* Future counseling sessions will help Beth to explore her feelings, develop coping skills, and to find meaningful and creative ways to express her feelings and concerns. A key component of the initial assessment does include a brief exploration into some of these aspects with the counselor asking Beth to reflect on her losses, to recall previous successful attempts to solve problems and deal with pain, and to evaluate levels of conditions that Beth would classify as bearable or unbearable. The counselor, upon assessment, needs to understand and help Beth understand what Beth's threshold is for her experience of suffering and desire for relief. Assessing current levels of lethality is fundamental to evaluating Beth's safety, and it is the first step to help Beth begin to recognize her own emotional responses as a continuum and regain a sense of control.

6. *Counseling relationship, commitment to treatment, and adjunct assessments.* The counselor establishes immediate rapport that is grounded in a genuine expressed concern for Beth's well-being, along with a clear assessment and outlined treatment goals for Beth to agree to evaluate. Additionally, the counselor works with Beth to commit to the counseling relationship and agree to a written step-by-step antisuicide contract for Beth to keep with her that includes the counselor's phone number, contact information, and local crisis line numbers. The counselor also recommends that Beth meet with her new primary care physician and have a complete physical and follow-up with postdelivery evaluations.

It is imperative that Beth's counselor work with her to teach her how to recognize in herself early warning signs of depression or thoughts of suicide in potential relapse situations (see Jamison, 1999). Jamison also emphasized that a successful counseling alliance keeps at the forefront the objective of helping the client to maintain strong feelings of self-worth, self-efficacy, and active participation in her own care. Being well informed about her own health, seeking out books and support groups, and continually educating herself are just a few ways that Beth can maintain an empowered coexistence with her mental health challenges. Finally, in her treatment for depression, an honest dialogue must be encouraged with Beth to navigate the waxing and waning suicidal feelings that often occur during the recovery process.

7. *Intervention strategies.* A possible appropriate intervention strategy with Beth might be grounded in a cognitive–behavioral approach as conceptualized by Linehan (1993) with dialectical behavior therapy (DBT) techniques. This model is based on a balance of acceptance and change with three fundamental assumptions about an individual such as Beth: She needs to be able to self-regulate interpersonal interactions; she needs to be able to identify and counter faulty beliefs and misplaced motivations; and she needs help to apply what she learns in counseling to her real-world experiences. The goals of a DBT intervention include the following: orienting the client to counseling, agreeing to treatment goals prior to the sessions, targeting all life-threatening behaviors, addressing problems, replacing maladaptive coping skills with healthy ones, and immediately attending to counseling-interrupting behaviors.

In addition, Linehan, Goodstein, Nielsen, and Chiles (1983) developed a Reasons for Living questionnaire that attempts to highlight attitudes that might prevent suicide attempts. An interesting aspect of this tool is its potential use both as an assessment tool and as an intervention strategy to uncover and evaluate strengths and fears. Key aspects of this survey include the following:

- levels of confidence and self-efficacy in handling change
- sense of responsibility to family
- impact of behavior on children
- fears and moral perspectives on suicide

Facilitated by her counselor, Beth can explore these feelings and contextualize them for herself, begin to focus on what beliefs have had positive outcomes, and identify and counter those thoughts that have contributed to her sense of hopelessness.

Beth's Family

Many studies conclude that social support is protective against depression (Colletta, 1983; Compas, Slavin, Wagner, & Vannatta, 1986; Lin, Ensel, & Kuo, 1979, all cited in Jacobs, et al., 1999). Although Beth's despondency had reached a crisis level, the ultimate sense of immediacy and attention shown by her husband was instrumental to her safety and will positively affect her future recovery. On the basis of her previous close and intimate relationships with family and friends, the counselor will need to help all of them find

281

creative ways to support Beth. Establishing set times to talk on the phone, regular visits, and using e-mail to facilitate dialogue and expression of feelings for Beth are just a few of the ways they can not only reconnect but *maintain* connections. One of the initial goals set by Beth, her counselor, and her husband is to make arrangements for family to visit and help with unpacking. Included in that goal is to help Beth arrange for supplemental child care and become more familiar with her neighbors and local social organizations.

Beth's husband will also benefit from counseling to address guilt, confusion, or blame he might experience as a result of feeling that he should have been more aware of Beth's emotional well-being. As previously noted, although themes and patterns have emerged related to suicidal risks and tendencies, crisis reactions are unique to each person and are embedded within many different contexts (e.g., cultural or spiritual). And, healthy interactions among spouses, family members, and loved ones often become obscured by conflicting meanings, competing needs, and misguided assumptions. In an attempt to rationalize and "make the best of" feelings of pain and confusion both Beth and her husband were experiencing, a disconnect occurred within and between each of them—in trying to protect one another and be strong for the other, Beth's cries for help and her husband's responses were muted. Eventually, Beth had become paralyzed by her own thinking, and options seemed no longer to exist (Jamison, 1999).

Upon reflection of how Beth's experience unfolded, it is imperative that the counselor (with Beth's permission) meet with Beth's family to both educate them and encourage them to seek other informational sources to learn more about suicidal risks, precipitants, and signs. With the counselor's skill to mediate feelings of blame or responsibility, a treatment goal for Beth's husband and the family might include considering what some of the possible indicators of emotional crisis were for Beth. The counselor can help them to categorize these to reflect on and to reconceptualize to use them as possible guideposts for needed future interventions during Beth's treatment. Possible indicators might include the following:

Changes in Ability to Reason
- inability to concentrate
- confusion, disorientation, or forgetfulness
- believing untrue things

Behavioral Changes
- not sleeping or sleeping too much
- change in appetite
- decline in communication
- withdrawing or becoming more combative

Emotional Indicators
- apathy and lack of motivation
- feelings of guilt or being a burden

- persistent statements about giving up or death
- feelings of hopelessness, helplessness, or uselessness

Physical Changes
- decline in personal care or hygiene
- significant weight loss
- chronic complaints of pain with no physical cause

National organizations, Web sites, and community groups are valuable resources for loved ones to continue to learn, maintain ongoing awareness, and convey continued support of Beth. In addition, through their learning, they will understand that the recent crisis intervention with Beth diffused immediate risk but is only one step in a long-term journey to prevent Beth from attempting suicide in the future. Ultimately, through their desire to actively support and gain understanding, Beth's family and friends become positive role models for the larger community to collectively respond to the needs of those at risk for suicide. Their collective experience both infuses and inspires the needed communal response to destigmatize mental illness and encourage open and skilled responses to those in crisis.

Beth's Community

Beth's story poignantly illuminates the profound individual and social implications of relocation and resulting disconnection from important support networks. Not only did Beth experience feelings of loss and isolation from loved ones, but she became further marginalized from her new local community because of a combination of grief, fear, confusion, and depression. This reinforcing dynamic of needing others and intimate relationships and needing to reach into one's own resources to establish and maintain healthy connections reflects both Levinson's (1986) process of individuation and Erikson's (1978) young adult task pursuit of intimacy over isolation. What these frameworks do not fully conceptualize within this context, however, is the profound larger social implications that are called into question to meet individual needs within a community response. In Beth's case, her new community was not aware of her presence. Incorporated into her treatment goals with her counselor might be to take steps to locate, access, and cultivate existing community resources.

While an emphasis on available public intervention and crisis resources is fundamental to this discussion on suicide, the point must be made that in Beth's case, the key issue of importance was her inability to access the resources that were available to her. As Lester (1997) emphasized, suicide is often the "result of a combination of events usually preceded by observable behaviors and warning signs" (p. 2). Therefore, a continued community effort to educate, inform, and support individuals and families about suicide is vital. Although individualized and appropriate crisis intervention

283

was accessed for Beth by her husband, O'Carroll (1990) asserted that the prevention of suicide requires a multidisciplinary effort, and "no single discipline or profession has all the necessary resources to address the problem of suicide adequately" (p. 500). Once again, the paradoxical nature of individual existence within a social context is illuminated. In our drive to be who we are as healthy individuals, we need to support one another to do so. The community needs to be able to recognize and support the intervention of loved ones and professionals alike to support the person in crisis as an individual.

Middle Age and Suicide: John

For the second time in a few weeks, John's wife receives a call from one of his coworkers asking her to pick John up at a nearby restaurant because he had too many drinks to drive himself home. While driving back home, John's wife starts crying and yelling that she has had enough of his problems. She tells John that he is just killing himself with the drinking, smoking, and his long hours at work. She tells him it is destroying her to watch him do this to himself. John explains that he is just "digging himself into a hole" because it is hard to keep up with all the new managers at work. He tells her that she does not understand what it is like for him and he is running out of ways to deal with the competition at work. They continue arguing until they arrive home.

John despondently tells his wife that he understands her threat to leave him and he says that he cannot stand himself either. He explains that somehow things just "got out of hand" and he cannot figure it all out. John's wife thought his heart attack a few years ago was a wake-up call for him, but John tells her it was more of an omen—a reminder that he is old, out of shape, and has little time to get his life back. He says that after the heart attack, he did not care about changing things. He is not doing the work he really wants to do, but it is too late. He tells his wife to go ahead and leave him while she still has a chance for a better life. John reminds her that because they do not have children, there is no point in staying together. She tells John she does love him, but she is just worn out by his bad moods, outbursts, and the lack of life they are living.

About 6:00 a.m. the next morning, John has chest pains and difficulty breathing. In the emergency room, John and his wife are told that he is experiencing erratic heart rhythms and will have to stay a few hours for observation given his medical history. John tells the doctor to just "let him die" because this is just another sign that he is on borrowed time anyway. John's wife starts crying, and the hospital's crisis counselor is called in to assess John's level of suicide risk and intervene with both John and his wife.

In recasting John's experiences within Erikson's (1978) framework for middle adulthood, his task struggle is evident between generativity and stagnation. John's sense of loss of a healthy (and youthful self) along with the loss of his "competitive edge" at work have contributed to a spiraling inward of self-absorption that has immobilized him. His increased alcohol consumption and lack of self-care have created a vicious cycle of physical decline that perpetuates both physical and emotional lethargy. John's belief that he has not lived up to his own goals and fulfilled the lowest predicted expectations of his parents (see Kahn, 1990; Viorst, 1986) captures the midlife crisis concept offered by Levinson et al. (1978). A cautionary reminder of the preponderance of statistics for rising suicide rates through the life span for men is needed at this point (see Centers for Disease Control and Prevention, 2002; Hendren, 1990; Lester, 1997).

Risks and Signs
- increased alcohol consumption
- outbursts at work and at home
- increased agitation
- persistent statements about giving up
- expressed feelings of loss and guilt

Life Circumstances Affecting Risk
- medical complications (heart attack)
- job/career dissatisfaction
- marital problems

John's Counselor

Overview. Determining the appropriate level of intervention with John is multifaceted because of his complicating medical condition. The counselor will need to maintain a heightened awareness of presenting symptoms. Given the increased alcohol use and escalating levels of agitation, the counselor needs to recognize in John what Jamison (1999) highlighted as the most "virulent mix of risk factors for suicide: depressed mood, morbid thinking, and 'wired' or agitated level of energy" (p. 112). In John's case, the counselor needs to make sure he is safe until his suicidal state abates and to incorporate substance abuse treatment protocols that may necessitate hospitalization, medication, or both. The counseling alliance should be grounded in trust and shared control, though issues of safety initially take precedence. According to Kahn (1990), "Because of the disillusionment of middle age establishing a therapeutic alliance depends more on the solid, commonsense understanding communicated to the patient than on the readiness to idealize one's helper" (p. 460).

The decision to hospitalize does not preclude the establishment of a *collaborative* alliance that may include John agreeing to a voluntary hospitalization. Offering immediate temporary relief to one who is encased in despair through cautious use of pharmacotherapy or hospitalization (Kahn, 1990) may be a necessary crisis intervention with John. Although issues related to hospitalization and pharmacological interventions are beyond the scope of this chapter, Kahn's point that "unless a complementary help-ing alliance is established, the ultimate risk of suicide remains high" (p. 460) is most relevant to this discussion. Kahn also emphasized that, related to age-appropriate perspectives, middle-age clients respond most positively to an alliance grounded in "common sense" (p. 460) with a partnership of direct and open communication. Further, other researchers claim that it is appropriate for the counselor to ask John directly about his own percep-tions of his suicidal risk, support system, and losses (see Blumenthal & Kupfer, 1990; Jamison, 1999).

Assessment and Intervention. Because John is in the hospital for observation after his cardiac incident, he will meet and be assessed by a variety of practitio-ners and care providers across disciplines. Given John's level of stress and despondence, the additional influence of repeated interruptions and result-ing confusion need to be considered as related risk factors during his initial assessment with the counselor. Therefore, Doyle's (1990) outline of key in-terview factors are worth applying to John's case. The counselor should imme-diately identify by professional title and refer to John by his last name; meet first with John alone before meeting with his wife; maintain continuous con-tact with John; inform John about issues of confidentiality; be resourceful and flexible; and recognize that John may test the counselor's commitment to the intervention and the relationship. After compiling a detailed history and securing permission from John to meet with his wife in order to gain addi-tional information, the counselor will also assess the following:

1. *Current plan and level of lethality.* John does not currently have a plan of action for suicide. His dependence on alcohol along with his access to a gun kept in the home, however, are increased risk fac-tors for John's level of lethality. As Lester (1997) noted, alcohol consumption is a contributing factor to suicide for several reasons, including lowering inhibitions, impairing judgment, aggravating depression, as a means of self-destruction, and by disrupting social relationships. Additionally, the counselor must be aware of the potential of deception and manipulation by John secondary to sub-stance abuse (Kahn, 1990). An integral part of implementing a treatment plan will need to include an agreement by John and his wife that during his treatment process he will need to agree to appropriate levels of supervision related to current crisis interven-tions and with adjunct substance abuse treatment. John must also agree to have his wife remove and properly dispose of the gun, dispose of any alcohol, and limit access to any medication in the home. With John's case, a multidimensional treatment approach is needed to address his psychological, physical, substance abuse, and marital needs.

2. *History, including past attempts and family incidence.* John has no history of past suicide attempts, but he does disclose that his mother and grandmother had each attempted suicide. His grandmother died by a self-inflicted gun shot. And although his mother survived a drug overdose attempt, John describes her as "reclusive and bedridden" for most of her life. She died of a heart attack at age 60. The counselor understands that heredity, personality, depression, and environmental factors are "interlocking domains" (Vaillant & Blumenthal, 1990), yet the statistical implications for increased suicide risk for John due to his family history must be kept at the forefront (Jamison, 1999). It is imperative that the counselor build a strong foundation to facilitate both immediate and long-term intervention success for John. Initially, the emphasis should be to support, empathize, and understand the crisis from John's point of view. Evolving goals should include brainstorming, goal setting, and implementing of action plans revolving around his psychosocial and medical needs.

3. *Support status.* As the counseling alliance begins to form, the counselor encourages active involvement with John's wife. A key component of a successful intervention will include John's wife seeking and utilizing resources for herself, including support group involvement and adjunct counseling. The counselor encourages John and his wife to think about family, friends, and coworkers who have been supportive during previous times of crisis. After careful consideration, a list is compiled with names and numbers of those people John's wife believes are steadfast. A written list serves as both a concrete reminder to John that he has strong support and as a resource for future assistance. And though John currently views many of his coworkers as competitors rather than allies, he is encouraged to build alliances with them as mentors for more mutual relationships.

4. *Risk factors (depression, mental status, substance abuse).* The overlap of predisposing risk factors, immediate precipitators, substance abuse, and health complications makes for a challenging treatment plan. But, as Hendren (1990) noted, the most important skill in assessing is the ability to interview effectively and should be grounded in a treatment plan that facilitates the client in accepting the counselor's help. Therefore, to better comprehend risk factors and evaluate their potential impact on John, the counselor must pursue the most accurate diagnosis by openly discussing and gauging these factors currently and historically. Skill and resourcefulness will be needed by the counselor to navigate and bridge parallel treatments that will arise from John's cardiac rehabilitation and substance abuse interventions and may influence shifting risk factors. The

pharmacological treatment of John's heart condition may contribute to mood fluctuations or necessitate a work leave, which in turn might contribute to additional feelings of loss of control.

Additionally, the need for numerous treatment appointments and potential scheduling conflicts will be frustrating for both John and his wife. As a result, the counselor should encourage a balanced evaluation of risk factors with a strengths-based assessment as offered by O'Leary (1998) and move beyond current recovery methods to seek novel resources within individuals and the larger society. In her review of the literature, O'Leary included as determinants of thriving factors such as hardiness; cognitive resources such as self-efficacy and appropriate appraisal; meaning making; and cultivating social supports. Along with assessing risks, John's counselor can work with him to reflect on previous examples of successful coping and problem solving from his past experiences. Long-term treatment goals should also include enhanced problem-solving skills through cognitive–behavioral, dialectical behavior, or psychodynamic strategies.

5. *Questions and probes.* It is of paramount importance to use questioning and probing techniques both to assess and intervene with potential suicidal crisis and to elicit vital information. Continued monitoring for perceptions and ideations must be embedded in any counseling approach or strategy. As Jamison (1999) emphasized, suicidal clients are less able to conceive of possible solutions and are immobilized in their thinking. Therefore, questioning must be appropriate to the needs and capabilities of the client as determined by the counselor with each interaction. Immediate needs necessitate keeping John safe and closely monitoring his emotional and physical well-being, along with providing support to his wife. Future interventions, however, might include reflecting on John's comments about his perceived failure in his parents' eyes, along with his sense of devalued career identity as a potential springboard for productive questioning. For example, with attentive support the counselor can help John to reconstruct his loss history and facilitate grief responses while encouraging John to discover what continues to be most vital for him regardless of his losses (Stillion & McDowell, 1996). This exploration might include reconnecting strategies with his wife and loved ones. Further, John's exclamation that he is not "doing the work he wanted to do" also provides profound productive intervention opportunities that capture the paradoxical sense of loss and potential for something new with encouragement to explore novel future goals.

6. *Counseling relationship, commitment to treatment, and adjunct assessments.* The counselor's initial goals of building a strong alliance, carefully evaluating and diagnosing, and establishing a no-suicide contract

that John will agree to are key. Some of the literature (Firestone, 1997; Lester, 1997) emphasizes the important components of on-going counselor availability, flexibility, resourcefulness, and follow-up with the suicidal client. With John's history of noncompliance with self-care after his heart attack, relapse into alcohol abuse, and escalating outbursts, the counselor must be careful to monitor John's level of commitment. The counselor must also function as a member of a team of practitioners interacting with and treating John and should therefore carefully maneuver overlaps and conflicts resulting from multiple interventions. The counselor must work closely with John to maintain both confidentiality and treatment priorities while helping him to successfully navigate his experiences with the health care system. Finally, the counselor must, as Doyle (1990) suggested, help John to understand "the nature, extent, and limits of the assistance the [counselor] offers" (p. 391) and help him to become aware of and utilize available resources embedded in his health care options, which include support groups, supplemental therapies including nutrition and exercise, and substance cessation programs.

7. *Intervention strategies.* An assortment of intervention strategy options too numerous and detailed to mention in this chapter exist for John and his counselor depending on the resulting assessment, diagnosis, prognosis, and treatment plan. Interventions that address John's acute needs—such as suicidal lethality and his heart arrhythmias—may include immediate clinical assessments with divergent approaches. His skilled counselor will need to both mediate his psychological needs and facilitate his physiological interventions through flexible attentiveness. This will include maintaining regular contact with John and his wife, securing permission to access related medical assessments where appropriate, and facilitating appropriate referrals and placements to address John's long-term treatment needs. Additionally, Jamison (1999) and Linehan et al. (1983) emphasized the importance of treatment compliance, ongoing education, and identifying maladaptive thoughts and replacing them with practiced and skill-developed actions.

An effective strategy for John is offered by Beck, Rush, Shaw, and Emery (1979) that includes a "crucial first stage" of the counselor stepping into the reality of the client. They advocated this technique as a guide to determine if hopelessness is based on a lack of positive expectations, the reality of medical disorders, social isolation, or pathological ways of viewing the world to discover appropriate areas of focus for intervention. Beck et al. (1979) emphasized that the counselor must be able to sense why John is thinking about suicide and added: "Such understanding and empathy not only enable the [counselor] to adapt his helping strategies to the specific needs of the [client] but communicate to the client that he is understood" (p. 213).

Within the initial crisis intervention, Beck et al. (1979) encouraged "stimulating patient curiosity" to diffuse the initial acuity and begin to sustain "continuity between sessions" (p. 213). These perspectives hold relevance fundamental to building a genuine and productive counseling alliance. John's counselor can validate his real and perceived losses, help him to acknowledge his losses and lost expectations, and begin to perceive of unrecognized possibilities with his health, marriage, and career.

John's Family

Although John's journey of recovery is grounded in his individual treatment needs and goals, his wife and the strength of their ongoing relationship will also benefit from interventions that enhance their relationship. Some research reveals that suicide rates are lowest among those who are married (Adam, 1990; Lester, 1997). But, Lester also found that married couples with a suicidal partner have difficulty communicating. Important treatment goals for John and his wife will need to include communication skill development, acquisition of tools for expressing feelings of frustration and anger, and assessment and plans of action to achieve both individual and mutual goals. The counselor may deem it appropriate to work only with John to sustain their established alliance and refer John and his wife to another counselor for marriage interventions. A cornerstone of interventions for John and his wife might include evaluating dimensions of their lifestyle that can counter suicidal trends as offered by Firestone (1997):

- recognizing the therapeutic value of friendship
- sharing activities and adventures with others
- searching for meaning and transcending goals
- considering existential and spiritual values
- developing unique priorities
- cultivating relationships with extended family

Additionally, John and his wife are encouraged by the counselor to reflect on and reassess why relationships with extended family members have been strained or severed. Further into counseling, they can begin to explore the impact of John's mood swings, alcohol abuse, and their relational difficulties with family members. John's wife is encouraged to slowly reconnect with the family members she believes to be most supportive. She is also encouraged to learn to identify warning signs (in John and herself) of potential crisis precipitants, such as increased arguing, feelings of frustration, isolation, changes in sleeping or eating patterns, and to respond to them with skills gained in counseling (or, when needed, seek out additional professional support).

John's Community

To reiterate a key point, Vaillant and Blumenthal (1990) noted that "social support is the single most important protective factor aside from appropriate treatment" (p. 21). For the purpose of this discussion, community is defined as the network of individuals one lives with, works with, or encounters on a regular basis who provide some form of assistance or connection. John's sense of autonomy and group membership have shifted with his different life stages and experiences. Each major life change or challenge elicits varying levels of identification and isolation within his work community and society as a whole. The stage development frameworks of Erikson (1978, 1982) and Levinson (1986) make clear the ongoing and symbiotic need of living as an individual within a variety of communities and the challenges inherent in maintaining both boundaries and connections.

For a person in crisis who is experiencing feelings of hopelessness and helplessness, an often immobilizing dichotomy exists. The profound sense of isolation experienced when one believes he or she is no longer needed or does not matter contributes to the severing of connections with both *others* and *self.* John, like many others in middle adulthood, question who they are and where they are in relation to others not only in their own age groups but also in comparison with those they are moving toward (older) and those they have moved away from (younger). As a result, John's sense of self within his work identity and as an aging male has become obscured by comparisons with past and future. Additionally, complicating medical conditions, alcohol dependence, and a strained marital relationship have made his perceptions of his world more ambiguous.

From both self-reports and communication with his wife, it is clear that John has coworkers and family who are concerned about him and have expressed a desire to encourage his recovery. They have agreed to attend support groups related both to substance abuse and to suicide prevention. They have also made an additional commitment to respect John's privacy within their roles but also work to advocate organizational awareness of crisis intervention at work and through their various leisure group memberships. John learns that a coworker's sister committed suicide, and he felt relieved that he was able to honestly share his feelings to both give and receive support. Some family members continue to distance themselves from John and his wife, and they both have discovered that societal stigmas are still attached to suicide. But, through continued counseling, ongoing education, and participation in advocacy groups, John, his wife, friends, and loved ones have joined together as a community not only to help John but also to help the community at large.

Suicide and Older Adults: Gloria

Community

Gloria's story begins where the previous case studies have ended—with a discussion about community and its potential impact on the adult in crisis and at risk for suicide. A brief review of the literature is appropriate at this point to capture the trends and themes with suicide and older adults. Vaillant and Blumenthal (1990) found that suicide in old age is "two times greater than the general population" (p. 7) and "In the elderly medical illness may contribute significantly to risk because of the convergence of multiple risk factors, including decreased social supports, more interpersonal losses . . . and the loss of dignity that may accompany growing older" (p. 6).

Hendren (1990) asserted that the highest suicide rates are for people over age 50, and Steffens and Blazer (1999) found that people 85 years and over have the highest prevalence of suicide. Stillion and McDowell (1996) noted that throughout history, older adults have shown higher suicide rates when compared with other age groups. Jamison (1999) claimed that many studies show that the elderly are inadequately treated for depression—a major cause of suicide in all age groups. Additionally, other researchers have found that older adults complete suicide attempts more than any other age group (Osgood & Thielman, 1990; Stillion & McDowell, 1996; Vaillant & Blumenthal, 1990), use more lethal means (Lester, 1997; Stillion & McDowell, 1996), and more often experience a chronic form of suicide that includes self-neglect through failure to eat or noncompliance with life-saving medication (Steffens & Blazer, 1999).

The controversies and complexities related to health and mental health access and allocation issues for older adults are varied and many. The scope of this chapter is too narrow to appropriately address the ever-growing and increasingly multifaceted components of service delivery systems and aging. I can only encourage readers to seek out related sources and discussions to more fully explore the reality of profound shifting trends secondary to our aging population. Recent estimates find that America's population of senior citizens will double by 2030 to 71 million (Centers for Disease Control and Prevention, 2002). Superimposing the suicide statistics onto expected population trends highlights the profound potential public health crisis of suicide and older adults. Communities large and small need to recognize and respond to the older adult in crisis. One currently successful approach that targets isolated seniors brings us back to Gloria and her postal carrier.

Gatekeeper programs have been successful at intervening on the behalf of isolated and frail older adults. Community members and workers such as utility employees, law enforcement providers, financial representatives, letter carriers, government workers, and others have been formally trained to recognize potential at-risk seniors. These gatekeepers make a referral to a designated agency, and a follow-up is made by appropriate services. It is not unusual for older adults to be alone and in crisis because of having no living family members and few sustained friendships. As a result, social interactions and bonding often occur with service staff such as bank tellers or supermarket cashiers. Typically, these casual encounters are the life-lines for many older adults.

Over the last few days, the postal carrier noticed that Gloria's mail has gone uncollected from the mailbox. After he rang the doorbell a few times, Gloria answered the door in wrinkled and stained clothing. She appeared disheveled and much thinner than the last time he saw her. Gloria seemed confused when he asked her how she was doing. She could not answer questions about the last time she ate, left the house, or spoke to anyone. Over the last 15 years, Gloria and the postal carrier have had many conversations about poetry and literature. Gloria, a retired English professor, often shared books and quotes with the postal carrier. Today she made a reference to herself as compared to "grapes withering on the vine" and that she was "seeking but could not find sustenance" in her current life. The postal carrier continued to make a mental note about how Gloria appeared and the comments she made in preparation to contact the local crisis intervention line (as he had been instructed to do as part of his gatekeeper training). Based on the following factors, he determined that it was imperative to phone and obtain immediate help for Gloria:

Risks and Signs
- sudden unkempt appearance
- sudden confusion and disorientation
- apathy and lack of motivation
- verbalization about thoughts of death

Life Circumstances Affecting Risk
- recent death of her husband
- decline in health due to diabetes complications
- isolation
- sensory deficit of vision loss

Gloria's Counselor

Overview. Even those willing to use available health resources often have difficulty navigating multiple agency barriers. The inability to cope with trauma and stress due to lack of information, resources, and pressures of guilt and responsibility only magnifies the problem of getting help. Gloria's experience reflects Erikson's (1978) conceptualization of the dynamic of older age tensing between integrity or despair. For Gloria, her lifetime of accomplishments are obscured by possible feelings of humiliation and loss of control related to her husband's death and decline in her own health. Bereavement, physical illness, functional disability, hopelessness, and depression have all converged to immobilize Gloria. Her ability to recognize her own need for help and seek help has been compromised because of disorientation arising from effects of inappropriate use of her insulin, extreme dehydration, and other possible undiagnosed conditions.

In response to the postal carrier's detailed call, a counselor is sent to meet with Gloria and assess her level of risk. The counselor has experience with aging clients and intends to secure Gloria's safety, elicit vital information, and—through a respectful and genuine interaction—help Gloria to feel valued and respected. Additionally, the counselor understands that owing to generational differences in communication styles, age-specific interviewing techniques might be used to respond to initial denial of suicidal ideation. According to Hendren (1990):

> Direct questions about suicide asked early in the interview are likely to be unanswered or answered in the negative. The interviewer should be patient and empathic as the older person tells of his or her life, losses, family, and concerns about bodily functions. (p. 249)

Finally, the experienced counselor must use appropriate tools and resources (including immediate appropriate medical assessments) to determine and differentiate delusion, depression, and dementia. Often the manifestations are similar, but causes can range from temporary to chronic and from single to multiple. Not unusually, the level of self-neglect necessitates hospitalization in an acute setting to complete a comprehensive assessment. The counselor's immediate goal is to secure Gloria's safety.

Assessment and Intervention. Interventions with Gloria may require a creative combination of direct questions and a more subtle understanding of her experience of pain and loss through her sharing of stories and memories. Ultimately, the facilitative goal is to enable Gloria to feel safe and experience trust. A detailed history may not be initially gathered because of Gloria's confusion and may need to be obtained with subsequent information from primary care providers. Determining levels of competence and Gloria's ability to give informed consent is questionable and will require both delicacy and detailed documentation to determine the following:

1. *Current plan and level of lethality.* Steffens and Blazer (1999) offered an important conceptualization that holds diagnostic relevance for Gloria and other isolated older adults, that of "passive death wishes," which they differentiate from chronic suicide:

    > Thoughts that one would rather be dead but [with] no intent, either directly or indirectly, to end one's life. Such thinking is common in the elderly and may or may not be associated with psychiat-

ric or medical illness . . . may carry thoughts of death with them on a daily basis, but never seriously entertain ideas of taking steps to end their life. (p. 446)

During the initial assessment the counselor determines that Gloria has not been eating and is extremely dehydrated—deprivations that can contribute to states of confusion. In an attempt to distinguish among confusion, delirium, and dementia, the counselor asks Gloria to respond to a brief mental status test. The results will reflect her disorientation to place and time, her awareness of her own confusion, expressed feelings of distress, and difficulty with thinking and memory that may result from depression or signal dementia of either permanent or reversible causes. The counselor continues to assess Gloria's presenting clinical features to differentiate between depression and dementia within the following general guidelines:

Depression	*Dementia*
Onset can be dated	Onset not apparent
Client complains of cognitive losses	Client may be unaware of losses
Client gives detailed complaints	Client is vague with complaints
Client feels defeated	Client struggles with tasks
Attention is preserved	Limited attention span
Variability on testing	Consistent poor results

Embedded in many of Gloria's responses are expressions of tremendous grief related to cumulative losses she has experienced over the last few years, which include the death of her husband, lost friendships, a secluded life, and a decline in her own health. Gloria repeatedly describes feeling exhausted and says she is too weak to try and get help or kill herself—she describes her current situation as a "dying limbo" and is just waiting to join her husband. With empathy and genuine respect, the counselor helps Gloria to consider accepting help and support to begin to regain her life.

2. *History, including past attempts and family incidence.* Gloria, with both direct responses and through reminiscent stories, conveys to the counselor a history of supportive and strong family members with no history of mental illness or suicide attempts. Gloria describes an "eccentric" great aunt who was on a perpetual journey around the world and lived to 100. It is clear to the counselor that Gloria's current self-reporting may not include all relevant historical facts, and she will continue to explore these with Gloria as their counseling alliance becomes stronger.

3. *Support status.* Gloria is able to explain to the counselor that she and her husband, married over 50 years, were inseparable and shared

many travels, adventures, and hobbies. The couple, however, had few close friends who have since died or moved. The counselor encourages Gloria to list others with whom she had regular contact, such as service providers or even her primary physician. Gloria explains that her health insurance changed and she has not seen her new doctor in over a year. She adds that she had limited social contact with anybody while she was caring for her husband. The counselor honors Gloria's original private lifestyle with her husband but also makes clear that her current life is one of isolation. The counselor attempts to help Gloria to return to a healthy and independent life. Gloria will need to consider how to accept the help of others to achieve this goal. In future sessions, the counselor will work with Gloria to identify those areas in which her autonomy will not be usurped but will instead be utilized to work toward better self-care.

4. *Risk factors (depression, mental status, substance abuse).* Gloria's profound symptoms of depression and loss contributed to her isolation from challenges such as limited transportation options, difficulty with meal preparation, and confusion with accessing medical care within her new insurance guidelines. Pervasive variables of neglect contribute to a lack of motivation to seek outside help. Further, depression and forgetfulness can cause changes in appetite and a vicious cycle of decline of health and sensory functions ensues. Poor self-care, including lack of dental care and vision care, and a decline in hearing are all contributing risk factors to escalating psychiatric distress—especially in isolation.

5. *Questions and probes.* Direct questioning and probing has become problematic for the counselor because of Gloria's fragility and exhaustion. The complex manifestations of confusion and related communicative difficulties also pose challenges for the counselor and Gloria. The counselor's primary goal is to establish the most supportive helping relationship that facilitates trust and aims to enhance appropriate intervention options. Patience and heightened sensitivity are required of the counselor, as is being aware of facial expression, body language, and embedded thematic narratives. Additionally, the counselor must be present in the immediacy of the interaction and be able to shift within the constructs of Gloria's reality at any given moment. By actively listening and checking for understanding, the counselor can reflect feelings while also clarifying. Both for Gloria and her counselor, the context of the relationship will shift secondary to Gloria's presenting confusion and disorientation. The alliance, however, can be strengthened by the honesty, caring, and genuineness of the counselor. The counselor determines that she will limit the current questioning to those areas of expressed despondency.

6. *Counseling relationship, commitment to treatment, and adjunct assessments.* The counselor determines that Gloria needs immediate medical assessment and intervention with probable hospitalization and is careful to work with Gloria in a strong and committed partnership to assist Gloria in accessing necessary services. The counselor will also function as liaison with the initial coordination of care (e.g., making appointments, arranging transportation, and securing a case manager). The counselor keeps at the forefront a commitment to Gloria that their agreed long-term goal is to help Gloria regain independence and facilitate Gloria being an active partner in her own care. They both commit to the initial intervention of the treatment process, which will include further evaluations and assessments with a multidisciplinary medical team. Gloria willingly agrees to admit herself to a hospital with her doctor's involvement. The counselor outlines the hospitalization process, offers timeline estimates for treatment, and assures Gloria that counseling will be available to her during and after her hospitalization.

7. *Intervention strategies.* The spectrum of services Gloria currently needs and may possibly require in the future include in-home support, transportation, managed care education, nutrition (including home-delivered meals), day health programs, and various interventions including mental health, physical therapy, and grief support. Within the counseling relationship, Gloria's counselor must be skilled at pivoting realities and memories and perhaps even relinquish linear conceptualizations to help Gloria reflect on what currently holds meaning for her. For example, selecting her own outfit and lipstick color may be the level of self-actualization Gloria achieves on a given day. Contextualizing the relationship within a phenomenological approach enhances the helping relationship by eliciting Gloria's desire to share her worldview without being directed to, oriented toward, or defined by the view of another. Many treatment interventions, especially within geriatric treatment plans, spend much time and effort orienting the client to the reality of the day and date. This, in fact, further confuses the client's place not only in the "outer world" but within her own inner world. If Gloria continues to experience cognitive decline, she will be better served within a trusted relationship not constrained by parameters and outcomes, and that will instead grow within the meaning-making of her worldview through strategies that might be grounded in reminiscence, music, or art.

Prevention and Postvention Strategies

An emphasis on the need for everyone—loved ones, coworkers, practitioners, and counselors—to be aware of warning signs of suicidal crisis and know how to effectively respond is evident. Lester (1997), Jamison (1999), and Firestone (1997) are a few of the many researchers who are attempting to dismantle myths, evaluate trends and statistics, caution against generalizations, and encourage ongoing education for individuals and society. Additionally, Lester (1997) focused on the most vital aspects of prevention as he suggested what to do when encountering someone who is in crisis or talks about suicide by (a) listening actively because a suicidal person is confused about what he or she wants and how to get it; (b) asking direct questions to show that you are taking the person seriously; (c) trying to determine the degree of intent; (d) staying with the person to facilitate seeking professional help; (e) being supportive and nonjudgmental; and (f) honoring the suicidal person's feelings.

Stillion and McDowell (1999) offered a framework of suicide prevention that outlines three levels: primary, which includes family and society; secondary, which includes intervention and treatment of overtly suicidal individuals; and tertiary, which consists of postvention work with survivors of suicide and loved ones of suicide victims. Various support and crisis programs exist that target specific populations, including the gatekeeper program noted earlier that serves seniors, peer support groups that target teens, and community education programs. O'Carroll (1990) asserted that primary prevention must be multidisciplinary and offered on a public level as an adjunct to clinical interventions. Jamison (1999) added that "everyone must be sensitized to identifying people at high risk for suicide" (p. 270) and that community-based suicide prevention programs have not had a demonstrable effect on suicide rates because they tend not to be used by the most severely depressed.

O'Leary (1998), as a member of the recent movement toward resiliency perspectives, however, offered a more optimistic view by asserting that it is necessary to identify new individual and social resources that can be used to identify a multidimensional set of relevant frameworks for future research and theoretical development. Perhaps additional inquiry into stage development and age-appropriate prevention strategies would hold more meaning and relevance for adults. For example, though their framework is conceptualized within adult learning theory, the work of Merriam and Caffarella (1999) might illuminate developmental aspects of adult needs within a counseling framework. The worldview, perception of needs, and perceived stressors of a younger adult who is building relationships and starting a family differ from the middle-aged person who is attempting to reconcile unmet expectations and differ also from the needs of a frail older adult. Applying age-delineated meanings and constructs to prevention programs may be one effective tool for more appropriate, successful, and productive suicide prevention.

In addressing elements of postvention, Firestone (1997) referred to the continued stigmatization of suicide survivors and the most typical reactions of shock, guilt, and anger. He elucidated the importance of the postvention process, which should include strategies extending beyond the initial stage of shock to a more complete psychotherapy program focusing on an exploration of sadness, development of an objective perspective, and the relief of suffering by diffusing anger. Additionally, he captured the importance of counselors considering themselves as survivors to recognize and more fully explore their own feelings of grief, guilt, or anger.

Stillion and McDowell (1996) proposed an additional postvention framework that differentiates between *diagnostic* and *therapeutic*. On the diagnostic level, they offered that trained staff can help survivors better process the "whys" through an attempt to understand the motivations of the deceased. Within the therapeutic postvention, Stillion and McDowell highlighted a more systematic process extended over time to facilitate survivors to work through special types of grief. They also believe that:

> Suicide is an event dangerous to the mental and physical health of surviving loved ones. . . . Postvention efforts need to be mobilized both to deal with the needs of individual survivors and to change conditions in society that exacerbate their grief. (pp. 231–232)

And although bereavement and grief research is available within postvention frameworks to better treat surviving loved ones, Jamison (1999) believed that little has been "written about the impact of suicide on friends and colleagues" (p. 299). Ultimately, Jamison framed her inquiry into postvention strategies optimistically by encouraging survivors and counselors to seek out what can be positive from what is awful. She encouraged a multifaceted emphasis on the support of friends, regaining faith, being patient over time, being consistent with counseling, establishing self-help groups, and redirecting energy toward political activities to raise awareness of and increase services for suicide prevention, intervention, and postvention.

Adaptations for Diversity

Supporting culturally competent counselors, being accessible, and accommodating diverse client needs are vital elements of all levels of crisis intervention. A commitment to a workforce representative of diverse client populations (e.g., targeted recruitment in areas in which there are a large number of clients who speak a particular language), establishing diversity advisory committees, implementing policies to support diversity efforts, and printing forms in a variety of languages are just a few ways to facilitate access and better utilization of services. An emphasis on outreach work with populations who often do not access services secondary to cultural dynamics might include, for example, regular monthly visits to housing complexes to seek out those who may be hesitant to initiate contact or be unaware of available mental health services.

Crisis responses are determined by culture (Lester, 1997). Although current statistical data exist that capture surface trends of suicide across race, they are generalized and limited due to broad categorizations. As a result, misreporting of attempted and completed suicide occurs within a variety of groups and populations. It is therefore crucial to continue community efforts to respond appropriately to diverse understandings of the meanings of suicide through the examples noted above. In addition, it is imperative that multidisciplinary research expands to include deeper conceptualizations of the existential meanings people hold related to life, death, suffering, and pain within these multiple perspectives. Exploring literature, rituals, and histories from psychosocial, sociological, or anthropological investigations are just a few pathways to gain insight into the beliefs and related needs of those in crisis specific to their understanding of the world.

Summary

Humans are social beings, yet it is clear that part of the struggle to establish and maintain healthy connections with others originates from a cohesive and *connected* sense of self. Many suicide researchers agree that human connectedness assumes the most critical importance with suicide (Jamison, 1999; Kahn, 1990; Vaillant & Blumenthal, 1990). While the research on suicide risk factors, precipitants, trends, and related demographics have not resulted in a unified theory of suicidality (Kahn, 1990), multiple frameworks and perspectives have significantly contributed to an enhanced understanding that suicide is complex and best understood within the context of a person's life (Doyle, 1990). Stage development theorists such as Erikson (1982) and Levinson (1986) conceptualized the dynamic of autonomy, connectivity, and growth within frameworks that attempt to capture the struggle *within* and *between* self and others across the life span.

In this chapter an attempt has been made to bridge perspectives and conceptualize the multilayered worldviews, stressors, and crisis responses to suicidal adults within three different age periods through case study examples. The goal of this framework is twofold: (a) to transcend surface descriptions and generalizations to more fully understand a client experiencing a suicidal crisis and (b) to provide the counselor with an additional context or view to more appropriately assess and intervene secondary to potential age-related interpretations. Yet, an important acknowledgment must be made that further inquiry and exploration is needed across cultures, religious faiths, belief systems, and numerous other aspects of the life experience to gain deeper knowledge about the impact of these perceptions on suicide risk, assessment, and intervention.

References

Adam, K. C. (1990). Environmental, psychosocial, and psychoanalytic aspects of suicidal behavior. In S. J. Blumenthal & D. J. Kupfer (Eds.), *Suicide over the life cycle: Risk factors, assessment, and treatment of suicidal patients* (pp. 39–96). Washington, DC: American Psychiatric Press.

Beck, A. T., Rush, A. J., Shaw, B. F., & Emery, G. (1979). *Cognitive therapy of depression.* New York: Guilford Press.

Blumenthal, S. J., & Kupfer, D. J. (Eds.). (1990). *Suicide over the life cycle: Risk factors, assessment, and treatment of suicidal patients.* Washington, DC: American Psychiatric Press.

Centers for Disease Control and Prevention. (2002). *National Center for Injury Prevention and Control: Suicide in the United States.* Retrieved February 6, 2003, from http://www.cdc.gov/ncipc/factsheets/suifacts.html

Doyle, B. B. (1990). Crisis management of the suicidal patient. In S. J. Blumenthal & D. J. Kupfer (Eds.), *Suicide over the life cycle: Risk factors, assessment, and treatment of suicidal patients* (pp. 381–424). Washington, DC: American Psychiatric Press.

Eastmond, D. V. (1991, Spring). Since Levinson: View of life cycle theory and adult education. *Journal of Adult Education, 19*(2), 3–10.

Erikson, E. H. (1978). *Adulthood.* New York: Norton.

Erikson, E. H. (1982). *The lifecycle completed: A review.* New York: Norton.

Firestone, R. W. (1997). *Suicide and the inner voice: Risk assessment, treatment, and case management.* Thousand Oaks, CA: Sage.

Gilligan, C. (1982). *In a different voice.* Cambridge, MA: Harvard University Press.

Hendren, R. L. (1990). Assessment and interviewing strategies for suicidal patients over the life cycle. In S. J. Blumenthal & D. J. Kupfer (Eds.), *Suicide over the life cycle: Risk factors, assessment, and treatment of suicidal patients* (pp. 235–252). Washington, DC: American Psychiatric Press.

Hughes, J., & Graham, S. (1990, Spring). Adult life roles. *Journal of Continuing Higher Education, 38,* 2–8.

Jacobs, D. G., Brewer, M., & Klein-Benheim, M. (1999). Suicide assessment: An overview and recommended protocol. In D. G. Jacobs (Ed.), *The Harvard Medical School guide to suicide assessment and intervention* (pp. 3–39). San Francisco: Jossey-Bass.

Jamison, K. R. (1999). *Night falls fast: Understanding suicide.* New York: Alfred A. Knopf.

Kahn, A. (1990). Principles of psychotherapy with suicidal patients. In S. J. Blumenthal & D. J. Kupfer (Eds.), *Suicide over the life cycle: Risk factors, assessment, and treatment of suicidal patients* (pp. 441–468). Washington, DC: American Psychiatric Press.

Lester, D. (1986). Genetics, twin studies, and suicide. *Suicide and Life-Threatening Behavior, 16,* 274–295.

Lester, D. (1997). *Making sense of suicide: An in-depth look at why people kill themselves.* Philadelphia: Charles Press.

301

Levinson, D. J. (1986). A conception of adult development. *American Psychologist, 41,* 3–13.

Levinson, D. J., Darrow, C. N., Klein, E. B., Levinson, M. H., & Mckee, B. (1978). *The seasons of a man's life.* New York: Ballantine.

Levinson, D. J., & Levinson, J. D. (1996). *The season's of a woman's life.* New York: Ballantine.

Linehan, M. M. (1993). *Cognitive–behavioral treatment of BPD.* New York: Guilford Press.

Linehan, M. M., Goodstein, J. L., Nielsen, S. L., & Chiles, J. A. (1983). Reasons for staying alive when you're thinking of killing yourself. *Journal of Consulting and Clinical Psychology, 51,* 276–286.

Loevinger, J. (1976). *Ego development: Conceptions and theories.* San Francisco: Jossey-Bass.

Maslow, A. H. (1968). *Toward a psychology of being* (2nd ed.). New York: Van Nostrand Reinhold.

Merriam, S. B., & Caffarella, R. S. (1999). *Learning in adulthood: A comprehensive guide* (2nd ed.). San Francisco: Jossey-Bass.

Moscicki, E. (1999). Epidemiology of suicide. In D. G. Jacobs (Ed.), *The Harvard Medical School guide to suicide assessment and intervention* (pp. 40–51). San Francisco: Jossey-Bass.

O'Carroll, P. W. (1990). Community strategies for suicide prevention and intervention. In S. J. Blumenthal & D. J. Kupfer (Eds.), *Suicide over the life cycle: Risk factors, assessment, and treatment of suicidal patients* (pp. 499–514). Washington, DC: American Psychiatric Press.

O'Leary, V. E. (1998). Strength in the face of adversity: Individual and social thriving. *Journal of Social Issues, 54,* 425–436.

Osgood, N. J., & Thielman, S. (1990). Geriatric suicidal behavior: Assessment and treatment. In S. J. Blumenthal & D. J. Kupfer (Eds.), *Suicide over the life cycle: Risk factors, assessment, and treatment of suicidal patients* (pp. 341–380). Washington, DC: American Psychiatric Press.

Pascual-Leone, J., & Irwin, R. R. (1998). Abstraction, the will, the self, and modes of learning in adulthood. In M. C. Smith & T. Pourchot (Eds.), *Adult learning and development: Perspectives from educational psychology* (pp. 35–66). Mahwah, NH: Erlbaum.

Peck, T. A. (1986). Women's self-definition in adulthood: From a different model. *Psychology of Women Quarterly, 10,* 274–284.

Rogers, C. R. (1961). *On becoming a person: A therapist's view of psychotherapy.* Boston: Houghton Mifflin.

Shneidman, E. (1999). Perturbation and lethality: A psychological approach to assessment and intervention. In D. G. Jacobs (Ed.), *The Harvard Medical School guide to suicide assessment and intervention* (pp. 83–97). San Francisco: Jossey-Bass.

Steffens, D. C., & Blazer, D. G. (1999). Suicide in the elderly. In D. G. Jacobs (Ed.), *The Harvard Medical School guide to suicide assessment and intervention* (pp. 443–462). San Francisco: Jossey-Bass.

Stillion, J. M., & McDowell, E. E. (1996). *Suicide across the life span: Premature exits.* (2nd ed.). Washington, DC: Taylor & Francis.

Vaillant, G. E., & Blumenthal, S. J. (1990). Introduction—suicide over the life cycle: Risk factors and life-span development. In S. J. Blumenthal & D. J. Kupfer (Eds.), *Suicide over the life cycle: Risk factors, assessment, and treatment of suicidal patients* (pp. 1–16). Washington, DC: American Psychiatric Press.

Viorst, J. (1986). *Necessary losses.* New York: Fawcett.

Chapter 11

Counseling Suicide Survivors

Dale Elizabeth Pehrsson and Mary Boylan

Death is often associated with an ending of pain. For those who commit suicide death may be the final and deliberate act to end one's own suffering either physical or emotional. But for the suicide survivors, those who continue to live after a deliberate final act of another, death is often associated with the beginning of suffering. This chapter focuses on suicide survivors, those who continue to live with the pain that often results when a loved one has deliberately died. It also addresses concerns that counselors need to consider when counseling suicide survivors.

Although personal and societal attitudes, cultural constructs, and religious views are changing and some are becoming more accepting of suicide, lingering issues must be addressed after the suicidal death of a family member or close friend. In addition to emotional and other personal needs, legal, medical, religious, financial, and social matters must also be addressed. Such a reactive and sudden sequence of events requires unique coping strategies. Reactions and strategies will not only differ among individuals but also differ across cultural groups.

Because the needs of these clients are unique, most counseling programs are likely to address their concerns either superficially or not at all. Therefore counselors are often not sufficiently trained to meet the needs of these clients caught in such circumstances. This chapter also addresses the needs of counselors who are also thrust into reacting to death by suicide. We address the need to develop and apply specialized counseling strategies to meet the needs of survivors, and we urge that counselors learn more about the diverse cultural perspectives concerning suicide. Some of these concerns are demonstrated in the following narrative as told by Delilah, a suicide survivor.

Delilah's Experience

I left her alone for just half an hour. I knew she was gloomy and even depressed but I really didn't know how awful things were. I went to the store for just a few minutes. When I returned, my mother was curled up on the kitchen floor. She appeared to be in pain but she wasn't. She was dead.

Why did I leave her alone? I should have seen it coming. My children needed milk. I had even run to the store and back. I was gone just half an hour. But that's all mom needed, half an hour and a bottle of drain cleaner.

Unfortunately, I wasn't the first to find her. Jackie was just 4 years old at the time but he knew his grandma was dead on the kitchen floor and worst of all he even knew how she died. I found him crying under his bed. I think Jackie's life changed that day. So did mine.

Of course, I called the police but when they got there I could hardly talk. Two detectives asked unending questions "Did your mother talk about committing suicide?" "Did you do anything to prevent this?" I didn't have answers; I still don't. I have questions. Why did I leave Mom alone? Why didn't I hide every potential poison? Why did she do it? Was it something I said or did? What caused her to kill herself? Why? There were so many "whys."

I had been worried about her and I had taken her to the doctor about her depression. Mom had talked about wanting to die. She did say, "Maybe some day I'll just end it all." But the doctor told me not to worry. He said, "It's good that she talks about it because when people talk about killing themselves, they never do."

My Mom had moved in with us about a year earlier. My sisters and my brother seemed glad that Jack and I were taking care of her. But then when she died, they blamed us. They said we should have seen it coming. We neglected her.

Of course they didn't say such things to our faces. They said it to everyone else in the family. Aunt Rosanna, Mom's younger sister, was the worst gossip under normal conditions but when Mom died, Aunt Rosanna outdid herself. Her remarks poisoned the entire family. She might as well have blamed me for murder. After the funeral they all stopped talking to us. But in some way they were right; I should have seen it coming.

Oh, the funeral! That was a huge problem. Mom and Dad had been devout Catholics. I called our parish right after I called the police. But when I told them it was suicide, no priest wanted anything to do with her. They refused to administer the last rites to her. Back in those days the Church refused Catholic burial for those who committed suicide. Suicide was an unforgivable mortal sin. We had to say goodbye to mom at the funeral parlor without any priest. She was buried in a grave that was not consecrated.

It's been many years now and your father and I hardly ever talk about it. It's good to talk about it now with you. Oh, you say, this is the first time I told you the details? Well, yes. It's very difficult to talk about it even now. You weren't there, were you? Of course not! I was 5 months pregnant at the time and you were born 4 months after your grandmother committed suicide. I'm so sorry you never got to meet your grandmother. (Delilah, now 73 years old, told this to her daughter. Delilah's mother committed suicide in 1963.)

Suicide Survivors

Delilah is one of many "suicide survivors." As defined by Schuyler (1973), a suicide survivor "is one who has sustained the loss of a significant person through death by suicide" (p. 313). We have probably all felt the terrible sense of loss and emptiness when someone we love dies. But when the loss results from suicide, many experience a far deeper wound, one that may never be fully felt. Some of the demands placed on suicide survivors may delay the bereavement process. Perhaps some distractions are not unwelcome. However, such unfelt feelings surface in many ways and may negatively affect families, work, school, and every level of personal relationships for many years to come.

The Consequences for Suicide Survivors

Suicide survivors are affected in many complex ways, and reactions vary from shock and denial to blame and guilt. Often this event initiates an endless search for answers (Lester, 2001; Pfeffer, Jiang, Kakuma, Hwang, & Metsch, 2002). In an earlier work, Hatton and McBride-Valente (1981) pointed out four common reactions to suicide. First, there is a prohibition of mourning by the family's social network. Second, there is a disruption in and inadequacy of the usual coping devices. Third, the isolation from friends and family may be long lasting and pervasive. And finally, there is a crisis in identity and personal sense of loss of control. The crisis may be extremely undermining. Some individuals may begin to doubt many of the beliefs on which they have built their lives. They may question their very sense of self. Those affected by the suicide of a loved one often suffer in silence—silence in the presence of others, silence during times they are alone.

Suicide survivors are also suicide victims. Helping suicide survivors can be one of the greatest challenges in a professional counselor's career. Counselors need to assist suicide survivors in accomplishing two major tasks. The first is to support survivors as they begin the grieving process. Survivors experience a wide range of feelings that often include denial, anger, self-blame, and guilt. Usually survivors need considerable time and opportunity to process these feelings and begin to accept the loss. The second task involves supporting survivors as they begin to reconstruct their lives without the person they lost. Although their ways of being and relating may dramatically and forever change, the event may offer an invitation for reflection and renewal (Lester, 2001).

The Experience of Survivors Is Unique

Survivors of a suicide most often encounter a situation for which they have no prior experience. It is not only tragic but also unique. Although suicide survivors may manifest grief similar to others who suffer from another's sudden and accidental death, the depth and complexity of feelings are different when suicide is the issue (Cerel, Fristad, Weller, & Weller, 2000). Lacking prior experiences and patterns of behavior, suicide survivors are often confused and disoriented, not knowing what to do and how to act in this very new situation (Shneidman, 1972). As Delilah experienced 40 years ago, suicide survivors deal with situations for which they are often not prepared. These include talking with police, coroners, caseworkers, and insurance agents. The activity and the barrage of inquiries, legal, financial, and personal, may deny time needed to feel the stirring emotions and may delay the beginnings of the healing process. Continuous explanations may even retraumatize survivors, especially those who discovered the body. Images of the incident may never fade. Even a 4-year-old may never forget.

The Traditional Rituals Are Altered

In many instances those who die by suicide are still denied religious ceremonies and burial in consecrated grounds (Kelleher, 1996; Schuyler, 1973). This is unfortunate because rituals, religious or otherwise, help to soothe transitions. When the Catholic Church rejected her mother, Delilah was denied a very soothing and transitional rite of passage. This is particularly true of religious rituals that help people deal with the transition from life to death.

Rituals are public displays that hold all types of relationships together, including the experiences of past, present, and future. Holidays and anniversaries also involve family traditions and rituals. Lindstrom (2002) found that the usual grieving time following the death of loved one was about 1 year. She explained that the "turning point" seems to be related to the annual cycle and to family rituals such as holidays during the first year after a loss. She also found that anxiety was reduced over time, and she suggested that anxiety appeared to have been reduced by the development of consistently successful coping strategies.

However, after a suicide the turning point may be much delayed. The factors that normally help in reducing anxiety are not necessarily available to a suicide survivor. Coping strategies may not be so quickly developed. Grief reduction appears to be related to family rituals, but family traditions often stop when they are too painfully connected to the suicide. In addition, religious rituals may be denied. Support from relatives and friends are also likely to help shorten the grieving process; in the case of a suicide, such relationships may change, most often not for the better. Attachments to community and social groups may be cut (Cerel et al., 2000). Families may deal with their anger and their shame by withdrawing from one another. Such changes may leave a wound that is long lasting, pervasive, and, perhaps, difficult to heal. Grieving in silence is the saddest grieving.

Grieving May Be Silent for Survivors

Delilah and her husband grieved in silence. They stopped talking about the suicide. Grieving in silence can lead to additional painful and dysfunctional coping strategies because feelings will express themselves one way or another. Regret and self-blame can emerge time and time again with questions such as "why" and "what if." Survivors become victims of their own blame, anxiety, self-condemnation, and reproach (Sommer-Rotenberg, 1998). Often, anger may result and be directed at the suicide victim or displaced to others; it can also be directed inward at the self, resulting in self-destructive behaviors.

Suicide disturbs survivors. It conflicts with the deepest need to promote personal survival. Sometimes, survivors just cannot understand and often cannot even feel their own numbed pain. When survivors cannot even talk about their loss, their emptiness may never be filled.

Bereavement May Be Complex for Survivors

All survivors of the death of a loved one mourn their loss. However, there is variance in the intensity of emotion and the pattern of mourning of survivors (Lester, 2001). How do survivors of a suicide respond? Until very recently, "society dictated that their grief be silent, hidden, and full of shame" (Kelleher, 1996, p. 69). While this is beginning to change, the family coping with the suicidal death of one of its members may face difficulties that are more complex than those accompanying other types of death (Calhoun, Selby, & Abernathy, 1984). These difficulties arise in part because the deceased died by choice and by a deliberate act (Kelleher, 1996). The bereaved individual may be pressured to return to engagements such as work and social contacts too soon and to avoid letting the loss interfere with the usual responsibilities. Expressions of grief are sometimes not viewed as socially acceptable and society admires the strength of those who do not express too much emotion (Lester, 2001). Yet according to Victoroff (1983), "The lives of survivors will forever be changed by the action of the deceased, as intense grief and guilt rouse and battle with its neutralizer, denial" (p. 203). Negative emotion may not be expressed because "The anger that the survivor experiences has no place for expression" (p. 205).

The most common emotion encountered in bereavement is depression; guilt and shame are common as well (Chance, 1988; Thompson, 1995). According to Lester (2001), "the two negative feelings that most differentiate the bereavement of a suicide from that of other kinds of death are (those of) shame and guilt" (p. 191). The feeling of shame can be a result of the survivor's fear of being associated with the act of suicide (Sommer-Rotenberg, 1998).

Feelings of guilt may occur after any death, but according to Sommer-Rotenberg (1998) "suicide leaves bereaved with especially acute feelings of self-denigration and self-recrimination. The continual weight of the unanswerable and relentless inner refrain—'If only I had done this, or if only I had not said that'—can become unbearable" (p. 240). During a normal grieving process guilt diminishes and the inevitability of death can be gradually accepted, but in the case of a suicidal death "the tendency to blame one's self, especially if there was conflict, is maximized" (Schuyler, 1973, p. 17).

Survivors of suicide have to come to terms with many negative feelings. They may become obsessed with thoughts of how they may have contributed to the suicidal act. They may accuse themselves of having failed to prevent the suicide (Shneidman, 2001). According to Schuyler (1973), survivors of suicide can be prone to self-destructive behaviors, which include suicide attempts and subsequent depressive episodes. Survivors experiencing more shame than guilt over a suicide are at risk for suicide themselves (Lester, 1998).

Issues of Social Stigma for Survivors

Although views are changing, social stigma continues to be associated with suicide within many cultures (Calhoun et al., 1984; Ginsberg, 1971; Sommer-Rotenberg, 1998). The social stigmas surrounding suicide often result in the survivors being isolated and lacking in social support (Calhoun et al., 1984; Kelleher, 1996; Lester, 2001; Schuyler, 1973; Sommer-Rotenberg, 1998). Delilah experienced isolation as her aunt, sisters, and brother blamed her and withdrew.

A suicide is often accompanied by secrecy and thus cannot be mourned openly for fear of social disapproval (Lester, 1998). Sommer-Rotenberg (1998) posited that when "a tragedy is not spoken of openly there can be no true sympathy, sharing, or healing" (p. 239).

Difficulty and complexity increase as a result of the negative perceptions and reactions of others toward those survivors who were closest to the suicide victim. Negative social reactions to suicide may result in a lower level of support offered to the survivors; in fact, social isolation can be a common occurrence following a suicidal death, and that negativity may be generalized. Because suicide is a more stigmatizing death than that from natural causes, there may be more negative views of the surviving family members (Calhoun et al., 1984; Schuyler, 1973). Such negativity may be a result of unconscious defenses to numb the pain when another commits suicide. One defense likely involves an attempt to forget and may take the form of strong avoidance of those who bring forth the memory of the deceased.

There is additional evidence that a suicide is "coded" as a social stigma and that it creates immense discomfort among many (even distant survivors). A study conducted by Calhoun, Selby, and Selby (1982) found that in the case of a hypothetical newspaper report on a child's suicide the parents were blamed more for the death occurring and were liked less than parents of a child whose death was a result of an illness. This study suggests that suicide is viewed by many as a stigmatizing death and "a type of death for which discomfort in interactions with the survivors is expected to be greater than for other types of death" (p. 259). Ginsberg (1971) found that, unlike the hypothetical case, knowing the family personally can make a difference in how an individual reacts to a survivor and that social perception may be less important when an individual is a personal acquaintance of the survivor.

Although social support is often denied, it is important for acceptance and healing. But survivors themselves often withdraw because they are unable to express the complexity of their feelings. Friends and family may withdraw as a survivor also withdraws. Survivors are often left alone. They "experience recurring grief reactions that leave them isolated, confused and depressed" (Thompson, 1995, p. 265). While some people possess the ability to talk themselves through a problem or concern, most benefit from having someone with whom they can share their problem (Kelleher, 1996). Over time and with effort, survivors can attempt to deal with and achieve release from issues of self-criticism and blame (Kelleher, 1996). According to Kelleher it is very important to "gradually re-establish the social routine's of one's life" (p. 74). Perhaps it may also be a time to establish new routines, new acquaintances, and new experiences.

The Influence of Parasuicide on Survivors

Some survivors have not only experienced the suicide, they may have had to deal with previous unsuccessful attempts, known as *parasuicides*. Delilah ran to the store and back because her mother had previously suggested suicide.

Parasuicide, often referred to as attempted suicide, is a suicide attempt that fails to result in death. Like a completed suicide, a parasuicide will also affect family and friends. No one can accurately ascertain the full impact of a suicide attempt on the relatives and friends of those displaying suicidal ideation (Kelleher, 1996). It is essential to gain an understanding of the cause of the suicidal behavior, which may be as a result of illness, alcohol, or drug use, or most often as a response to a perceived distressing circumstance. The challenge for the family is to "reorder their relationship and their domestic situation" (Kelleher, 1996, p. 75). The family should be encouraged to seek assistance and advice from counseling professionals. A history of suicide attempts is the strongest predictive risk factor for future suicide attempts or suicide completions in all age groups (Brent, Baugher, Bridge, Chen, & Chiappetta, 1999; Lewisohn, Rohde, & Seeley, 1996; Neiger

311

& Hopkins, 1988). Between one in three (Lewinsohn et al., 1996) and four out of every five people who kill themselves have made a previous attempt (Martin & Dixon, 1986). Fifty percent of female completers have made at least one previous attempt (Lewinsohn et al., 1996). Each attempted suicide often becomes more lethal in nature (Borowsky, Ireland, & Resnick, 2001; Capuzzi, 1994; Capuzzi & Golden, 1988). Survivors of those who have completed suicide after a series of attempts (parasuicides) may have even greater guilt than those who were surprised by the event. They may blame themselves even more. Delilah most likely blamed herself because she "should have seen it coming" given her mother's "history."

Suicide Survivors and Development

Suicides by children and young adults are likely to have a dramatic effect on peers. According to the National Institute of Mental Health (World Health Organization, 2000), the suicide rate in 1999 among children, ages 10–14, was approximately 192 deaths among 19,608,000 children in this age group. In this group, four males committed suicide for every female. Among adolescents, ages 15–19, the suicide rate was 1,615 deaths among 19,594,000 adolescents. In this group five males committed suicide for every female. For young people, 15–24 years old, suicide is the third leading cause of death. Persons under age 25 accounted for 14% of all suicides in 1999. From 1952 to1995 the incidence of suicide among adolescents nearly tripled. Among young adults, ages 20 to 24, the suicide rate was 12.7/100,000, or 2,285 deaths among 17,594,000 in this age group. One female to six males in the 20–24 age group committed suicide (Centers for Disease Control and Prevention, 1996). Thus, as suicide statistics increase with age the number of those affected by a suicide also increases. There are likely to be more suicide survivors affected by the death of a young adult than by the death of a young child.

However, young children can be affected deeply by suicide. According to Delilah, "I think Jackie's life changed that day." Without delving further into that statement we can surmise that Delilah regrets very much that Jackie suffered that experience.

Although Lester (2001) addressed the paucity of literature on children as suicide survivors, he continued to point out that children may experience similar feelings and symptoms as do adults but have different behaviors. Their feelings may be deep and long lasting. Some children can be so traumatized and disturbed that their behaviors may become symbolically antisocial. They are likely to express their feelings through actions rather than verbally. They are likely to be extremely confused and may very inappropriately displace their feelings. Children are more likely to act out, whereas adults are more equipped with cognitive and linguistic skills that may enable them to intellectualize their feelings and, in time, perhaps to talk about the suicide. Children will usually lack defenses such as intellectualizing that may work for a while for adults.

The suicide of a parent deeply affects a child. Cain and Fast (1972) studied case materials for 45 disturbed children all of whom had one parent who committed suicide. The children experienced guilt related to the death of parents. The guilt was as a result of many issues. Some children experienced hostility toward the suicidal parents, and others felt partially responsible when death occurred through suicide. If the parent suffered from long-term depression and had made the child feel guilty during the illness, the child was more likely to feel more guilt for the occurrence of the suicide. If the parent had been severely distressed and the child had received warnings against upsetting the parent, the child assumed a large responsibility for the suicide. The child felt the most devastating effects if the parent had made more than one suicide attempt and the child had wished the parent had completed the suicide. Some children also expressed feelings that they must have been naughty or demonstrating "bad" behaviors that led to their parent's suicide. Others felt that they must somehow have disappointed the parent; some felt they should have been able to stop the parent from committing suicide. Thus, "suicide not only kills victims, but victimizes and 'kills' many of those who were touched by their lives and consequently by their deaths" (Parsons, 1996, p. 77).

Even though the majority of adolescent suicides occur at home (Malley, Kush, & Bogo, 1994), many occur elsewhere. The death of a peer can have very negative effects on children and adolescents, but when an adolescent discovers the body of a suicide victim, an adolescent's emotional and relational development can be impaired. Further, the effect of finding the body is most often traumatizing and has far-reaching ramifications for families, school personnel, and populations and influences entire communities (Kelleher, 1996).

The Impact of Sibling Suicide

Some children and adults are suicide survivors of siblings. Aunt Rosanna, "the worst gossip under normal conditions," seemed to outdo herself when Delilah's mother committed suicide. Gossip is often a symptom of underlying issues or anger and pain. Aunt Rosanna was a sibling suicide survivor.

According to Linn-Gust (2001), sibling survivors are the "forgotten mourners." In many cases siblings form the strongest of relationships. From genes to experiences, siblings most often have more in common with one another than with anyone else. They may have had deep positive feelings toward one another, but the effect of the suicide may be even more devastating if their feelings were mutually negative.

Young sibling suicide survivors not only lose their brother or sister, they frequently lose their parents, perhaps for a time, perhaps forever. Parents may permanently change as a result of the suicide of one of their children. A child's role in the family may change suddenly and permanently. Parents may be so caught up in their own grief and neglect their living child or, at the other extreme, they may overprotect the survivor and impose outlandish controls motivated by fear of further loss.

Parents may change also as a result of the suicide of a family member especially if the victim lived in the same house. Delilah claims that her life changed as a result of her mother's suicide. One can only guess what the effects were on her children, including her yet to be born daughter.

In addition to the high rate of adolescent suicide in the United States, Americans age 65 years and older (Conwell & Brent, 1995) have extremely high suicide rates. More older men than women commit suicide, and more widowed or divorced men commit suicide. However, the suicide of a sister or a brother at any age can be so traumatic that it may invite thoughts of suicide. One of the major concerns about suicide survivors is that they may enter into deep depression and may be prone to suicide themselves. This is especially true of an older person who has experienced the loss of a deep relationship.

Implications for Counselors Who Counsel Survivors

Although suicides have most likely been a fact of life prior to recorded history, we can find accounts of suicides in societies for the last two millennia (Shneidman, 2001). The World Health Organization ranks suicide as the second leading cause of death worldwide, with approximately 800,000 cases of suicide reported each year (Parker, 1998). Because of cultural and international differences in collecting data and differences in the classifications of a death as a suicide, this estimate may in fact be too low. Despite this high incidence of suicide worldwide, it is only relatively recently that a need to address the consequences of being a suicide survivor has been recognized by the counseling and mental health profession (Lester, 2001). Although suicide may be a singular act, it results in plural effects (Parsons, 1996). There are an estimated 50,000 suicides in the United States each year. Reason dictates that there are at least 200,000 survivor victims created each year whose lives are shattered by that event (Shneidman, 2001).

Although there are no accurate records to determine the number of suicide survivors, we estimate that each suicide deeply affects, on an average, four to six others intimately. According to the National Center for Health Statistics (Hoyert, Kochanek, & Murphy, 1999), about 31,000 suicides are committed in the United State annually. If on the average there are five survivors for each event, then each year there are 155,000 suicide survivors. Over a period of just 10 years there will be 1,550,000 survivors. Since 1963 when Delilah's mother died, the number of suicide survivors in the United States may have grown to as many as 4,650,000. Approximately 1 out of every 60 Americans is a suicide survivor. Many, perhaps most, of these victims continue to deal with the pain. Certainly counselors will treat some suicide survivors even if the presenting problem does not appear to be related to suicide.

According to Chance (1988), survivors of suicide "are amongst the most difficult and challenging patients that mental health professionals will see" (p. 30). The survivor will be seeking answers to the reasons for a suicide, and issues of responsibility, culpability, meaning, purpose, relationships, influences, feelings of guilt, shame, love, and rage all need to be examined in the counseling process. Survivors also have to confront their philosophical beliefs surrounding death and their own mortality and the place of an afterlife should they hold such a belief. Chance (1988) stated that, ultimately, we as counselors "must challenge the belief that surviving a suicide leaves one with a ruined life. Although there is a scar that may be evident to others to some degree, the wound itself can heal given the proper care" (p. 33).

The majority of suicide survivors do not immediately seek the assistance of a professional counselor if the support of family, relatives, and friends is considered sufficient (Kelleher, 1996; Lester, 2001). However, some may seek professional help later without realizing that part of their present concerns may be related to unresolved issues about a suicide. Therefore, counselors are likely to be involved in dealing with suicide survivors more often than is reported in the literature.

Many professional counselors, unfortunately, are not aware of the special needs of these clients and lack strategies for counseling suicide survivors (Lester, 2001). They may have some training in counseling death survivors, but suicide survivors present multifaceted challenges. Lester (2001) posited that "particular attention needs to be paid to the training and education of mental health professionals in the skill and art of bereavement counseling and the intricacies of conducting survivor groups" (p. 209). However, suicide survivors differ from other death survivors because the bereavement is exacerbated by social stigma and a resulting loss of self-esteem related to an inability to have prevented the suicide (Jamison, 1999).

Counselor Preparedness and Self-Awareness

Three overriding areas, important for all situations, seem to be particularly important for counselors in dealing with suicide survivors. These include belief, knowledge, and strategies. Counselors need to examine their personal beliefs about the suicide, gain knowledge of the processes involved in grieving, and develop and improve strategies for coping with one of their unmatched challenges. In a parallel way, counselors need to apply these characteristics to better help the client. Counselors need to become aware of their client's beliefs, knowledge, and strategies. Counselors need to understand their client's personal belief about suicide, gain knowledge of their client's way of grieving, and understand the client's present coping strategies. Because of the relationships between the counselor and the client, we discuss beliefs, knowledge, and strategies as they apply both to counselors and to suicide survivor clients.

Counselor Understanding of Beliefs

Counselors need to examine their own beliefs regarding suicide specifically and death in general. Such beliefs are likely attached to the counseling–client relationship. Specifically, counselor's beliefs about death, religion, and spirituality will affect their effectiveness with such clients. Roger, Gueulette, Abbey-Hide, Carney, and Werth (2001) found that religious affiliation does have a significant influence on one's views of rational suicide. Religious beliefs can affect how counselors interact with clients. According to Chance (1988), bias can limit our own effectiveness because "to the extent we are able, our tolerance and theirs will set the range of possibilities" (p. 31). Professional counselors need to consider their own philosophical beliefs toward suicide and avoid being judgmental (Lester, 2001). To truly assist the individual, we as counselors must place aside our own beliefs and biases and attend to the special needs of suicide survivors.

Counselors should reflect on and develop a keen awareness of their own philosophical and religious beliefs, and this is especially important in counseling suicide survivors. Although it is obvious that counselors should try to function within their clients' frames of reference, it may be particularly difficult to do so if there are covert preconceptions about suicide.

Counselor Knowledge of Grief

Humans experience grief. It is a universal process, "part of the human existential plight and dignity" (Lindstrom, 2002, p. 20). Grief is a profound experience unfortunately common to human existence. Although most humans would likely desire to avoid grief, there is a positive side that involves opportunities for awareness of self-worth and a renewal of the search for meaning (Lindstrom, 2002).

Some who grieve never seem to fully recover; others do. Some recoveries take a very long time, others less. There appears to be a process that has been observed, studied, and developed into a field known as grief counseling. Grief counseling is a discipline that, since the early work of Kubler-Ross (1969), has advanced and is still developing. Kubler-Ross offered as a basic premise that individuals have five stages to complete within the overall process of grieving. The stages are denial, anger, bargaining, depression, and acceptance. Other authors, for example Bowlby (1982), developed models with different numbers of stages. Suicide survivors as grievers would seem to go through a similar process. However, they may not (Lindstrom, 2002). Whether stages exist in any absolute progression or not, there is a process, and counselors need to assist the client in moving through this process. Further, the process as previously theorized does not necessarily exist in any absolute series of stages. The process may be more individual and unique for each person than previously thought. Counselors should be cautious about "knowing" what the process should be for each individual. Any approach to helping a client move through the putative "right and absolute process" may conflict with diversity issues involving gender as well as cultural differences. A counselor's process will be best guided by the client's process (as long as that process is not in itself life threatening or otherwise devastating).

Most humans experience enormous sadness at various times in their lives. The fatality of a loved one is ordinarily followed by grief. One may be even anticipating a sick friend's death and may even deliberately set aside a time for grieving. But when grief follows a suicide, it is often not only unanticipated but also extremely shocking. Even though grief is a vastly common experience, grief counseling is a specialty for which counselors need advanced training. The counseling process becomes even more specialized when counseling a suicide survivor.

Counseling Strategies With Survivors

The most common method for treating adult suicide survivors involves groups (Lester, 2001). According to Kelleher (1996), these self-help groups have emerged from the survivors themselves recognizing their own need "to organize their own response to suicide loss" (p. 69).

Such self-help groups may help counselors understand processes that are unique to this population. Counselors who are interested in this area would do well to consider joining and participating in such groups as a member, not as an authority. Listening to and observing suicide survivors may be one of the best ways to learn about this unique experience. It is likely to provide the counselor with strategies.

Based on Schuyler's (1973) suggestions, there are several guidelines that may help develop strategies in dealing with survivors of suicide:

- Guide the survivor to reach an understanding of the death that allows for maintaining self-worth and continuation of the search for meaning.
- Counsel in a nonjudgmental, accepting atmosphere.
- Encourage the survivor to mourn the death and to plan a future life without the deceased.
- Monitor the suicide survivor for suicidal ideation.
- Make special efforts to identify and encourage support from client's family and other social groups (Conyne, 1987).

It should be very apparent that suicide survivors are a unique population and present special challenges for a therapist. There are no stages and there is no timeline for any one client in the processes of grieving and healing. Individual process is also affected by cultural backgrounds involving beliefs, knowledge, and strategies.

Adaptations for Diversity

Delilah is a New Yorker and her story takes place within a culture influenced by Italian American Catholicism. Her family origin is European. She is a native of New York City and is acculturated to the "East Coast" way of being. Her experiences and those of her friends, family, and other suicide survivors affected by her mother's death would likely have been quite different in other cultures. How would this process differ in Ireland or in Japan? Would suicidal death be handled differently in Mexico or Norway? How would the process contrast in various parts of the United States? How would the experience vary had Delilah and her family been Latter-Day Saints or Jewish rather than Catholic? To what extent would it be a different story if Delilah had been an atheist? Would the story differ if Delilah had been gay? What if Delilah were a man? What role does gender, age, or race play in survivor grief? Does this matter?

The questions raised above are critical. As we explore the possible answers, we gain a better understanding of the suicide victim as well as the survivors. Various cultural and religious beliefs will profoundly influence the experience of being a suicide survivor. It will also influence how the counselor counsels the survivor. Survivors have their own unique cultural and life experiences. The client's experiences are distinctive and, when shared, tell counselors about the world of those we counsel.

Cultural and gender differences in suicide rates must be considered. Self-inflicted injuries explained approximately 814,000 deaths in 2000 (World Health Organization, 2000). If each person who committed suicide left only one survivor, these individuals worldwide would need support. Suicide is a global issue.

Cultural and Religious Factors Among Survivors

The variation in suicide rates internationally can be attributed to cultural and religious systems. For example, in Norway where suicide is considered disgraceful and an unacceptable choice of actions, suicide is rare. Within most cultures where there are strong religious taboos against it, there are few suicides. Ireland is an exception to this trend (Kelleher, 1996).

Strong rural community support, a strong sense of tradition, and a high regard for family also seem to be important factors in low levels of suicides. In many religions suicide is considered sinful and a disgrace (Jilek-Aall, 1988). For example, funeral oration and rituals were delayed or changed if someone within a Jewish community committed suicide (Jamison, 1999).

Suicide within some religious and cultural contexts is considered more shameful than in others. In such cases the client might have a need for secrecy, which could impede the grieving process.

Religious and cultural attitudes may influence suicide behavior and the survivor's reaction. In Japan suicide is sometimes considered to be an honorable deed and even an acceptable way to deal with issues. Japanese people have a long history and tradition of ritualized suicide (Jilek-Aall, 1988). In addition, some Eskimo, Norse, Samoan, and Crow Indian cultures view suicide as an act of self-sacrifice (Jamison, 1999).

Completion rates among European American adolescent men are higher than any other ethnic group (Metha, Weber, & Webb, 1998). In the past, African American adolescents generally lived within tight social networks of support that create insulating factors against self-harm. However, from 1980 to 2000, the suicide rates for African American adolescent males showed a 200% increase (Capuzzi, 2002).

From sovereign nation to nation, suicide rates vary highly among first nation peoples. Various Apache tribes rank as high as 43 per 100,000 (Capuzzi, 2002), whereas the Navajo's suicide rate parallels the national average at a rate of 11 to 13 per 100,000 (Popenhagen & Qualley, 1998). Difficulties such as poverty, joblessness, chemical dependency, availability of firearms, and child abuse seem major causative factors to suicide. Native American communities have different rituals and beliefs about death and suicide (Crofoot Graham, 2002). A perceptive counselor does not assume that all ethnic and cultural clusters act the same in their rituals and mourning practices.

The client's appearance can be deceiving. How a client looks is only a partial representation of the client's personal, cultural, religious, and racial needs. For example, a client may seem as if he or she is acculturated to mainstream American society, but his or her social and religious beliefs might be culturally very Japanese or Mexican. The counselor needs to find out what the client needs. The survivor's perspective on suicide, death, and loss is unique; so, although the survivor may belong to a particular religious or ethnic group, reactions may be different. Making sweeping assumptions can impede successful counseling. The impact of a suicide, though poignant, may be more acceptable and not seen as a shameful event within some cultures. However, a counselor would be wise to make no assumptions about the cultural or religious influences on the survivor. The wise counselor should ask what the suicide means to the survivor.

Gender Factors for Counselor Consideration

Men are more likely to complete suicides than are women, the rate being four to one (Vannatta, 1997). Females are three times more apt to engage in non-lethal suicidal attempt (Canetto, 1997). The suicide attempt of girls is nine times that of boys. Boys successfully complete suicides at a rate of five for every girl's suicide (Kalafat, 1990). Males use violent means, such as firearms, hanging, and automobile accidents, more often than do females (Popenhagen & Qualley, 1998). The mode of death and the frequency of attempts add to the pain that the survivors must endure. A more violent death can impact survivors who often suffer from feelings of heightened anger, guilt, and relief.

Counselor Diversity Competencies

Early on in the professional history of counselors, Wren (1962) called for a change for counselors. He proposed that counselors move from the focus on monocultural counseling to counseling within a cross-cultural context. Ibrahim and Arredondo (1986) put forth professional standards addressing the cross-cultural needs of clients. Later, the Association for Counselor Education and Supervision and the Association for Multicultural Counseling and Development developed guidelines for counselors to embrace (DeLucia-Waack, 1996). Whether in the counseling or counselor education setting, our profession is currently focusing on implementing strategies that address cultural competencies for practitioners. We seek ways that better address the challenge of addressing the rich cultural perspectives of our clients. While professional standards continue to emerge, the diversity needs of our clients are being identified within multiple contexts (Arredondo, 1999; Arredondo & Arciniega, 2001).

To better practice culturally competent counseling, we offer several essential guidelines. First, counselors need to reflect and have self-awareness regarding their own worldview and cultural contexts. Self-aware counselors understand their own lived experience. They embrace their own worldview from a social, cultural, racial, and ethnic perspective. They acknowledge their own blind spots and covert assumptions when working with others who are either similar to or different from them (Arredondo & Arciniega, 2001). Second, counselors need to incorporate knowledge of their client's worldview, cultural and social contexts, and specific information that affects their needs. Finally, counselors should use assessment tools that are client based and not Euro Americentric in nature. The world is becoming more and more connected. More and more often it is not unusual for counselors in one country to counsel clients who have migrated from another country (Sue & Sue, 1999).

To meet the cultural needs of our survivor clients, we propose a framework of practical suggestions for counseling survivors in a competent manner.

- Remember that the client's appearance can be deceiving; it is only a partial representation of the client's personal, cultural, religious, and racial needs.
- Keep in mind that the client's perspective on suicidal death and loss is uniquely his or her own.

- Consider that the survivors of suicide will respond individually and seek support that fits within their unique cultural worldviews.
- Note that bereavement experiences will also vary because of historical, religious, legal, and financial factors.
- Remember that responses of family and friends and mourning rituals vary widely, often within the same culture.
- Keep focused on the fact that each suicidal situation will have its own history and context and no two survivor reactions will be the same.
- Recognize your own feelings related to the emotional impact of the event.
- Stay current and attend conferences on counseling suicide survivors.
- Keep in mind that clients are the experts of their lived experience. No one understands the perspective of life and death or the effect of a suicide better than the client.

Summary

In this chapter we have presented historical and current perspectives related to counseling survivors of suicide. The issues are complex. Anger, unanswered questions, guilt, and unrecognized mourning often compound grief. The interventions and the skills that the counselor must demonstrate are also complex. Suicide is an international phenomenon that affects individuals from all cultures; cultural factors vary.

The needs of suicide survivors vary. Counselors must be prepared to deal with the consequences of a suicidal act on survivors. All clients present themselves with a unique set of issues in counseling. A skilled counselor understands that clients address issues in their own ways and "one size does not fit all." The survival of individuals affected by suicide is a global phenomenon that affects us all to the core of our humanity.

References

Arredondo, P. (1999). Multicultural competencies as tools to address oppression and racism. *Journal of Counseling & Development, 11,* 102–109.

Arredondo, P., & Arciniega, M. (2001). Strategies and techniques for counselor training based on the multicultural competencies. *Journal of Multicultural Counseling and Development, 29,* 263–274.

Borowsky, I. W., Ireland, M., & Resnick, M.D. (2001). Adolescent suicide attempts: Risk and protectors. *Pediatrics, 107,* 485–494.

Bowlby, J. (1982). *Attachment and loss: Vol. 1. Attachment* (2nd ed.). London: Hogarth Press.

Brent, D. A., Baugher, M., Bridge, J., Chen, T., & Chiappetta, L. (1999). Age and sex-related risk factors for adolescent suicide. *Journal of the American Academy of Child and Adolescent Psychiatry, 38,* 1497–1505.

Cain, A. C., & Fast, I. (1972). Children have disturbed reactions to parent's suicide: Distortions of guilt, communication and identification. In A.C. Cain
(Ed.), *Survivors of suicide* (pp. 93–111). Springfield, IL: Charles C Thomas.

Calhoun, L.G., Selby, J. W., & Abernathy, C. B. (1984). Suicidal death: Social
reactions to bereaved survivors. *Journal of Psychology, 116*, 255–261.

Calhoun, L. G., Selby, J. W., & Selby, L. E. (1982). The psychological aftermath of suicide: An analysis of current evidence. *Clinical Psychology Review, 2*, 409–420.

Canetto, S. S. (1997). Meanings of gender and suicidal behavior during
adolescence. *Suicide & Life Threatening Behavior 27*, 339–351.

Capuzzi, D. (1994). *Suicide prevention in the schools: Guidelines for middle and
high school settings.* Alexandria, VA: American Counseling Association.

Capuzzi, D. (2002). Legal and ethical challenges in counseling suicidal
student. *Professional School Counseling, 6*, 36–45.

Capuzzi, D., & Golden, L. (1988). *Preventing adolescent suicide.* Muncie, IN:
Accelerated Development.

Centers for Disease Control and Prevention. (1996). *Violence surveillance summary series, No. 2.* Atlanta, GA: Author.

Cerel, J., Fristad, M. A., Weller, E. B., & Weller, R. A. (2000, April). Suicide-
bereaved children and adolescents: II. Parental and family functioning.
Journal of the American Academy of Child and Adolescent Psychiatry, 39, 437–444.

Chance, S. (1988). Surviving suicide. *Bulletin of the Menninger Clinic, 52*, 30–39.

Conwell, Y., & Brent, D. (1995). Suicide and aging: Patterns of psychiatric
diagnosis. *International Psychogeriatrics, 7*, 149–164.

Conyne, R. K. (1987). *Primary prevention counseling: Empowering people and systems.* Muncie, IN: Accelerated Development.

Crofoot Graham, T. L. (2002). Using reasons for living to connect to American Indian healing traditions. *Journal of Sociology and Social Welfare, 29*,
55–75.

DeLucia-Waack, J. L. (Ed.). (1996). *Multicultural counseling competencies: Implications for training and practice.* Alexandria, VA: Association for Counselor
Education and Supervision.

Ginsberg, G. P. (1971). Public conceptions and attitudes about suicide.
Journal of Health and Social Behavior, 12, 200–207.

Hatton, C. L., & McBride-Valente, S. (1981). Bereavement group for parents
who suffered a suicidal loss of a child. *Suicide and Life Threatening Behaviors, 11*, 141–150.

Hoyert, D. L., Kochanek, K. D., & Murphy, S. L. (1999). Deaths: Final data for
1997. In *Vital statistics of the United States: National vital statistics report*
(Vol. 47, No. 19, DHHS Publication No. PHS 99-1120). Hyattsville, MD:
National Center for Health Statistics.

Ibrahim, F. A., & Arredondo, P. M. (1986). Ethical standards for cross-cultural counseling: Counselor preparation, practice, assessment, and research. *Journal of Counseling & Development, 64*, 349–354.

Jamison, K. R. (1999). *Night falls fast.* New York: Alfred A. Knopf.

Jilek-Aall, L. (1988). Suicidal behavior among youth: A cross-cultural comparison. *Transcultural Psychiatric Research Review, 25,* 87–105.

Kalafat, J. (1990). Adolescent suicide and the implications for school response programs. *School Counselor, 37,* 359–370.

Kelleher, M. J. (1996). *Suicide and the Irish.* Cork, Ireland: Mercier Press.

Kubler-Ross, E. (1969). *On death and dying.* New York: Macmillan.

Lester, D. (1998). The association of shame and guilt with suicidality. *Journal of Social Psychology, 138,* 535–536.

Lester, D. (Ed.). (2001). *Suicide prevention: Resources for the millennium.* Ann Arbor, MI: Sheridan Books.

Lewisohn, P. M., Rohde, P., & Seeley, J. R. (1996). Adolescent suicidal ideation and attempts: Prevalence, risk factors and clinical implications. *Clinical Psychology: Science and Practice, 3,* 25–46.

Lindstrom, T. C. (2002). "It ain't necessarily so": Challenging mainstream thinking about bereavement. *Family Community Health, 25*(1), 11–21.

Linn-Gust, M. (2001). *Do they have bad days in heaven: Surviving the suicide loss of a sibling.* Atlanta, GA: Bolton Press.

Malley, P. B., Kush, F., & Bogo, R. (1994). School-based adolescent suicide prevention and intervention programs: A survey. *School Counselor, 42,* 130–136.

Martin, N. K., & Dixon, P. N. (1986). Adolescent suicide: Myths, recognition and evaluation. *School Counselor, 33,* 265–271.

Metha, A., Weber, B., & Webb, L. D. (1998). Youth suicide prevention: A survey and analysis of policies and efforts in the fifty states. *Suicide and Life Threatening Behavior, 2,* 150–164.

Neiger, B. L., & Hopkins, R. W. (1988). Adolescent suicide: Character traits of high-risk teenagers. *Adolescence, 23,* 469–475.

Parker, S. (1998). Seeing suicide as preventable: A national strategy emerges. *Christian Science Monitor, 90,* 3–4.

Parsons, R. D. (1996). Student suicide: The counselor's postvention role. *Elementary School Guidance and Counseling, 31*(1), 77–81.

Pfeffer, C. R., Jiang, H., Kakuma, T., Hwang, J., & Metsch, M. (2002). Group intervention for children bereaved by the suicide of a relative. *Journal of the American Academy of Child and Adolescent Psychiatry, 41,* 505–513.

Popenhagen, M. P., & Qualley, R. A. (1998). Adolescent suicide: Detention, intervention and prevention. *Professional School Counseling, 1,* 30–35.

Roger, J. R., Gueulette, C. M., Abbey-Hide, J., Carney, J. V., & Werth, J. L. (2001). Rational suicide: An empirical investigation of counselor attitudes. *Journal of Counseling & Development, 79,* 365–372.

Schuyler, D. (1973). Counseling suicide survivors: Issues and answers. *Omega, 4,* 313–321.

Shneidman, E. S. (1972). *Death and the college student.* New York: Behavioral Publications.

Shneidman, E. S. (Ed.). (2001). *Comprehending suicide: Landmarks in 20th century suicidology*. Washington, DC: American Psychological Association.

Sommer-Rotenburg, D. (1998). Suicide and language. *Canadian Medical Association Journal, 3*, 239–240.

Sue, D. W., & Sue, D. (1999). *Counseling the culturally different* (3rd ed.). New York: Wiley.

Thompson, R. A. (1995). Being prepared for suicide or sudden death in schools: Strategies to restore equilibrium. *Journal of Mental Health Counseling, 17*, 264–278.

Vannatta, R. A. (1997). Adolescent gender differences in suicide-related behaviors. *Journal of Youth and Adolescence, 26*, 559–568.

Victoroff, V. (1983). *The suicide patient: Recognition, intervention, management*. Oradell, NJ: Medical Economics Books.

World Health Organization (2000). The world wealth report 2001 mental health: New understanding, new hope. Retrieved February 22, 2003, from http://www.who.int/whr2001/2001/main/en/chapter2/002g.html

Wren, C. G. (1962). The culturally encapsulated counselor. *Harvard Educational Review, 32*, 444–449.

Epilogue

Now that you have finished reading this book, it is my hope that you feel better prepared to work with suicidal clients and that you have found the contents applicable to counseling with the clients in your specific setting. It is also my hope that you will give some thought to what you need to do, after reflecting on the content of this book, to competently and successfully work with clients who present with risk factors and signs and symptoms that are indicative of the potential for suicide attempts or completions. I have a number of suggestions that I would like you to consider.

First, I think it is important to do an assessment of the extent and nature of the formalized education and supervised practice you have experienced that would prepare you for working with this clientele. One way of doing such a self-assessment is to review the content areas included in this text and ask yourself some pertinent questions. "Do I need to learn more about risk and protective factors, depression, assessment, or ethical and legal issues before I agree to work with a client who may be suicidal?" "Do I have a comprehensive grasp of treatment options?" "Would I be more effective with children, adolescents, adults, or survivors as clients?" "How much supervised practice have I experienced while counseling suicidal clients and how much more do I need?" The answers to these, and other questions you could ask, should assist you in identifying courses, seminars, professional conferences, and supervision options that would better prepare you to meet future counseling responsibilities with the suicidal, or potentially suicidal, client.

Second, I believe it is critically important to engage in some introspection to determine whether or not you need to commit to some personal counseling prior to agreeing to counsel a client experiencing suicidal ideation. If you have prejudices, losses, unresolved grief issues, or apprehensions that might impede the progress you could make with a suicidal client, such issues should be thoroughly assessed and addressed in the context of your own "work" with a professional counselor. How can you provide a healing environment in which your client can progress if you have not done your own personal work? How can you assist a client in coping with unresolved grief or loss if you are simultaneously struggling with similar concerns?

Third, because counseling vulnerable clients can be time consuming, stressful, and demanding, boundary setting is also an important consideration that you need to think about prior to agreeing to work with suicidal clients. Consideration should always be given to the number of such clients that should simultaneously be part of your case load, whether you want them to call you or a crisis number if they experience difficulty coping between scheduled sessions, and how much work you want to do as a member of a crisis team that may be called on to assist survivors after a loss due to suicide. You may even want to consider whether you want to work with potentially suicidal clients independently or conjointly with a trusted colleague.

Networking with other professionals who can assist and support you in the process of providing clients with a comprehensive constellation of services is a fourth consideration that should be thought through prior to doing any work with clients who are suicidal or who have made prior suicide attempts. You may need to enlist the assistance of a psychiatrist or nurse practitioner to do an additional assessment of the client's depression so that medication can be prescribed, monitored, and integrated into the counseling process. Additionally, it may be appropriate to refer to a nutritionist who can assist in the process of determining whether a change in eating patterns would help a client overcome difficulty with depression. Knowing the right police officer to call on for the purpose of removing a weapon from a suicidal client is critical; this should be someone who has prior training and experience in working with such a client. Knowing the names of case workers from the agency in your community that provides protective services for children and families can be crucial, for the purpose of obtaining immediate assistance, when it is not safe to send a suicidal client back into the home. Such networking with professionals in the community must be done ahead of time; this is time consuming and continuous because professionals move in and out of agencies and communities.

Peer support is also an essential aspect of competent, safe, and successful service delivery to the suicidal or potentially suicidal client. This peer support can take a variety of forms. For example, if you are counseling with a client who presents challenges you are not sure you are properly addressing, knowing other counselors with whom you can do case consultation can help you enhance the quality of the counseling you are providing. Participating as a member of a support group composed of other counselors and therapists can make it much easier to relieve the stress that often builds as you work in an intense way with a vulnerable client. Continuing to engage in your own personal work with a counselor can also prevent the possibility of allowing your own needs or unresolved issues to block your capacity to assist your client. Meeting on a regular basis with a supervisor is another example of the possibilities for peer support that can enhance your effectiveness with a client.

There are many aspects of self-care that should also be uppermost in the mind of anyone who has interest in counseling suicidal clients. Overwork, high stress, lack of exercise, poor eating habits, weight gain or loss, neglect of recreational activities and timeout with friends and family members, dissatisfaction with work or the work environment, among others, are not only areas for consideration by your clients but also areas of self-assessment and consideration for the practitioner. Counselors who do not do a good job of taking care of their own physical, emotional, and spiritual health cannot expect to do a good job of teaching clients to take care of themselves. It is quite easy to let the cycle leading to burnout and less than competent work with clients build to the point that it could be necessary to take a leave from your position or your private practice.

This book was conceptualized to provide the reader with a comprehensive overview of what counselors need to know about counseling potentially suicidal (and suicidal) clients. This knowledge and skills base can only be applied to the work of the counselor as it is translated and shared through the person of the counselor. It is essential that counselors take care of themselves so they can be competent, effective, and facilitative of the health and wellness of a group of clients who deserve the best the profession can provide.

Index

T